Game Plan for the
GMAT

Your Proven Guidebook
for Mastering the GMAT Exam
in 40 Short Days

*Complete coverage of math, verbal, analytical writing
and integrated reasoning sections*

Brandon Royal

Published by Maven Publishing

MAVEN

1st Edition: This printing, April 2014

Published by:

Maven Publishing
4520 Manilla Road S.E.
Calgary, Alberta, Canada T2G 4B7
www.mavenpublishing.com

Library and Archives Canada Cataloguing in Publication:

Royal, Brandon
Game plan for the GMAT : your proven guidebook for mastering the GMAT exam in 40 short days / by Brandon Royal.

Issued in print and electronic formats.

ISBN 978-1-897393-39-0 (paperback)
ISBN 978-1-897393-38-3 (ebook)

1. Graduate Management Admission Test--Study guides. 2. Business--Problems, exercises, etc. I. Title.

HF1118.R6975 2012   650.076   C2012-906872-1

Technical Credits:
Cover design: George Foster, Fairfield, Iowa, USA
Editing: Victory Crayne, Laguna Woods, California, USA

The book's cover was set in Minion. The interior text was set in Scala and Scala Sans.

CONTENTS

Your 40-Day Game Plan for the GMAT   **6**

Quiz – True or False   **13**

Chapter 1:   The GMAT Exam   **15**

What's on the GMAT Exam? ◆ How is the GMAT Scored? ◆ Your Target Score ◆ How does the Computer Exam Work? ◆ Exam Tactics

Chapter 2:   Problem Solving   **21**

Overview

Official Exam Instructions for Problem Solving • Strategies and Approaches

Review of Basic Math

Flowcharting the World of Numbers ◆ Number Definitions ◆ The Four Basic Operations ◆ Common Fractions and their Percentage Equivalents ◆ Rules for Odd and Even Numbers ◆ Rules for Positive and Negative Numbers ◆ Common Squares, Cubes, and Square Roots ◆ Divisibility Rules ◆ Exponents ◆ Radicals ◆ Basic Geometry Formulas ◆ Probability, Permutations & Combinations

Multiple-Choice Problems

Distance-Rate-Time Problems ◆ Age Problems ◆ Average Problems ◆ Work Problems ◆ Picture Frame, Rug, or Border Problems ◆ Mixture Problems ◆ Group Problems ◆ Matrix Problems ◆ Price-Cost-Volume-Profit Problems ◆ Least-Common-Multiple Word Problems ◆ General Algebraic Word Problems ◆ Function Problems ◆ Algebraic Fractions ◆ Fractions and Decimals ◆ Percentage Problems ◆ Ratios and Proportions ◆ Squares and Cubes ◆ Exponent Problems ◆ Radical Problems ◆ Inequality Problems ◆ Prime Number Problems ◆ Remainder Problems ◆ Symbolism Problems ◆ Coordinate Geometry Problems ◆ Plane Geometry Problems ◆ Solid Geometry Problems ◆ Probability Problems ◆ Enumeration Problems ◆ Permutation Problems ◆ Combination Problems ◆ Answers and Explanations

Chapter 3:   Data Sufficiency   **171**

Overview

Official Exam Instructions for Data Sufficiency ◆ Strategies and Approaches ◆ How are Answers Chosen in Data Sufficiency? ◆ How do the Big Seven Numbers Work?

Multiple-Choice Problems

Odds and Evens ◆ Averaging ◆ Positives and Negatives ◆ Integers and Non-Integers ◆ Squares and Cubes ◆ Factors and Multiples ◆ Prime Numbers ◆ Factoring ◆ Inequalities ◆ Statistics ◆ Answers and Explanations

Chapter 4:   Sentence Correction   **199**

Overview

Official Exam Instructions for Sentence Correction ◆ Strategies and Approaches

Review of Sentence Correction

Overview ◆ 100-Question Quiz on Grammar, Diction, and Idioms ◆ Review of Grammatical Terms ◆ Diction Review ◆ 200 Grammatical Idioms ◆ Style Review ◆ Answers to the 100-Question Quiz on Grammar, Diction, and Idioms

Multiple-Choice Problems

Subject-Verb Agreement ◆ Pronoun Usage ◆ Modification ◆ Parallelism ◆ Comparisons ◆ Verb Tenses ◆ Answers and Explanations

Chapter 5:   Critical Reasoning   **277**

Overview

Official Exam Instructions for Critical Reasoning ◆ Strategies and Approaches

Review of Critical Reasoning

Defining Terms ◆ The ABCs of Argument Structure ◆ Evaluating Arguments ◆ The "Big Six" Assumption Categories

Multiple-Choice Problems

Comparison and Analogy Assumptions ◆ Cause-and-Effect Assumptions ◆ Representativeness Assumptions ◆ Implementation Assumptions ◆ Number-based Assumptions ◆ Logic-based Assumptions ◆ Bolded-Statement Problems ◆ Answers and Explanations

Chapter 6:   Reading Comprehension   **333**

Overview

Official Exam Instructions for Reading Comprehension ◆ Strategies and Approaches

Review of Reading Comprehension

Passage Type ◆ Passage Content ◆ Passage Structure ◆ Passage Question Types ◆ Common Wrong Answer Choices ◆ The Relationship Between Passage Question Types and Common Wrong Answer Choices

Multiple-Choice Problems

Sample Passage ◆ Social Science Passage ◆ Science Passage ◆ Answers and Explanations

Chapter 7:   Analytical Writing Workshop   **363**

Overview

Official Exam Instructions for the Analytical Writing Assessment ◆ Strategies and Approaches

Review of Analytical Writing

Frequently Asked Questions ◆ The 4-Step Approach for Writing an Argument Essay ◆ Using the Assumption Cracker

Essay Exercises

◆ Two Analysis of an Argument Essays ◆ Outlines and Proposed Solutions

Chapter 8:   Integrated Reasoning Workshop   **379**

Overview

Official Exam Instructions for Integrated Reasoning ◆ Strategies and Approaches

Review of Integrated Reasoning with Exercises

Frequently Asked Questions ◆ Understanding Basic Graphs ◆ Quiz on Basic Graphs ◆ Line Graphs, Pie Charts, and Bar Charts ◆ Exercises: Grand Hotel, Work Force, and Magna Fund ◆ Correlation Analysis ◆ Quiz on Correlation Analysis

Appendix I – GMAT and MBA Informational Websites   **401**

Registering for the GMAT Exam ◆ MBA Fairs & Forums ◆ MBA Social Networks ◆ GMAT Courses ◆ Other GMAT & MBA Websites ◆ Information on Business School Rankings

Appendix II – Contact Information for the World's Leading Business Schools   **405**

U.S. Business Schools ◆ Canadian Business Schools ◆ European Business Schools ◆ Australian Business Schools ◆ Asia-Pacific Business Schools ◆ Latin and South American Business Schools ◆ South African Business Schools

Quiz – Answers   **411**

On a Personal Note   **413**

Praise for *Game Plan for the GMAT*   **415**

About the Author

YOUR 40-DAY GAME PLAN FOR THE GMAT

Your 40-day game plan consists of tackling GMAT study with two goals in mind. The first goal involves doing the problems in this book. This will set the conceptual framework and help you not only build technical competence by familiarizing yourself with the types of math problems on the exam but also recognize special problem solving approaches and shortcuts. The second goal involves completing additional practice problems and/or tests that can be obtained from the GMAC website (www.gmac.com).

The GMAC (Graduate Management Admission Council) provides two options for practicing on past exam questions and obtaining scores out of 800. The first option is to practice on "retired" paper exams (in pdf file format) and the second is to practice on GMATPrep® software, the latter being proprietary computer adaptive tests designed to simulate the feel of the actual exam. Practicing on the paper exams can be viewed as a bridge between mastering the problems in this book and completing the final GMATPrep® software. Some readers may choose to skip the paper exams and go directly to the computer adaptive tests. Note that the two GMATPrep® exams are offered as free downloads from the GMAC website. Paper tests are sold in packets of three for US$29.99 per packet.

Studying for the math and verbal sections of the GMAT exam requires some 100 hours of study time. This book's content is conveniently divided into topics. The following checklist provides an overview of all topical areas within the individual chapters of Problem Solving, Data Sufficiency, Sentence Correction, Critical Reasoning, Reading Comprehension, Analytical Writing, and Integrated Reasoning. Boxes may be checked upon completing of each topic. Each day's study requires two to three hours of daily study time, and as a practical matter, total study time will vary between 80 to 120 hours for the entire 40 days.

MATH SECTION:

	Problem No.
Day 1: Problem Solving	
❑ Distance-Rate-Time Problems (pages 51–52)	1–6
❑ Age Problems (page 53)	7
❑ Average Problems (pages 53–54)	8–10
❑ Work Problems (pages 54–55)	11–13
Day 2: Problem Solving	
❑ Picture Frame, Rug, or Border Problems (page 55)	14
❑ Mixture Problems (page 56)	15–17
❑ Group Problems (pages 57–58)	18–20
❑ Matrix Problems (pages 58–59)	21–23

	Problem No.
Day 3: Problem Solving	
❑ Price-Cost-Volume-Profit Problems (pages 59–61)	24–28
❑ Least-Common-Multiple Word Problems (page 61)	29
❑ General Algebraic Word Problems (pages 62–63)	30–33
❑ Function Problems (page 63)	34
Day 4: Problem Solving	
❑ Algebraic Fractions (page 64)	35–36
❑ Fractions and Decimals (page 65)	37–39
❑ Percentage Problems (pages 66–68)	40–46
❑ Ratios and Proportions (pages 68–70)	47–52
Day 5: Problem Solving	
❑ Squares and Cubes (page 70)	53–54
❑ Exponent Problems (pages 71–73)	55–62
❑ Radical Problems (pages 74–75)	63–65
❑ Inequality Problems (page 75)	66
Day 6: Problem Solving	
❑ Prime Number Problems (pages 75–76)	67–68
❑ Remainder Problems (page 76)	69–70
❑ Symbolism Problems (page 77)	71
❑ Coordinate Geometry Problems (pages 77–78)	72–74
Day 7: Problem Solving	
❑ Plane Geometry Problems (pages 79–82)	75–84
❑ Solid Geometry Problems (page 83)	85
❑ Probability Problems (pages 83–86)	86–91
❑ Enumeration Problems (page 86)	92

Day 8: Problem Solving/Data Sufficiency

❑ Permutation Problems (pages 87–88)   93–96

❑ Combination Problems (pages 88–89)   97–100

❑ Odds and Evens (page 178)   1–2

❑ Averaging (page 178)   3

Day 9: Data Sufficiency

❑ Positives and Negatives (page 178)   4

❑ Integers and Non-Integers (page 179)   5–6

❑ Squares and Cubes (page 179)   7

❑ Factors and Multiples (pages 179–180)   8–9

Day 10: Data Sufficiency

❑ Prime Numbers (page 180)   10–11

❑ Factoring (pages 180–181)   12–13

❑ Inequalities (pages 181–182)   14–20

❑ Statistics (page 183)   21–22

Day 11: Review of Problems

❑ Review any of the math problems that you had trouble with the first time round. This may require that you make notes in your own notebook.

Day 12: Review of Problems

❑ Spend a second day reviewing any of the multiple-choice math problems that you had trouble with the first time round.

Day 13: Paper Test #1

❑ Using one of the GMAC paper tests, complete both Problem Solving sections contained in that exam. Also, correct each of these sections using the answers provided at the back of that test. The math section of each paper exam consists of two Problem Solving sections and one Data Sufficiency section. Note that on the actual exam these two problem types are intermixed and covered within the single 75-minute math section.

Day 14: Paper Test #2

❑ Using another of the GMAC paper tests, complete both Problem Solving sections contained in that exam. Also, correct each of these sections using the answers provided with the back of that test.

Day 15: Paper Tests #1–2

❑ Using both of your selected GMAC paper tests, complete the single Data Sufficiency section contained in each of these exams and correct them using the answers provided at the back of each test.

Day 16: Paper Tests #1–2

❑ Calculate a score out of 800 for the math (quantitative) section of each of these two exams. You have completed both the Problem Solving and the Data Sufficiency sections for each test. Spend time reviewing any math problem that you failed to answer correctly on any of these six test sections.

Day 17: Computer Test #1

❑ Complete the math section of one of the two free downloadable GMATPrep® Software exams.

Day 18: Review of Computer Test #1

❑ Review the answers to the problems on this first adaptive test.

Day 19: Computer Test #2

❑ Complete the math section of the *other* free downloadable GMATPrep® Software exam.

Day 20: Review of Computer Test #2

❑ Review the answers to the problems on this second and final adaptive test. Spend any extra time reviewing basic concepts.

VERBAL SECTION (PLUS ANALYTICAL WRITING AND INTEGRATED REASONING):

Problem No.

Day 21: Sentence Correction

❑ 100-Question Quiz (pages 201–205)   Q1–33

Day 22: Sentence Correction

❑ 100-Question Quiz (pages 205–210)   Q34–66

Day 23: Sentence Correction

❑ 100-Question Quiz (pages 210–215)   Q67–100

Day 24: Sentence Correction

❑ Subject-Verb Agreement (pages 246–248)   1–5

❑ Pronoun Usage (pages 248–249)   6–8

❑ Modification (pages 250–251)   9–11

Day 25: Sentence Correction

❑ Parallelism (pages 251–252)   12–14

❑ Comparisons (pages 253–256)   15–23

❑ Verb Tenses (pages 256–259)   24–29

Day 26: Critical Reasoning

❑ Comparison and Analogy Assumptions (pages 294–295)   1–3

❑ Cause-and-Effect Assumptions (pages 295–298)   4–9

❑ Representativeness Assumptions (pages 298–301)   10–14

Day 27: Critical Reasoning

❑ Implementation Assumptions (pages 301–302)   15–17

❑ Number-based Assumptions (pages 303–305)   18–23

❑ Logic-based Assumptions (pages 306–308)   24–29

❑ Bolded-Statement Problems (page 309)   30

Problem No.

Day 28: Reading Comprehension

   ❏ Sample Passage (pages 345–346)   1–5

   ❏ Social Science Passages (pages 348–349)   6–9

   ❏ Science Passages (pages 350–352)   10–13

Day 29: Analytical Writing

   ❏ Argument Essays (pages 371–372)   1–2

Day 30: Integrated Reasoning

   ❏ Understanding Basic Graphs (pages 384–385)   1

   ❏ Line Graphs, Bar Charts, and Pie Charts (pages 387–390)   2–9

   ❏ Correlation Analysis (page 394)   10

Day 31: Review of Problems

   ❏ Review any of the verbal problems or quiz questions that you had trouble with the first time round. This may require that you make notes in your own notebook.

Day 32: Review of Problems

   ❏ Spend a second day reviewing any of the verbal multiple-choice problems or quiz questions that you had trouble with the first time round.

Day 33: Paper Test #1

   ❏ Using one of the GMAC paper tests, complete the Sentence Correction, Critical Reasoning, and Reading Comprehension sections contained in that exam. Also, correct each of these sections using the answers provided at the back of that test. The verbal section of each paper exam consists of separate sections for all three verbal types, presented in multiple-choice format. Note that on the actual exam these problem types are intermixed and covered within the single 75-minute verbal section.

Day 34: Review of Paper Test #1

   ❏ Calculate a score out of 800 for the verbal section of your first paper exam. Spend time reviewing any verbal problem that you failed to answer correctly.

Day 35: Paper Test #2

❏ Using another of the GMAC paper tests, complete the Sentence Correction, Critical Reasoning, and Reading Comprehension sections contained in that exam. Also, correct each of these sections using the answers provided at the back of that test.

Day 36: Review of Paper Test #2

❏ Calculate a score out of 800 for the verbal section of your second paper exam. Spend time reviewing those verbal problems that you failed to answer correctly.

Day 37: Computer Test #1

❏ Complete the verbal section of one of the two free downloadable GMATPrep® Software exams, including the Integrated Reasoning section.

Day 38: Review of Computer Test #1

❏ Review the answers to the problems on this first computer test.

Day 39: Computer Test #2

❏ Complete the verbal section of the *other* free downloadable GMATPrep® Software exam.

Day 40: Review of Computer Test #2

❏ Review the answers to the problems on this second and final computer test. Spend any extra time reviewing basic concepts. The day before the test should be reserved for light study only. Rather than thinking about what you might not know, reflect on how much you do know and how far you've come.

QUIZ – TRUE OR FALSE

Try these ten basic, but occasionally tricky, math and verbal problems. See pages 411–412 for solutions.

1. If the ratio of gold coins to non-gold coins in a rare coin collection is 1:5, then 20 percent of the total coin collection is represented by gold coins. ❑ True ❑ False

2. The probability of tossing a normal six-sided die twice and getting at least one six is calculated as $\frac{1}{6} + \frac{1}{6} = \frac{1}{3}$. ❑ True ❑ False

3. A store item that has been discounted first by 20 percent and then by 30 percent is now selling at 50 percent of its original price. ❑ True ❑ False

4. The ratios of the length of the sides of a right triangle with corresponding angle measures of 30°–60°–90° is 1–2–$\sqrt{3}$. ❑ True ❑ False

5. Multiplying a number by 1.2 is the same as dividing that same number by 0.8 ❑ True ❑ False

6. The following is a grammatically correct sentence: "Jonathan not only likes tennis but also golf." ❑ True ❑ False

7. The statement "some doctors are rich people" does not imply reciprocality because "some rich people might not be doctors." ❑ True ❑ False

8. The Analysis of an Argument essay is more effective if written using some personal examples and anecdotes. ❑ True ❑ False

9. Whereas the conclusion and evidence of an argument are always explicit, the assumption of an argument may or may not be explicit. ❑ True ❑ False

10. Arguably the best way to read a GMAT Reading Comprehension passage is to read line by line, starting from the top and proceeding to the bottom. ❑ True ❑ False

CHAPTER 1

THE GMAT EXAM

Chance favors the prepared mind.
—Louis Pasteur

What's on the GMAT Exam?

The GMAT exam is a 3½-hour, four-section standardized exam consisting of Math, Verbal, Writing, and Integrated Reasoning sections. See *Exhibit 1.1*. Except for the Writing section (essay format) and Integrated Reasoning (true/false, yes/no, online fill-ins), the Math and Verbal sections follow an entirely multiple-choice format.

Exhibit 1.1   GMAT Exam Snapshot

Section	No. of questions	Time allowed
Analytical Writing	1 topic	30 minutes
Integrated Reasoning	12	30 minutes
Break		5 minutes
Math (Quantitative)	37	75 minutes
Break		5 minutes
Verbal	41	75 minutes
	Total Time	3.5 hours + two 5-minute breaks

Exam Breakdown

Analytical Writing Assessment (30 minutes)
- Analysis of an Argument (1 essay)

Integrated Reasoning (30 minutes)
- Graphic Interpretation, Table Analysis,
Multi-Source Reasoning, and Two-Part Analysis (12 questions)

Math (Quantitative) Section (75 minutes)
- Problem Solving (23–24 questions)
- Data Sufficiency (13–14 questions)
Total number of questions: 37 (28 scored, 9 unscored*)

Verbal Section (75 minutes)
- Sentence Correction (14–15 questions)
- Critical Reasoning (14–15 questions)
- Reading Comprehension (4 passages, 12–14 questions)
Total number of questions: 41 (30 scored, 11 unscored*)

*There are 20 unscored questions shared between the Math and Verbal sections of the GMAT exam; either 9 Quantitative and 11 Verbal Questions or 10 questions from each section are unscored.

NOTE ⤹ Within each Math and Verbal section, the different types of problems are intermixed. That is, on the math section, Problem Solving and Data Sufficiency problems are intermixed. On the verbal section, Reading Comprehension, Critical Reasoning, and Sentence Correction problems are also intermixed.

How is the GMAT Scored?

You actually receive five scores from taking the GMAT exam: 1) Total score, 2) Math (Quantitative) score, 3) Verbal score, 4) AWA (Analytical Writing Assessment) score, and 5) Integrated Reasoning score. Your Total score ranges from 200 to 800. Scores on individual Math and Verbal sections range from 0 to 60 and are accompanied by a corresponding percentile rank. Your AWA score (out of 6.0) and Integrated Reasoning score (out of 8) is totally independent of your Math, Verbal, or Total score (Math + Verbal). See *Exhibits 1.2–1.4.*

Scaled scores: Scaled scores above 50 (out of 60) on the Math section or above 44 (out of 60) on the Verbal section correspond to the 99th percentile. This means that only 1 percent of all test takers can achieve either of these respective scores and, as such, these scores are rare. A scaled score of 750 out of 800 on the combined test corresponds to the 99th percentile.

EXHIBIT 1.2   GMAT SCORING SNAPSHOT

Section	Scaled scoring	Percentile rank
Analytical Writing	0.0 to 6.0	0% to 90%
Integrated Reasoning	1 to 8	0% to 90%
Math (Quantitative)	0 to 60	0% to 99%
Verbal	0 to 60	0% to 99%
Total (Math + Verbal)	200 to 800	0% to 99%

Your Target Score

Naturally, for the purposes of applying to business school, the higher your GMAT Total score the better. Let's say that a scaled score of 700 (700 out of 800 corresponds to the 90th percentile) is considered a really good score and is what most candidates aim for if applying to top business schools. There is some credence given to the idea that everyone applying to a leading business school is equal in the admissions process after scoring in the 90th percentile or higher. In other words, if you get rejected with a score of 700 or above, the problem lies not with your GMAT score, but with another part of your application. In terms of applying to business school, particularly top business schools, admissions officers typically view GMAT scores (scaled scores) as falling into four arbitrary categories.

Score:	*What this likely means:*
Less than 500:	Not acceptable; take the exam over again.
Between 500 and 600:	Marginal—low for a top business school, although you could still get accepted.
Between 600 and 700:	In the ballpark for a top business school.
Greater than 700:	Excellent!

Remember: The GMAT score is one of several factors that go into the admissions process. In the often-quoted words of admissions officers at large: "A high GMAT score does not guarantee acceptance and a low GMAT score does not necessarily preclude it."

EXHIBIT 1.3   GMAT TOTAL QUANTITATIVE & VERBAL TEST SCORES

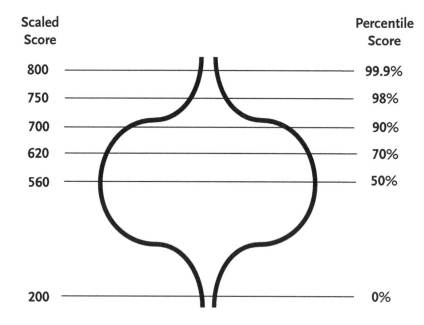

Scaled Score		Percentile Score
800		99.9%
750		98%
700		90%
620		70%
560		50%
200		0%

Source: GMAC.com – Percentages of examinees tested (including repeaters) who scored below specified total scores

The Analytical Writing Assessment (AWA) Section

The first half hour of the GMAT exam consists of a writing segment called *Analysis of an Argument*. This essay writing exercise requires a test taker to *break down* an argument by explaining why it is weak. Graders (one human and one electronic e-grading machine called an e-rater) score the essay based on essay content, organization, and grammar. Scores are assigned out of 6.0 based on intervals of 0.5 points. Your AWA score is an average of both individual scores (human and machine graded) obtained on the argument essay. *See Exhibit 1.4.*

EXHIBIT 1.4   GMAT ANALYTICAL WRITING TEST SCORES

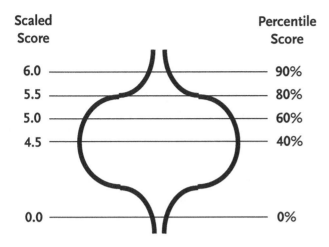

Source: GMAC.com – Percentages of examinees tested (including repeaters) who scored below specified total scores

The Integrated Reasoning Section

The second half hour of the GMAT exam involves a new section (as of June 2012) called Integrated Reasoning. This section consists of four different types of reasoning questions that test a candidate's ability to hone in relevant information and to see relationships among various data presented in different formats. Test takers are required to navigate "letters, numbers, and pictures"—letters being words, numbers being math, and pictures being graphs (e.g., line graphs, pie charts, and bar charts). Scores are assigned out of 8 in intervals of 1. See *Exhibit 1.5*.

EXHIBIT 1.5   GMAT INTEGRATED REASONING TEST SCORES

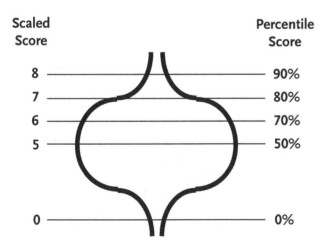

Source: GMAC.com – Percentages of examinees tested (including repeaters) who scored below specified total scores

Although it is unclear how business schools use AWA scores and integrated reasoning scores in the admissions process, the most likely possibility is that they are used in borderline admission decisions.

How does the Computer Exam Work?

The GMAT computer exam is adaptive. When starting work on a given Math or Verbal section, each person is assumed to be an average test taker and the test presents questions of average difficulty (i.e., 500-level test questions). Should the test taker get these questions correct, he or she is given a series of more difficult problems. As soon as the test taker misses a question, he or she is given an easier question. Eventually, and in theory, there will come a point at which the test taker can neither get a harder question right nor get an easier question wrong. It is here that the test draws a line, so to speak, and assigns a score. If, for example, a test taker cannot get 720-level problems correct but can get 680-level problems correct, the test assumes that the score to be assigned is 700.

It is not possible to skip a question on the computer exam without entering an answer; an answer must be entered for every question attempted before attempting additional questions. It is also not possible to go back to a previous problem or previous section.

Exam Tactics

Mastering the GMAT exam is really a function of mastering two things: content and context. Content refers to the ability to do questions with technical proficiency. Context is about everything else including becoming familiar with the computer, coping with a mix of questions, dealing with time pressure, and maintaining concentration and stamina.

As with many other academic pursuits, content is best mastered a little at a time; cumulative practice is preferable. Candidates should try working for at least 15 minutes every day for about a three-month period. If you wait until each weekend in order to try and do, say, two to three hours of GMAT study, you may find your efforts short-changed.

Each section of the GMAT exam is designed to be completed. Under no circumstances should a test taker allow an exam to finish without entering answer choices for all multiple-choice problems. A common question is, "How can I speed up on my Math or Verbal section?" There are effectively two ways to do this. The first is to do problems quicker; the second is to "skip" problems by guessing at an answer and moving on to the next problem. In order to do problems quicker, a candidate has to master content so that individual questions seem easier. And that's what *Game Plan for the GMAT* is really all about.

Technically, we cannot skip a problem on the GMAT. By skipping problems, we meaning guessing at them. In terms of skipping (guessing at) problems, we can skip problems randomly or in blocks. Most of us are good at some types of problems and weaker at others. Learning to identify those types of problems that we are unlikely to get correct gives us the option of skipping them altogether. What if we are fairly certain that we won't be able to finish an entire Math section of 37 problems or a Verbal section of 41 problems? Because problems toward the end of a GMAT section are deemed less important than earlier problems, in terms of skipping (guessing at) problems, one strategy is to "truncate" the exam. This means we simply proceed as if the Math section contains, say, 32 (not 37) problems, and the Verbal section contains, say, 35 (not 41) problems. Upon doing 32 math problems (or 35 verbal problems), feel free to guess on the remaining problems in light of time running out.

Maximize your chances of maintaining your concentration during the exam. Think one section at a time, one problem at a time, and only about the specific part of the problem that is before you.

CHAPTER 2

PROBLEM SOLVING

Math Class is tough.
—Barbie's original voice chip by Mattell

OVERVIEW

Official Exam Instructions for Problem Solving

Directions

Solve the problem and indicate the best of the answer choices given.

Numbers

All numbers used are real numbers.

Figures

A figure accompanying a problem solving question is intended to provide information useful in solving the problem. Figures are drawn as accurately as possible EXCEPT when it is stated in a specific problem that the figure is not drawn to scale. Straight lines may sometimes appear jagged. All figures lie in a plane unless otherwise indicated.

Strategies and Approaches

The following is a 4-step approach for math Problem Solving.

1. *Identify the type of problem and the appropriate math principle behind the problem at hand.*

    There are many different types of math problems on the GMAT. Each math problem in this book comes with a *classification* to highlight what category the problem belongs to and a *snapshot* to highlight why that particular problem was chosen, as well as any special problem-solving approach or math principle that is deemed relevant.

2. *Decide which approach to use to solve the problem—algebra, picking numbers, backsolving, approximation, or eyeballing.*

    There are both direct problem-solving approaches and indirect problem-solving approaches. The direct or algebraic approach involves applying actual math principles or formulas. Because we may not always know the correct algebraic method, we need an indirect or alternative approach. Other times, an indirect approach is plainly easier to apply than the algebraic approach. There are four alternative approaches for Problem Solving and these include: picking numbers, backsolving, approximation, and eyeballing.

3. *After performing calculations, always check again for what is being asked for.*

    Avoid making reading comprehension errors on the math section. Always re-read the question before choosing an answer, particularly if you have been engrossed in performing a longer computation.

4. *Employ elimination or guessing strategies, if necessary and when possible.*

    Guess if you must but employ guessing or elimination techniques.

Here are examples of each of the four indirect or alternative problem-solving approaches including guessing/elimination techniques.

i)   Picking Numbers

If a and b are even integers, which of the following is an odd integer?

A) $ab + 2$
B) $a(b - 1)$
C) $a(a + 5)$
D) $3a + 4b$
E) $(a + 3)(b - 1)$

Choice E. This key strategy involves first picking numbers and then substituting them into the answer choices. Whenever a problem involves variables, we may consider using this strategy. For this particular problem, pick the numbers $a = 2$ and $b = 4$ because both are even integers, yet both are still small and manageable numbers. Now substitute. Answer choice E is correct. You can be confident that if it works for your chosen set of numbers, it will also work for all other numbers as well. There is no need to try other numbers.

$ab + 2$	$(2 \times 4) + 2 = 10$ even
$a(b - 1)$	$2(4 - 1) = 6$ even
$a(a + 5)$	$2(2 + 5) = 14$ even
$3a + 4b$	$(3 \times 2) + (4 \times 4) = 22$ even
$(a + 3)(b - 1)$	$(2 + 3)(4 - 1) = 15$ odd

ii)   Backsolving

If $(x + 2)^2 = -4 + 10x$, then which of the following could be the value of x?

A)   2
B)   1
C)   0
D)   −1
E)   −2

Choice A. The key to using backsolving is to use the answer choices and see if they work. In this respect, backsolving is like picking numbers except that the numbers we pick are one or more of the actual answer choices. Look for the answer which makes both sides equal. In this particular problem, we may choose to start testing on any single answer choice. Choice A is as good a starting point as any.

Choice A.
$(2 + 2)^2 = -4 + 10(2)$
$16 = 16$; This is the correct answer since both sides are equal.

Choice B.
$(1 + 2)^2 = -4 + 10(1)$; $9 = 6$. This is a wrong answer since both sides are not equal.

Choice C.

$(0 + 2)^2 = -4 + 10(0)$; $4 = -4$. This is a wrong answer since both sides are not equal.

Choice D.

$(-1 + 2)^2 = -4 + 10(-1)$; $1 = -14$. This is a wrong answer since both sides are not equal.

Choice E.

$(-2 + 2)^2 = -4 + 10(-2)$; $0 = -24$. This is a wrong answer since both sides are not equal.

iii) Approximation

Approximately what percentage of the world's forested area is represented by Finland given that Finland has 53.42 million hectares of forested land of the world's 8.076 billion hectares of forested land.

A)   0.0066%
B)   0.066%
C)   0.66%
D)   6.6%
E)   66%

Choice C. Approximation is a strategy that helps us arrive at less than an exact number and the inclusion in this problem of the word "approximately" is an obvious clue. First, 8.076 billion is 8,076 million. Next, 8,076 million rounds to 8,000 million and 53.42 million rounds to 53 million. Dividing 53 million by 8,000 million we arrive at 0.0066 (53M/8,000M). We convert this decimal figure to a percentage by multiplying by 100 (or moving the decimal point two places to the right) and adding a percent sign in order to obtain our answer of 0.66%. Note that the shortcut method involves comparing 53 million to 1% of 8,000 million or 80 million. Since 53 million is approximately two-thirds of 80 million then the answer is some two-thirds of 1% or 0.66%.

iv) Eyeballing

If the figure below is a square with a side of 4 units, what is the area of the enclosed circle, expressed to the nearest whole number?

A) π
B)   4
C)   8
D)   13
E)   16

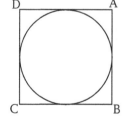

Choice D. Eyeballing is a parallel technique to be used on diagrams. Note that whatever the area of this circle may be, it must be less than the area of this square. The area of the square (in square units) is: $A = s^2 = 4 \times 4 = 16$. Therefore, the area of the circle is a little less than 16. Choice D is the only close answer. For the record, the near exact area of the circle is: $A = \pi r^2 = 3.14(2)^2 = 12.56$ or 13. Note that the decimal approximation for π is 3.14 while the fractional approximation is $\frac{22}{7}$.

v) Elimination and Guessing

A broker invested her own money in the stock market. During the first year, she increased her stock market wealth by 50 percent. In the second year, largely as a result of a slump in the stock market, she suffered a 30 percent decrease in the value of her stock investments. What was the net increase or decrease on her overall stock investment wealth by the end of the second year?

A) −5%
B) 5%
C) 15%
D) 20%
E) 80%

Choice B. Numerical answers to multiple-choice problems are presented in ascending or descending order in terms of size. If you must guess, the key strategies of elimination include: (1) eliminate an answer that looks different from the others, (2) eliminate answers which look too big or too small, i.e., extreme answers, and (3) eliminate answers which contain the same or similar numbers as given in the question or are easy derivatives of the numbers used in the problem. By easy derivatives, think in terms of addition and subtraction, not multiplication and division. For example, eliminate −5% because it is negative, and thus different from the other positive numbers. Eliminate 80% because it is much bigger than any other number (extreme). Eliminate 20% because it is an easy derivative of the numbers mentioned in the question, (i.e., 50% less 30%). You would then guess choices B or C. The actual answer is obtained by multiplying 150% by 70% and subtracting 100% from this total. That is: $150\% \times 70\% = 105\%$; $105\% - 100\% = 5\%$.

Remember that these are classic guessing strategies. They are, however, not infallible.

REVIEW OF BASIC MATH

Flowcharting the World of Numbers

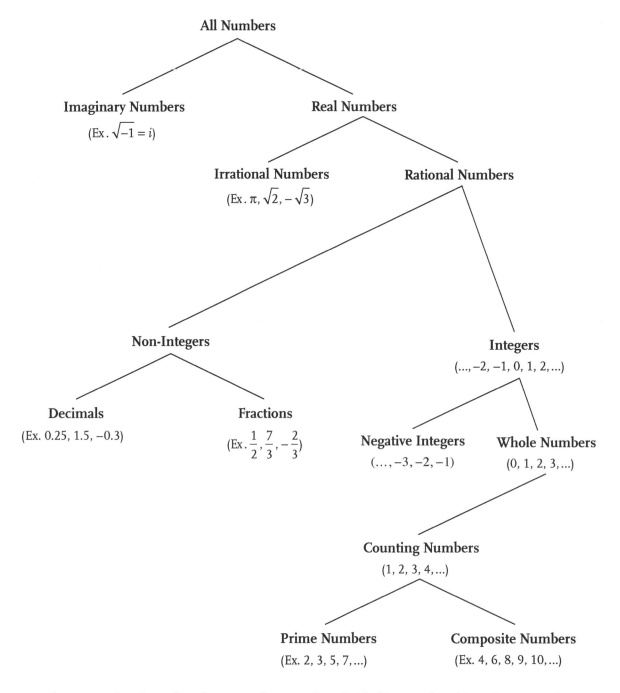

In reference to the above flowchart, numbers are first divided into real and imaginary numbers. *Imaginary* numbers are not a part of everyday life (nor are they tested on the GMAT). *Real* numbers are further divided into rational and irrational numbers. *Irrational* numbers are numbers which cannot be expressed as simple integers, fractions, or decimals; non-repeating decimals are always irrational numbers of which π may be the most famous. *Rational* numbers include integers and non-integers. *Integers* are positive and negative whole numbers while *non-integers* include decimals and fractions.

Number Definitions

Real numbers: Any number which exists on the number line. Real numbers are the combined group of rational and irrational numbers.

Imaginary numbers: Any number multiplied by i, the imaginary unit: $i = \sqrt{-1}$. Imaginary numbers are the opposite of real numbers and are not part of our everyday life.

Rational numbers: Numbers which can be expressed as a fraction whose top (the numerator) and bottom (the denominator) are both integers. Note that every whole number is a rational number because any whole number can be written as a fraction (that is, any number can itself be placed over the number one.)

Irrational numbers: Numbers which can't be expressed as a fraction whose top (the numerator) and bottom (the denominator) are integers. Square roots of non-perfect squares (such as $\sqrt{2}$) are irrational, and π is irrational. An irrational number may be described as a non-repeating decimal or, stated another way, an irrational number has endless non-repeating digits to the right of its decimal point.

Integers: Integers consist of those numbers which are multiples of 1: $\{ \ldots, -2, -1, 0, 1, 2, 3, \ldots \}$. Integers are "integral"—they contain no fractional or decimal parts.

Non-integers: Non-integers are those numbers which contain fractional or decimal parts. E.g., $\frac{1}{2}$ and 0.125 are non-integers.

Whole numbers: Non-negative integers: $\{0, 1, 2, 3, \ldots \}$. Note that 0 is a whole number, but it's technically a non-negative whole number, given that it is neither positive nor negative).

Counting numbers: The subset of whole numbers which excludes 0: $\{1, 2, 3, \ldots \}$.

Prime numbers: Prime numbers are a subset of the counting numbers. They include those non-negative integers which have two and only two factors; that is, the factors 1 and themselves. The first 10 primes are 2, 3, 5, 7, 11, 13, 17, 19, 23, and 29. Note that 1 is not a prime number as it only has one factor, i.e., 1. Also, the number 2 is not only the smallest prime but also the only even prime number.

Composite numbers: A positive number that has more than two factors other than 1 and itself. Also, any non-prime number greater than 1. Examples include: 4, 6, 8, 9, 10, etc. Note that 1 is not a composite number and the number 4 is the smallest composite number.

Fraction: A fraction is a mathematical term that is usually expressed in the form $\frac{a}{b}$, where a is the numerator and b is the denominator. Although most everyday fractions are between 0 and positive 1, fractions can be greater than 1 and they can also be negative.

Decimal: Decimal means "based on ten." Each place or position left of the decimal point is 10 times bigger than the previous place or position. Each place or position right of the decimal point is 10 times smaller than the previous place or position. The exact opposite is true in the case of negative numbers. Whole numbers are typically written without a decimal place.

Factors: A factor is an integer that can be divided evenly into another integer ("divided evenly" means that there is no remainder). For example, the factors of 12 are 1, 2, 3, 4, 6, and 12.

Multiples: A multiple is a number that results from a given integer being multiplied by another integer. Example: Multiples of 12 include 12, 24, 36, 48, etc. Proof: $12 \times 1 = 12$, $12 \times 2 = 24$, $12 \times 3 = 36$, and $12 \times 4 = 48$, etc. Note that whereas a factor of any number is less than or equal to the number in question, a multiple of any number is equal to or greater than the number itself. That is, any non-zero integer has a finite number of factors but an infinite number of multiples.

The Four Basic Operations

The four basic arithmetic operations are addition, subtraction, multiplication, and division. The results of these operations are called sum, difference, product, and quotient, respectively. Two additional operations involve exponents and radicals.

Addition

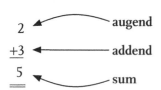

Subtraction

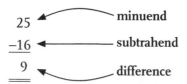

Multiplication

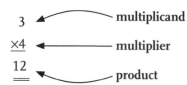

Division

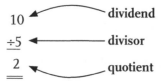

Exponents

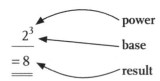

Radicals

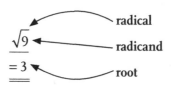

CHART OF COMMON FRACTIONS AND THEIR PERCENTAGE EQUIVALENTS

Exercise – Fill in the missing percentages to change common fractions into their percentage equivalents.

$$\frac{1}{1} = 100\%$$

$$\frac{1}{2} = 50\% \qquad \frac{2}{2} = 100\%$$

$$\frac{1}{3} = ?\% \qquad \frac{2}{3} = ?\% \qquad \frac{3}{3} = 100\%$$

$$\frac{1}{4} = ?\% \qquad \frac{2}{4} = 50\% \qquad \frac{3}{4} = ?\% \qquad \frac{4}{4} = 100\%$$

$$\frac{1}{5} = ?\% \qquad \frac{2}{5} = ?\% \qquad \frac{3}{5} = ?\% \qquad \frac{4}{5} = ?\% \qquad \frac{5}{5} = 100\%$$

$$\frac{1}{6} = ?\% \qquad \frac{2}{6} = ?\% \qquad \frac{3}{6} = 50\% \qquad \frac{4}{6} = ?\% \qquad \frac{5}{6} = ?\% \qquad \frac{6}{6} = 100\%$$

$$\frac{1}{7} = ?\% \qquad \frac{2}{7} = ?\% \qquad \frac{3}{7} = ?\% \qquad \frac{4}{7} = ?\% \qquad \frac{5}{7} = ?\% \qquad \frac{6}{7} = ?\% \qquad \frac{7}{7} = 100\%$$

$$\frac{1}{8} = ?\% \qquad \frac{2}{8} = ?\% \qquad \frac{3}{8} = ?\% \qquad \frac{4}{8} = 50\% \qquad \frac{5}{8} = ?\% \qquad \frac{6}{8} = ?\% \qquad \frac{7}{8} = ?\% \qquad \frac{8}{8} = 100\%$$

$$\frac{1}{9} = ?\% \qquad \frac{2}{9} = ?\% \qquad \frac{3}{9} = ?\% \qquad \frac{4}{9} = ?\% \qquad \frac{5}{9} = ?\% \qquad \frac{6}{9} = ?\% \qquad \frac{7}{9} = ?\% \qquad \frac{8}{9} = ?\% \qquad \frac{9}{9} = 100\%$$

$$\frac{1}{10} = ?\% \qquad \frac{2}{10} = ? \qquad \frac{3}{10} = ?\% \qquad \frac{4}{10} = ? \qquad \frac{5}{10} = 50\% \qquad \frac{6}{10} = ? \qquad \frac{7}{10} = ? \qquad \frac{8}{10} = ? \qquad \frac{9}{10} = ? \qquad \frac{10}{10} = 100\%$$

Solutions – Common fractions and their percentage equivalents.

$$\frac{1}{1} = 100\%$$

$$\frac{1}{2} = 50\% \qquad \frac{2}{2} = 100\%$$

$$\frac{1}{3} = 33\tfrac{1}{3}\% \qquad \frac{2}{3} = 66\tfrac{2}{3}\% \qquad \frac{3}{3} = 100\%$$

$$\frac{1}{4} = 25\% \qquad \frac{2}{4} = 50\% \qquad \frac{3}{4} = 75\% \qquad \frac{4}{4} = 100\%$$

$$\frac{1}{5} = 20\% \qquad \frac{2}{5} = 40\% \qquad \frac{3}{5} = 60\% \qquad \frac{4}{5} = 80\% \qquad \frac{5}{5} = 100\%$$

$$\frac{1}{6} = 16\tfrac{2}{3}\% \qquad \frac{2}{6} = 33\tfrac{1}{3}\% \qquad \frac{3}{6} = 50\% \qquad \frac{4}{6} = 66\tfrac{2}{3}\% \qquad \frac{5}{6} = 83\tfrac{1}{3}\% \qquad \frac{6}{6} = 100\%$$

$$\frac{1}{7} = 14.3\% \qquad \frac{2}{7} = 28.6\% \qquad \frac{3}{7} = 42.9\% \qquad \frac{4}{7} = 57.1\% \qquad \frac{5}{7} = 71.4\% \qquad \frac{6}{7} = 85.7\% \qquad \frac{7}{7} = 100\%$$

$$\frac{1}{8} = 12.5\% \qquad \frac{2}{8} = 25\% \qquad \frac{3}{8} = 37.5\% \qquad \frac{4}{8} = 50\% \qquad \frac{5}{8} = 62.5\% \qquad \frac{6}{8} = 75\% \qquad \frac{7}{8} = 87.5\% \qquad \frac{8}{8} = 100\%$$

$$\frac{1}{9} = 11.11\% \qquad \frac{2}{9} = 22.22\% \qquad \frac{3}{9} = 33.33\% \qquad \frac{4}{9} = 44.44\% \qquad \frac{5}{9} = 55.55\% \qquad \frac{6}{9} = 66.66\% \qquad \frac{7}{9} = 77.77\% \qquad \frac{8}{9} = 88.88\% \qquad \frac{9}{9} = 100\%$$

$$\frac{1}{10} = 10\% \qquad \frac{2}{10} = 20\% \qquad \frac{3}{10} = 30\% \qquad \frac{4}{10} = 40\% \qquad \frac{5}{10} = 50\% \qquad \frac{6}{10} = 60\% \qquad \frac{7}{10} = 70\% \qquad \frac{8}{10} = 80\% \qquad \frac{9}{10} = 90\% \qquad \frac{10}{10} = 100\%$$

Rules for Odd and Even Numbers

	Scenario 1:	*Scenario 2:*
Even + Even = Even	$2 + 2 = 4$	$-2 + -2 = -4$
Odd + Odd = Even	$3 + 3 = 6$	$-3 + -3 = -6$
Even + Odd = Odd	$2 + 3 = 5$	$-2 + -3 = -5$
Odd + Even = Odd	$3 + 2 = 5$	$-3 + -2 = -5$
Even − Even = Even	$4 - 2 = 2$	$-4 - (-2) = -2$
Odd − Odd = Even	$5 - 3 = 2$	$-5 - (-3) = -2$
Even − Odd = Odd	$6 - 3 = 3$	$-6 - (-3) = -3$
Odd − Even = Odd	$5 - 2 = 3$	$-5 - (-2) = -3$
Even × Even = Even	$2 \times 2 = 4$	$-2 \times -2 = 4$
Odd × Odd = Odd	$3 \times 3 = 9$	$-3 \times -3 = 9$
Even × Odd = Even	$2 \times 3 = 6$	$-2 \times -3 = 6$
Odd × Even = Even	$3 \times 2 = 6$	$-3 \times -2 = 6$
Even ÷ Even = Even	$4 \div 2 = 2$	$-4 \div -2 = 2$
Odd ÷ Odd = Odd	$9 \div 3 = 3$	$-9 \div -3 = 3$
Even ÷ Odd = Even	$6 \div 3 = 2$	$-6 \div -3 = 2$
Odd ÷ Even = *Not Possible	$5 \div 2 = 2\frac{1}{2}$	$-5 \div -2 = 2\frac{1}{2}$

*With reference to the previous two examples, an odd number divided by an even number does not result in either an even or odd integer; it results in a non-integer.

Rules for Positive and Negative Numbers

	Scenario 1:	*Scenario 2:*
Positive + Positive = Positive	$2 + 2 = 4$	
Negative + Negative = Negative	$-2 + (-2) = -4$	
Positive + Negative = Depends	$4 + (-2) = 2$	$2 + (-4) = -2$
Negative + Positive = Depends	$-2 + 4 = 2$	$-4 + 2 = -2$
Positive − Positive = Depends	$4 - 2 = 2$	$2 - 4 = -2$
Negative − Negative = Depends	$-2 - (-4) = 2$	$-4 - (-2) = -2$
Positive − Negative = Positive	$2 - (-2) = 4$	
Negative − Positive = Negative	$-4 - 2 = -6$	
Positive × Positive = Positive	$2 \times 2 = 4$	
Negative × Negative = Positive	$-2 \times -2 = 4$	
Positive × Negative = Negative	$2 \times -2 = -4$	
Negative × Positive = Negative	$-2 \times 2 = -4$	
Positive ÷ Positive = Positive	$4 \div 2 = 2$	
Negative ÷ Negative = Positive	$-4 \div -2 = 2$	
Positive ÷ Negative = Negative	$4 \div -2 = -2$	
Negative ÷ Positive = Negative	$-4 \div 2 = -2$	

Common Squares, Cubes, and Square Roots

Basic Squares from 1 to 30			Basic Cubes from 1 to 10
$1^2 = 1$	$11^2 = 121$	$21^2 = 441$	$1^3 = 1$
$2^2 = 4$	$12^2 = 144$	$22^2 = 484$	$2^3 = 8$
$3^2 = 9$	$13^2 = 169$	$23^2 = 529$	$3^3 = 27$
$4^2 = 16$	$14^2 = 196$	$24^2 = 576$	$4^3 = 64$
$5^2 = 25$	$15^2 = 225$	$25^2 = 625$	$5^3 = 125$
$6^2 = 36$	$16^2 = 256$	$26^2 = 676$	$6^3 = 216$
$7^2 = 49$	$17^2 = 289$	$27^2 = 729$	$7^3 = 343$
$8^2 = 64$	$18^2 = 324$	$28^2 = 784$	$8^3 = 512$
$9^2 = 81$	$19^2 = 361$	$29^2 = 841$	$9^3 = 729$
$10^2 = 100$	$20^2 = 400$	$30^2 = 900$	$10^3 = 1000$

Also:

$10^1 = 10$
$10^2 = 100$
$10^3 = 1,000$
$10^4 = 10,000$
$10^5 = 100,000$
$10^6 = 1,000,000$
$10^9 = 1$ billion
$10^{12} = 1$ trillion

NOTE ↫ In most English-speaking countries today (particularly the U.S., Great Britain, Canada, and Australia), one billion equals 1,000,000,000 or 10^9, or one thousand millions. In many other countries including France, Germany, Spain, Norway, and Sweden, the word "billion" indicates 10^{12}, or one million millions. Although Britain and Australia have traditionally employed the international usage of 10^{12}, they have now largely switched to the U.S. version of 10^9.

In short, for GMAT purposes, a billion equals 10^9 and a trillion equals 10^{12}.

Common Square Roots

$\sqrt{1} = 1$

$\sqrt{2} = 1.4$

$\sqrt{3} = 1.7$

$\sqrt{4} = 2$

$\sqrt{5} = 2.2$

Pop Quiz

See pages 84–85 for solutions.

Review – Converting Fractions

Convert the following fractions to their percentage equivalents:

$\frac{1}{3} =$ $\frac{2}{3} =$ $\frac{1}{6} =$ $\frac{5}{6} =$ $\frac{1}{8} =$

$\frac{3}{8} =$ $\frac{5}{8} =$ $\frac{7}{8} =$ $\frac{1}{9} =$ $\frac{5}{9} =$

Review – Converting Decimals

Convert the following decimals, which are greater than 1, into fractional equivalents.

$1.2 =$ $1.25 =$ $1.33 =$

Simplify each expression below without multiplying decimals or using a calculator. (Hint: Translate each decimal into a common fraction and then multiply and/or divide.)

$(1.25)(0.50)(0.80)(2.00) =$

$$\frac{(0.7500)(0.8333)}{(0.6250)} =$$

$$\frac{(0.2222)}{(0.3333)(0.6666)} =$$

Review – Common Squares from 13 to 30

Fill in the missing numbers to complete the Pythagorean triplets below. A Pythagorean triple consists of three positive integers a, b, and c, such that $a^2 + b^2 = c^2$.

3 : 4 : 5

5 : 12 : ___

7 : ___ : 25

8 : 15 : ___

Review – Common Square Roots

Put the following statements in order, from largest to smallest value. (Hint: Approximate each square root to one decimal point.)

I. $1 + \sqrt{5}$

II. $2 + \sqrt{3}$

III. $3 + \sqrt{2}$

Review – Exponents and Radicals

Put the following statements in order, from largest to smallest value.

I. 4

II. 4^2

III. $\sqrt{4}$

IV. $\frac{1}{4}$

V. $\left(\frac{1}{4}\right)^2$

VI. $\sqrt{\frac{1}{4}}$

Divisibility Rules

No.	Divisibility Rule	Examples
1	Every number is divisible by 1.	15 divided by 1 equals 15.
2	A number is divisible by 2 if it is even.	24 divided by 2 equals 12.
3	A number is divisible by 3 if the sum of its digits is divisible by 3.	651 is divisible by 3 since 6 + 5 + 1 = 12 and "12" is divisible by 3.
4	A number is divisible by 4 if its last two digits form a number that is divisible by 4.	1,112 is divisible by 4 since the number "12" is divisible by 4.
5	A number is divisible by 5 if the number ends in 5 or 0.	245 is divisible by 5 since this number ends in 5.
6	A number is divisible by 6 if it is divisible by both 2 and 3.	738 is divisible by 6 since this number is divisible by both 2 and 3, and the rules that govern the divisibility of 2 and 3 apply.
7	No clear rule.	Not applicable.
8	A number is divisible by 8 if its last three digits form a number that is divisible by 8.	2,104 is divisible by 8 since the number "104" is divisible by 8.
9	A number is divisible by 9 if the sum of its digits is divisible by 9.	4,887 is divisible by 9 since 4 + 8 + 8 + 7 = 27 and 27 is divisible by 9.
10	A number is divisible by 10 if it ends in 0.	990 is divisible by 10 because 990 ends in 0.

Exponents

Here are the ten basic rules governing exponents:

Rule 1 $a^b \times a^c = a^{b+c}$

             Example $2^2 \times 2^2 = 2^{2+2} = 2^4$

Rule 2 $a^b \div a^c = a^{b-c}$

             Example $2^6 \div 2^2 = 2^{6-2} = 2^4$

Rule 3 $(a^b)^c = a^{b \times c}$

             Example $(2^2)^3 = 2^{2 \times 3} = 2^6$

Rule 4 $(ab)^c = a^c b^c$

             Example $6^2 = (2 \times 3)^2 = 2^2 \times 3^2$

Rule 5 $\dfrac{a^c}{b^c} = \left(\dfrac{a}{b}\right)^c$

             Example $\dfrac{4^5}{2^5} = \left(\dfrac{4}{2}\right)^5 = 2^5$

Rule 6 $a^{-b} = \dfrac{1}{a^b}$

             Example $2^{-3} = \dfrac{1}{2^3}$

Rule 7   i) $a^{1/2} = \sqrt{a}$

Example $(4)^{1/2} = \sqrt{4} = 2$

ii) $a^{1/3} = \sqrt[3]{a}$

Example $(27)^{1/3} = \sqrt[3]{27} = 3$

iii) $a^{2/3} = \left(\sqrt[3]{a}\right)^2$

Example $(64)^{2/3} = \left(\sqrt[3]{64}\right)^2 = 4^2 = 16$

Rule 8 $a^b + a^b = a^b(1+1) = a^b(2) = 2a^b$

Example $2^{10} + 2^{10} = 2^{10}(1+1) = 2^{10}(2) = 2^{10}(2^1) = 2^{11}$

Rule 9 $a^b + a^c \neq a^{b+c}$

Example $2^2 + 2^3 \neq 2^{2+3}$

Rule 10 $a^b - a^c \neq a^{b-c}$

Example $2^5 - 2^2 \neq 2^{5-2}$

Radicals

Here are the ten basic rules governing radicals:

Rule 1 $\left(\sqrt{a}\right)^2 = a$

Example $\left(\sqrt{4}\right)^2 = 4$

Proof $\sqrt{4} \times \sqrt{4} = \sqrt{16} = 4$

Rule 2 $\sqrt{a} \times \sqrt{b} = \sqrt{a \times b}$

Example $\sqrt{4} \times \sqrt{9} = \sqrt{36}$

Proof $\sqrt{4} = 2; \sqrt{9} = 3.$
Thus, $2 \times 3 = 6$

Rule 3 $\sqrt{a} \div \sqrt{b} = \sqrt{\dfrac{a}{b}}$

Example $\sqrt{100} \div \sqrt{25} = \sqrt{4}$

Proof $\sqrt{100} = 10; \sqrt{25} = 5.$
Thus, $10 \div 5 = 2$

Rule 4 $\dfrac{\sqrt[c]{a}}{\sqrt[c]{b}} = \sqrt[c]{\dfrac{a}{b}}$

Example $\dfrac{\sqrt[3]{64}}{\sqrt[3]{8}} = \sqrt[3]{\dfrac{64}{8}}$

Proof $\sqrt[3]{64} = 4; \sqrt[3]{8} = 2.$
Thus, $4 \div 2 = 2$

Rule 5 $b\sqrt{a} + c\sqrt{a} = (b + c)\sqrt{a}$

Example $3\sqrt{4} + 2\sqrt{4} = 5\sqrt{4}$

Proof $\sqrt{4} = 2.$
Thus, $3(2) + 2(2) = 5(2)$

Rule 6 $b\sqrt{a} - c\sqrt{a} = (b - c)\sqrt{a}$

Example $5\sqrt{9} - 2\sqrt{9} = 3\sqrt{9}$

Proof $\sqrt{9} = 3.$ Thus, $5(3) - 2(3) = 3(3)$

Rule 7 $$\frac{b}{\sqrt{a}} = \frac{b}{\sqrt{a}} \times \frac{\sqrt{a}}{\sqrt{a}} = \frac{b\sqrt{a}}{a}$$

Example $$\frac{6}{\sqrt{3}} = \frac{6}{\sqrt{3}} \times \frac{\sqrt{3}}{\sqrt{3}} = \frac{6\sqrt{3}}{\sqrt{9}} = \frac{6\sqrt{3}}{3} = 2\sqrt{3}$$

In the calculation directly above, we multiply both the numerator and denominator of the original fraction by $\sqrt{3}$ $\left(\text{i.e.,} \frac{6}{\sqrt{3}} \times \frac{\sqrt{3}}{\sqrt{3}}\right)$ in order to remove the radical from the denominator of this fraction.

Rule 8 $$\frac{\sqrt{a}+1}{\sqrt{a}-1} = \frac{\sqrt{a}+1}{\sqrt{a}-1} \times \frac{\sqrt{a}+1}{\sqrt{a}+1}$$

Example $$\frac{\sqrt{2}+1}{\sqrt{2}-1} = \frac{\sqrt{2}+1}{\sqrt{2}-1} \times \frac{\sqrt{2}+1}{\sqrt{2}+1} = 3 + 2\sqrt{2}$$

In the calculation directly above, we multiply both the numerator and denominator of the fraction by $\sqrt{2}+1$ $\left(\text{i.e.,} \frac{\sqrt{2}+1}{\sqrt{2}-1} \times \frac{\sqrt{2}+1}{\sqrt{2}+1}\right)$ in order to remove the radical from the denominator of this fraction.

$$\frac{\sqrt{a}-1}{\sqrt{a}+1} = \frac{\sqrt{a}-1}{\sqrt{a}+1} \times \frac{\sqrt{a}-1}{\sqrt{a}-1}$$

Example $$\frac{\sqrt{2}-1}{\sqrt{2}+1} = \frac{\sqrt{2}-1}{\sqrt{2}+1} \times \frac{\sqrt{2}-1}{\sqrt{2}-1} = 3 - 2\sqrt{2}$$

By multiplying both the numerator and denominator of the fraction by $\sqrt{2}-1$ $\left(\text{i.e.,} \frac{\sqrt{2}-1}{\sqrt{2}+1} \times \frac{\sqrt{2}-1}{\sqrt{2}-1}\right)$ we can remove the radical from the denominator of this fraction.

Rule 9 $\qquad \sqrt{a} + \sqrt{b} \neq \sqrt{a+b}$

Example $\quad \sqrt{16} + \sqrt{9} \neq \sqrt{25}$

Proof $\qquad \sqrt{16} = 4; \sqrt{9} = 3.$
Thus, $4 + 3 \neq 5$

Rule 10 $\qquad \sqrt{a} - \sqrt{b} \neq \sqrt{a-b}$

Example $\quad \sqrt{25} - \sqrt{16} \neq \sqrt{9}$

Proof $\qquad \sqrt{25} = 5; \sqrt{16} = 4.$
Thus, $5 - 4 \neq 3$

Basic Geometry Formulas

Circles

Circumference:

Circumference = $\pi \times$ diameter

$C = \pi d$ or $C = 2\pi r$
[where r = radius and Q = center point]

Area:

Area = $\pi \times$ radius^2

$A = \pi r^2$

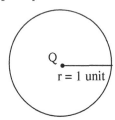

r = 1 unit

Triangles

Area:

Area = $\dfrac{\text{base} \times \text{height}}{2}$

$A = \dfrac{bh}{2}$

The Pythagorean Theorem:

$c^2 = a^2 + b^2$
[where c is the length of the hypotenuse and a and b are the length of the legs]

3 : 4 : 5 Triangle

In a $3:4:5$ triangle, the ratios of the length of the sides are always $3:4:5$ units.

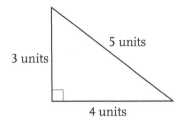

45°–45°–90° Triangle

In a 45°–45°–90° triangle, the ratios of the length of the sides are $1:1:\sqrt{2}$ units. A right-isosceles triangle is another name for a 45°–45°–90° triangle.

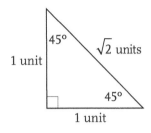

30°–60°–90° Triangle

In a 30°–60°–90° triangle, the ratios of the lengths of the sides are $1:\sqrt{3}:2$ units.

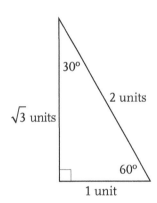

Squares

Perimeter:

Perimeter = 4 × side

$P = 4s$

Example $P = 4(2) = 8$ units

Area:

Area = side^2

$A = s^2$

Example $A = (2)^2 = 4$ units^2

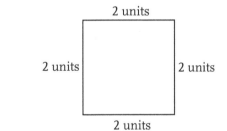

Rectangles

Perimeter:

Perimeter = (2 × length) + (2 × width)

$P = 2l + 2w$

Example $P = 2(4) + 2(2) = 12$ units

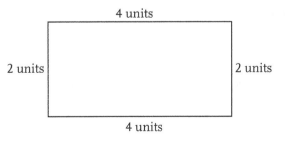

Area:

Area = length × width

$A = lw$

Example $A = 4 \times 2 = 8 \text{ units}^2$

Cubes

Surface Area:

Surface Area = 6 × side^2

$SA = 6s^2$

Example $SA = 6(2)^2 = 24 \text{ units}^2$

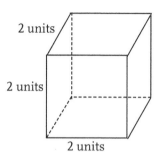

Volume:

Volume = side^3

$V = s^3$

Example $V = 2^3 = 8 \text{ units}^3$

Rectangular Solids

Surface Area:

Surface Area = 2(length × width) + 2(length × heigth) + 2(width × height)

$SA = 2lw + 2lh + 2wh$

Example $SA = 2(4 \times 2) + 2(4 \times 3) + 2(2 \times 3) = 52 \text{ units}^2$

Volume:

Volume = length × width × height

$V = lwh$

Example $V = 4 \times 2 \times 3 = 24 \text{ units}^3$

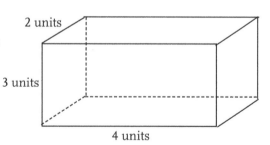

Circular Cylinders

Surface Area:

Surface Area = $2\pi \, (\text{radius})^2 + \pi(\text{diameter})(\text{height})$

Surface Area = $2\pi r^2 + \pi dh$

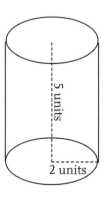

Example $SA = 2\pi(2)^2 + \pi(4)(5)$

$SA = 8\pi + 20\pi = 28\pi \text{ units}^2$

Volume:

Volume $= \pi r^2 h$

Example $V = \pi(2)^2(5) = 20\pi \text{ units}^3$

Cone

Volume:

Volume $= \frac{1}{3}Bh = \frac{1}{3}\pi r^2 h$

Example $V = \frac{1}{3}\pi(3)^2(6) = 18\pi \text{ units}^3$

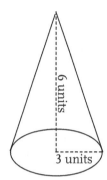

Pyramids

Volume:

Volume $= \frac{1}{3}Bh$

[where B is the area of the base and h is the height]

Example $V = \frac{1}{3}(20)(3) \text{ units}^3$

Note: The formula for all tapered solids is the same: $V = \frac{1}{3}Bh$, where B is the area of the base and h is the perpendicular distance from the base to the vertex.

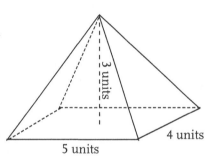

Sphere

Surface Area:

Surface Area $= 4\pi r^2$

Example $SA = 4\pi(3)^2 = 36\pi \text{ units}^2$

Volume:

Volume $= \frac{4}{3}\pi r^3$

Example $V = \frac{4}{3}\pi(3)^3 = 36\pi \text{ units}^3$

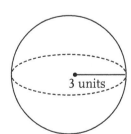

Probability, Permutations & Combinations

Overview

Exhibits 2.1–2.2 are strategic flowcharts for use in both previewing and reviewing the material in this section. First, what is the difference between probability and permutations and combinations? Probabilities are expressed as fractions or decimals between 0 and 1 (where 1 is the probability of certainty and 0 is the probability of impossibility) or, alternatively, as percentages between 0% and 100% (where 100% is the probability of certainty and 0% is the probability of impossibility). Permutations and combinations, on the other hand, result in outcomes greater than or equal to 1. Frequently they result in quite large outcomes such as 10, 36, 720, etc.

Probability:

In terms of probability, a quick rule of thumb is to determine first whether we are dealing with an "and" or "or" situation. "And" means multiply and "or" means addition. For example, if a problem states "what is the probability of *x* and *y*," we multiply individual probabilities together. If a problem states "what is the probability of *x* or *y*," we add individual probabilities together.

Moreover, if a probability problem requires us to <u>multiply</u>, we must ask one further question: "Are the events independent or are the events dependent?" *Independent* means that two events have no influence on one another and we simply multiply individual probabilities together to arrive at a final answer. *Not independent (or dependent)* events mean that the occurrence of one event has an influence on the occurrence of another event and this influence must be taken into account.

Likewise, if a problem requires us to <u>add</u> probabilities, we must ask one further question: "Are the events mutually exclusive or non-mutually exclusive?" *Mutually exclusive* means that two events cannot occur at the same time and there is no "overlap" present. If two events have no overlap, we simply add probabilities. *Not mutually exclusive* means that two events can occur at the same time and that overlap is present. If two events do contain overlap, this overlap must not be double counted.

Permutations and Combinations:

With respect to permutations and combinations, permutations are ordered groups while combinations are unordered groups. Order matters in permutations; order does not matter in combinations. For example, AB and BA are considered different outcomes in permutations, but are considered a single outcome in combinations. In real-life, examples of permutations include telephone numbers, license plates, electronic codes, and passwords. Examples of combinations include selection of members for a team or lottery tickets. In the case of lottery tickets, for instance, the order of numbers does not matter; we just need to get all the numbers, usually six of them.

As a practitioner's rule, the words "arrangements" or "possibilities" imply permutations; the words "select" or "choose" imply combinations.

Factorials:

Factorial means that we engage multiplication such that:

     Example: $4! = 4 \times 3 \times 2 \times 1$

     Example: $7! = 7 \times 6 \times 5 \times 4 \times 3 \times 2 \times 1$

Zero factorial equals one and one factorial also equals one:

     Example: $0! = 1$

     Example: $1! = 1$

Coins, Dice, Marbles, and Cards:

Problems in this chapter include reference to coins, dice, marbles, and cards. For clarification purposes: The two sides of a coin are heads and tails. A die has six sides numbered from 1 to 6, with each having an equal likelihood of appearing subsequent to being tossed. The word "die" is singular; "dice" is plural. Marbles are assumed to be of a single, solid color. A deck of cards contains 52 cards divided equally into four suits—clubs, diamonds, hearts, and spades—where each suit contains 13 cards including ace, king, queen, jack, 10, 9, 8, 7, 6, 5, 4, 3, and 2. Card problems have not appeared on the GMAT in recent years.

EXHIBIT 2.1   PROBABILITY FLOWCHART

The numbers at the bottom of the chart denote the applicable probability formula.

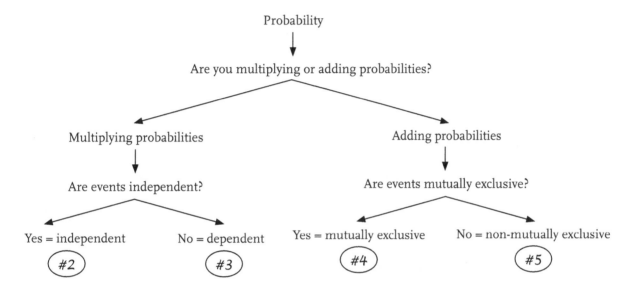

EXHIBIT 2.2   PERMUTATIONS AND COMBINATIONS FLOWCHART

The numbers at the bottom of the chart denote the applicable permutation or combination formula.

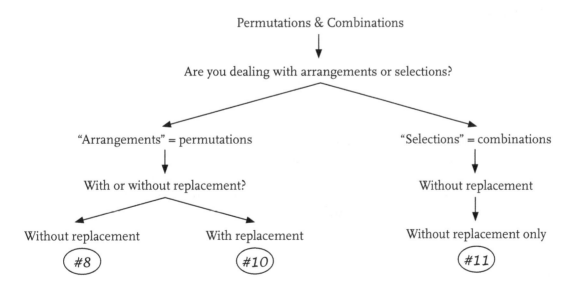

Basic Probability Formulas

Here at a glance are the basic probability, permutation, and combination formulas used in this chapter and which are applicable to the GMAT.

Universal Formula

#1 $\text{Probability} = \dfrac{\text{Selected Events(s)}}{\text{Total Number of Possibilities}}$

Example: You buy 3 raffle tickets and there are 10,000 tickets sold. What is the probability of winning the single prize?

$$\text{Probability} = \frac{3}{10,000}$$

Special Multiplication Rule

#2 $P(A \text{ and } B) = P(A) \times P(B)$

[Where the probability of A and B equals the probability of A times the probability of B]

If events are independent (that is, one event has no influence on the other), we simply multiply them together.

Example: What is the probability of tossing a coin twice and obtaining heads on both the first and second toss?

$$\frac{1}{2} \times \frac{1}{2} = \frac{1}{4}$$

General Multiplication Rule

#3 $P(A \text{ and } B) = P(A) \times P(B/A)$

[Where the probability of A and B equals the probability of A times the probability of B, given that A has already occurred]

If events are not independent (that is, one event has an influence on the other), we must adjust the second event based on its influence from the first event.

Example: A bag contains six marbles, three blue and three green. What is the probability of blindly reaching into the bag and pulling out two green marbles?

$$\frac{3}{6} \times \frac{2}{5} = \frac{6}{30} = \frac{1}{5}$$

Special Addition Rule

(#4) $P(A \text{ or } B) = P(A) + P(B)$

[Where the probability of A or B equals the probability of A added to the probability of B]

If events are mutually exclusive (that is, there is no overlap), then we just add the probability of the events together.

Example: The probability that Sam will go to high school at Montcalm Academy is 50 percent, while the probability that he will go to Crescent Heights High School is 25 percent. What is the probability that he will choose to go to high school at either Montcalm Academy or Crescent Heights High School?

50% + 25% = 75%

General Addition Rule

(#5) $P(A \text{ or } B) = P(A) + P(B) - P(A \text{ and } B)$

[Where the probability of A or B equals the probability of A added to the probability of B minus the probability of A and B]

If events are not mutually exclusive (that is, there is overlap), then we must subtract out the overlap subsequent to adding the events.

Example: The probability that tomorrow will be rainy is 30 percent. The probability that tomorrow will be windy is 20 percent. What is the probability that tomorrow's weather will be either rainy or windy?

30% + 20% − (30% × 20%)
30% + 20% − 6%
50% − 6% = 44%

With regard to the General Addition Rule, the reason that we subtract out the overlap is because we do not want to count it twice. When two events overlap, both events contain that same overlap. Thus, it must be subtracted once in order not to "double" count it.

NOTE ✑ Let's quickly contrast what is commonly referred to as the inclusive "or" and the exclusive "or." The problem used in support of probability formula #5 is governed by an inclusive "or." It is reasonable to assume that tomorrow's weather can be <u>both</u> rainy and windy. The problem is effectively asking: "What is the probability that tomorrow's weather will be either rainy or windy, or both rainy and windy?" The inclusive "or" occurs whenever there is overlap. The problem used in support of probability formula #4 effectively asks: "What is the probability that Sam will choose to go to high school at Montcalm Academy or Crescent Heights High School, but not both high schools?" The choice between going to high school at two different locations is a mutually exclusive one, and we treat that particular problem as involving an exclusive "or."

Complement Rule

(#6) $P(A) = 1 - P(not\ A)$

[Where the probability of A equals one minus the probability of A not occurring]

The Complement Rule of probability describes the *subtracting* of probabilities rather than the adding or multiplying of probabilities. To calculate the probability of an event using this rule, we ask: "What is the probability of a given event not occurring?" Then we subtract this result from 1.

Example: What is the probability of rolling a pair of dice and not rolling double sixes?

The probability of rolling double sixes:

$$\frac{1}{6} \times \frac{1}{6} = \frac{1}{36}$$

The probability of not rolling double sixes:

$$1 - \frac{1}{36} = \frac{35}{36}$$

Rule of Enumeration

(#7) If there are x ways of doing one thing, y ways of doing a second thing, and z ways of doing a third thing, then the number of ways doing all these things is $x \times y \times z$. This is known as the Rule of Enumeration.

NOTE ๑ Technically, the Rule of Enumeration does not fall under the umbrella of "probability" or "permutation" or "combination." For practical reasons, however, it is most often discussed along with probability.

Example: Fast-Feast Restaurant offers customers a set menu with a choice of one of each of the following: 2 different salads, 3 different soups, 5 different entrees, 3 different desserts, and coffee or tea. How many possibilities are there with respect to how a customer can take his or her meal?

$2 \times 3 \times 5 \times 3 \times 2 = 180$

Permutations

(#8) Without replacement $_{n}P_{r} = \dfrac{n!}{(n-r)!}$

[Where n = total number of items and r = number of items we are taking or arranging]

Example: How many two-letter codes can be made from the letters A, B, C, and D if the same letter cannot be displayed more than once in any given code?

$$_{n}P_{r} = \frac{n!}{(n-r)!}$$

$$_{4}P_{2} = \frac{4!}{(4-2)!} = \frac{4!}{2!} = \frac{4 \times 3 \times \cancel{2 \times 1}}{\cancel{2 \times 1}} = 4 \times 3 = 12$$

#9 $_n P_n = n!$

[Shortcut formula when all items are taken together]

Example: How many ways can a person display (or arrange) four different books on a shelf?

$$_n P_r = \frac{n!}{(n-r)!}$$

$$_4 P_4 = \frac{4!}{(4-4)!} = \frac{4!}{0!} = \frac{4!}{1} = 4! = 4 \times 3 \times 2 \times 1 = 24$$

Also, shortcut formula: $n! = 4! = 24$

#10 (With replacement n^r

Example: How many four-digit codes can be made from the numbers 1, 2, 3, and 4, if the same numbers can be displayed more than once in a given code?

$$n^r \qquad 4^4 = 256$$

NOTE ᴥ Permutation with replacement (that is, n^r) technically falls under the Rule of Enumeration. It is included here for ease of presentation. For a problem to be considered a permutation, the permutation formula must be applicable.

Combinations

#11 $_n C_r = \frac{n!}{r!(n-r)!}$

[Where n = total number of items taken and r = the number of items we are choosing or selecting]

Example: How many ways can a person choose three of four colors for the purpose of painting the inside of a house?

$$_n C_r = \frac{n!}{r!(n-r)!}$$

$$_4 C_3 = \frac{4!}{3!(4-3)!} = \frac{4!}{3! \times (1)!} = \frac{4 \times \cancel{3 \times 2 \times 1}}{\cancel{3 \times 2 \times 1} \times 1} = 4$$

Additional formulas:

Joint Permutations

#12 $_n P_r \times _n P_r = \frac{n!}{(n-r)!} \times \frac{n!}{(n-r)!}$

Example: A tourist plans to visit three of five Western European cities and then proceed to visit two of four Eastern European cities. At the planning stage, how many itineraries are possible?

$$_5P_3 \times {_4}P_2$$

$$\frac{5!}{(5-3)!} \times \frac{4!}{(4-2)!}$$

$$\frac{5!}{2!} \times \frac{4!}{2!}$$

$$\frac{5 \times 4 \times 3 \times \cancel{2 \times 1}}{\cancel{2 \times 1}} \times \frac{4 \times 3 \times \cancel{2 \times 1}}{\cancel{2 \times 1}}$$

$$60 \times 12 = 720$$

Multiplying outcomes, rather than adding them, is consistent with the treatment afforded by the Rule of Enumeration.

Joint Combinations

(#13) $\quad _nC_r \times {_n}C_r = \dfrac{n!}{r!(n-r)!} \times \dfrac{n!}{r!(n-r)!}$

Example: A special marketing task force is to be chosen from five professional golfers and five professional tennis players. If the final task force chosen is to consist of three golfers and three tennis players, then how many different task forces are possible?

$$_5C_3 \times {_5}C_3$$

$$\frac{5!}{3!(5-3)!} \times \frac{5!}{3!(5-3)!}$$

$$\frac{5!}{3!(2)!} \times \frac{5!}{3!(2)!}$$

$$\frac{5 \times 4 \times \cancel{3 \times 2 \times 1}}{\cancel{3 \times 2 \times 1} \times 2 \times 1} \times \frac{5 \times 4 \times \cancel{3 \times 2 \times 1}}{\cancel{3 \times 2 \times 1} \times 2 \times 1}$$

$$10 \times 10 = 100$$

Repeated Letters or Numbers (Permutations)

(#14) $\dfrac{n!}{x!\,y!\,z!}$ {where x, y, and z are different but identical letters or numbers]

Example: How many four-numeral codes can be created using the four numbers 0, 0, 1, and 2?

$$\frac{4!}{2!} = \frac{4 \times 3 \times \cancel{2 \times 1}}{\cancel{2 \times 1}} = 12$$

Note that 2! denotes the two zeros which represent repeated numbers.

MULTIPLE-CHOICE PROBLEMS

Distance-Rate-Time Problems

1. **River Boat ( )**

    A river boat leaves Silver Town and travels upstream to Gold Town at an average speed of 6 kilometers per hour. It returns by the same route at an average speed of 9 kilometers per hour. What is the average speed for the round-trip in kilometers per hour?

    A)   7.0
    B)   7.1
    C)   7.2
    D)   7.5
    E)   8.0

2. **Run-Run ( )**

    If Susan takes 9 seconds to run y yards, how many *minutes* will it take her to run x yards at the same rate?

    A) $\dfrac{xy}{9}$

    B) $\dfrac{9x}{60y}$

    C) $\dfrac{60xy}{9}$

    D) $\dfrac{xy}{540}$

    E) $\dfrac{540x}{y}$

3. **Forgetful Timothy ( )**

    Timothy leaves home for school, riding his bicycle at a rate of 9 miles per hour. Fifteen minutes after he leaves, his mother sees Timothy's math homework lying on his bed and immediately leaves home to bring it to him. If his mother drives at 36 miles per hour, how far (in terms of miles) must she drive before she reaches Timothy?

    A) $\dfrac{1}{3}$
    B)   3
    C)   4
    D)   9
    E)   12

51

4. P & Q

P and Q are the only two applicants qualified for a short-term research project that pays 600 dollars in total. Candidate P has more experience and, if hired, would be paid 50 percent more per hour than candidate Q would be paid. Candidate Q, if hired, would require 10 hours more than candidate P to do the job. Candidate P's hourly wage is how many dollars greater than candidate Q's hourly wage?

A) $10
B) $15
C) $20
D) $25
E) $30

5. Submarine

On a reconnaissance mission, a state-of-the-art nuclear powered submarine traveled 240 miles to reposition itself in the proximity of an aircraft carrier. This journey would have taken 1 hour less if the submarine had traveled 20 miles per hour faster. What was the average speed, in miles per hour, for the actual journey?

A) 20
B) 40
C) 60
D) 80
E) 100

6. Sixteen-Wheeler

Two heavily loaded sixteen-wheeler transport trucks are 770 kilometers apart, sitting at two rest stops on opposite sides of the same highway. Driver A begins heading down the highway driving at an average speed of 90 kilometers per hour. Exactly one hour later, Driver B starts down the highway toward Driver A, maintaining an average speed of 80 kilometers per hour. How many kilometers *farther* than Driver B, will Driver A have driven when they meet and pass each other on the highway?

A) 90
B) 130
C) 150
D) 320
E) 450

Age Problems

7. **Elmer ( )**

    Elmer, the circus Elephant, is currently three times older than Leo, the circus Lion. In five years from now, Leo the circus Lion will be exactly half as old as Elmer, the circus Elephant. How old is Elmer today?

    A)   10
    B)   15
    C)   17
    D)   22
    E)   25

Average Problems

8. **Three's Company ( )**

    The average (arithmetic mean) of four numbers is $4x + 3$. If one of the numbers is x, what is the average of the other three numbers?

    A) $x + 1$
    B) $3x + 3$
    C) $5x + 1$
    D) $5x + 4$
    E) $15x + 12$

9. **Fourth Time Lucky ( )**

    On his first 3 tests, Rajeev received an average score of N points. If on his fourth test, he exceeds his previous average score by 20 points, what is his average score for his first 4 tests?

    A) N
    B) $N + 4$
    C) $N + 5$
    D) $N + 10$
    E) $N + 20$

10. Vacation (🌶🌶)

P persons have decided to rent a van to tour while on holidays. The price of the van is *x* dollars and each person is to pay an equal share. If *D* persons cancel their trip thus failing to pay their share, which of the following represents the *additional* number of dollars per person that each remaining person must pay in order to still rent the van?

A) Dx

B) $\dfrac{x}{P-D}$

C) $\dfrac{Dx}{P-D}$

D) $\dfrac{Dx}{P(P-D)}$

E) $\dfrac{x}{P(P-D)}$

Work Problems

11. Disappearing Act (🌶🌶)

Working individually, Deborah can wash all the dishes from her friend's wedding banquet in 5 hours and Tom can wash all the dishes in 6 hours. If Deborah and Tom work together but independently at the task for 2 hours, at which point Tom leaves, how many remaining hours will it take Deborah to complete the task alone?

A) $\dfrac{4}{15}$

B) $\dfrac{3}{11}$

C) $\dfrac{4}{3}$

D) $\dfrac{15}{11}$

E) $\dfrac{11}{2}$

12. Exhibition (🌶️🌶️)

If it takes 70 workers 3 hours to disassemble the exhibition rides at a small amusement park, how many hours would it take 30 workers to do this same job?

A) $\dfrac{40}{3}$

B)   11

C)   7

D) $\dfrac{7}{3}$

E) $\dfrac{9}{7}$.

13. Legal (🌶️🌶️🌶️)

A group of 4 junior lawyers require 5 hours to complete a legal research assignment. How many hours would it take a group of three legal assistants to complete the same research assignment assuming that a legal assistant works at two-thirds the rate of a junior lawyer?

A)   13
B)   10 .
C)   9
D)   6
E)   5

Picture Frame, Rug, or Border Problems

14. Persian Rug (🌶️🌶️)

A Persian rug set on a dining room floor measures *a* inches by *b* inches, which includes the actual rug design and a solid colored border *c* inches. Which algebraic expression below represents the *area* of the solid colored <u>border</u> in square inches?

A) $ab - 4c$

B) $a + b - [(a - c) + (b - c)]$

C) $2a + 2b - [2(a - 2c) + 2(b - 2c)]$

D) $ab - (a - c)(b - c)$

E) $ab - (a - 2c)(b - 2c)$.

Mixture Problems

15. Nuts ( )

A wholesaler wishes to sell 100 pounds of mixed nuts at $2.50 a pound. She mixes peanuts worth $1.50 a pound with cashews worth $4.00 a pound. How many pounds of cashews must she use?

A)   40
B)   45
C)   50
D)   55
E)   60

16. Gold ( )

An alloy weighing 24 ounces is 70 percent gold. How many ounces of pure gold must be added to create an alloy that is 90 percent gold?

A)   6
B)   9
C)   12
D)   24
E)   48

17. Evaporation ( )

How many liters of water must be evaporated from 50 liters of a 3-percent sugar solution to get a 10-percent solution?

A)   35

B) $33\frac{1}{3}$

C)   27

D) $16\frac{2}{3}$

E)   15

Group Problems

18. **Standardized Test ( )**

    If 85 percent of the test takers taking an old paper and pencil GMAT exam answered the first question on a given math section correctly, and 75 percent of the test takers answered the second question correctly, and 5 percent of the test takers answered neither question correctly, what percent answered *both* correctly?

    A)   60%
    B)   65% ·
    C)   70%
    D)   75%
    E)   80%

19. **Language Classes ( )**

    According to the admissions and records office of a major university, the schedules of X first-year college students were inspected and it was found that S number of students were taking a Spanish course, F number of students were taking a French course, and B number of students were taking both a Spanish and a French Course. Which of the following expressions gives the percentage of students whose schedules were inspected who were taking *neither* a Spanish course *nor* a French course?

    A) $100 \times \dfrac{X}{B+F+S}$

    B) $100 \times \dfrac{B+F+S}{X}$

    C) $100 \times \dfrac{X-F-S}{X}$

    D) $100 \times \dfrac{X+B-F-S}{X}$ ·

    E) $100 \times \dfrac{X-B-F-S}{X}$

20. German Cars (𝄞𝄞𝄞)

The *New Marketing Journal* conducted a survey of wealthy German car owners. According to the survey, all wealthy car owners owned one or more of the following three brands: BMW, Mercedes, or Porsche. Respondents' answers were grouped as follows: 45 owned BMW cars, 38 owned Mercedes cars, and 27 owned Porsche cars. Of these, 15 owned both BMW and Mercedes cars, 12 owned both Mercedes and Porsche cars, 8 owned both BMW and Porsche cars, and 5 persons owned all three types of cars. How many different individuals were surveyed?

A)   70
B)   75
C)   80
D)   110
E)   130

Matrix Problems

21. Single (𝄞𝄞)

In a graduate physics course, 70 percent of the students are male and 30 percent of the students are married. If two-sevenths of the male students are married, what fraction of the female students is single?

A) $\dfrac{2}{7}$

B) $\dfrac{1}{3}$

C) $\dfrac{1}{2}$

D) $\dfrac{2}{3}$

E) $\dfrac{5}{7}$

22. Batteries (🌶🌶🌶)

One-fifth of the batteries produced by an upstart factory are defective and one-quarter of all batteries produced are rejected by the quality control technician. If one-tenth of the non-defective batteries are rejected by mistake, and if all the batteries not rejected are sold, then what percent of the batteries sold by the factory are defective?

A)   4%
B)   5%
C)   6%
D)   8%
E)   12%

23. Experiment (🌶🌶🌶)

Sixty percent of the rats included in an experiment were female rats. If some of the rats died during an experiment and 70 percent of the rats that died were male rats, what was the ratio of the death rate among the male rats to the death rate among the female rats?

A)   7 : 2
B)   7 : 3
C)   2 : 7
D)   3 : 7
E)   Cannot be determined from the information given

Price-Cost-Volume-Profit Problems

24. Garments (🌶)

If s shirts can be purchased for d dollars, how many shirts can be purchased for t dollars?

A) sdt

B) $\dfrac{ts}{d}$

C) $\dfrac{td}{s}$

D) $\dfrac{d}{st}$

E) $\dfrac{s}{dt}$

25. Pete's Pet Shop (🌶🌶)

At Pete's Pet Shop, 35 cups of bird seed are used every 7 days to feed 15 parakeets. How many cups of bird seed would be required to feed 9 parakeets for 12 days?

A)   32
B)   36
C)   39
D)   42
E)   45

26. Sabrina (🌶🌶)

Sabrina is contemplating a job switch. She is thinking of leaving her job paying $85,000 per year to accept a sales job paying $45,000 per year plus 15 percent commission for each sale made. If each of her sales is for $1,500, what is the least number of sales she must make per year if she is not to lose money because of the job change?

A)   57
B)   177
C)   178
D)   377
E)   378

27. Delicatessen (🌶🌶)

A large delicatessen purchased p pounds of cheese for c dollars per pound. If d pounds of the cheese had to be discarded due to spoilage and the delicatessen sold the rest for s dollars per pound, which of the following represents the gross profit on the sale of the purchase? (gross profit equals sales revenue minus product cost)

A) $(s - c)(p - d)$
B) $s(p - d) - cp$
C) $c(p - d) - sd$
D) $d(s - c) - pc$
E) $pc - ds$

28. Prototype (🌶🌶🌶)

A Prototype fuel-efficient car (P-Car) is estimated to get 80% more miles per gallon of gasoline than does a traditional fuel-efficient car (T-Car). However, the P-Car requires a special type of gasoline that costs 20% more per gallon than does the gasoline used by a T-Car. If the two cars are driven the same distance, what percent less than the money spent on gasoline for the T-Car is the money spent on gasoline for the P-Car?

A) $16\frac{2}{3}\%$

B) $33\frac{1}{3}$

C) 50%

D) 60%

E) $66\frac{2}{3}\%$

Least-Common-Multiple Word Problems

29. Lights (🌶🌶)

The Royal Hawaiian Hotel decorates its Rainbow Christmas Tree with non-flashing white lights and a series of colored flashing lights—red, blue, green, orange, and yellow. The red lights turn red every 20 seconds, the blue lights turn blue every 30 seconds, the green lights turn green every 45 seconds, the orange lights turn orange every 60 seconds, and yellow lights turn yellow every 1 minute and 20 seconds. The manager plugs the tree in for the first time on December 1st precisely at midnight and all lights begin their cycle at exactly the same time. If the five colored lights flash simultaneously at midnight, what is the next time all five colored lights will all flash together at the exact same time?

A) 0:03 AM
B) 0:04 AM
C) 0:06 AM
D) 0:12 AM
E) 0:24 AM

General Algebraic Word Problems

30. Hardware (🌶)

Hammers and wrenches are manufactured at a uniform weight per hammer and a uniform weight per wrench. If the total weight of two hammers and three wrenches is one-third that of 8 hammers and 5 wrenches, then the total weight of one wrench is how many times that of one hammer?

A) $\dfrac{1}{2}$

B) $\dfrac{2}{3}$

C)   1

D) $\dfrac{3}{2}$

E)   2

31. Snooker (🌶 🌶)

A snooker tournament charges $45.00 for VIP seats and $15.00 for general admission ("regular" seats). On a certain night, a total of 320 tickets were sold, for a total cost of $7,500. How many *fewer* tickets were sold that night for VIP seats than for general admission seats?

A)   70
B)   90
C)   140
D)   230
E)   250

32. Chili Paste (🌶 🌶)

Each week a restaurant serving Mexican food uses the same volume of chili paste, which comes in either 25-ounce cans or 15-ounce cans of chili paste. If the restaurant must order 40 more of the smaller cans than the larger cans to fulfill its weekly needs, then how many *smaller* cans are required to fulfill its weekly needs?

A)   60
B)   70
C)   80
D)   100
E)   120

33. Premium ( )

The price of 5 kilograms of premium fertilizer is the same as the price of 6 kilograms of regular fertilizer. If the price of premium fertilizer is y cents per kilogram more than the price of regular fertilizer, what is the price, in cents, per kilogram of premium fertilizer?

A) $\dfrac{y}{30}$

B) $\dfrac{5}{6}y$

C) $\dfrac{6}{5}y$

D) $5y$

E) $6y$

Function Problems

34. Function ( )

If $f(x) = \sqrt{x}$ and $g(x) = \sqrt{x^2 + 7}$, what is the value of $f(g(3))$?

A)   1
B)   2
C)   3
D)   4
E)   5

Algebraic Fractions

35. Rescue ( )

If $a = \dfrac{b-d}{c-d}$, then $d =$

A) $\dfrac{b+a}{c+a}$

B) $\dfrac{b-a}{c-a}$

C) $\dfrac{bc-a}{bc+a}$

D) $\dfrac{b-ac}{1-a}$

E) $\dfrac{b-ac}{a-1}$

36. Hodgepodge ( )

The expression $\dfrac{\dfrac{1}{h}}{1-\dfrac{1}{h}}$, where h is not equal to 0 and 1, is equivalent to which of the following?

A) $1-h$

B) $h-1$

C) $\dfrac{1}{h-1}$

D) $\dfrac{1}{1-h}$

E) $\dfrac{h}{h-1}$

Fractions and Decimals

37. Mirage (🌶)

Which of the following has the greatest value?

A) $\dfrac{10}{11}$

B) $\dfrac{4}{5}$

C) $\dfrac{7}{8}$

D) $\dfrac{21}{22}$

E) $\dfrac{5}{6}$

38. Deceptive (🌶)

Dividing 100 by 0.75 will lead to the same mathematical result as multiplying 100 by which number?

A) 0.25
B) 0.75
C) 1.25
D) 1.33
E) 1.75

39. Spiral (🌶🌶)

In a certain sequence, the first term is 2, and each successive term is 1 more than the reciprocal of the term that immediately precedes it. What is the fifth term in this sequence?

A) $\dfrac{13}{8}$

B) $\dfrac{21}{13}$

C) $\dfrac{8}{5}$

D) $\dfrac{5}{8}$

E) $\dfrac{8}{13}$

Percentage Problems

40. Discount (🌶)

A discount of 10 percent on an order of goods followed by a discount of 30 percent amounts to

- A) the same as one 13 percent discount
- B) the same as one 27 percent discount
- C) the same as one 33 percent discount
- D) the same as one 37 percent discount
- E) the same as one 40 percent discount

41. Inflation (🌶)

An inflationary increase of 20 percent on an order of raw materials followed by an inflationary increase of 10 percent amounts to

- A) the same as one 22 percent inflationary increase
- B) the same as one 30 percent inflationary increase
- C) the same as an inflationary increase of 10 percent followed by an inflationary increase of 20 percent
- D) less than an inflationary increase of 10 percent followed by an inflationary increase of 20 percent
- E) more than an inflationary increase of 10 percent followed by an inflationary increase of 20 percent

42. Gardener (🌶)

A gardener increased the length of his rectangle-shaped garden by 40 percent and decreased its width by 20 percent. The area of the new garden

- A) has increased by 20 percent
- B) has increased by 12 percent
- C) has increased by 8 percent
- D) is exactly the same as the old area
- E) cannot be expressed in percentage terms without actual numbers

43. Microbrewery ( )

Over the course of a year, a certain microbrewery increased its beer output by 70 percent. At the same time, it decreased its total working hours by 20 percent. By what percent did this factory increase its output per hour?

A) 50%
B) 90%
C) 112.5%
D) 210%
E) 212.5%

44. Squaring Off ( )

If the sides of a square are doubled in length, the area of the original square is now how many times as large as the area of the resultant square?

A) 25%
B) 50%
C) 100%
D) 200%
E) 400%

45. Diners ( )

A couple spent $264 in total while dining out and paid this amount using a credit card. The $264 figure included a 20 percent tip which was paid on top of the price of the food which already included a sales tax of 10 percent. What was the actual price of the meal before tax and tip?

A) $184
B) $200
C) $204
D) $216
E) $232

46. Investments (🌶🌶)

A lady sold two small investment properties, A and B, for $24,000 each. If she sold property A for 20 percent more than she paid for it, and sold property B for 20 percent less than she paid for it, then, in terms of the net financial effect of these two investments (excluding taxes and expenses), we can conclude that the lady

A) broke even
B) had an overall gain of $1,200
C) had an overall loss of $1,200
D) had an overall gain of $2,000
E) had an overall loss of $2,000

Ratios and Proportions

47. Earth Speed (🌶🌶)

The Earth travels around the Sun at an approximate speed of 20 miles per second. This speed is how many kilometers per hour? [1km = 0.6 miles]

A) 2,000
B) 12,000
C) 43,200
D) 72,000
E) 120,000

₉ 48. Rum & Coke (🌶🌶)

A drink holding 6 ounces of an alcoholic drink that is 1 part rum to 2 parts coke is added to a jug holding 32 ounces of an alcoholic drink that is 1 part rum to 3 parts coke. What is the ratio of rum to coke in the resulting mixture?

A) 2:5
B) 5:14
C) 3:5
D) 4:7
E) 14:5

49. Millionaire

For every \$20 that a billionaire spends, a millionaire spends the equivalent of 20 cents. For every \$4 that a millionaire spends, a yuppie spends the equivalent of \$1. The ratio of money spent by a yuppie, millionaire, and billionaire can be expressed as

A)   1 : 4 : 400
B)   1 : 4 : 100
C)   20 : 4 : 1
D)   100 : 4 : 1
E)   400 : 4 : 1

50. Deluxe

At Deluxe paint store, Fuchsia paint is made by mixing 5 parts of red paint with 3 parts of blue paint. Mauve paint is made by mixing 3 parts of red paint with 5 parts blue paint. How many liters of blue paint must be added to 24 liters of Fuchsia to change it to Mauve paint?

A)   9
B)   12
C)   15
D)   16
E)   18

51. Rare Coins

In a rare coin collection, all coins are either pure gold or pure silver, and there is initially one gold coin for every three silver coins. With the addition of 10 more gold coins to the collection, the ratio of gold coins to silver coins is 1 to 2. Based on this information, how many total coins are there now in this collection (after the acquisition)?

A)   40
B)   50
C)   60
D)   80
E)   90

52. Coins Revisited ( )

In a rare coin collection, one in six coins is gold, and all coins are either gold or silver. If 10 silver coins were to be subsequently traded for an additional 10 gold coins, the ratio of gold coins to silver coins would be 1 to 4. Based on this information, how many gold coins would there be in this collection after the proposed trade?

A) 50
B) 60
C) 180
D) 200
E) 300

Squares and Cubes

53. Plus-Zero ( )

If $x > 0$, which of the following *could* be true?

I. $x^3 > x^2$

II. $x^2 = x$

III. $x^2 > x^3$

A) I only
B) I & II
C) II & III
D) All of the above
E) None of the above

54. Sub-Zero ( )

If $x < 0$, which of the following *must* be true?

I. $x^2 > 0$

II. $x - 2x > 0$

III. $x^3 + x^2 < 0$

A) I only
B) I & II
C) II & III
D) All of the above
E) None of the above

Exponent Problems

55. Solar Power ($\mathcal{S}$)

The mass of the sun is approximately 2×10^{30} kg and the mass of the moon is approximately 8×10^{12} kg. The mass of the sun is approximately how many times the mass of the moon?

A) 4.0×10^{-18}

B) 2.5×10^{17}

C) 4.0×10^{18}

D) 2.5×10^{19}

E) 4.0×10^{42}

56. Bacteria ($\mathcal{S}\mathcal{S}$)

A certain population of bacteria doubles every 10 minutes. If the number of bacteria in the population initially was 10^5, then what was the number in the population 1 hour later?

A) $2(10^5)$

B) $6(10^5)$

C) $(2^6)(10^5)$

D) $(10^6)(10^5)$

E) $(10^5)^6$

57. K.I.S.S. ($\mathcal{S}\mathcal{S}$)

If a is a positive integer, then $3^a + 3^{a+1} =$

A) 4^a

B) $3^a - 1$

C) $3^{2a} + 1$

D) $3^a(a-1)$

E) $4(3^a)$

58. Triplets (⌇⌇)

$3^{10} + 3^{10} + 3^{10} =$

A) 3^{11}

B) 3^{13}

C) 3^{30}

D) 9^{10}

E) 9^{30}

59. The Power of 5 (⌇⌇⌇)

If $5^5 \times 5^7 = (125)^x$, then what is the value of x?

A)   2
B)   3
C)   4
D)   5
E)   6

60. M&N (⌇⌇⌇)

If $m > 1$ and $n = 2^{m-1}$, then $4^m =$

A) $16n^2$

B) $4n^2$

C) n^2

D) $\dfrac{n^2}{4}$

E) $\dfrac{n^2}{16}$

61. Incognito ( )

Which of the following fractions has the greatest value?

A) $\dfrac{25}{(2^4)(3^3)}$

B) $\dfrac{5}{(2^2)(3^3)}$

C) $\dfrac{4}{(2^3)(3^2)}$

D) $\dfrac{36}{(2^3)(3^4)}$

E) $\dfrac{76}{(2^4)(3^4)}$

62. Chain Reaction ( )

If $x - \dfrac{1}{2^6} - \dfrac{1}{2^7} - \dfrac{1}{2^8} = \dfrac{2}{2^9}$, then $x =$

A) $\dfrac{1}{2}$

B) $\dfrac{1}{2^3}$

C) $\dfrac{1}{2^4}$

D) $\dfrac{1}{2^5}$

E) $\dfrac{1}{2^9}$

Radical Problems

63. Simplify (🌶)

$$\sqrt{\frac{12 \times 3 + 4 \times 16}{6}} =$$

A) $\dfrac{5\sqrt{6}}{3}$

B) $\sqrt{22}$

C) $\sqrt{6} + 4$

D) $\dfrac{8\sqrt{15}}{3}$

E) $16\dfrac{2}{3}$

64. Tenfold (🌶)

$$\frac{\sqrt{10}}{\sqrt{0.001}} =$$

A)   10,000
B)   1,000
C)   100
D)   1
E)   Can be expressed only as a non-integer

65. Strange ( )

The expression $\dfrac{1-\sqrt{2}}{1+\sqrt{2}}$ is equivalent to which of the following?

A) $\quad -3+2\sqrt{2}$

B) $\quad 1-\dfrac{2}{3}\sqrt{2}$

C) $\quad 0$

D) $\quad 1+\dfrac{2}{3}\sqrt{2}$

E) $\quad 3+2\sqrt{2}$

Inequality Problems

66. Two-Way Split ( )

If $-x^2+16<0$, which of the following must be true?

A) $\quad -4>x>4$
B) $\quad -4<x>4$
C) $\quad -4<x<4$
D) $\quad -4\le x\ge 4$
E) $\quad -4\ge x\ge 4$

Prime Number Problems

67. Primed ( )

The "primeness" of a positive integer x is defined as the positive difference between its largest and smallest prime factors. Which of the following has the greatest primeness?

A) $\quad 10$
B) $\quad 12$
C) $\quad 14$
D) $\quad 15$
E) $\quad 18$

68. Odd Man Out (⌇⌇)

If *P* represents the product of the first 13 positive integers, which of the following must be true?

I.   *P* is an odd number.
II.   *P* is a multiple of 17.
III.   *P* is a multiple of 24.

A)   I only
B)   II only
C)   III only
D)   None of the above
E)   All of the above

Remainder Problems

69. Remainder (⌇⌇)

When the integer *k* is divided by 7, the remainder is 5. Which of the following expressions below when divided by 7, will have a remainder of 6?

I. $4k + 7$

II. $6k + 4$

III. $8k + 1$

A)   I only
B)   II only
C)   III only
D)   I and II only
E)   I, II and III

70. Double Digits (⌇⌇)

How many two-digit whole numbers yield a remainder of 3 when divided by 10 and also yield a remainder of 3 when divided by 4?

A)   One
B)   Two
C)   Three
D)   Four
E)   Five

Symbolism Problems

71. Visualize ( )

For all real numbers V, the operation $V*$ is defined by the equation $V* = V - \dfrac{V}{2}$. If $(V*)* = 3$, then $V =$

A)   12
B)   6
C)   4
D) $\sqrt{12}$
E)   −12

Coordinate Geometry Problems

72. Masquerade ( )

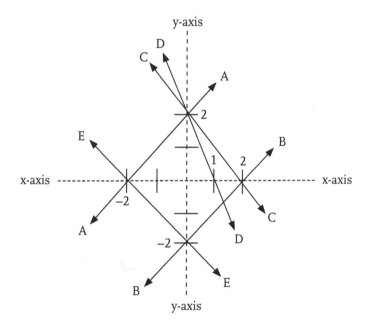

Which of the above lines fit the equation $y = -2x + 2$?

A)   Line A
B)   Line B
C)   Line C
D)   Line D
E)   Line E

73. **Boxed In** ( )

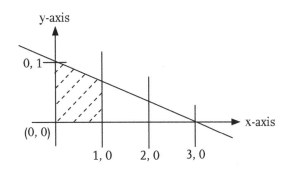

In the rectangular coordinate system above, the shaded region is bounded by a straight line. Which of the following is NOT an equation of one of the boundary lines?

A) $x = 0$

B) $y = 0$

C) $x = 1$

D) $x - 3y = 0$

E) $y + \frac{1}{3}x = 1$

74. **Intercept** ( )

In the rectangular coordinate system, what is the x-intercept of a line passing through $(10,3)$ and $(-6,-5)$?

A)   4
B)   2
C)   0
D)   −2
E)   −4

Plane Geometry Problems

75. Magic ( )

What is the ratio of the circumference of a circle to its diameter?

A) π
B) 2π
C) π^2
D) $2\pi r$
E) varies depending on the size of the circle

76. Kitty Corner ( )

The figure below is a cube with each side equal to 2 units. What is the length (in units) of diagonal BD? (Note: BD is drawn diagonally from bottom left-hand corner in the front to top right-hand corner at the back.)

A) $2\sqrt{2}$
B) $2\sqrt{3}$
C) $3\sqrt{2}$
D) $3\sqrt{3}$
E) $4\sqrt{3}$

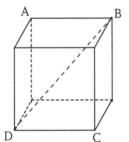

77. Lopsided ( )

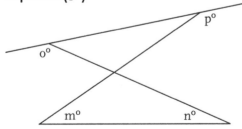

Note: Figure not drawn to scale

In the figure above, $m + n = 110$. What is the value of $o + p$?

A) 70
B) 110
C) 250
D) 270
E) 330

78. Diamond ( )

The figure below is a square. What is its perimeter (measured in units)?

A) $6\sqrt{2}$
B)   9
C)   12
D) $12\sqrt{2}$
E)   18

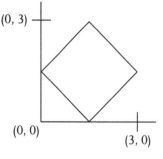

79. AC ( )

In the right triangle ABD below, AC is perpendicular to BD. If $AB = 5$ and $AD = 12$, then AC is equal to?

A) $\dfrac{30}{13}$

B) $\sqrt{12}$

C)   4

D) $2\sqrt{5}$

E) $\dfrac{60}{13}$

80. Circuit ( )

A rectangular circuit board is designed to have a width of W inches, a length of L inches, a perimeter of P inches, and an area of A square inches. Which of the following equations must be true?

A) $2W^2 + PW + 2A = 0$

B) $2W^2 - PW + 2A = 0$

C) $2W^2 - PW - 2A = 0$

D) $W^2 + PW + A = 0$

E) $W^2 - PW + 2A = 0$

81. Victorian ( )

A professional painter is painting the window frames of an old Victorian House. The worker has a ladder that is exactly 25 feet in length which he will use to paint two sets of window frames. To reach the first window frame, he places the ladder so that it rests against the side of the house at a point exactly 15 feet above the ground. When he finishes, he proceeds to reposition the ladder to reach the second window so that now the ladder rests against the side of the house at a point exactly 24 feet above the ground. How much *closer* to the base of the house has the bottom of the ladder now been moved?

A)   7
B)   9
C)   10
D)   13
E)   27

82. QR ( )

If segment QR in the cube below has length $4\sqrt{3}$ inches, what is the volume of the cube (in cubic inches)?

A)   16
B)   27
C)   64
D)   81
E)   125

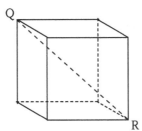

83. Cornered (𝄢𝄢𝄢)

Viewed from the outside inward, the figure below depicts a square-circle-square-circle, each enclosed within the other. If the area of square ABCD is 2 square units, then which of the following expresses the area of the darkened corners of square EFGH?

A) $2 - \dfrac{1}{4}\pi$

B) $2 - \dfrac{1}{2}\pi$

C) $1 - \dfrac{1}{4}\pi$

D) $\dfrac{1}{2} - \dfrac{1}{8}\pi$

E) $1 - \dfrac{1}{2}\pi$

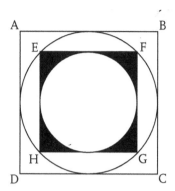

84. Woozy (𝄢𝄢𝄢)

In the equilateral triangle below, each side has a length of 4 units. If PQ has a length of 1 unit and TQ is perpendicular to PR, what is the area of region QRST?

A) $\dfrac{1}{3}\sqrt{3}$

B) $3\sqrt{3}$

C) $\dfrac{7}{2}\sqrt{3}$

D) $4\sqrt{3}$

E) $15\sqrt{3}$

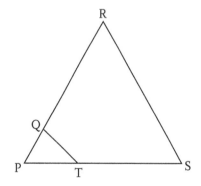

Solid Geometry Problems

85. Sphere (𝄢𝄢𝄢)

A sphere has a radius of x units. If the length of this radius is doubled, then how many times larger, in terms of volume, is the resultant sphere as compared with the original sphere?

A)   1
B)   2
C)   4
D)   8
E)   16

Probability Problems

86. Four Aces (𝄢)

Which of the following represents the probability of selecting four cards at random from a deck of cards and getting four aces? (the cards are to be selected one after the other without replacing any of the cards)

A) $\dfrac{1}{52} \times \dfrac{1}{52} \times \dfrac{1}{52} \times \dfrac{1}{52}$

B) $\dfrac{1}{52} \times \dfrac{1}{51} \times \dfrac{1}{50} \times \dfrac{1}{49}$

C) $\dfrac{4}{52} \times \dfrac{3}{51} \times \dfrac{2}{50} \times \dfrac{1}{49}$

D) $\dfrac{4}{52} \times \dfrac{3}{52} \times \dfrac{2}{52} \times \dfrac{1}{52}$

E) $\dfrac{4}{52} \times \dfrac{4}{52} \times \dfrac{4}{52} \times \dfrac{4}{52}$

87. **Orange & Blue ( )**

There are 5 marbles in a bag—2 are orange and 3 are blue. If two marbles are pulled from the bag, what is the probability that the first will be orange and the second will be blue?

A) $\dfrac{6}{25}$

B) $\dfrac{3}{10}$

C) $\dfrac{2}{5}$

D) $\dfrac{3}{5}$

E) $\dfrac{7}{10}$

88. **Exam Time ( )**

A student is to take her final exams in two subjects. The probability that she will pass the first subject is $\dfrac{3}{4}$ and the probability that she will pass the second subject is $\dfrac{2}{3}$. What is the probability that she will pass one exam or the other exam?

A) $\dfrac{5}{12}$

B) $\dfrac{1}{2}$

C) $\dfrac{7}{12}$

D) $\dfrac{5}{7}$

E) $\dfrac{11}{12}$

89. Sixth Sense ( )

What is the probability of rolling a six on either the first or second toss of a dice?

A) $\dfrac{1}{36}$

B) $\dfrac{5}{18}$

C) $\dfrac{1}{6}$

D) $\dfrac{11}{36}$

E) $\dfrac{1}{3}$

90. Exam Time Encore ( )

A student is to take her final exams in three subjects. The probability that she will pass the first subject is $\frac{3}{4}$, the probability that she will pass the second subject is $\frac{2}{3}$, and the probability that she will pass the third subject is $\frac{1}{2}$. What is the probability that she will pass at least one of these three exams?

A) $\dfrac{1}{4}$

B) $\dfrac{11}{24}$

C) $\dfrac{17}{24}$

D) $\dfrac{3}{4}$

E) $\dfrac{23}{24}$

91. Coin Toss (⌇⌇⌇)

What is the probability of tossing a coin five times and having heads appear at most three times?

A) $\dfrac{1}{16}$

B) $\dfrac{5}{16}$

C) $\dfrac{2}{5}$

D) $\dfrac{13}{16}$

E) $\dfrac{27}{32}$

Enumeration Problems

92. Hiring (⌇)

A company seeks to hire a sales manager, a shipping clerk, and a receptionist. The company has narrowed its candidate search and plans to interview all remaining candidates including 7 persons for the position of sales manager, 4 persons for the position of shipping clerk, and 10 persons for the position of receptionist. How many different hirings of these three people are possible?

A) $7 + 4 + 10$

B) $7 \times 4 \times 10$

C) $21 \times 20 \times 19$

D) $7! + 4! + 10!$

E) $7! \times 4! \times 10!$

Permutation Problems

93. Fencing ( )

Four contestants representing four different countries advance to the finals of a fencing championship. Assuming all competitors have an equal chance of winning, how many possibilities are there with respect to how a first-place and second-place medal can be awarded?

A)   6
B)   7
C)   12
D)   16
E)   24

94. Alternating ( )

Six students—3 boys and 3 girls—are to sit side by side for a makeup exam. How many ways could they arrange themselves given that no two boys and no two girls can sit next to one another?

A)   12
B)   36
C)   72
D)   240
E)   720

95. Banana ( )

Which of the following leads to the correct mathematical solution for the number of ways that the letters of the word BANANA could be arranged to create a six-letter code?

A) $6!$

B) $6! - (3! + 2!)$

C) $6! - (3! \times 2!)$

D) $\dfrac{6!}{3! + 2!}$

E) $\dfrac{6!}{3! \times 2!}$

96. Table ( )

How many ways could three people sit at a table with five seats in which two of the five seats will remain empty?

A)   8
B)   12
C)   60
D)   118
E)   120

Combination Problems

97. Singer ( )

For an upcoming charity event, a male vocalist has agreed to sing 4 out of 6 "old songs" and 2 out of 5 "new songs." How many ways can the singer make his selection?

A)   25
B)   50
C)   150
D)   480
E)   600

98. Outcomes ( )

Given that $_nP_r = \dfrac{n!}{(n-r)!}$ and $_nC_r = \dfrac{n!}{r!(n-r)!}$, where n is the total number of items and r is the number of items taken or chosen, which of the following statements are *true* in terms of the number of outcomes generated?

I. $_5P_3 > {_5P_2}$

II. $_5C_3 > {_5C_2}$

III. $_5C_2 > {_5P_2}$

A)   I only
B)   I & II only
C)   I & III only
D)   II & III only
E)   I, II & III

99. Reunion (🌶🌶🌶)

If 11 people meet at a reunion and each person shakes hands exactly once with each of the others, what is the total number of handshakes?

A) $11 \times 10 \times 9 \times 8 \times 7 \times 6 \times 5 \times 4 \times 3 \times 2 \times 1$
B) $10 \times 9 \times 8 \times 7 \times 6 \times 5 \times 4 \times 3 \times 2 \times 1$
C) 11×10
D)   55
E)   45

100. Display (🌶🌶🌶)

A computer wholesaler sells eight different computers and each is priced differently. If the wholesaler chooses three computers for display at a trade show, what is the probability (all things being equal) that the two most expensive computers will be among the three chosen for display?

A) $\dfrac{15}{56}$

B) $\dfrac{3}{28}$

C) $\dfrac{1}{28}$

D) $\dfrac{1}{56}$

E) $\dfrac{1}{168}$

ANSWERS AND EXPLANATIONS

Review – Converting Fractions

$$\frac{1}{3} = 33\frac{1}{3}\% \qquad \frac{2}{3} = 66\frac{2}{3}\% \qquad \frac{1}{6} = 16\frac{2}{3}\% \qquad \frac{5}{6} = 83\frac{1}{3}\%$$

$$\frac{1}{8} = 12.5\% \qquad \frac{3}{8} = 37.5\% \qquad \frac{5}{8} = 62.5\% \qquad \frac{7}{8} = 87.5\%$$

$$\frac{1}{9} = 11.11\% \qquad \frac{5}{9} = 55.55\%$$

Review – Converting Decimals

The answer to the first question is found by adding 1 to the fractional equivalent of 0.2.

$$0.2 = \frac{1}{5} \quad \text{Thus, } 1.2 = 1 + \frac{1}{5} = 1\frac{1}{5} = \frac{6}{5}$$

The answer to the second question is found by adding 1 to the fractional equivalent of 0.25.

$$0.25 = \frac{1}{4} \quad \text{Thus, } 1.25 = 1 + \frac{1}{4} = 1\frac{1}{4} = \frac{5}{4}$$

The answer to the third question is found by adding 1 to the fractional equivalent of 0.33.

$$0.33 = \frac{1}{3} \quad \text{Thus, } 1.33 = 1 + \frac{1}{3} = 1\frac{1}{3} = \frac{4}{3}$$

Each of the following three "fraction" problems equals 1!

$$\frac{5}{4} \times \frac{5}{10} \times \frac{8}{10} \times \frac{2}{1} = \frac{400}{400} = 1$$

$$\frac{\frac{3}{4} \times \frac{5}{6}}{\frac{5}{8}} = \frac{\frac{15}{24}}{\frac{5}{8}} = \frac{15}{24} \times \frac{8}{5} = \frac{120}{120} = 1$$

$$\frac{\dfrac{2}{9}}{\dfrac{1}{3} \times \dfrac{2}{3}} = \frac{\dfrac{2}{9}}{\dfrac{2}{9}} = \frac{2}{9} \times \frac{9}{2} = \frac{18}{18} = 1$$

Review – Common Squares from 13 to 30

Fill in the missing numbers to complete the Pythagorean triplets below. Refer to problem 81 (page 81), titled *Victorian*, for more on Pythagorean triplets.

3 : 4 : 5

5 : 12 : 13

7 : 24 : 25

8 : 15 : 17

Review – Common Square Roots

The answer to this square root problem is III, II & I. These statements are, in fact, in order from smallest to largest value, but the question asks to order the values from smallest to largest.

I. $1 + 2.2 = 3.2$
II. $2 + 1.7 = 3.7$
III. $3 + 1.4 = 4.4$

Review – Exponents and Radicals

The order of values, from largest to smallest, is as follows: II, I, III, VI, IV, and V. In terms of actual values, here is a listing:

I. 4

II. $4^2 = 16$

III. $\sqrt{4} = 2$

IV. $\dfrac{1}{4}$

V. $\left(\dfrac{1}{4}\right)^2 = \dfrac{1}{16}$

VI. $\sqrt{\dfrac{1}{4}} = \dfrac{1}{2}$

1. River Boat (🌶)

Choice C
Classification: Distance-Rate-Time Problem
Snapshot: The easiest way to solve this problem is to supply a hypothetical distance over which the river boat travels. This problem may be referred to as a "hypothetical distance D-R-T problem."

To find a hypothetical distance over which the river boat travels, take the Lowest Common Multiple (L-C-M) of 6 and 9. In other words, assume that the distance is 18 kilometers each way. If the boat travels upstream ("going") at 6 kilometers per hour, it will take 3 hours to complete its 18-kilometer journey. If the boat travels downstream ("returning") at 9 kilometers per hour, it will take 2 hours to complete its 18-kilometer journey.

$$R = \frac{D}{T} = \frac{18+18}{2+3} = \frac{36}{5} = 7.2 \text{ kilometers per hour}$$

The trap answer (choice D) is 7.5 kilometers per hour, which is derived from simply averaging 9 kilometers per hour and 6 kilometers per hour. That is:

$$R = \frac{D}{T} = \frac{9+6}{2} = \frac{15}{2} = 7.5 \text{ kilometers per hour}$$

NOTE ⮞ For the record, the *algebraic method* used to solve this problem is as follows:

$$R = \frac{D_1 + D_2}{T_1 + T_2}$$

$$R = \frac{x+x}{\dfrac{x}{6} + \dfrac{x}{9}}$$

$$R = \frac{2x}{\dfrac{3x+2x}{18}} = \frac{2x}{\dfrac{5x}{18}} = \frac{36x}{5x} = \frac{36}{5} = 7.2 \text{ kilometers per hour}$$

2. Run-Run (🌶🌶)

Choice B
Classification: Distance-Rate-Time Problem
Snapshot: This D-R-T problem expresses its answer in terms of an algebraic expression. Often, such problems also require time conversions, from seconds to minutes or from minutes to hours (and vice versa).

The problem is asking for time, where $T = \frac{D}{R}$. We have algebraic expressions for both speed and distance. Speed is $\frac{y}{9}$ seconds (not 9 seconds over y yards) and distance is x yards.

Therefore: $T = \dfrac{D}{R}$

$$T = \frac{x \text{ yards}}{\dfrac{y \text{ yards}}{9 \text{ sec}}}$$

$$T = x \ \cancel{\text{yards}} \times \frac{9 \text{ seconds}}{y \ \cancel{\text{yards}}} = \frac{9x \text{ seconds}}{y}$$

$$T = \frac{9x \ \cancel{\text{seconds}}}{y} \times \frac{1 \text{ min}}{60 \ \cancel{\text{seconds}}} = \frac{9x}{60y} \text{ minutes} \qquad \text{[converting from seconds to minutes]}$$

NOTE ✎ When solving for <u>distance</u> or <u>rate</u>, we *multiply* by 60 when converting from minutes to hours (or seconds to minutes) and *divide* by 60 when converting from hours to minutes (or minutes to seconds). When solving for <u>time</u>, we *divide* by 60 when converting from minutes to hours (or seconds to minutes) and *multiply* by 60 when converting from hours to minutes (or minutes to seconds).

Additional Examples:

i)   Solving for <u>distance</u>:

    Example   At the rate of d miles per q minutes, how many <u>miles</u> does a bullet train travel in x hours?

$$D = R \times T$$

$$D = \frac{d \text{ miles}}{q \ \cancel{\text{minutes}}} \times x \ \cancel{\text{hours}} \times \frac{60 \ \cancel{\text{minutes}}}{1 \ \cancel{\text{hour}}} = \frac{60dx}{q} \text{ miles}$$

ii)   Solving for <u>rate</u> (or speed):

    Example   A bullet train completes a journey of d miles. If the journey took q minutes, what was the train's <u>speed</u> in miles per hour?

$$R = \frac{D}{T}$$

$$R = \frac{d \text{ miles}}{q \ \cancel{\text{minutes}}} \times \frac{60 \ \cancel{\text{minutes}}}{1 \text{ hour}} = \frac{60d}{q} \text{ miles per hour}$$

iii) Solving for <u>time</u>:

Example   Another bullet train completes a journey of d miles. If this train traveled at a rate of z miles per minute, how many <u>hours</u> did the journey take?

$$T = \frac{D}{R}$$

$$T = \frac{d \ \text{\sout{miles}}}{z \ \text{\sout{miles} / \sout{minute}}} \times \frac{1 \ \text{hour}}{60 \ \text{\sout{minutes}}} = \frac{d}{60z} \ \text{hours}$$

3. Forgetful Timothy (👣👣)

Choice B
Classification: Distance-Rate-Time Problem
Snapshot: *Forgetful Timothy* may be called a "catch up D-R-T problem." A slower individual (or machine) starts first and a faster second person (or machine) must catch up.

Like so many difficult D-R-T problems, the key is to view distance as a constant. In other words, the applicable formulas include: $D_1 = R_1 \times T_1$ and $D_2 = R_2 \times T_2$, where $D_1 = D_2$. The solution, therefore, is to set the two formulas equal to one another such that $R_1 \times T_1 = R_2 \times T_2$.

	Rate		Time		Distance
Timothy	9	×	T	=	$9T$
Mother	36	×	$T - \frac{1}{4}$	=	$36\left(T - \frac{1}{4}\right)$

Note that since time here is measured in hours, 15 minutes should be translated as $\frac{1}{4}$ hour.

First, we solve for T:

$$D_{1 \ \text{Timothy}} = D_{2 \ \text{Mother}}$$

$$(R_1 \times T_1)_{\ \text{Timothy}} = (R_2 \times T_2)_{\ \text{Mother}}$$

$$9T = 36\left(T - \frac{1}{4}\right)$$

$$9T = 36T - 9$$

$$9T - 36T = -9$$

$$-27T = -9$$

$$T = \frac{-9}{-27}$$

$$T = \frac{1}{3} \ \text{hour}$$

Second, we solve for D:

So, if Timothy rode for $\frac{1}{3}$ hour at 9 m.p.h., the distance he covered was 3 miles. It is also true that his mother drove for 3 miles:

$$D = 36 \text{ m.p.h.} \times (\tfrac{1}{3} \text{ hrs} - \tfrac{1}{4} \text{ hrs})$$

$$D = 36 \text{ m.p.h.} \times \tfrac{1}{12} \text{ hrs} = 3 \text{ miles}$$

4.   P & Q (𝄞𝄞𝄞)

Choice A
Classification: Distance-Rate-Time Problem
Snapshot: In this D-R-T problem, output is a constant, although the rates and times of two working individuals differ and must be expressed relative to each other.

The formula, $D_1 = R_1 \times T_1$, links candidate P and candidate Q in so far as distance or output is a constant (i.e., in this case, "total pay" is $600). Set $P = R_1 \times T_1$ and $Q = R_2 \times T_2$. If the work rate of candidate Q is 100 percent or 1.0, then the work rate of candidate P is 150% or 1.5. If candidate P takes T hours, then candidate Q takes $T + 10$ hours.

$$D_{1 \text{ Candidate P}} = D_{2 \text{ Candidate Q}}$$

$$(R_1 \times T_1)_{\text{ Candidate P}} = (R_2 \times T_2)_{\text{ Candidate Q}}$$

$$1.5(T) = 1.0(T + 10)$$

$$1.5T = T + 10$$

$$0.5T = 10$$

$$T = \frac{10}{0.5}$$

$$T = 20 \text{ hours}$$

Candidate P takes 20 hours (i.e., 10 + 10). Thus, candidate P's hourly rate is: $600 ÷ $20 hours = $30 per hour. Candidate Q's time in hours to complete the research equals $T + 10$ or 20 + 10 = 30 hours. Likewise, candidate Q's hourly rate is, $600 ÷ 30 hours = $20 per hour. Therefore, since candidate P earns $30 per hour and candidate Q earns $20 per hour, candidate P earns $10 more dollars per hour than candidate Q does.

5. Submarine (🌶🌶🌶)

Choice C
Classification: Distance-Rate-Time Problem
Snapshot: *Submarine* is a complicated word problem and one which involves factoring. Again, the key is to view "distance" as a constant where $D_1 = D_2$. The key, therefore, is to set the two formulas equal to one another such that $R_1 \times T_1 = R_2 \times T_2$.

	Rate		Time		Distance
Actual	R	×	T	=	240
Hypothetical	$R + 20$	×	$T - 1$	=	240

We now have two distinct equations:

    i) $R \times T = 240$
    ii) $(R + 20)(T - 1) = 240$

We need to substitute for one of the variables (i.e., R or T) in order to solve for the remaining variable. Practically, we want to find R, so we solve for R in the second equation by first substituting for T in the second equation.

To do this, we solve for T in the first equation ($T = \frac{240}{R}$) in order to substitute for T in the second equation:

$$(R + 20)\left(\frac{240}{R} - 1\right) = 240$$

$$240 - R + \frac{20(240)}{R} - 20 = 240$$

Next multiply through by R.

$$(R)(240) - (R)(R) + (\cancel{R})\left(\frac{20(240)}{\cancel{R}}\right) - (R)(20) = (R)(240)$$

$$240R - R^2 + 4{,}800 - 20R = 240R$$

$$-R^2 - 20R + 4{,}800 = 0$$

Next multiply through by −1.

$$(-1)(-R^2) - (-1)(20R) + (-1)(4{,}800) = (-1)(0)$$

$$R^2 + 20R - 4{,}800 = 0$$

Factor for R.

$(R + 80)(R - 60) = 0$

$R = -80$ or 60

$R = 60$

We choose 60 and ignore –80 because it is a negative number and time (or distance) can never be negative.

An alternative approach involves *backsolving*. The algebraic setup follows:

Slower time – faster time = 1 hour

$$\frac{240}{R} - \frac{240}{R + 20} = 1 \text{ hour}$$

Now backsolve. That is, take the various answer choices and substitute them into the formula above and see which results in an answer of 1 hour. Our correct answer is 60 m.p.h.

$$\frac{240}{60} - \frac{240}{60 + 20} = 1$$

$$\frac{240}{60} - \frac{240}{80} = 1$$

$$4 - 3 = 1 \text{ hour}$$

6. Sixteen-Wheeler (🌶🌶🌶)

Choice B

Classification: Distance-Rate-Time Problem

Snapshot: This problem is a variation of a "two-part D-R-T" problem. Distance is a constant, although individual distances and rates and times are different. The applicable formula is: $D = (R_1 \times T_1) \times (R_2 \times T_2)$. Distance is a constant because the combined distances traveled by the two drivers will always be the same.

$D = \text{Distance}_{(\text{Driver A})} + \text{Distance}_{(\text{Driver B})}$

$D = (\text{Rate}_1 \times \text{Time}_1) + (\text{Rate}_2 \times \text{Time}_2)$

The distance covered by Driver A is $90(T + 1)$. The distance covered by Driver B is $80T$.

$80T + 90(T + 1) = 770$ [where T equals the time of Driver B]

$80T + 90T + 90 = 770$

$170T = 680$

$T = \dfrac{680}{170}$

$T = 4 \text{ hours}$

Given that Driver B took 4 hours, Driver A took 5 hours (i.e., $T + 1$). We now calculate how far each person has traveled and take the difference:

Driver A:

$$D = R \times T$$
$$D = 90(T + 1) = 90(4 + 1) = 90(5)$$
$$D = 450 \text{ kilometers}$$

Driver B:

$$D = R \times T$$
$$D = 80T = 80(4)$$
$$D = 320 \text{ kilometers}$$

Finally, $450 - 320 = 130$ kilometers

NOTE ⤸ This problem could also have been solved by expressing "time" in terms of Driver A:

$$90T + 80(T - 1) = 770$$
$$90T + 80T - 80 = 770$$
$$170T = 850$$
$$T = \frac{850}{170}$$
$$T = 5 \text{ hours}$$

In this case, we can confirm that whereas Driver A took 5 hours, Driver B took 4 hours. Driver A drove for 5 hours at 90 kilometers per hour (450 miles). Driver B drove for 4 hours at 80 kilometers per hour (320 miles). The <u>difference</u> in distances driven is 130 kilometers.

7.   Elmer (🌶)

Choice B
Classification: Age Problem
Snapshot: In cases where an age problem states, "Alan is twice as old as Betty," the math translation is $A = 2B$, not $2A = B$. In cases where an age problem states, "10 years from now Sam will be twice as old as Tania," the math translation is $S + 10 = 2(T + 10)$. In this latter situation, remember to add 10 years to both sides of the equation because both individuals will have aged 10 years.

First Equation:

Elmer is currently three times older than Leo.
$E = 3L$

Second Equation:

> In five years from now, Leo will be exactly half as old as Elmer.
> $2(L + 5) = E + 5$

Next, we substitute for the variable E in order to solve for L. That is, substitute $3L$ (First Equation) for the variable E (Second Equation).

$$2(L + 5) = 3L + 5$$
$$2L + 10 = 3L + 5$$
$$-L = -5$$
$$(-1)(-L) = (-1)(-5) \qquad [\text{multiply through by } -1]$$
$$L = 5$$

Therefore, since Leo, the circus Lion, is 5 years old, this means that Elmer, the circus Elephant, is 15 years old. This calculation is derived from the first equation, $E = 3L$.

8. Three's Company ( )

Choice D
Classification: Average Problem
Snapshot: If the average of eight numbers is 7, their sum must be 56. This simple revelation provides a key step in solving most average problems.

$$\text{Average} = \frac{\text{Sum of Terms}}{\text{Number of Terms}}$$

$$\text{Average} = \frac{4(4x + 3) - x}{3}$$

$$\text{Average} = \frac{16x + 12 - x}{3} = \frac{15x + 12}{3} = 5x + 4$$

9. Fourth Time Lucky ( )

Choice C
Classification: Average Problem
Snapshot: This average problem requires a solution in the form of an algebraic expression.

$$\text{Average} = \frac{\text{Sum of Terms}}{\text{Number of Terms}}$$

$$\text{Average} = \frac{3N + (N + 20)}{4}$$

$$\text{Average} = \frac{4N + 20}{4} = \frac{4N}{4} + \frac{20}{4} = N + 5$$

Note that since Rajeev received an average score of N points on his first 3 tests, his total points is $3N$.

10. Vacation (🌶🌶)

Choice D
Classification: Average Problem
Snapshot: This special type of average problem may be referred to as a "dropout problem." Specifically, we want to know how much *additional* money each individual must pay as a result of others dropping out. This problem type also requires mastery of algebraic fractions.

First Equation:

$$\frac{x}{P}$$ represents the amount each person was originally going to pay before the dropouts.

Second Equation:

$$\frac{x}{P-D}$$ represents the total amount each person has to pay after the dropouts.

Accordingly, $\frac{x}{P-D} - \frac{x}{P}$ will yield the additional amount that each person must pay. Note that the amount that each person has to pay after the dropouts is greater per person than the amount before.

Therefore we subtract the First Equation from the Second Equation, not the other way around. The algebra here requires dealing with algebraic fractions that can be a bit confusing. Multiply each term through by the common denominator of $P(P - D)$.

$$\frac{x}{P-D} - \frac{x}{P}$$

$$\frac{P(\cancel{P-D})\dfrac{x}{\cancel{P-D}} - \cancel{P}(P-D)\dfrac{x}{\cancel{P}}}{P(P-D)}$$

$$\frac{Px - \left[(P-D)x\right]}{P(P-D)}$$

$$\frac{\cancel{Px} - \cancel{xP} + Dx}{P(P-D)}$$

$$\frac{Dx}{P(P-D)}$$

NOTE ✍ See problem 36 (page 64), titled *Hodgepodge*, which provides another example of working with algebraic fractions.

11. Disappearing Act (👣 👣)

Choice C
Classification: Work Problem
Snapshot: This problem is a "walk-away work problem." Two people (or two machines) will set to work on something and, after a stated period of time, one of the individuals gets up and leaves (or one of the machines breaks down), forcing the remaining person (or machine) to finish the task.

Since an hour is an easy unit to work with, think in terms of how much of the task each person working alone could complete in just one hour. Deborah could do the job in 5 hours, so she does $\frac{1}{5}$ of the job in an hour; Tom could do the job in 6 hours, so he does $\frac{1}{6}$ of the job in one hour. Working together for 2 hours, they complete $\frac{11}{15}$ of that job, which leaves $\frac{4}{15}$ of the task for Deborah to complete alone. Deborah can complete $\frac{4}{15}$ of the task in $1\frac{1}{3}$ hours.

The solution unfolds in three steps:

i)   Amount of work they both will do in 2 hours:

$$2\left(\frac{1}{5}+\frac{1}{6}\right)=2\left(\frac{6}{30}+\frac{5}{30}\right)=2\left(\frac{11}{30}\right)=\frac{22}{30}=\frac{11}{15}$$

ii)   Amount of work left to do:

$$1-\frac{11}{15}=\frac{4}{15}$$

iii) Time it takes Deborah to complete the task alone:

$$\text{Time}=\frac{\text{Amount of Work}}{\text{Deborah's Work Rate}}$$

$$T=\frac{\frac{4}{15}}{\frac{1}{5}}=\frac{4}{15}\times\frac{5}{1}=\frac{20}{15}=\frac{4}{3}=1\frac{1}{3}\text{ hours}$$

NOTE ❧ The general formula for work problems is "$\frac{1}{A}+\frac{1}{B}=\frac{1}{T}$," where A and B represent the time it takes a given person or machine to individually complete a task and T represents the total time it takes both persons or machines to complete the task working together but independently.

12. Exhibition (👣 👣)

Choice C
Classification: Work Problem
Snapshot: For problems that involve the work rates for a group of individuals (or machines), calculate first the work rate for a single person (or machine) and then multiply this rate by the number of persons (or machines) in the new group. The time necessary to complete the new task will be 1 divided by this number.

Solution in four steps:

Find how much of the job 70 workers could do in 1 hour.

Result: If 70 workers can do the job in 3 hours then the 70 workers can do $\frac{1}{3}$ of the job in one hour.

Find out how much of the job a single worker can do in 1 hour.

Result: $\frac{1}{70} \times \frac{1}{3} = \frac{1}{210}$. This is the hourly work rate for an individual worker.

Multiply this rate by the number of new workers.

Result: $30 \times \frac{1}{210} = \frac{30}{210} = \frac{1}{7}$. This is the work rate for the group of new workers.

Take the reciprocal of this number and voila—the answer!

Result: $\frac{1}{7}$ becomes $\frac{7}{1} = 7$ hours

Alternative solution:

If 70 men could do the work in 3 hours, then how long would it take 30 men to the do the same job?

$$30H = 70 \times 3$$
$$30H = 210$$
$$H = \frac{210}{30} = 7 \text{ hours}$$

13. Legal (👣 👣 👣)

Choice B
Classification: Work Problem
Snapshot: Again, the key is to think in terms of a *work rate* for a single individual. Next, multiply this figure by the total number of new group members to find a "group rate." Finally, take the reciprocal of this number to arrive at total hours; alternatively, divide 1 by this number to arrive at total hours.

Five steps:

i)   Find how much of the job 4 junior lawyers could do in 1 hour.

   If 4 junior lawyers can do the job in 5 hours then the 4 junior lawyers can do $\frac{1}{5}$ of the job in one hour.

ii)   Find out how much of the job a single worker can do in 1 hour.

   Result: $\frac{1}{4} \times \frac{1}{5} = \frac{1}{20}$. This is the work rate for a single junior lawyer.

iii)   Adjust this work rate for the rate of legal assistants versus junior lawyers.

   Result: $\frac{1}{20} \times \frac{2}{3} = \frac{2}{60}$. This is the adjusted work rate for a single legal assistant.

iv)   Multiply this rate by the number of legal assistants.

   Result: $3 \times \frac{2}{60} = \frac{6}{60}$. This is the work rate for the group of three legal assistants.

v)   Take the reciprocal of this number and voila—the answer!

   Result: $\frac{6}{60}$ becomes $\frac{60}{6} = 10$ hours

Alternative solution:

$$3 \times \frac{2}{3} \times H = 4 \times 5$$

$$\frac{6}{3} H = 20$$

$$\frac{\cancel{3}}{\cancel{6}} \times \frac{\cancel{6}}{\cancel{3}} H = \frac{3}{6} \times 20$$

$$H = \frac{60}{6} = 10 \text{ hours}$$

14. Persian Rug ( )

Choice E
Classification: Picture Frame or Border Problem
Snapshot: Don't forget that a frame or border surrounding a picture or carpet contains a border on all sides.

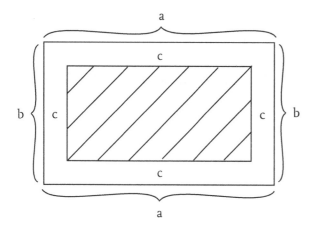

The key is to subtract the area of the entire rug (rug plus border) from the area of the rug itself (rug minus border).

i) Find the area of the entire rug (including the border) in square inches.

Answer: $a \times b$ or ab

ii) Find the area of the rug itself (without the border) in square inches.

Answer: $(a - 2c)(b - 2c)$

iii) Find the area of the strip (in square inches) by subtracting the area of the rug (excluding border) from the area of entire rug (including border).

Answer: $ab - (a - 2c)(b - 2c)$

The answer is not choice D, which assumes that the frame is only on one side of the picture. A border on a rectangle or square object occurs on all sides of the object. Answer choice C represents the difference in perimeters. This would have been the correct answer had the question asked, "Which algebraic expression below represents the positive difference in the measure of the perimeter of the rug and the rug design?"

15. Nuts ( )

Choice A
Classification: Mixture Problem
Snapshot: This is a dry mixture. We need to calculate the <u>amounts</u> of <u>two</u> different <u>nut</u> mixtures to arrive at a final mixture.

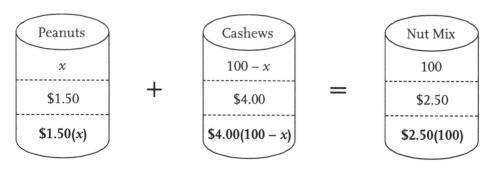

$1.50(x) + $4.00(100 - x) = $2.50(100)$

$1.50x + $400 - $4.00x = 250

$-$2.5x = -150

$(-1)(-$2.5x) = (-1)(-$150)$

$2.5x = 150

$x = \dfrac{$150}{$2.5}$

$x = 60$ pounds of peanuts

Therefore, $100 - 60 = 40$ pounds of cashews

The following is an alternative solution using a *two-variables, two-equations* approach. Substitute for one of the variables, x or y, and solve. Here the variable x represents peanuts while the variable y represents cashews.

i) $1.50x + $4.00y = $2.50(100)$
ii) $x + y = 100$

"Put equation ii) into equation i) and solve for y." That is, substitute for the variable "x" in equation i), using $x = 100 - y$ per equation ii). Although we could substitute for either variable, we prefer to substitute for x and solve for y given that the final answer is expressed in terms of cashew nuts.

$1.50(100 - y) + $4.00y = $2.50(100)$
$150 - $1.5y + $4.00y = 250
$-$100 = -$2.5y$
$2.5y = 100
$y = 40$ pounds of cashews

NOTE ✎ Mixture problems are best solved using the *barrel method*, which summarizes information similar to a 3-row by 3-column table.

This problem garners one-chili rating partly because it is easy to backsolve, especially given the fact that the answer is choice A and we would likely begin choosing answer choices beginning with choice A. From the information given in the problem, we know we are looking for a final mixture that costs $2.50 per pound. We also know the individual prices per pound. Choice A tells us that we have 40 pounds of cashews and, by implication, 60 pounds of peanuts. Will this give us an answer of $2.50? Yes it does, and the answer choice A is confirmed.

```
40 pounds × $4.00 = $160.00    Cashews
60 pounds × $1.50 =  $90.00    Peanuts
                    $250.00
Total pounds          100
Price per pound      $2.50
```

16. Gold ( )

Choice E
Classification: Mixture Problem
Snapshot: This is a dry mixture involving percentages. We need to calculate the amount of <u>pure gold</u> that needs to be added to arrive at a final alloy. When adding pure gold, we use 100%. If we were to add a pure non-gold alloy, the percentage would be 0%.

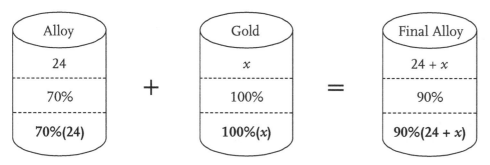

$70\%(24) + 100\%(x) = 90\%(24 + x)$

$16.80 + x = 21.6 + 0.90x$

$0.1x = 4.8$

$x = \dfrac{4.8}{0.1}$

$x = 48$ ounces of pure gold

17. Evaporation ( )

Choice A
Classification: Mixture Problem
Snapshot: This is a wet mixture. We need to calculate the amount of pure water that needs to be subtracted to arrive at a final solution. The percentage for pure water is 0 percent because pure water (whether added or subtracted) lacks any "mixture." This causes the middle term in the equation to drop out.

We need to calculate the amount of <u>pure water</u> that needs to be <u>subtracted</u> to arrive at a final solution.

Water/Sugar		Water		Final Mixture
50		x		$50 - x$
3%	−	0%	=	10%
3%(50)		0%(x)		10%(50 − x)

$3\%(50) - 0\%(x) = 10\%(50 - x)$

$1.5 - 0 = 5 - 0.10x$

$-3.5 = -0.10x$

$0.10x = 3.5$

$x = \dfrac{3.5}{0.1}$

$x = 35$ liters of pure water

NOTE ⤖ In the above equation, we simply reverse the equation and change the signs, so that "$-3.5 = -0.10x$" becomes "$0.10x = 3.5$." Another way to derive this algebraically is as follows:

$-3.5 = -0.10x$

$(-1)(-3.5) = (-1)(-0.10x)$ [multiply both sides by -1]

$3.5 = 0.10x$

$0.10x = 3.5$ [simply switch terms around; that is, if A = B, then B = A]

In short, when solving for a single variable such as x, our practical goal is to get x on one side of the equation and all other terms on the opposite side of the equation. Typically, this involves isolating x on the left-hand side of the equation (left of the equals sign) while placing all the other terms on the right-hand side of the equation (right of the equals sign). There are two essential rules to keep in mind when manipulating elements of a formula to in order to achieve this objective. The first rule is that bringing any number (or term) across the equals sign, changes the sign of that number (or term). That is, positive numbers become negative and negative numbers become positive. The second rule is that whatever we do to one term in an equation, we must do to every other term in that same equation (in order to maintain the equivalent value of all terms in the equation). So, in the above equation, we may choose to multiply each side of the equation by -1 in order to cancel the negative signs. We do this because we always want to solve for a positive x value.

18. Standardized Test (👣👣)

Choice B
Classification: Group Problem
Snapshot: This category of problem deals most often with situations which are not mutually exclusive and will therefore contain overlap; this overlap must not be double counted, otherwise the number of members or items in a group will exceed 100 percent due to mutual inclusivity. In short, group problems will either give you *neither* and ask for *both* or give you *both* and ask for *neither*.

The Venn Diagram below lends a pictorial. Note that 100 percent is what is in the "box"; it includes Q1 & Q2 and *neither*. But it must not include *both* because *both* represents overlap that must be subtracted out, otherwise the overlap will be double counted. In other words, either Q1 may include the 65% as part of its 85% or Q2 may include the 65% as part of its 75%, but Q1 and Q2 cannot both claim it. Another way to view this problem is to break it up analytically as follows: The number of students who only got Q1 correct is 20% (85% – 65%) while the number of students who only got Q2 correct is 10% (75% – 65%). Since 65% of students got both questions correct, the number of students that got one or the other question correct is: 20% + 10% + 65% = 95%. And 5% of students got neither question correct.

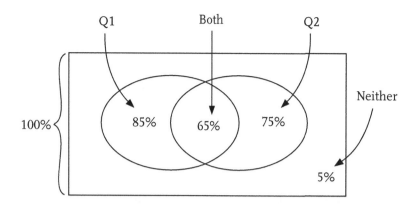

The following is the mathematical solution to this problem.

Two-Groups Formula	Solve
+ Group A	+ 85%
+ Group B	+ 75%
− Both	− x%
+ Neither	+ 5%
Total	100%

Calculation:

Group A + Group B − Both + Neither = Total
$85\% + 75\% - x + 5\% = 100\%$
$165\% - x = 100\%$
$x = 65\%$

NOTE ❧ Some group problems involve two overlapping circles and some involve three overlapping circles. The formulas below are the key to solving these types of problems with a minimum of effort.

Summary of templates:

Two-Groups Formula		Solve
Add:	Group A	x
Add:	Group B	x
Less:	Both	<x>
Add:	Neither	x
	Total	xx

Three-Groups Formula		Solve
Add:	Group A	x
Add:	Group B	x
Add:	Group C	x
Less:	A & B	<x>
Less:	A & C	<x>
Less:	B & C	<x>
Add:	All of A & B & C	x
Add:	None of A or B or C	x
	Total	xx

19. Language Classes (🌶🌶🌶)

Choice D
Classification: Group Problem
Snapshot: This type of Group Problem requires that we express our answer in algebraic form.

This problem is more difficult and garners a three-chili rating in so far as it requires an answer that is expressed in terms of an algebraic expression.

Use the classic *two-groups formula:*

Group A + Group B – Both + Neither = Total

Applied to the problem at hand:

Spanish + French – Both + Neither = Total Students

$S + F - B + N = X$

$N = X + B - F - S$

Therefore, expressed as a percent:

$$\text{Neither} = 100\% \times \frac{X + B - F - S}{X}$$

20. German Cars (🌶🌶🌶)

Choice C
Classification: Group Problem
Snapshot: This problem involves three overlapping circles. There are two ways to solve this problem. One employs the "three-groups" formula, while the other involves using the Venn-diagram approach. For the purpose of answering this question in two minutes, it is highly recommended that candidates use the "three-groups" formula.

I. Three-Groups Formula

The three-groups formula is preferable because it is clearly fastest, relying directly on the numbers found right in the problem. In short, the total number of individuals owning a single car are added together, the number of individuals owning exactly two of these cars is subtracted from this number, and, finally, the number of people owning all three of these cars are added back. The calculation follows:

Three-Groups Formula		Solve
Add:	BMW	45
Add:	Mercedes	38
Add:	Porche	27
Less:	BMW & Mercedes	<15>
Less:	BMW & Porche	<12>
Less:	Mercedes & Porche	<8>
Add:	BMW & Mercedes & Porche	5
Add:	None of BMW & Mercedes & Porche	0
	Total	80

Calculation:

B + M + P − BM − BP − MP + BMP + None = Total
45 + 38 + 27 − 15 − 12 − 8 + 5 + 0 = x
$x = 80$

II.   The Venn-diagram Approach

The Venn-diagram approach is highly analytical and requires breaking the problem down into non-overlapping areas while finding individual values for all seven areas. That's right!—seven distinct areas are created when three groups overlap.

27 + 16 + 12 + 10 + 7 + 3 + 5 = 80
BMW only + Mercedes only + Porsche only − [(BMW & Mercedes) − (Mercedes & Porsche) − (BMW & Porsche)] + (BMW & Mercedes & Porsche).

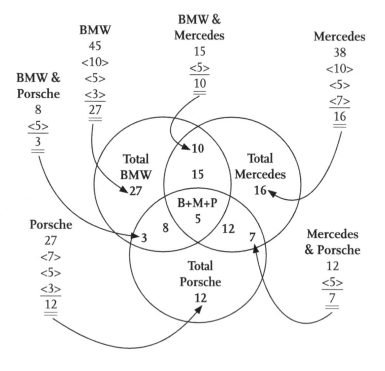

110

21. Single ()

Choice D
Classification: Matrix Problem
Snapshot: A matrix can be used to summarize data, particularly data that is being contrasted across two variables and that can be sorted into four distinct outcomes. Use a table with nine boxes and fill in numbers that total down and across.

Two-thirds of the women are single (i.e., $\frac{20}{30} = \frac{2}{3}$). For this problem, assume for simplicity's sake that there are 100 students in the course and fill in the given information, turning percentages into numbers. If 70% of the students are male, then 30% must be female. If we assume there are 100 students, then 70 are male and 30 are female. Note that if two-sevenths of the male students are married, then 20 male students are married; that is, two-sevenths of 70 students equals 20 students.

First, fill in the information derived directly from the problem:

	Male	Female	
Married	20		30
Single		?	
	70	?	100

Second, complete the matrix by filling in the remaining numbers, ensuring that numbers total both down and across. Boxes marked with question marks denote key information (i.e., numbers) needed to solve the problem.

	Male	Female	
Married	20	10	30
Single	50	20	70
	70	30	100

22. Batteries (🌶🌶🌶)

Choice A
Classification: Matrix Problem
Snapshot: To solve difficult matrix problems try "picking numbers," particularly the number 100, if possible.

To obtain the percent of batteries sold by the factory that are defective, we fill in the information per the matrix below to obtain $\frac{3}{75}$ or $\frac{1}{25}$ or 4%. As in the previous problem, the technique of picking the number "100" greatly simplifies the task at hand.

First, fill in the information directly deducible from the problem:

	Defective	Not Defective	
Rejected		$\frac{1}{10}(80) = 8$	$\frac{1}{4}(100) = 25$
Not Rejected	?		?
	$\frac{1}{5}(100) = 20$	80	100

Second, complete the matrix. Boxes marked with question marks denote key numbers needed to solve the problem at hand.

	Defective	Not Defective	
Rejected	17	8	25
Not Rejected	3	72	75
	20	80	100

23. Experiment (🌶🌶🌶)

Choice A
Classification: Matrix Problem
Snapshot: This is a difficult, "odd-ball" matrix problem. Although it is possible to employ a traditional matrix, a guesstimate must be made regarding one of the numbers.

There are two ways to solve this problem: the "picking numbers" approach and the "algebraic" approach.

I.   Picking Numbers Approach

Let's pick numbers. Say the total number of rats that are originally alive is 100, of which 60 are female and 40 are male. Let's say that 50 rats die, which means 15 were female and 35 were male. Calculation for dead rats is: 30% × 50 = 15 female rats versus 70% × 50 = 35 male rats.

	Male	Female	
Rats that Died	35	15	*50
Rats that Lived			
	40	60	100

Complete the matrix by deducing the remaining numbers.

	Male	Female	
Rats that Died	35	15	*50
Rats that Lived	5	45	**50
	40	60	100

Note that the figure "*50" is merely a guesstimate; the figure "**50" is a plug number. If there were 100 rats and 50 died, then 50 must have lived.

As it turns out, data about the number of rats that lived is not useful in the problem at hand; the focus is on the number of rats that died. We are able to calculate the ratio that represents the death rate among male rats to the death rate among female rats as follows:

$$\frac{\dfrac{\text{male rat deaths}}{\text{male rats (total)}}}{\dfrac{\text{female rat deaths}}{\text{female rats (total)}}} = \frac{\dfrac{35}{40}}{\dfrac{15}{60}} = \frac{35}{40} \times \frac{60}{15} = 7:2$$

II. Algebraic Approach

$$\frac{\begin{array}{c}0.7 \text{ died (male)}\\ \hline 0.4 \text{ total (male)}\end{array}}{\begin{array}{c}0.3 \text{ died (female)}\\ \hline 0.6 \text{ total (female)}\end{array}} = \frac{0.7 \,\text{died}}{0.4 \,\text{total}} \times \frac{0.6 \,\text{total}}{0.3 \,\text{died}} = \frac{0.42^{\,7}}{0.12^{\,2}} = \frac{7}{2} = 7:2$$

The trap answer, per choice B, may be calculated in two ways. The first involves using numbers we previously obtained through the picking numbers approach. In this case: $\frac{35}{15} = \frac{7}{3} = 7:3$. However, this ratio is not correct because it involves dividing the estimated number of dead male rats by the number of dead female rats. We need to instead divide the death rate of male rats by the death rate of female rats.

Another way of obtaining trap answer choice B is as follows:

$$\frac{\begin{array}{c}\text{male rat deaths}\\ \hline \text{male rats (total)}\end{array}}{\begin{array}{c}\text{female rat deaths}\\ \hline \text{female rats (total)}\end{array}} = \frac{\begin{array}{c}70\% \times 40\%\\ \hline 40\%\end{array}}{\begin{array}{c}30\% \times 60\%\\ \hline 60\%\end{array}} = \frac{\begin{array}{c}28\%\\ \hline 40\%\end{array}}{\begin{array}{c}18\%\\ \hline 60\%\end{array}} = \frac{28\%}{40\%} \times \frac{60\%}{18\%} = 7:3$$

The problem here involves multiplying the respective death rates for male and female rats by the percentage of male and female rats. However, this is erroneous since we do not know how many rats died. In other words, we are dealing with two different groups of rats. The first group represents the total number of rats and the second group represents the rats that died. No direct link can be drawn between these two groups so we cannot directly multiply these percentages.

24. Garments ( )

Choice B
Classification: Price-Cost-Volume-Profit Problem
Snapshot: When Price-Cost-Volume-Profit problems are presented in the form of algebraic expressions, it is best to first find a per unit figure. Typically, this involves finding a dollar per unit or dollar per individual or usage per unit or usage per individual.

This problem requires us to calculate "number of units" (or "volume"). Start with the basic "cost" formula and solve for "number of units" as follows:

$$\text{Total Cost} = \text{Cost}_{\text{per unit}} \times \text{Number of units}$$

$$\text{Therefore, Number units} = \frac{\text{Total Cost}}{\text{Cost}_{\text{per unit}}}$$

$$\text{Number of units} = \frac{{}^{t}\,\text{dollars}}{\dfrac{{}^{d}\,\text{dollars}}{{}^{s}\,\text{shirts}}}$$

$$\text{Number of units} = t \ \cancel{\text{dollars}} \times \frac{s \ \text{shirts}}{d \ \cancel{\text{dollars}}}$$

$$\text{Number of units} = \frac{ts}{d} \ \text{shirts}$$

In summary, since the "price per unit" equals d/s, we divide t by d/s to arrive at ts/d.

25. Pet's Pet Shop (🌶🌶)

Choice B
Classification: Price-Cost-Volume-Profit Problem
Snapshot: The key here is to find a "usage per unit" figure, then work outward.

This problem requires that we calculate a "usage per unit" figure.

$$\text{Cups per bird per day} = \frac{\dfrac{35 \ \text{cups}}{15 \ \text{birds}}}{7 \ \text{days}}$$

$$\text{Cups per bird per day} = \frac{35 \ \text{cups}}{15 \ \text{birds}} \times \frac{1}{7 \ \text{days}}$$

$$\text{Cups per bird per day} = \frac{1}{3} \ \text{cups per bird per day}$$

Therefore, the number of cups of bird seed needed to feed 9 birds for 12 days is:

$\frac{1}{3}$ cups per bird per day $\times$ 9 birds $\times$ 12 days $=$ 36 cups

26. Sabrina (🌶🌶)

Choice C
Classification: Price-Cost-Volume-Profit Problem
Snapshot: This problem tests break-even point in terms of total revenue.

The difference between Sabrina's current base salary, $85,000, and $45,000 is $40,000. Divide $40,000 by 15%($1,500) to get 177.77 sales. In the equation below, x stands for the number of sales.

$$\text{Revenue}_{\text{Option 1}} = \text{Revenue}_{\text{Option 2}}$$

$$\$85,000 = \$45,000 + 0.15(\$1,500)(x)$$
$$\$85,000 - \$45,000 = 0.15(\$1,500)(x)$$
$$\$40,000 = 0.15(\$1,500)(x)$$
$$\$40,000 = \$225x$$

$$\$225x = \$40,000$$

$$x = \frac{\$40,000}{\$225}$$

$$x = 177.77$$

Therefore, $x = 178$ unit sales

When dividing $40,000 by $225 (commission) per sale, the dollar signs cancel, leaving the answer as the number of sales (or units).

NOTE ∞ Don't be tricked by tempting wrong answer choice B. A total of 177 sales isn't enough to break even. This number must be rounded up to 178 in order to avoid losing money. The actual number of sales is discrete, and can only be represented by whole numbers, not decimals.

27. Delicatessen ( )

Choice B
Classification: Price-Cost-Volume-Profit Problem
Snapshot: This type of problem shows how to calculate gross profit (or gross margin) when expressed in algebraic terms.

A variation of the "profit" formula is:

$$\text{Profit} = (\text{Price}_{\text{per unit}} \times \text{No. of units}) - (\text{Cost}_{\text{per unit}} \times \text{No. of units})$$

$$\text{Profit} = s\frac{\text{dollars}}{\text{pound}} \times \left(p \; \text{pounds} - d \; \text{pounds} \right) - \left(c \frac{\text{dollars}}{\text{pound}} \times p \; \text{pounds} \right)$$

$$\text{Profit} = s(p - d) - cp$$

NOTE ∞ First, in terms of units, "pounds" cancel out and leave dollars, which of course is the unit measurement for profit. Second, "gross profit" is *sales revenue* minus *product cost*. Sales revenue is price per unit multiplied by the number of units: $s(p - d)$. Product cost is cp. Therefore, gross profit is $s(p - d) - cp$.

28. Prototype ( )

Choice B
Classification: Price-Cost-Volume-Profit Problem
Snapshot: This problem highlights the concepts of *efficiency* and *cost efficiency*.

First, we set up the problem conceptually:

$$\left(1.0 \frac{\text{dollar}}{\text{gallon}} \times 1.0 \; \text{gallon} \right) - x \; \text{dollar savings} = \left(1.2 \frac{\text{dollar}}{\text{gallon}} \times \frac{5}{9} \; \text{gallons} \right)$$

Question: Where does the fraction $\frac{5}{9}$ come from? An 80 percent increase in efficiency can be expressed as $\frac{180\%}{100\%}$ or $\frac{9}{5}$. The reciprocal of $\frac{9}{5}$ is $\frac{5}{9}$. This means that the P-Car needs only five-ninths as much fuel to drive the same distance as does the T-Car.

Second, we solve for x, which represents the cost savings when using the P-Car.

Let's convert $1.2 to $\frac{6}{5}$ for simplicity.

$$\$(1.0)(1.0) - \$x = \$\left(\frac{6}{5}\right)\left(\frac{5}{9}\right)$$

$$\$1.0 - \$x = \$\left(\frac{6}{\cancel{5}}\right)\left(\frac{\cancel{5}}{9}\right)$$

$$\$1 - \$x = \$\frac{2}{3}$$

$$-\$x = -\$1 + \$\frac{2}{3}$$

$$-\$x = -\$\frac{1}{3}$$

$$(-1)(-\$x) = (-1)(-\$\tfrac{1}{3}) \qquad \text{[multiply both sides by } -1\text{]}$$

$$\$x = \$\frac{1}{3} \qquad \text{[dollar signs cancel]}$$

$$x = \frac{1}{3} = 33\frac{1}{3}\%$$

Since we save one-third of a dollar for every dollar spent, our percentage savings is $33\frac{1}{3}\%$. Therefore, although the cost of gas for the T-Car is more expensive, it results in an overall cost efficiency.

For the record, whereas 80% represents how much more <u>efficient</u> the P-Car is compared to the T-Car, the correct answer, $33\frac{1}{3}\%$ represents how much more <u>cost efficient</u> the P-Car is compared to the T-Car.

29. Lights (🌶🌶)

Choice D
Classification: Least-Common-Multiple Word Problem
Snapshot: This problem highlights the use of prime factorization in solving L-C-M word problems. To find the point at which a series of objects "line up," find the least common multiple of the numbers involved.

There are two ways to solve L-C-M problems: prime factorization and trial and error. Prime factorization is a direct approach that allows us to find the least common multiple by breaking down each component number into its prime factors. Then we multiply all the different prime factors together, including the largest "cluster" of any distinct prime factor to arrive at the least common multiple. The chart on the following page identifies these clusters through the use of underlining.

I. Prime Factor Method

Color	Prime Factors
Red	$2 \times 2 \times \underline{5} = 20$ seconds
Blue	$2 \times 3 \times 5 = 30$ seconds
Green	$\underline{3 \times 3} \times 5 = 45$ seconds
Orange	$2 \times 2 \times 3 \times 5 = 60$ seconds
Yellow	$\underline{2 \times 2 \times 2 \times 2} \times 5 = 80$ seconds

Therefore: $\underline{2 \times 2 \times 2 \times 2} \times \underline{3 \times 3} \times \underline{5} = 720$ seconds (or 12 minutes)

II. Trial-and-Error Method

Color	Flash Time	Cycles	Time
Red	20 seconds	3 cycles	1 minute
Blue	30 seconds	2 cycles	1 minute
Green	45 seconds	4 cycles	3 minutes
Orange	60 seconds	1 cycle	1 minute
Yellow	80 seconds	3 cycles	4 minutes

The trial-and-error method pivots on cycles. "How can the number of seconds for "Flash Time" be turned into cycles?" Observing the numbers in the "Time" column, we ask, "What is the least common multiple of 1 minute, 1 minute, 3 minutes 1 minute, and minutes?" "Voila!" The answer is 12 minutes.

30. Hardware ( )

Choice A
Classification: General Algebraic Word Problem
Snapshot: This problem further highlights the need to translate words into math. If we have twice as many pencils as crayons, the algebraic expression is $P = 2C$, not $2P = C$.

The total weight of 2 hammers and 3 wrenches is one-third that of 8 hammers and 5 wrenches:

$$3(2H + 3W) = 8H + 5W$$
$$6H + 9W = 8H + 5W$$
$$4W = 2H$$
$$W = \frac{2}{4}H$$
$$W = \frac{1}{2}H$$

Choosing the correct answer is perhaps the trickiest step because the mathematical result may seem counterintuitive and may be interpreted in reverse. Since $W = \frac{1}{2}H$ or $2W = H$, this means that two wrenches are as heavy as one hammer. Stated another way, a single wrench is half the weight of one hammer.

31. Snooker (🎣🎣)

Choice C
Classification: General Algebraic Word Problem
Snapshot: The classic way to solve GMAT algebraic word problems is to identify two distinct equations and then substitute for one of the variables.

Set-up: x = general admission seat tickets and y = VIP seat tickets

First equation:

$x + y = 320$
$y = 320 - x$ [Solve for y in terms of x.]

Second equation:

$\$15x + \$45y = \$7,500$
$\$x + \$3y = \$500$ [Simplify by dividing each term by the number 15.]

"Put the first equation into the second equation." That is, we substitute for the variable y in the first equation and solve for x.

$\$x + \$3(320 - x) = \$500$
$\$x + \$960 - \$3x = \$500$
$-\$2x = -\$460$
$(-1)(-\$2x) = (-1)(-\$460)$
$\$2x = \$460$
$x = \dfrac{\$460}{\$2}$
$x = 230$ tickets

Therefore, using the first equation (or, equally, the second equation), we substitute, $x = 230$, and solve for VIP seats:

$230 + y = 320$
$y = 90$

Finally, the difference between 230 and 90 is 140. This represents how many *more* general admission seat tickets were sold than VIP seat tickets, or equally, how many *fewer* VIP seat tickets were sold than general admission seat tickets.

32. Chili Paste (🌶🌶)

Choice D
Classification: General Algebraic Word Problem
Snapshot: Some word problems can be solved using a single variable as opposed to the classic two-variable problem solving approach. Four scenarios are possible in terms of solving this particular problem. In each scenario, let x = small cans and y = large cans.

Scenario 1: $15x = 25(x - 40)$ [where x = small cans]

$x = 100$ small cans

Scenario 2: $25y = 15(y + 40)$ [where y = large cans]

$y = 60$ large cans

$x = 100$ small cans

Scenario 3: $\dfrac{x}{15} - \dfrac{x}{25} = 40$ [where x = weekly needs]

$x = 1,500$ ounces

Thus, $1,500 \div 15 = 100$ small cans

This problem is solved using a single variable; the weekly needs of the restaurant is expressed in terms of x.

Scenario 4: i) $x = y + 40$ [where x = small cans]

ii) $y = \frac{15}{25}x$ (or $x = \frac{25}{15}y$)

Substituting equation ii) into equation i) above:

Thus, $x = \frac{3}{5}x + 40$

$x = 100$ small cans

Scenario 4 employs a classic two-variable, two equations approach. The second equation in this scenario is tricky because it utilizes a fractional relationship involving the volume of small cans to large cans, i.e., $\frac{15}{25}$ ounces.

NOTE ⚹ *Chili Paste* is an interesting problem and one which highlights multiple solutions. That's what's really interesting about math—"you can get downtown by taking many different roads." In other words, there are often multiple approaches to use to arrive at one single correct answer.

33. Premium (🌶🌶)

Choice E
Classification: General Algebraic Word Problem
Snapshot: This problem involves three variables and requires an answer expressed in terms of a third variable, in this case y.

Likely the easiest way to solve this problem is to identify two equations and substitute for one of the variables.

First Equation:

$5P = 6R$

The price of 5 kilograms of premium fertilizer is the same as the price of 6 kilograms of regular fertilizer.

Second Equation:

$P - y = R \quad \text{or} \quad R = P - y$

The price of premium fertilizer is y cents per kilogram more than the price of regular fertilizer.

Now we substitute for R in the first equation and solve for P:

$5P = 6(P - y)$
$5P = 6P - 6y$
$-P = -6y$
$(-1)(-P) = (-1)(-6y)$
$P = 6y$

34. Function ($\int$)

Choice B
Classification: Function Problem
Snapshot: This problem tackles compound functions. A function is a process that turns one number into another number. Usually this involves just plugging one number into a formula. The letter "f" is commonly used to designate a function, although any variable could be used.

Let's refer to the two equations as follows:

First equation: $\qquad f(x) = \sqrt{x}$

Second equation: $\qquad g(x) = \sqrt{x^2 + 7}$

Start by substituting "3" into the second equation:

$f(g(x))$ means apply g first, and then apply f to the result.

$g(x) = \sqrt{x^2 + 7}$
$g(3) = \sqrt{(3)^2 + 7} = \sqrt{9 + 7} = \sqrt{16} = 4$

Next, substitute "4" into the first equation:

$$f(x) = \sqrt{x}$$
$$f(4) = \sqrt{4} = 2$$

NOTE ❧ Here are two additional function problems.

Q1: Assuming identical information with respect to the original problem, what would be the solution to $g(f(9))$?

$g(f(x))$ means apply f first, and then apply g to the result.

First, simply substitute "9" into the first equation:

$$f(x) = \sqrt{x}$$
$$f(9) = \sqrt{9} = 3$$

Second, substitute "3" into the second equation:

$$g(x) = \sqrt{x^2 + 7}$$
$$g(3) = \sqrt{x^2 + 7} = \sqrt{(3)^2 + 7} = \sqrt{9 + 7} = \sqrt{16} = 4$$

Q2: What is $f(x)g(x)$ if $f(9) = \sqrt{x}$ and $g(3) = \sqrt{x^2 + 7}$?

$f(x)g(x)$ means apply f and g separately, and then multiply the results.

$$f(9) = \sqrt{x} = \sqrt{9} = 3$$
$$g(3) = \sqrt{x^2 + 7} = \sqrt{(3)^2 + 7} = \sqrt{9 + 7} = \sqrt{16} = 4$$

Result: $f(x)g(x) = 3 \times 4 = 12$

35. Rescue (🌶)

Choice D
Classification: Algebraic Fraction Problem
Snapshot: This problem highlights the "factoring out of a common term" as a key to solving algebraic fraction problems.

$$a(c - d) = b - d$$
$$ac - ad = b - d$$

$$d - ad = b - ac$$

$$d(1 - a) = b - ac$$

$$d = \frac{b - ac}{1 - a}$$

36. Hodgepodge ( )

Choice C

Classification: Algebraic Fraction Problem

Snapshot: Solving algebraic fraction problems often requires the ability to deal with common denominators.

First, we need to simplify the expression $1 - \frac{1}{h}$, which can be recast as $\frac{1}{1} - \frac{1}{h}$. A key step is to pick a common denominator for each individual fraction and the product of both denominators can serve as the common denominator. In this case, "$1h$" will serve as the common denominator for "h" and "1":

$$1 - \frac{1}{h} = \frac{1}{1} - \frac{1}{h} = \frac{(1h)\dfrac{1}{1} - \dfrac{1}{h}(1h)}{(1)(h)} = \frac{h - 1}{h}$$

Now the simplified calculation becomes:

$$\frac{\dfrac{1}{h}}{\dfrac{h-1}{h}} = \frac{1}{h} \times \frac{h}{h-1} = \frac{1}{h-1}$$

Likely, the trickiest step with this problem is simplifying the fraction in the denominator of the fraction. Take this very simple example:

$$\frac{\dfrac{1}{2} - \dfrac{1}{3}}{}$$

$$\frac{{}^{3}6\left(\dfrac{1}{2}\right) - {}^{2}6\left(\dfrac{1}{3}\right)}{(2)(3)}$$

$$\frac{3 - 2}{6} = \frac{1}{6}$$

In this simple example, we instinctively place the difference (that is, the integer 1) over the common denominator (that is, 6). It is easy to forget this step when dealing with the more difficult algebraic expression presented in this problem.

37. Mirage ( )

Choice D
Classification: Fractions and Decimals
Snapshot: This problem tests the ability to determine the size of a fraction a conceptual way, without having to perform calculations.

Whenever we add the same number to both the numerator and denominator of a fraction <u>less</u> than 1, we will always create a <u>bigger</u> fraction. In this problem, we are effectively adding 1 to both the numerator and denominator. Take the fraction $\frac{1}{2}$ for example. If we add 1 to both the numerator and denominator of this fraction, the fraction becomes conspicuously larger.

$$\frac{1}{2} = 50\% \qquad \frac{1+1}{2+1} = \frac{2}{3} = 66\frac{2}{3}\%$$

Therefore, 50% becomes $66\frac{2}{3}\%$.

This memorable example adds 1 million to both the numerator and denominator of a fraction less than 1:

$$\frac{1}{2} = 50\% \qquad \frac{1+1,000,000}{2+1,000,000} = \frac{1,000,001}{1,000,002} \cong 100\%$$

Therefore, 50% becomes almost 100%.

Alternatively, adding the same number to both the numerator and denominator of a fraction <u>greater</u> than 1 will always result in a <u>smaller</u> fraction.

Which of the following has the greatest value?

A) $\frac{11}{10}$ B) $\frac{5}{4}$ C) $\frac{8}{7}$ D) $\frac{22}{21}$ E) $\frac{6}{5}$

Choice B has the greatest value while choice D has the smallest value.

38. Deceptive ( )

Choice D
Classification: Fractions and Decimals
Snapshot: Dividing by any number is exactly the same as multiplying by that number's reciprocal (and also multiplying by any number is exactly the same as dividing by that number's reciprocal).

Dividing 100 by 0.75 is the same as multiplying 100 by the reciprocal of 0.75. The reciprocal of 0.75 is 1.33, not 1.25!

39. Spiral ( )

Choice A
Classification: Fractions and Decimals
Snapshot: This problem highlights reciprocals in the context of a numerical sequence.

The first five terms in this sequence unfold as follows:

$$2 \rightarrow \frac{3}{2} \rightarrow \frac{5}{3} \rightarrow \frac{8}{5} \rightarrow \frac{13}{8}$$

First term: 2

Second term: $1+\dfrac{1}{2}=\dfrac{3}{2}$

Third term: $1+\dfrac{2}{3}=\dfrac{5}{3}$

Fourth term: $1+\dfrac{3}{5}=\dfrac{8}{5}$

Fifth term: $1+\dfrac{5}{8}=\dfrac{13}{8}$

40. Discount ( )

Choice D
Classification: Percentage Problem
Snapshot: Percentage problems are easily solved by expressing the original price in terms of 100 percent.

A 10% discount followed by a 30% discount amounts to an overall 37% discount based on original price.

$90\% \times 70\% = 63\%$
$100\% - 63\% = 37\%$

Note that we cannot simply add 10% to 30% to get 40% because we cannot add (or subtract) the percents of different wholes.

41. Inflation ( )

Choice C
Classification: Percentage Problem
Snapshot: The commutative property of multiplication states that *order* doesn't matter when multiplying numbers.

$120\% \times 110\% = 132\%$
$110\% \times 120\% = 132\%$

It does not matter the *order* in which we multiply numbers; the result remains the same. In this case, a 20% inflationary increase followed by a 10% inflationary increase is the same as an inflationary increase of 10% followed by an inflationary increase of 20%. Either way, we have an overall inflationary increase of 32%.

In contrast with the previous problem, titled *Discount*, this problem does not require the actual amount of overall increase, but rather the relationship between the two inflationary increases. For the record, a 10% discount followed by a 30% discount is the same as a 30% discount followed by a 10% discount. Test: $0.9 \times 0.7 = 0.63$; $0.63 \times 100\% = 63\%$ and $0.7 \times 0.9 = 0.63$; $0.63 \times 100\% = 63\%$. Either way, we have an overall discount of 37%.

NOTE ⤖ The *commutative law* of mathematics states that order doesn't matter. This law holds for addition and multiplication, but it does <u>not</u> hold for subtraction or division. Here are some examples.

Addition:

Multiplication:

$$a + b = b + a$$
$$2 + 3 = 3 + 2$$

$$a \times b = b \times a$$
$$2 \times 3 = 3 \times 2$$

BUT NOT:

Subtraction:

Division:

$$a - b \neq b - a$$
$$4 - 2 \neq 2 - 4$$

$$a \div b \neq b \div a$$
$$4 \div 2 \neq 2 \div 4$$

42. Gardener (🌶)

Choice B
Classification: Percentage Problem
Snapshot: The concepts of percentage increase and decrease are applied to a simple geometry problem.

View the area of the original rectangular garden as having a width and length of 100%. The new rectangular garden has a length of 140% and a width of 80%. A 20% decrease in width translates to a width of 80% of the original width.

Area of original garden:

Area = lw = 100% × 100% = 100%

Area of resultant garden:

Area = lw = 140% × 80% = 112%

Percent change is as follows:

$$\frac{\text{New} - \text{Old}}{\text{Old}} \qquad \frac{112\% - 100\%}{100\%} = \frac{12\%}{100\%} = 12\%$$

NOTE ⤳ The calculation below is technically more accurate. The percent signs (i.e., %) cancel out and 0.12 must be multiplied by 100% in order to turn this decimal into a percentage and to reinstate the percentage sign in the final answer.

$$\frac{112\% - 100\%}{100\%} = \frac{12\%}{100\%} = 0.12$$

$$0.12 \times 100\% = 12\%$$

As a final note, an even more concise calculation for this problem results from the use of decimals.

$$1.4 \times 0.8 = 2.12$$
$$2.12 - 1.0 = 1.12 \times 100\% = 112\%$$
$$112\% - 100\% = 12\%$$

43. Microbrewery ( )

Choice C

Classification: Percentage Problem

Snapshot: This problem highlights the difference between "percentage increase" and "percentage of an original number."

Note that this problem is in essence asking about productivity: productivity = output ÷ work hours. Use 100% as a base, and add 70% to get 170% and then divide 170% by 80% to get 212.5%. An even simpler calculation involves the use of decimals:

$$\frac{1.7}{0.8} = 2.125$$

$$2.125 \times 100\% = 212.5\%$$

Now calculate the percent increase:

$$\frac{New - Old}{Old} \qquad \frac{212.5\% - 100\%}{100\%} = \frac{112.5\%}{100\%} = 112.5\%$$

Encore! What if the wording to this problem had been identical except that the last sentence read:

The year-end factory output per hour is what percent of the beginning of the year factory output per hour?

A) 50%
B) 90%
C) 112.5%
D) 210%
E) 212.5%

The answer would be choice E. This problem is not asking for a percent increase, but rather "percentage of an original number."

Percentage of an original number:

$$\frac{\text{New}}{\text{Old}} \qquad \frac{212.5\%}{100\%} = 212.5\%$$

Again, the calculation below is more accurate. The percent signs (i.e., %) cancel out and 2.125 must be multiplied by 100% in order to turn this decimal into a percentage and to reinstate the percentage sign in the final answer.

$$\frac{212.5\%}{100\%} = 2.125$$

$$2.125 \times 100\% = 212.5\%$$

NOTE ✑ The fact that two of the answer choices, namely choices C and E, are 100% apart alerts us to the likelihood that a distinction needs to be made between "percentage increase" and "percentage of an original number."

44. Squaring Off (🥿🥿)

Choice A
Classification: Percentage Problem
Snapshot: A number of tricky geometry problems can be solved by picking numbers such as 1, 100, or 100 percent.

Area of original square:

$$\text{Area} = \text{side}^2$$

$$A = s^2$$

$$A = (1)^2 = 1 \text{ square unit}$$

Area of resultant square:

$$\text{Area} = \text{side}^2$$

$$A = s^2$$

$$A = (2)^2 = 4 \text{ square units}$$

$$\frac{\text{Original Square}}{\text{Resultant Square}} = \frac{1}{4} = 25\%$$

NOTE ✑ As a matter of form, we generally express a larger number in terms of a smaller number. For example, we tend to say that A is three times the size of B rather than saying that B is one-third the size of A. But it's not technically incorrect to express the smaller value in terms of the larger value. Here, the resultant square is four times the size of the original square. It is equally correct to say that the smaller (original) square figure is one quarter (or 25 percent) the size of the larger (resultant) square.

45. Diners (🌶🌶)

Choice B
Classification: Percentage Problem
Snapshot: This problem highlights a subtle mathematical distinction. In terms of percentages, and increase from 80 percent to 100 percent is not the same as an increase from 100 percent to 120 percent.

Ho, ho—this nice, round number represents the cost before tax (and tip).

Let x be the cost of food *before tip:*

$$\frac{x}{\$264} = \frac{100\%}{120\%}$$

$$120\%(x) = 100\%(\$264)$$

$$\frac{1}{\cancel{120\%}} \times \cancel{120\%}(x) = \frac{1}{120\%} \times \$264(100\%)$$

$$x = \frac{\$264(100\%)}{120\%}$$

$$x = \frac{\$264(1.0)}{1.2}$$

$$x = \$220$$

Now let x be the cost of food *before tip and tax:*

$$\frac{x}{\$220} = \frac{100\%}{110\%}$$

$$110\%(x) = 100\%(\$220)$$

$$\frac{1}{\cancel{110\%}} \times \cancel{110\%}(x) = \frac{1}{110\%} \times \$220(100\%)$$

$$x = \frac{\$220(100\%)}{110\%}$$

$$x = \frac{\$220(1.0)}{1.1}$$

$$x = \$200$$

NOTE ✎ The shortcut method is to divide $264 by 1.2 and then by 1.1. That is, $[(\$264 \div 1.2) \div 1.1)] = \$200$. An even quicker method is to divide $264 by 1.32. This results from: $\$264 \div (1.2 \times 1.1) = \$264 \div 1.32 = \$200$.

46. Investments (🌶️🌶️)

Choice E

Classification: Percentage Problem

Snapshot: You cannot add or subtract the percents of different wholes. Case in point: Twenty percent of a big number results in a larger value than 20 percent of a small number.

Below are the calculations for gain and loss expressed as proportions:

Gain on sale of Property A:

$$\frac{120\%}{100\%} = \frac{\$24,000}{x}$$

$$120\%(x) = 100\%(\$24,000)$$

$$\frac{1}{\cancel{120\%}} \times \cancel{120\%}(x) = \frac{1}{120\%} \times 100\%(\$24,000)$$

$$x = \frac{\$24,000(100\%)}{120\%}$$

$$x = \frac{\$24,000(1.0)}{1.2}$$

$$x = \$20,000$$

Gain: $\$24,000 - \$20,000 = \$4,000$

This gain represents the sales price less original purchase price.

Loss on the sale of Property B:

$$\frac{100\%}{80\%} = \frac{x}{\$24,000}$$

$$100\%(\$24,000) = 80\%(x)$$

$$80\%(x) = 100\%(\$24,000)$$

$$\frac{1}{\cancel{80\%}} \times \cancel{80\%}(x) = \frac{1}{80\%} \times 100\%(\$24,000)$$

$$x = \frac{\$24,000(100\%)}{80\%}$$

$$x = \frac{\$24,000(1.0)}{0.8}$$

$$x = \$30,000$$

Loss: $\$30,000 - \$24,000 = \$6,000$

This loss represents the original purchase price less the amount received from the sale.

Therefore, we have an overall net loss of $2,000 ($6,000 loss and $4,000 gain). The following provides shortcut calculations:

Calculation of gain:

$24,000 ÷ 1.2 = $20,000
Gain: $24,000 − $20,000 = $4,000

Calculation of loss:

$24,000 ÷ 0.8 = $30,000
Loss: $30,000 − $24,000 = $6,000

Again, we have an overall net loss of $2,000 ($6,000 loss and $4,000 gain).

47. Earth Speed (🌶🌶)

Choice E
Classification: Ratios and Proportions
Snapshot: This problem illustrates how quantities expressed in certain units can be changed to quantities in other units by smartly multiplying by 1.

This problem proves a bit more cumbersome. Here's a three-step approach:

i)   Visualize the end result:

$$\frac{20 \text{ miles}}{1 \text{ second}} \times \underline{\quad} \times \underline{\quad} = \frac{? \text{ km}}{\text{hour}}$$

ii)   Anticipate the canceling of units:

$$\frac{20 \text{ miles}}{1 \text{ second}} \times \frac{\text{seconds}}{\text{hour}} \times \frac{\text{km}}{\text{mile}} = \frac{? \text{ km}}{\text{hour}}$$

iii)   Enter conversions and cancel units:

$$\frac{20 \text{ } \cancel{\text{miles}}}{1 \text{ } \cancel{\text{second}}} \times \frac{3{,}600 \text{ } \cancel{\text{seconds}}}{1 \text{ hour}} \times \frac{1 \text{ km}}{0.6 \text{ } \cancel{\text{mile}}} = \frac{? \text{ km}}{\text{hour}}$$

Per the above equation, 1 hour equals 3,600 seconds and 1 kilometer equals 0.6 miles.

$$\frac{20 \times 3{,}600}{0.6} = \frac{72{,}000}{0.6} = 120{,}000 \text{ kilometer/hour}$$

48. Rum & Coke ( )

Choice B
Classification: Ratios and Proportions
Snapshot: Part-to-part ratios are not the same as part-to-whole ratios. If the ratio of married to non-married people at a party is $1:2$, the percentage of married persons at the party is one out of every three persons or $33\frac{1}{3}$ percent (not 50 percent).

The trap answer is choice A because it erroneously adds component parts of the two different ratios. That is, $1:2 + 1:3$ does not equal $1 + 1:2 + 3 = 2:5$. This could only be correct if ratios represented identical volumes. We cannot simply add two ratios together unless we know the numbers behind those ratios.

	Total	Rum	Coke
Solution #1	6	2	4
Solution #2	32	8	24
Totals		10	28
		Simplify☺	
Final Ratio		5	14

The ratio of $10:28$ simplifies to $5:14$.

Supporting Calculations:

$6 \times \frac{1}{3} = 2$ Two ounces of rum in solution #1

$6 \times \frac{2}{3} = 4$ Four ounces of Coke in solution #1

$32 \times \frac{1}{4} = 8$ Eight ounces of rum in solution #2

$32 \times \frac{3}{4} = 24$ Twenty-four ounces of Coke in solution #2

49. Millionaire ( )

Choice A
Classification: Ratios and Proportions
Snapshot: Triple ratios (3 parts) are formed by making the middle term of equivalent size.

Correct answers would include any and all multiples of $1:4:400$, including $2:8:800$, $4:16:1600$, etc. However, the latter choices are not presented as options here.

Visualize the solution:

Billionaire	Millionaire	Yuppie
$20 ◀ – – – – – – – – – ▶ $0.20		
	$4 ◀ – – – – – – – – – ▶ $1	

Do the math:

	Billionaire	Millionaire	Millionaire	Yuppie
Original Ratio	$20	$0.20	$4	$1
Adjusting Multipliers	×20	×20	×1	×1
Resultant Ratio	$400	$4	$4	$1

Equivalent

Choose the answer:

B to M to Y → $400 to $4 to $1

∴ Y to M to B → $1 to $4 to $400

NOTE ✎ Triple ratios (e.g., A : B : C) are formed from two pairs of ratios by making sure the "middle terms" are of equivalent size.

50. Deluxe (🌶🌶🌶)

Choice D

Classification: Ratios and Proportions

Snapshot: *Deluxe* is clearly a difficult ratio problem. The first step is to break the 24 liters of fuchsia into "red" and "blue." This requires using a part-to-whole ratio (i.e., three-eighths blue and five-eighths red; $\frac{3}{8}$ and $\frac{5}{8}$ respectively). Our final ratio is a part-to-part ratio, comparing red and blue paint in fuchsia to the red and blue paint in mauve.

First, we know that there are 24 liters of fuchsia in a ratio of 5 parts red to 3 parts blue. We break down this amount into the actual amount of red and blue in 24 liters of fuchsia.

Blue: 5 parts red to 3 parts blue.

$$\frac{3}{5+3} = \frac{3}{8} \quad \rightarrow \quad \frac{3}{8} \times 24 = 9 \text{ liters of blue paint}$$

Red: 5 parts red to 3 parts blue.

$$\frac{5}{5+3} = \frac{5}{8} \quad \rightarrow \quad \frac{5}{8} \times 24 = 15 \text{ liters of red paint}$$

So the final formula, expressed as a proportion, becomes:

$$\frac{15\,\text{red}}{9\,\text{blue} + x\,\text{blue}} = \frac{3\,\text{red}}{5\,\text{blue}}$$

$5(15) = 3(9 + x)$

$75 = 3(9 + x)$

$75 = 27 + 3x$
$3x + 27 = 75$

$3x = 48$

$x = 16$ liters of blue paint

51. Rare Coins ( )

Choice E
Classification: Ratios and Proportions
Snapshot: This problem highlights two different problem solving approaches for ratio-type problems: the "two-variable, two-equations" approach and the "multiples" approach.

I.   Two-Variable, Two-Equations Approach

Using this approach, we identify two equations and substitute one variable for another. G represents gold coins; S represents silver coins.

First equation:

$$\frac{1}{3} = \frac{G}{S} \qquad or \qquad S = 3G$$

Second equation:

$$\frac{G + 10}{S} = \frac{1}{2} \qquad or \qquad S = 2(G + 10)$$

Since $S = 3G$ and $S = 2(G + 10)$, we can substitute for one of these variables and solve for the other.

$2(G + 10) = 3G$

$2G + 20 = 3G$

$G = 20$ and, therefore, $S = 60$

We substitute $G = 20$ into either of the two original equations and obtain $S = 60$. Finally, 20 (gold coins) *plus* 60 (silver coins) *plus* 10 (gold coins added) *equals* 90 total coins.

II.   Multiples Approach

The secret behind this approach is to view x as representing multiples of the actual number of coins. Given a ratio of 1 to 3, we can represent the actual number of gold coins versus non-gold coins as $1x$ and $3x$ respectively. The solution is as follows:

$$\frac{1x + 10}{3x} = \frac{1}{2}$$

$$2(1x + 10) = 3x$$

$$2x + 20 = 3x$$

$$x = 20$$

Substituting 20 for x in the original equals:

$$\frac{\text{coins (gold)}}{\text{coins (silver)}} = \frac{1x}{3x} = \frac{1(20)}{3(20)} = \frac{20}{60}$$

Thus, 20 (gold coins) *plus* 60 (silver coins) *plus* 10 (gold coins added) *equals* 90 total coins.

NOTE ⚭ In the event of guessing, since the final ratio is 2 to 1, this means that the total number of coins must be a multiple of 3. Only answer choices C (60) or E (90) could, therefore, be correct.

52. Coins Revisited (🌶🌶🌶)

Choice B
Classification: Ratios and Proportions
Snapshot: *Coins Revisited* differs from the previous problem, *Rare Coins*, in that the total number of coins in the collection (per *Coins Revisited*) does not change. Mathematically, 10 coins are subtracted from the denominator while coins 10 coins are added to the numerator. In this particular problem, the second statement, "If 10 more gold coins were to be subsequently traded...," is treated mathematically no different than if an actual trade had occurred.

The secret to this particular problem lies in first translating the part-to-whole ratio of 1 to 6 to a part-to-part ratio of 1 to 5.

I.   Two-Variable, Two-Equations Approach

First equation:

$$\frac{1}{5} = \frac{G}{S} \qquad S = 5G$$

Second equation:

$$\frac{G + 10}{S - 10} = \frac{1}{4} \qquad 4(G + 10) = 1(S - 10)$$

Since $S = 5G$ and $4(G + 10) = 1(S - 10)$, we can substitute and solve for G (or S).

$$4(G + 10) = 1(5G - 10)$$
$$4G + 40 = 5G - 10$$
$$-G = -50$$
$$(-1)(-G) = (-1)(-50)$$
$$G = 50 \text{ and, therefore, } S = 250$$

Thus, there are 60 gold coins after the trade (i.e., 50 gold coins plus 10 gold coins added).

II. Multiples Approach

Here $1x$ and $5x$ can be viewed as representing multiples of the actual number of gold coins and silver coins, respectively. The solution is as follows:

$$\frac{1x + 10}{5x - 10} = \frac{1}{4}$$
$$4(1x + 10) = 1(5x - 10)$$
$$4x + 40 = 5x - 10$$
$$x = 50$$

Substituting 50 for x in the original equals:

$$\frac{\text{coins (gold)}}{\text{coins (non-gold)}} = \frac{1x}{5x} = \frac{1(50)}{5(50)} = \frac{50}{250}$$

Thus, 50 (gold coins) *plus* 10 gold coins added equals 60 coins.

NOTE ✍ For the record, there are 300 gold coins in the collection (both before and after the proposed trade). Before the trade, there are 50 gold coins and 250 silver coins. After the trade, there would be 60 gold coins and 240 silver coins.

53. Plus-Zero (🧦)

Choice D
Classification: Squares and Cubes
Snapshot: First, consider which of the seven numbers—2, –2, 1, –1, $\frac{1}{2}$, $-\frac{1}{2}$, and 0—satisfy each of the conditions presented in statements I through III. When a problem states $x > 0$, three numbers should immediately come to mind: 2, 1, and $\frac{1}{2}$.

Statement I:

Could x^3 be greater than x^2?
Answer—yes.

Example $2^3 > 2^2$

Proof $8 > 4$

Statement II:

Could x^2 be equal to x?
Answer—yes.

Example $1^2 = 1$

Proof $1 = 1$

Statement III:

Could x^2 be greater than x^3?
Answer—yes.

Example $\left(\dfrac{1}{2}\right)^2 > \left(\dfrac{1}{2}\right)^3$

Proof $\dfrac{1}{4} > \dfrac{1}{8}$

54. Sub-Zero ($\mathcal{S}\,\mathcal{S}$)

Choice B
Classification: Squares and Cubes

Snapshot: When a problem states $x < 0$, three numbers should immediately come to mind: $-2, -1,$ and $-\dfrac{1}{2}$.

Statement I:

Is x^2 greater than 0?
Answer—absolutely. As long as x is negative, it will, when squared, become positive.

Statement II:

Is $x - 2x$ greater than 0?
Answer—absolutely. As long as x is negative, the expression "$x - 2x$" will be greater than zero.

Statement III:

Is $x^3 + x^2$ less than 0?
Answer—not necessarily.

Example $\left(-\dfrac{1}{2}\right)^3 + \left(-\dfrac{1}{2}\right)^2$

$-\dfrac{1}{8} + \dfrac{1}{4} = \dfrac{1}{8}$

$\dfrac{1}{8} > 0$

55. Solar Power ( )

Choice B
Classification: Exponent Problem
Snapshot: This problem tests the ability to manipulate exponents.

$$\dfrac{2 \times 10^{30}}{8 \times 10^{12}} = 0.25 \times 10^{18} = 2.5 \times 10^{17}$$

Note that by moving the decimal one place to the right (i.e., 0.25 to 2.5), we reduce the power of the exponent by one (i.e., 10^{18} becomes 10^{17}).

56. Bacteria ( )

Choice C
Classification: Exponent Problem
Snapshot: This problem shows how exponents can be used to express the multiplicative power of numbers.

Visualize the solution. We start with $(10)^5$ then multiply by 2 for each 10-minute segment. Since there are six 10-minute segments in one hour, we arrive at $[2 \times 2 \times 2 \times 2 \times 2 \times 2 \times (10^5)]$. Thus, $(2^6)(10^5)$ represents the number of bacteria after one hour.

57. K.I.S.S. ( )

Choice E
Classification: Exponent Problem
Snapshot: Picking numbers may be used as an alternative approach in solving exponent problems.

I.   Algebraic Method

$3^a + 3^{a+1}$

$3^a + 3^a \times 3^1$

$3^a(1 + 3^1)$ [factor out 3^a from both terms]

$3^a(1 + 3)$

$3^a(4)$ or $4(3^a)$ [the use of brackets here is simply a matter of form]

II. Picking Numbers Method

Another method that can be used to solve this problem is substitution, which involves picking numbers. Take the original expression: $3^a + 3^{a+1}$. Substitute the "easiest integer." That is, let's substitute $a = 1$.

Therefore, $3^1 + 3^{1+1} = 3^1 + 3^2 = 3 + 9 = 12$. We ask ourselves: "Which answer choice gives us 12 when we substitute $a = 1$ into that equation?" Answer: Choice E.

Proof: $4(3^a) = 4(3^1) = 12$.

58. Triplets (🦶🦶)

Choice A
Classification: Exponent Problem
Snapshot: Consistent with Exponent Rule 8 (see page 37), we can simplify this expression by factoring out a common term (i.e., 3^{10}).

$3^{10} + 3^{10} + 3^{10}$
$3^{10}(1 + 1 + 1)$
$3^{10}(3)$
$3^{10} \times 3^1 = 3^{11}$

NOTE ⤚ Here's a bonus question:

$$\frac{2^{15} - 2^{14}}{2} = ?$$

A) 1   B) 2   C) 2^7 D) 2^{13} E) 2^{14}

Calculation:

$$\frac{2^{15} - 2^{14}}{2} = \frac{2^{14}(2^1 - 1)}{2} = \frac{2^{14}(2 - 1)}{2} = \frac{2^{14}(1)}{2} = \frac{2^{14}}{2^1} = 2^{13}$$

Choice D is therefore correct.

59. The Power of 5 (🦶🦶🦶)

Choice C
Classification: Exponent Problem
Snapshot: This problem highlights the multiplying of exponents consistent with Exponent Rule 3—"power of a power" (see page 36).

$5^5 \times 5^7 = (125)^x$

$5^{12} = (125)^x$ Per Exponent Rule 1

$$5^{12} = (5^3)^x \qquad \text{Per Exponent Rule 3}$$

$$5^{12} = (5^3)^4 \qquad \text{Therefore, } x = 4$$

$$5^{12} = 5^{12}$$

Note that in the penultimate step above, given that the bases are equal in value, the exponents must also be equal in value. That is, in terms of exponents, $12 = 3x$ and $x = 4$. Here's a somewhat easier scenario:

$$10^3 \times 10^5 = (100)^x$$

$$10^8 = (100)^x \qquad \text{Per Exponent Rule 1}$$

$$10^8 = (10^2)^x \qquad \text{Per Exponent Rule 3}$$

$$10^8 = (10^2)^4 \qquad \text{Therefore, } x = 4$$

$$10^8 = 10^8$$

Note that with respect to exponents, $8 = 2x$ and $x = 4$.

60. M&N ( )

Choice B
Classification: Exponent Problem
Snapshot: This problem highlights a more difficult exponent problem containing two variables, m and n. It also highlights Exponent Rule 4 (see page 36).

There are two ways to solve this problem. The first is the *algebraic method* and the second is the *picking numbers* method.

I. Algebraic Method

$$n = 2^{m-1}$$

$$n = 2^m \times 2^{-1} = \frac{2^m}{2^1}$$

$$2n = 2^m$$

$$4^m = (2 \times 2)^m = 2^m \times 2^m \qquad \text{Per Exponent Rule 4}$$

$$4^m = 2n \times 2n = 4n^2 \qquad \text{Note: } 2n = 2^m$$

Note that in the penultimate step above, $4^m = 2^m \times 2^m$, and since $2^m = 2n$, the final calculation becomes $2n \times 2n$.

II. Picking Numbers Method

Since $m > 1$, pick $m = 2$, such that $n = 2^{m-1} = 2^{2-1} = 2^1 = 2$.

When $m = 2$, it is also true that $4^m = 4^2 = 16$. So the question becomes: "When $m = 2$ which answer, A thru E, when substituting $n = 2$, will result in an answer of 16?"

Choice B is correct: $4n^2 = 4(2)^2 = 16$.

61. Incognito (🦶🦶🦶)

Choice E
Classification: Exponent Problem
Snapshot: This problem shows how fractions can be simplified through factoring. This treatment is consistent with Exponent Rule 8 (see page 37).

The key is to first factor out "$(2^2)(3^2)$" from each of the denominators.

A) $\dfrac{25}{(2^4)(3^3)} \rightarrow \dfrac{25}{(2^2)(3^1)} = \dfrac{25}{12} = 2\dfrac{1}{12}$

B) $\dfrac{5}{(2^2)(3^3)} \rightarrow \dfrac{5}{(1)(3^1)} = \dfrac{5}{3} = 1\dfrac{2}{3}$

C) $\dfrac{4}{(2^3)(3^2)} \rightarrow \dfrac{4}{(2^1)(1)} = \dfrac{4}{2} = 2$

D) $\dfrac{36}{(2^3)(3^4)} \rightarrow \dfrac{36}{(2^1)(3^2)} = \dfrac{36}{18} = 2$

E) $\dfrac{76}{(2^4)(3^4)} \rightarrow \dfrac{76}{(2^2)(3^2)} = \dfrac{76}{36} = 2\dfrac{4}{36} = 2\dfrac{1}{9}$

NOTE ✎ In terms of guessing on GMAT math problems, there is one technique worth keeping in mind for use on "Which of the following" questions (also known as "WOTF" math questions). In this question type, test makers tend to manifest answers deep in the answer choices, meaning that choices D and E have a disproportional chance of ending up as correct answers. Why is this? "Which of the following" questions require the test taker to work with the answer choices, and most candidates logically work from choices A to E. For test-taking purposes, this presents two opportunities. If we need to guess on these questions, it is best to guess choices D or E. Also, it is judicious to start checking answers in reverse order, starting with choice E.

62. Chain Reaction (🦶🦶🦶)

Choice D
Classification: Exponent Problem
Snapshot: This follow-up problem is a more difficult problem than the preceding one, but the suggested approach is identical.

If, $x - \dfrac{1}{2^6} - \dfrac{1}{2^7} - \dfrac{1}{2^8} = \dfrac{2}{2^9}$ then $x = \dfrac{2}{2^9} + \dfrac{1}{2^8} + \dfrac{1}{2^7} + \dfrac{1}{2^6}$

Now factor out $\dfrac{1}{2^6}$ from each of the terms in the denominator:

So $x = \dfrac{1}{2^6}\left(\dfrac{2}{2^3} + \dfrac{1}{2^2} + \dfrac{1}{2^1} + 1 \right)$

$x = \dfrac{1}{2^6}\left(\dfrac{2}{8} + \dfrac{1}{4} + \dfrac{1}{2} + 1 \right)$

$x = \dfrac{1}{2^6}\left(1 + 1 \right) = \dfrac{1}{2^6}(2) = \dfrac{1}{2^5}$

63. Simplify ( )

Choice A
Classification: Radical Problem
Snapshot: This problem illustrates how to simplify radicals and brings into play Radical Rule 7 (see page 39).

$$\sqrt{\dfrac{(12 \times 3) + (4 \times 16)}{6}} = \sqrt{\dfrac{36 + 64}{6}} = \sqrt{\dfrac{100}{6}} = \sqrt{\dfrac{50}{3}}$$

$$\dfrac{\sqrt{50}}{\sqrt{3}} = \dfrac{\sqrt{25 \times 2}}{\sqrt{3}} = \dfrac{\sqrt{25} \times \sqrt{2}}{\sqrt{3}} = \dfrac{5\sqrt{2}}{\sqrt{3}}$$

$$\dfrac{5\sqrt{2}}{\sqrt{3}} \times \dfrac{\sqrt{3}}{\sqrt{3}} = \dfrac{5\sqrt{2 \times 3}}{\sqrt{9}} = \dfrac{5\sqrt{6}}{3}$$

Note that you cannot break up the radical at the addition sign into two parts:

$$\neq \dfrac{\sqrt{12 \times 3} + \sqrt{4 \times 16}}{6} = \dfrac{\sqrt{36} + \sqrt{64}}{6} = \dfrac{6 + 8}{6} = \dfrac{14}{6} = 2\dfrac{1}{3} \quad \text{This result is incorrect!}$$

64. Tenfold ( )

Choice C
Classification: Radical Problem
Snapshot: This problem highlights Radical Rule 3 (see page 38).

$$\frac{\sqrt{10}}{\sqrt{0.001}} = \sqrt{\frac{10}{0.001}} = \sqrt{10,000} = 100$$

65. Strange ( )

Choice A
Classification: Radical Problem
Snapshot: This problem illustrates how the "multiplicative inverse" can be used to simplify radical equations—it illustrates Radical Rule 8 (see page 39).

The solutions approach is to multiply the denominator of the fraction by its multiplicative inverse.

$$\left(\frac{1-\sqrt{2}}{1+\sqrt{2}}\right) = \left(\frac{1-\sqrt{2}}{1+\sqrt{2}}\right) \times \left(\frac{1-\sqrt{2}}{1-\sqrt{2}}\right)$$

$$\left(\frac{1-\sqrt{2}}{1+\sqrt{2}}\right) \times \left(\frac{1-\sqrt{2}}{1-\sqrt{2}}\right) = \frac{1-\sqrt{2}-\sqrt{2}+\sqrt{4}}{1-\sqrt{2}+\sqrt{2}-\sqrt{4}} = \frac{1-2\sqrt{2}+\sqrt{4}}{1-\sqrt{4}}$$

$$\frac{1-2\sqrt{2}+\sqrt{4}}{1-\sqrt{4}} = \frac{1-2\sqrt{2}+2}{1-2} = \frac{3-2\sqrt{2}}{-1}$$

$$\frac{3-2\sqrt{2}}{-1} = \frac{3-2\sqrt{2}}{-1} \times \frac{-1}{-1} = \frac{-3+2\sqrt{2}}{+1} = -3+2\sqrt{2}$$

66. Two-Way Split ( )

Choice A
Classification: Inequality Problem
Snapshot: This problem tests our ability to combine two inequalities into one expression using a single variable x. Also, when multiplying through by a negative number, we reverse the direction of the inequality sign.

Note that another correct answer could have been expressed as following: $x < -4$ or $x > 4$, which is an alternative way of writing the former expression.

$-x^2 + 16 < 0$

$(-1)(x^2) + 16 < 0$

$(-1)(-1)(x^2) + (-1)16 > (-1)0$ [multiply each term through by -1]

$x^2 - 16 > 0$

Therefore, $x < -4$ or $x > 4$. When combining these two inequalities into one expression, we write it as: $-4 > x > 4$. Note that in the penultimate step of our calculation above, we multiply each term of the equation by -1 in order to cancel the negative sign in front of x. In multiplying through by -1, we must remember to reverse the inequality sign.

67. Primed (🌶)

Choice C
Classification: Prime Number Problem
Snapshot: To review prime numbers and prime factorization.

"x"	Factors	Prime Factors	"Primeness"
A) 10	1, 2, 5, 10	2, 5	$5 - 2 = 3$
B) 12	1, 2, 3, 4, 6, 12	2, 3	$3 - 2 = 1$
C) 14	1, 2, 7, 14	2, 7	$7 - 2 = 5$
D) 15	1, 3, 5, 15	3, 5	$5 - 3 = 2$
E) 18	1, 2, 3, 6, 9, 18	2, 3	$3 - 2 = 1$

68. Odd Man Out (🌶🌶)

Choice C
Classification: Prime Number Problem
Snapshot: This problem highlights the mathematical reason for why one number is or is not a multiple of another number.

First, let's visualize P as: $1 \times 2 \times 3 \times 4 \times 5 \times 6 \times 7 \times 8 \times 9 \times 10 \times 11 \times 12 \times 13$
This is also the equivalent of 13! (or 13 factorial)

Statement I is false. P is an even number. As long as we have a least one even number in our multiplication sequence, the entire product will be even. Remember an even number times an odd or even number is always an even number. For the record, P actually equals 6,227,020,800.

Statement II is false while statement III is true. The key here is to look at the prime factors of P. These include: 2, 3, 5, 7, 11, and 13. For P to be a multiple of any number, that number must not contain any prime number that isn't already contained in P. What are the distinct prime factors of 17?

Factorization	Prime Factors	Distinct Prime Factors
$17 = 1 \times 17$	17	17
$24 = 1 \times 24$		
$24 = 1 \times 8 \times 3$		
$24 = 1 \times 2 \times 2 \times 2 \times 3$	2, 2, 2, 3	2, 3

The number 17 has as its (only) prime factor, the number 17. Since P does not contain this number, it will not be a multiple of 17. It's as simple as that. Think of prime factors as the "DNA" of any number. Any number x will not be a multiple of y if y contains any distinct prime number not included in x. Stated another way, x will be a multiple of y only if x contains, at a minimum, the same number of distinct prime factors as y does. For example, the number 6 is a multiple of 3 because 3 contains no prime numbers that aren't already included in 6 (i.e., 2, 3). The number 6 is not a multiple of 5 because 5 has a prime factor 5, which is not shared as a prime factor of the number 6.

P is a multiple of 24 because P contains all of the distinct prime numbers that 24 has (i.e, 2,3).

69. Remainder ( )

Choice E
Classification: Remainder Problem
Snapshot: Picking numbers is as sure-fire technique for solving multiple and remainder problems.

A key step in this problem involves picking a number for k based on the original information that k, when divided by 7, leaves a remainder 5. This number is 12. We now substitute 12 for k.

I. $4k + 7$ $4k + 7 = 4(12) + 7 = 55$
$$55 \div 7 = 7, \text{ with a remainder of } 6$$

II. $6k + 4$ $6k + 4 = 6(12) + 4 = 76$
$$76 \div 7 = 10, \text{ with a remainder of } 6$$

III. $8k + 1$ $8k + 1 = 8(12) + 1 = 97$
$$97 \div 7 = 13, \text{ with a remainder of } 6$$

70. Double Digits ( )

Choice D
Classification: Remainder Problem
Snapshot: When faced with multi-step divisibility problems (A divided by B leaves x but A divided by C leaves y), find only those numbers that satisfy the first scenario then use this short-list of numbers to determine the solution to the next scenario.

The key to this problem is to do one part at a time rather than trying to combine the information. For example, list all two-digit numbers that when divided by 10 leave 3. These numbers include: 13, 23, 33, 43, 53, 63, 73, 83, and 93. Next, examine these numbers and determine which of these, when divided by 4, will leave a remainder of 3. These numbers include: 23, 43, 63, and 83.

Numbers	Reminder
13	1
23	3⇐
33	1
43	3⇐
53	1
63	3⇐
73	1
83	3⇐
93	1

71. Visualize (𝄞𝄞)

Choice A
Classification: Symbolism Problem
Snapshot: Learning to visualize the solution is the key to conquering symbolic or "make-believe" operations.

Set the problem up conceptually by first visualizing the solution:

$$V* = V - \frac{V}{2}$$

$$(V*)* = V - \frac{V}{2} - \left(\frac{V - \frac{V}{2}}{2} \right)$$

$$3 = V - \frac{V}{2} - \left(\frac{V - \frac{V}{2}}{2} \right)$$

Calculate the outcome algebraically:

$$(2)3 = (2)V - (2)\frac{V}{2} - (2)\left(\frac{V - \frac{V}{2}}{2} \right) \qquad \text{Multiply each term in the equation by 2.}$$

$$6 = 2V - V - \left(V - \frac{V}{2} \right)$$

146

$$6 = 2V - V - V + \frac{V}{2}$$

$$(2)6 = (2)2V - (2)V - (2)V + (\cancel{2})\frac{V}{\cancel{2}}$$ Once again, multiply each term through by 2.

$$12 = 4V - 2V - 2V + V$$

$$V = 12$$

72. Masquerade (🌶)

Choice D
Classification: Coordinate Geometry Problem
Snapshot: Positive lines slope upward ("forward slashes"); negative lines slope backward ("back slashes"). Graphs with slopes less than one (coefficients consisting of positive or negative fractions between +1 and −1) are flat and closer to the x-axis. Graphs with slopes greater than one (coefficients greater than +1 or less than −1) are more upright and closer to the y-axis.

Compare the general slope formula, $y = mx + b$, to the equation in this problem: $y = -2x + 2$. For the general slope formula, m is equal to the slope and b is equal to the y-intercept. In the equation at hand, the slope is −2. A negative slope tells us that the graph is moving northwest-southeast; a slope of negative 2 tells us that the graph drops two units for every one unit it runs. The y-intercept is 2. This means that one point is (0,2).

Lines A and B are out because they have positive slopes and we are looking for a negative slope. We are looking for a y-intercept of 2 so Line E (choice E) is out. Focus on Lines C and D. Since the slope is −2, this means it drops two units for every one unit it runs and, because it is negative, it is moving northwest-southeast (note that if it had a positive slope, the graph would move southwest-northeast). You may be able to pick out Line D as the immediate winner. If not, test both the y-intercept and x-intercept to be absolutely sure. To test the y-intercept, which we already can see is (0,2), we set x equal to zero: $y = -2(0) + 2$, and 2 is our answer. Line D intersects the y-axis at (0,2) as anticipated. To test the x-intercept, we set y equal to zero: $0 = -2x + 2$, and 1 is our answer. Line D intersects the x-axis at (1,0). Thus, equation Line D is the clear winner based on its slope and its y-intercept and x-intercept.

NOTE ⤚ Need additional proof? Whenever you know two points on a line, you can figure out the slope. Using the two points above, (0,2) and (1,0), we can find the slope of our line. Slope equals rise over run. Algebraically, it doesn't matter which point is subtracted from the other:

$$\text{slope} = \frac{\text{rise}}{\text{run}} = \frac{\text{rise}_2 - \text{rise}_1}{\text{run}_2 - \text{run}_1} = \frac{2-0}{0-1} = \frac{2}{-1} = -2$$

Is −2 the slope that we are looking for? Yes.

147

73. Boxed In (🌶)

Choice D
Classification: Coordinate Geometry Problem
Snapshot: This problem highlights basic information regarding coordinate geometry. The slope of a horizontal line is "$y = ...$". The slope of a vertical line is "$x = ...$". The slope of the y-axis is $x = 0$. The slope of the x-axis is $y = 0$.

Go through each answer choice. Choices A, B, C, and E represent boundary lines. Choice A, $x = 0$, is the y-axis. Choice B, $y = 0$, is the x-axis. Choice C, $x = 1$, forms the right boundary; the equation $y = -\frac{1}{3}x + 1$ forms the top boundary. To test the inappropriateness of choice D, $x - 3y = 0$, try placing various points into the equation. Any set of points on the line should be able to satisfy the equation. For example, take $(3,0)$. Now substitute $x = 3$ and $y = 0$ into the equation in choice D, $x - 3y = 0$. You get $3 - 3(0) = 0$. This doesn't make sense and cannot be the correct equation. Try choice E, $y + \frac{1}{3}x = 1$. Substitute $(3,0)$ and we get $0 + \frac{1}{3}(3) = 1$. This works—it is the proper equation and forms the roof, or top line, of the marked area.

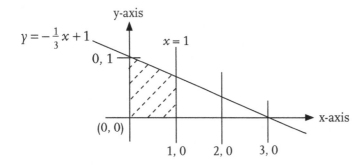

74. Intercept (🌶 🌶)

Choice A
Classification: Coordinate Geometry Problem
Snapshot: The slope formula is $y = mx + b$, where m is defined as the slope or gradient and b is defined as the y-intercept.

Start by visualizing the slope formula: $y = mx + b$. Let's determine the slope first. Slope m equals "rise over run."

$$\text{slope} = \frac{\text{rise}}{\text{run}} = \frac{\text{rise}_2 - \text{rise}_1}{\text{run}_2 - \text{run}_1} = \frac{3 - (-5)}{10 - (-6)} = \frac{8}{16} = \frac{1}{2}$$

The slope formula now reads: $y = \frac{1}{2}x + b$. To find b, let's put in the coordinates of the first point: $3 = \frac{1}{2}(10) + b$; $b = -2$. The complete slope formula becomes: $y = \frac{1}{2}x - 2$.

To find the x-intercept, we set $y = 0$.

$$y = \frac{1}{2}x - 2$$

$$0 = \frac{1}{2}x - 2$$

$$-\frac{1}{2}x = -2$$

$$x = 4$$

75. Magic (⌇)

Choice A

Classification: Plane Geometry Problem

Snapshot: This problem tests the simple definition of π.

Circumference = $\pi \times$ diameter. Since $C = \pi d$, the ratio of a circle's circumference to its diameter is: $\frac{\pi d}{d} = \pi$. This is the very definition of Pi; Pi is the ratio of the circumference of a circle to its diameter. The circumference of a circle is uniquely $\cong 3.14$ times as big as its diameter. This is always true. Choice D cannot be correct. A ratio is a ratio and, as such, does not vary with the size of the circle. For the record, the fractional equivalent of Pi is $\frac{22}{7}$.

76. Kitty Corner (⌇)

Choice B

Classification: Plane Geometry Problem

Snapshot: A diagonal drawn inside a square or a cube always forms a right-isosceles triangle, and the relationship between the relative lengths of the sides of a right-isosceles triangle is $1 : 1 : \sqrt{2}$.

View the triangular wedge. The height is 2, the base is $2\sqrt{2}$, and the hypotenuse is x. Using the Pythagorean Theorem:

$$a^2 + b^2 = c^2$$

$$(2)^2 + (2\sqrt{2})^2 = (x)^2$$

$$4 + 8 = x^2$$

$$x^2 = 12$$

$$x = \sqrt{12} = \sqrt{4 \times 3} = \sqrt{4} \times \sqrt{3} = 2\sqrt{3}$$

You may wonder, "How do we know the base is $2\sqrt{2}$?" The base of the triangle is really the hypotenuse of the right isosceles triangle, which is at the very bottom of the cube. Because all sides of the cube are 2 units in length, the hypotenuse of the bottom triangle is $2\sqrt{2}$. This information is critical to finding the hypotenuse of the triangle represented by x.

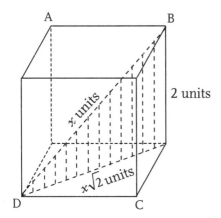

77. Lopsided (🌶)

Choice C
Classification: Plane Geometry Problem
Snapshot: This problem illustrates how to find the measures of angles indirectly.

Since $m + n = 110$ degrees; thus $x = 70$ degrees because a triangle n-m-x equals 180. Also triangle y-x-z also measures 180 degrees. The measure of $o + p$ is found by setting the measures of y-x-z equal to 180 degrees. Thus, $x = 70$; $y = 180 - o$; $z = 180 - p$. Finally, $180 = 70 + (180 - o) + (180 - p)$ and $o + p = 250$ degrees.

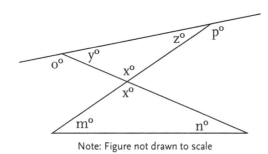

Note: Figure not drawn to scale

78. Diamond (🌶 🌶)

Choice A
Classification: Plane Geometry Problem
Snapshot: This problem requires an understanding of right-isosceles triangles and the ability to calculate the length of a single side when given the hypotenuse.

Either of the two dotted lines within the square serves to divide the square into two right-isosceles triangles. Since each dotted line has a length of 3 units, each side has a length of $\frac{3}{\sqrt{2}}$. This calculation can be a bit tricky. Given that the ratios of the lengths of the sides of a right-isosceles triangle are $1 : 1 : \sqrt{2}$, we can use a ratio and proportion to calculate the length of the hypotenuse (the dotted line in the diagram that follows):

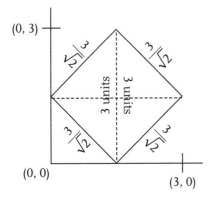

Standard ratio: $1 : 1 : \sqrt{2}$

Per this problem: $x : x : 3$

Ratio solved: $\dfrac{3}{\sqrt{2}} : \dfrac{3}{\sqrt{2}} : 3$

Calculation:

$$\dfrac{1}{\sqrt{2}} :: \dfrac{x}{3}$$

$$1(3) = x(\sqrt{2})$$

$$\dfrac{1}{\sqrt{2}} \times 3 = \dfrac{1}{\sqrt{2}} \times x(\sqrt{2})$$

$$\dfrac{3}{\sqrt{2}} = \dfrac{x(\cancel{\sqrt{2}})}{\cancel{\sqrt{2}}}$$

$$x = \dfrac{3}{\sqrt{2}}$$

Calculating the perimeter:

$$P = 4s$$

$$P = 4 \times \dfrac{3}{\sqrt{2}} = \dfrac{12}{\sqrt{2}} \text{ units}$$

We typically simplify radicals in order to eliminate having a radical in the denominator of a fraction. This dovetails with Radical Rule 3 (see page 32).

$$\dfrac{12}{\sqrt{2}} = \dfrac{12}{\sqrt{2}} \times \dfrac{\sqrt{2}}{\sqrt{2}} = \dfrac{12\sqrt{2}}{\sqrt{4}} = \dfrac{12\sqrt{2}}{2} = 6\sqrt{2} \text{ units}$$

79. AC (🐦🐦)

Choice E

Classification: Plane Geometry Problem

Snapshot: This tricky geometry problem requires viewing a triangle from different perspectives. In order to find the height of the triangle at hand, we flip the triangle vertically.

In the original diagram, the measure of BD is easy to calculate using the Pythagorean formula:

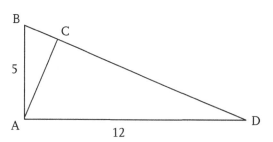

$$c^2 = a^2 + b^2$$
$$c^2 = (12)^2 + (5)^2$$
$$c^2 = 144 + 25$$
$$c^2 = 169$$
$$c^2 = \sqrt{169}$$
$$c = 13$$

Therefore the measure of BD is 13. As seen in the diagram below, we now know the measures of all sides of the triangle. We can also calculate the area of the triangle:

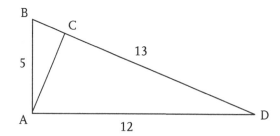

$$\text{Area} = \frac{bh}{2} = \frac{12 \times 5}{2} = 30 \text{ units}^2$$

When the diagram is flipped, it is easy to calculate the height (AC) given that the area is 30 square units and the base is 13 units.

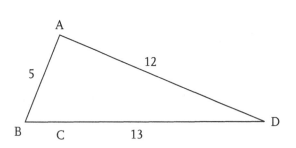

$$A = \frac{bh}{2}$$
$$30 = \frac{bh}{2}$$
$$30 = \frac{13 \times h}{2}$$
$$60 = 13 \times h$$
$$h = \frac{60}{13} \text{ units}$$

80. Circuit (🌶🌶)

Choice B
Classification: Plane Geometry Problem
Snapshot: This problem introduces geometry problems where the solution is expressed in algebraic terms. It also requires that we remain flexible and be able to work with variables expressed as capital letters as well as lower case letters.

Two formulas are needed to solve this problem:

$$A = l \times w \quad \text{and} \quad P = 2l + 2w$$

Of course, cosmetically speaking, this is the same as writing each variable with a capital letter, where A is area, L is length, W is width, and P is perimeter of a given rectangle.

$$A = L \times W \quad \text{and} \quad P = 2L + 2W$$

Since none of the answer choices have reference to the variable of length, we substitute for the variable L as follows:

$$P = 2L + 2W \qquad \text{and} \qquad L = \frac{A}{W}$$

$$\text{so } P = 2\left(\frac{A}{W}\right) + 2W$$

Multiplying each term of the equation by W:

$$(W)P = (W)2\left(\frac{A}{\cancel{W}}\right) + (W)2W$$

$$PW = 2A + 2W^2$$

$$2W^2 - PW + 2A = 0$$

81. Victorian (🌶🌶)

Choice D
Classification: Plane Geometry Problem
Snapshot: The Pythagorean Theorem, $a^2 + b^2 = c^2$, can always be used to find the length of the sides of any right triangle. "Pythagorean triplets" are integers which satisfy the Pythagorean Theorem. The four common Pythagorean triplets that appear on the GMAT include: $3:4:5$; $5:12:13$; $8:15:17$; and $7:24:25$.

This is a classic problem that can be solved using the Pythagorean formula: $a^2 + b^2 = c^2$, where a, b, and c are sides of a triangle and c is the hypotenuse. In this problem, we concentrate on the first window and find the distance from the base of the house as follows: $(15)^2 + (x)^2 = (25)^2$ so $x = 20$. Then we concentrate on the second window and find the distance from the base of the house as follows: $(24)^2 + (x)^2 = (25)^2$ so $x = 7$. Don't forget that the ladder has been moved closer by 13 feet, not 7 feet.

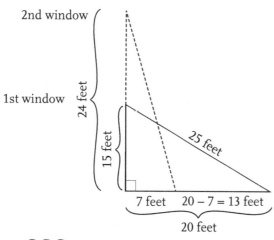

82. QR (🎵🎵🎵)

Choice C

Classification: Plane Geometry Problem

Snapshot: This difficult problem works in reverse of the previous one. Whereas the previous problem, titled *Victorian,* gave the measure of a side and asked us to calculate the *longest diagonal,* this problem gives the measure the longest diagonal and asks us find the measure of a side, en route to finding volume.

$$a^2 + b^2 = c^2$$

$$x^2 + \left(x\sqrt{2}\right)^2 = \left(4\sqrt{3}\right)^2$$

$$x^2 + (x^2)(\sqrt{4}) = (16)(\sqrt{9})$$

$$x^2 + 2x^2 = 48$$

$$3x^2 = 48$$

$$x^2 = 16$$

$$x = 4$$

Therefore, $V = s^3 = (4)^3 = 64 \text{ inches}^3$.

NOTE ↩ The base of the internal triangle formed is the hypotenuse of a right-isosceles triangle. Also, the answer to $x^2 = 16$ is $+4$ and -4, but we discard the -4 because distance cannot be negative.

83. Cornered (🎵🎵🎵)

Choice C

Classification: Plane Geometry Problem

Snapshot: This problem combines circle, square, and triangle geometry. Often the key to calculating the area of the "odd-ball" figures lies in subtracting one figure from another.

Here, the solution lies in subtracting the area of the smaller (inner) circle from the area of the smaller (inner) square.

Area of outer square:

$$A = s^2$$
$$2 = s^2$$
$$s = \sqrt{2}$$

Area of inner square:

$$A = s^2$$
$$A = (1)^2 = 1 \text{ unit}^2$$

Note that above we pick the number 1 in so far as it is the "simplest" of integers.

Area of inner circle:

$$A = \pi r^2 = \pi(\tfrac{1}{2})^2 = \tfrac{1}{4}\pi \text{ units}^2$$

Area of darkened corners equals area of inner square **less** area of inner circle:

$$A = 1 - \tfrac{1}{4}\pi \text{ units}^2$$

Explanation:

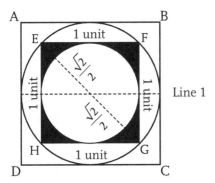

The key to this problem lies in first finding the length of one side of square ABCD. Obviously, if the area of ABCD is 2 square units, the length of one side of square ABCD is calculated as the square root of 2 or $\sqrt{2}$. Line AB equals $\sqrt{2}$, and, therefore, Line 1 is also $\sqrt{2}$. Line 1 may be viewed as the diameter of the outer circle. It is also the diagonal of square EFGH. EG also equals $\sqrt{2}$, and, hence, EH and HG equal 1 unit (because the ratios of the length of the sides in an isosceles right triangle with angle measures of

$45°–45°–90°$ is $1–1–\sqrt{2}$. We can now calculate the measure of square EFGH (where each side equals 1 unit) and the area of the inner circle (with its radius of $\frac{1}{2}$ unit). That is, the length of a side of the inner square equals the diameter of the inner circle. The diameter is twice the radius or, more directly, the radius is one-half the diameter.

84. Woozy (🌶🌶🌶)

Choice C
Classification: Plane Geometry Problem
Snapshot: This problem combines the geometry of equilateral triangles and $30°–60°–90°$ triangles.

Conceptually, we want to subtract the area of the smaller triangle PQT from the area of the larger equilateral triangle PRS. Note that in a $30°–60°–90°$ triangle, the ratios of the lengths of the sides are $1 : \sqrt{3} : 2$ units.

Area of triangle PRS equals:

$$A = \frac{bh}{2} = \frac{4 \times 2\sqrt{3}}{2} = \frac{8\sqrt{3}}{2} = 4\sqrt{3}$$

Area of triangle PQT equals:

$$A = \frac{bh}{2} = \frac{1 \times \sqrt{3}}{2} = \frac{\sqrt{3}}{2} = \frac{1}{2}\sqrt{3}$$

Therefore:

$$4\sqrt{3} - \frac{1}{2}\sqrt{3} = \frac{8}{2}\sqrt{3} - \frac{1}{2}\sqrt{3} = \frac{7}{2}\sqrt{3}$$

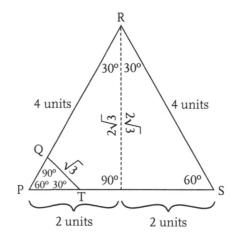

85. Sphere (🌶🌶🌶)

Choice D
Classification: Solid Geometry Problem
Snapshot: A number of very difficult geometry problems can be solved by picking small manageable numbers.

The best approach is to pick and substitute numbers. Say, for example, that the radius of the original sphere is 2 units, then:

Original sphere:

$$\text{Volume} = \frac{4}{3}\pi r^3$$

Example: $V = \frac{4}{3}\pi(2)^3 = \frac{32}{3}\pi \text{ units}^3$

New sphere:

$$\text{Volume} = \frac{4}{3}\pi r^3$$

Example: $V = \frac{4}{3}\pi(4)^3 = \frac{256}{3}\pi \text{ units}^3$

Final calculation:

$$\frac{\text{New}}{\text{Original}} = \frac{\dfrac{256}{3}\pi \text{ units}^3}{\dfrac{32}{3}\pi \text{ units}^3} = \frac{\overset{8}{\cancel{256}}}{\underset{1}{\cancel{3}}} \times \frac{\overset{1}{\cancel{3}}}{\underset{1}{\cancel{32}}} = 8 \text{ times}$$

86. Four Aces ( )

Choice C
Classification: Probability Problem
Snapshot: This problem presents a classic application of the General Multiplication Rule of probability. Selecting a card "without replacement" affects or influences the probability of the next card being chosen because the first card is missing from the deck. On the other hand, selecting a card "with replacement" does not affect or influence the probability of the next card being chosen because replacing a given card restores the deck to its prior state.

On the first pick, there is a $\frac{4}{52}$ chance of selecting an ace. On our second pick, there is a $\frac{3}{51}$ chance of selecting an ace because there is one fewer ace to choose from and one fewer card in the deck. On the third pick, there is a $\frac{2}{50}$ chance of selecting an ace because there is one fewer ace to choose from and one fewer card in the deck. Finally, there is a $\frac{1}{49}$ chance of selecting an ace because there is only one ace to choose from with exactly 49 cards left in the deck.

For the record, answer choice E would have been the correct answer if we had selected our four aces with replacement. Such would be the case if the problem had asked: "What is the probability of selected four aces in a row if we replace each card before selecting the next one?" Choice A would be the correct answer if we were to choose any single card with replacement. For example: "What is the probability of selecting the ace of spades four times in a row from a random deck of cards, if we replace that card in the deck after selecting it?" Choice B would have been the correct answer if we had to select these four aces in a specific order and had done so without replacing each card. Such would be the case if the problem had asked: "What is the probability of selecting the ace of spades, followed by the ace of hearts, followed by the ace of clubs, and followed by the ace of diamonds, if we do not replace each card after selecting it?"

NOTE ✑ There are two sets of terms that are key to understanding how to distinguish among basic probability problems. The first set of terms is "mutually exclusive" and "not mutually exclusive." The second set of terms is "independent" and "not independent (dependent)." *Mutually exclusive* means that two events or outcomes do not overlap with one another or cannot occur at the same time. *Not mutually exclusive* means that two events or outcomes do overlap with one another or can occur at the same time. *Independent* means that two events or outcomes do not influence one another and occur randomly relative to each other. *Not independent (or dependent)* means that two events or outcomes influence one another and that the occurrence of one event has an affect on the occurrence of another event.

Here are some simple real-life examples to illuminate these terms. Say we are putting on a business conference and inviting attendees as well as guest speakers. The assignment of VIP seating and non-VIP seating is a mutually exclusive outcome. Either a person is in the VIP seats or he or she is not. The same holds true for determining who is an in-state versus out-of-state attendee. An attendee is either in-state or out-of-state with no overlap possible. However, in classifying attendees by profession, we might have overlap between who is a manager and who is an engineer and who is a salesperson and who is an entrepreneur. Obviously, some attendees might fall into more than one category. These categories would, therefore, not be mutually exclusive.

Two tasks might be independent and have no influence on one another. For example, in preparing for the conference, it wouldn't make any difference whether we made name tags first and then made copies of the conference handouts or made copies of the conference handouts and then made name tags. These events represent separate tasks that have no bearing on one another. On the other hand, two tasks may not be independent of one another; they may, in fact, be dependent on one another. This is true of events that must occur in a certain sequence. In preparing for the conference, we must plan the conference first before inviting speakers to speak at the conference. Likewise, attendees must be registered for the conference, before they can be admitted to the conference and before they ever fill out conference evaluation forms, which are handed out at the end of the conference. In other words, the filling out of a conference evaluation form is dependent upon a person actually attending the conference, which, in turn, is dependent upon a person having first registered for the conference.

87. Orange & Blue ( )

Choice B
Classification: Probability Problem
Snapshot: This problem also employs the General Multiplication Rule (refer to Probability Rule 3, page 46). The use of the word "and" in this problem is a signal that we need to multiply probabilities, not add probabilities. The probability of choosing the first orange marble will influence the probability of choosing the first blue marble because there will be one fewer marble to choose from (selection without replacement).

The probability of first choosing an orange marble is $\frac{2}{5}$. The probability of then choosing a blue marble is $\frac{3}{4}$.

$$\frac{2}{5} \times \frac{3}{4} = \frac{6}{20} = \frac{3}{10}$$

Note that the trap answer, choice A, involves forgetting to subtract one marble from the denominator of the second fraction:

$$\frac{2}{5} \times \frac{3}{5} = \frac{6}{25}$$

NOTE ⤶ Suppose this problem had instead asked: "There are 5 marbles in a bag—2 are orange and 3 are blue. If two marbles are pulled from the bag, what is the probability that at least one will be orange?"

Here, answer choice E would be correct. The simplest way to view this problem is to think in terms of what we don't want. At least one orange marble means that we want anything but two blue marbles.

Probability of getting two blue marbles:

$$\frac{3}{5} \times \frac{2}{4} = \frac{6}{20} = \frac{3}{10}$$

Therefore, the probability of getting at least one orange marble is the same as one minus the probability of getting two blue marbles.

$$P(A) = 1 - P(\text{not } A)$$

$$1 - \frac{3}{10} = \frac{7}{10}$$

Another way to solve this follow-up problem is using the direct method, which entails writing out all possibilities and adding up the results that we are looking for. There are four possible outcomes when we choose two marbles at random. Three of these outcomes yield at least one orange marble:

Orange, Blue: $\quad \frac{2}{5} \times \frac{3}{4} = \frac{6}{20}$

Blue, Orange: $\quad \frac{3}{5} \times \frac{2}{4} = \frac{6}{20}$ $\left. \right\}$ $\frac{14}{20} \Rightarrow \frac{7}{10}$

Orange, Orange: $\quad \frac{2}{5} \times \frac{1}{4} = \frac{2}{20}$

Blue, Blue: $\quad \frac{3}{5} \times \frac{2}{4} = \frac{6}{20}$

Note that the total of all of the above possibilities equals 1 (i.e., $\frac{6}{20} + \frac{6}{20} + \frac{2}{20} + \frac{6}{20} = \frac{20}{20}$) because there are no other possibilities other than the four outcomes presented here.

88. Exam Time (🌶️🌶️)

Choice E
Classification: Probability Problem
Snapshot: The use of the word "or" in this problem (i.e., "pass one exam <u>or</u> the other exam") is a signal that probabilities are to be added, not multiplied. The probability of two non-mutually exclusive events A <u>or</u> B occurring is calculated by adding the probability of the first event to the second event and then subtracting out the overlap between the two events.

$$\frac{9}{12} + \frac{8}{12} - \frac{6}{12} = \frac{11}{12}$$

The General Addition Rule states: $P(A \text{ or } B) = P(A) + P(B) - P(A \text{ and } B)$. The probability of passing the first exam is added to the probability of passing the second exam, less the probability of passing both exams. If we don't make this subtraction, we will double count the possibility that she will pass both exams. In this case, we can calculate the overlap as $\frac{3}{4} \times \frac{2}{3} = \frac{6}{12} = \frac{1}{2}$ because we assume the two events are independent. One way to prove this result is to recognize that the probability of passing either exam (including both exams) is everything other than failing both exams. The probability of failing both exams is $\frac{1}{4} \times \frac{1}{3} = \frac{1}{12}$. Therefore, the probability of passing either exam is $1 - \frac{1}{12} = \frac{11}{12}$.

Note that situations involving A or B do not necessarily preclude the possibility of both A and B. If we simply add probabilities we inadvertently double count the probability of A and B. We should only count overlap once and, therefore, we must subtract it out. See problems 18–20, pages 57–58.

89. Sixth Sense (🌶️🌶️)

Choice D
Classification: Probability Problem
Snapshot: The use of the word "or" signals the need to add probabilities (i.e., "first _or_ second toss of a dice"). The only other question to be asked is whether there is a need to subtract out overlap. That is, "Are the two events mutually exclusive?" As it turns out, they are not mutually exclusive and this overlap must be subtracted out. This problem also employs the General Addition Rule. The overlap created by the possibility of rolling a six on both the first and the second roll of the dice must be taken into account.

Second Roll

		1	2	3	4	5	6
	1	1,1	1,2	1,3	1,4	1,5	**1,6**
	2	2,1	2,2	2,3	2,4	2,5	**2,6**
First Roll	3	3,1	3,2	3,3	3,4	3.5	**3,6**
	4	4,1	4,2	4,3	4,4	4,5	**4,6**
	5	5,1	5,2	5,3	5,4	5,5	**5,6**
	6	**6,1**	**6,2**	**6,3**	**6,4**	**6,5**	**6,6**

As seen in the chart, there are of course thirty-six possible outcomes when we toss a pair of dice (or equally if we role a single die twice). With respect to how we can get at least one six, we have 11 outcomes: (6,1), (6,2), (6,3), (6,4), (6,5), (1,6), (2,6), (3,6), (4,6), (5,6), and (6,6). See numbers in bold above.

To solve this problem using the formula for the General Addition Rule:

$$P(A \text{ or } B) = P(A) + P(B) - P(A \text{ and } B)$$

$$\frac{1}{6} + \frac{1}{6} - \frac{1}{36}$$

$$\frac{6}{36} + \frac{6}{36} - \frac{1}{36}$$

$$\frac{12}{36} - \frac{1}{36} = \frac{11}{36}$$

Note that we can't just add $\frac{1}{6}$ and $\frac{1}{6}$ to get $\frac{12}{36}$ or $\frac{1}{3}$, which incidentally is answer choice E. To do so would fail to account for, and properly remove, the overlap created when double sixes are rolled.

After all, what is the probability of getting a six on the first roll of a dice? Answer: (6,1), (6,2), (6,3), (6,4), (6,5), and (6,6). The probability of event A is $\frac{6}{36}$ or $\frac{1}{6}$. What is the probability of getting a six on the second roll of a dice? Answer: (1,6), (2,6), (3,6), (4,6), (5,6), and (6,6). The probability of event B is $\frac{6}{36}$ or $\frac{1}{6}$. Note that "double sixes" is included in both event A and event B. This overlap must be subtracted out. To be clear, the probability of getting a six on the first or second roll of a dice does include the possibility of getting sixes on the first and second rolls (i.e., double sixes), but this outcome can only be counted once.

Another way this problem could have been asked is: "What is the probability of rolling two normal six-sided dice and getting at least one six?" This problem could be solved using the Complement Rule of probability. The probability of rolling <u>at least</u> one six is the same as the probability of "one minus the probability of rolling no sixes."

The probability of rolling no sixes is:

$$\frac{5}{6} \times \frac{5}{6} = \frac{25}{36}$$

The probability of rolling at least one six is:

$$1 - \frac{25}{36} = \frac{11}{36}$$

NOTE ⬿ Answer choice B would have been the correct answer had the problem asked: "What is the probability of rolling a single dice twice and getting <u>exactly</u> one six?" Perhaps the simplest way to arrive at the correct answer is to write out the possibilities. There are eleven ways to get exactly one six: (6,1), (6,2), (6,3), (6,4), (6,5), (6,6), (1,6), (2,6), (3,6), (4,6), (5,6), and (6,6). Alternatively, we could choose to subtract out $\frac{1}{36}$ from the previous calculation (i.e., $\frac{11}{36}$) in order to remove the probability of rolling double sixes. Note that in the following calculation, the "first" six is removed because it represents overlap while the "second" six is removed because it represents the actual probability of rolling double sixes.

$$\frac{1}{6} + \frac{1}{6} - \frac{1}{36} - \frac{1}{36} = \frac{10}{36} = \frac{5}{18}$$

90. Exam Time Encore (🌶🌶🌶)

Choice E
Classification: Probability Problem
Snapshot: This problem involves three overlapping probabilities and is best solved using the Complement Rule of probability. The direct mathematical approach is more cumbersome, but parallels the solution to *German Cars*, problem 20 (page 58).

I.   Shortcut Approach

Using the Complement Rule, the probability of total failure is calculated as one minus the probability of failing all three exams:

i)   The probability of <u>not</u> passing the first exam:

$$P(\text{not } A) = 1 - P(A) \qquad 1 - \frac{3}{4} = \frac{1}{4}$$

ii) Below is the probability of <u>not</u> passing the second exam:

$$P(\text{not } B) = 1 - P(B) \qquad 1 - \frac{2}{3} = \frac{1}{3}$$

iii) Below is the probability of <u>not</u> passing the third exam:

$$P(\text{not } C) = 1 - P(C) \qquad 1 - \frac{1}{2} = \frac{1}{2}$$

iv) The probability of <u>failing all three</u> exams:

$$P(\text{not } A \text{ or } B \text{ or } C) \qquad \frac{1}{4} \times \frac{1}{3} \times \frac{1}{2} = \frac{1}{24}$$

v)   The probability of <u>passing at least one</u> exam:

$$P(A) = 1 - P(\text{not } A) \qquad 1 - \frac{1}{24} = \frac{23}{24}$$

II. Direct Approach

The direct method is much more cumbersome. Mathematically it is solved by calculating the probability of passing only one of the three exams, two of the three exams, and all of the three exams.

1.   Probability of passing <u>exam one</u> but not exams two or three:

$$P(A) \times P(\text{not } B) \times P(\text{not } C) \qquad \frac{3}{4} \times \frac{1}{3} \times \frac{1}{2} = \frac{3}{24}$$

2.   Probability of passing <u>exam two</u> but not exams one or three:

$$P(\text{not } A) \times P(B) \times P(\text{not } C) \qquad \frac{1}{4} \times \frac{2}{3} \times \frac{1}{2} = \frac{2}{24}$$

3.   Probability of passing <u>exam three</u> but not exams one or two:

$$P(\text{not } A) \times P(\text{not } B) \times P(C) \qquad \frac{1}{4} \times \frac{1}{3} \times \frac{1}{2} = \frac{1}{24}$$

4.   Probability of passing <u>exams one</u> and <u>two</u> but not exam three:

$$P(A) \times P(B) \times P(\text{not } C) \qquad \frac{3}{4} \times \frac{2}{3} \times \frac{1}{2} = \frac{6}{24}$$

5. Probability of passing <u>exams one</u> and <u>three</u> but not exam two:

$P(A) \times P(\text{not } B) \times P(C)$ $\qquad \dfrac{3}{4} \times \dfrac{1}{3} \times \dfrac{1}{2} = \dfrac{3}{24}$

6. Probability of passing <u>exams two</u> and <u>three</u> but not exam one:

$P(\text{not } A) \times P(B) \times P(C)$ $\qquad \dfrac{1}{4} \times \dfrac{2}{3} \times \dfrac{1}{2} = \dfrac{2}{24}$

7. Probability of passing <u>all three</u> exams:

$P(A) \times P(B) \times P(C)$ $\qquad \dfrac{3}{4} \times \dfrac{2}{3} \times \dfrac{1}{2} = \dfrac{6}{24}$

8. Probability of <u>not passing any</u> of the three exams:

$P(\text{not } A) \times P(\text{not } B) \times P(\text{not } C)$ $\qquad \dfrac{1}{4} \times \dfrac{1}{3} \times \dfrac{1}{2} = \dfrac{1}{24}$

The above are all the possibilities regarding the outcomes of one student taking three exams. Adding the first seven of eight possibilities above will result in the correct answer using the direct approach.

Proof: $\qquad \dfrac{3}{24} + \dfrac{2}{24} + \dfrac{1}{24} + \dfrac{6}{24} + \dfrac{3}{24} + \dfrac{2}{24} + \dfrac{6}{24} = \dfrac{23}{24}$

Note that the total of all eight outcomes above will total to 1 because 1 is the sum total of all probabilistic possibilities.

Proof: $\qquad \dfrac{3}{24} + \dfrac{2}{24} + \dfrac{1}{24} + \dfrac{6}{24} + \dfrac{3}{24} + \dfrac{2}{24} + \dfrac{6}{24} + \dfrac{1}{24} = \dfrac{24}{24} = 1$

91. Coin Toss (🌶🌶🌶)

Choice D
Classification: Probability Problem
Snapshot: To highlight how the words "at most" also trigger the Complement Rule of probability.

The easiest way to approach this problem is to think in terms of what we don't want. "At most three heads" means that we want anything except all heads or four heads. This includes the following:

We don't want all heads: $\qquad$ HHHHH $\quad \Big\} \quad \dfrac{1}{32}$

We don't want four heads: $\qquad$ HHHHT $\dfrac{1}{32}$

HHHTH $\dfrac{1}{32}$

HHTHH $\dfrac{1}{32}$

HTHHH $\dfrac{1}{32}$

THHHH $\dfrac{1}{32}$

$\dfrac{5}{32}$

$\dfrac{6}{32}$

Therefore, the probability of getting "at most three heads" is one minus the probability of getting all heads or four heads:

Thus, $1-\left(\dfrac{1}{32}+\dfrac{5}{32}\right)=1-\dfrac{6}{32}=\dfrac{26}{32}=\dfrac{13}{16}$

NOTE ⁕ For summary purposes, let's try one more example in order to contrast the three phrases—"exactly," at least," and "at most."

1) Suppose a question asks: "A coin is tossed three times. What is the probability of getting <u>exactly</u> one head?"

Again, GMAT problems involving the word "exactly" can usually be solved by the "trial-and-error" method. This means simply writing out all the possibilities. For instance, we know that there are eight possibilities and that each of the eight outcomes has exactly a one-eighth chance of occurring.

Example: $\frac{1}{2}\times\frac{1}{2}\times\frac{1}{2}=\frac{1}{8}$.

HHH	TTT
HHT	TTH
HTH	THT
THH	HTT

We can easily confirm the answer by adding up those outcomes in which we have exactly two heads: HHT, HTH, and THH. Three occurrences out of eight are possible. The answer becomes $\frac{3}{8}$ or 37.5%.

2) What if the question had asked: "A coin is tossed three times. What is the probability of getting <u>at least</u> one head?"

The answer would be $\frac{7}{8}$ or 87.5%. We can easily confirm this result by adding up those outcomes in which we get at least one head: HHH, HHT, HTH, THH, TTH, THT, and HTT. Note that this answer represents everything except "triple tails" (i.e., TTT). A quicker way to solve this problem would be to use the Complement Rule. "One minus the probability of getting all tails" would also give us "at least one head."

$$1-\left(\dfrac{1}{2}\times\dfrac{1}{2}\times\dfrac{1}{2}\right)=\dfrac{8}{8}-\dfrac{1}{8}=\dfrac{7}{8}$$

3) Finally, what if the question had asked: "A coin is tossed three times. What is the probability of getting <u>at most</u> one head?"

The answer would be $\frac{4}{8}$ or 50%. We can easily confirm this result by adding up those outcomes in which we get at most one head: HTT, THT, TTH, and TTT. Note that this answer also includes the possibility of getting all tails (i.e., TTT).

92. Hiring ( )

Choice B
Classification: Permutation Problem (Noted Exception)
Snapshot: This particular problem falls under neither the umbrella of probability nor permutation nor combination. It is included here because it is frequently mistaken for a permutation problem.

$$7 \times 4 \times 10 = 280$$

The solution requires only that we multiply together all individual possibilities. Multiplying 7 (candidates for sales managers) by 4 (candidates for shipping clerk) by 10 (candidates for receptionist) would result in 280 possibilities.

NOTE ✑ This problem is about a series of choices. It utilizes the "multiplier principle" and falls within the Rule of Enumeration. The permutation formula cannot be used with this type of problem. This problem is concerned with *how many options we have*, not *how many arrangements are possible,* as is the case with a permutation problem.

93. Fencing ( )

Choice C
Classification: Permutation Problem
Snapshot: This problem is a permutation, not a combination, because order does matter. If country A wins the tournament and country B places second, it is a different outcome than if country B wins and country A places second.

$$_n P _r = \frac{n!}{(n-r)!}$$

$$_4 P _2 = \frac{4!}{(4-2)!} = \frac{4 \times 3 \times \cancel{2 \times 1}}{\cancel{2!}} = 12$$

NOTE ✑ Consider this follow-up problem. A teacher has four students in a special needs class. She must assign four awards at the end of the year: math, English, history, and creative writing awards. How many ways could she do this assuming that a single student could win multiple awards?

$$n^r = 4^4 \qquad 4 \times 4 \times 4 \times 4 = 256$$

She has four ways she could give out the math award, four ways she could give out the English award, four ways to give out the history award, and four ways to give out the creative writing award. Refer to Probability Rule 10, page 49.

94. Alternating (🌶️🌶️)

Choice C

Classification: Permutation Problem

Snapshot: This problem is foremost a joint permutation, in which we calculate two individual permutations and multiply those outcomes together. This problem also introduces the "mirror image" concept of permutations given that we do not know whether a boy or girl sits in the first seat and this will double the possible outcomes.

There are two possibilities with respect to how the girls and boys can sit for the make-up exam. A boy will sit in the first, third, and fifth seats and a girl will sit in the second, fourth, and sixth seats or a girl will sit in the first, third, and fifth seats and a boy will sit in the second, fourth, and sixth seats.

Scenario 1	Scenario 2
B G B G B G	G B G B G B
$\dfrac{3}{B_1} \times \dfrac{3}{G_1} \times \dfrac{2}{B_2} \times \dfrac{2}{G_2} \times \dfrac{1}{B_3} \times \dfrac{1}{G_3}$ *or* $\dfrac{3}{G_1} \times \dfrac{3}{B_1} \times \dfrac{2}{G_2} \times \dfrac{2}{B_2} \times \dfrac{1}{G_3} \times \dfrac{1}{B_3}$	

With reference to the scenario 1 above, how many ways can each seat be filled (left to right)? Answer: The *first* seat can be filled by one of three boys, the *second* seat can be filled by one of three girls, the *third* seat can filled by one of two remaining boys, the *fourth* seat can be filled by one of two remaining girls, the *fifth* seat will be filled by the final boy, and the *sixth* seat will be filled by the final girl.

With reference to the scenario 2 above, how many ways can each seat be filled (left to right)? Answer: The *first* seat can be filled by one of three girls, the *second* seat can be filled by one of three boys, the *third* seat can filled by one of two remaining girls, the *fourth* seat can be filled by one of two remaining boys, the *fifth* seat will be filled by the final girl, and the *sixth* seat will be filled by the final boy.

Therefore:

$$(3 \times 3 \times 2 \times 2 \times 1 \times 1) + (3 \times 3 \times 2 \times 2 \times 1 \times 1)$$
$$36 + 36 = 72$$

In short, the answer is viewed as:

$$(3! \times 3!) + (3! \times 3!)$$
$$2(3! \times 3!)$$
$$2[(3 \times 2 \times 1) \times (3 \times 2 \times 1)] = 72$$

NOTE ✍ There are two common variations stemming from this type of permutation problem:

i)   Three boys and three girls are going to sit for a make-up exam. The girls are to sit in the first, second, and third seats while the boys must sit in the fourth, fifth, and sixth seats. How many possibilities are there with respect to how the six students can be seated?

Answer: $3! \times 3! = 6 \times 6 = 36$ possibilities

ii) Three boys and three girls are going to sit for a make-up exam. If there are no restrictions on how the students may be seated, how many possibilities are there with respect to how they can be seated?

Answer: $6! = 6 \times 5 \times 4 \times 3 \times 2 \times 1 = 720$ possibilities

95. Banana ( )

Choice E
Classification: Permutation Problem

Snapshot: This problem highlights the handling of "repeated letters" (or "repeated numbers"). The formula for calculating permutations with repeated numbers or letters is $\frac{n!}{x!\,y!\,z!}$, where x, y, and z are distinct but identical numbers or letters.

$$\frac{n!}{x!\,y!} = \frac{6!}{3! \times 2!} = \frac{6 \times 5 \times 4 \times \cancel{3 \times 2 \times 1}}{(\cancel{3 \times 2 \times 1}) \times (2 \times 1)} = 60$$

The word "banana" has three "a's" and two "n's"—3! denotes the three "a's" while 2! denotes the two "n's."

96. Table ( )

Choice C
Classification: Permutation Problem
Snapshot: This problem deals with the prickly issue of "empty seats."

$$\frac{5!}{2!} = \frac{5 \times 4 \times 3 \times \cancel{2 \times 1}}{\cancel{2 \times 1}} = 60$$

NOTE ❧ The answer to this problem is similar in approach to that of the previous problem, *Banana*. In permutation theory, "empty seats" are analogous to "identical numbers" (or "identical letters").

Also the geometric configuration of a table should not mislead. The solution to this problem would be identical had we been dealing with a row of five seats.

97. Singer ( )

Choice C
Classification: Combination Problem
Snapshot: Joint Combinations are calculated by multiplying the results of two individual combinations.

First, break the combination into two calculations. First, the "old songs," and second, the "new songs."

$$_nC_r = \frac{n!}{r!(n-r)!}$$

$$_6C_4 = \frac{6!}{4!(6-4)!} = \frac{6!}{4!(2)!} = \frac{6 \times 5 \times \cancel{4 \times 3 \times 2 \times 1}}{\cancel{4 \times 3 \times 2 \times 1} \times (2 \times 1)} = 15$$

Thus, 15 represents the number of ways the singer can choose to sing four of six songs.

$$_nC_r = \frac{n!}{r!(n-r)!}$$

$$_5C_2 = \frac{5!}{2!(5-2)!} = \frac{5!}{2!(3)!} = \frac{5 \times 4 \times \cancel{3 \times 2 \times 1}}{2 \times 1 \times (\cancel{3 \times 2 \times 1})} = 10$$

Thus, 10 represents the number of ways the singer could chose to sing three of five old songs. Therefore, the joint combination equals $15 \times 10 = 150$.

In summary, the outcome of this joint combination is:

$$_nC_r \times _nC_r = \frac{n!}{r!(n-r)!} \times \frac{n!}{r!(n-r)!}$$

$$_6C_4 \times _5C_2 = \frac{6!}{4!(6-4)!} \times \frac{5!}{2!(5-2)!}$$

$$_6C_4 \times _5C_2 = \frac{6!}{4!(2)!} \times \frac{5!}{2!(3)!}$$

$$_6C_4 \times _5C_2 = \frac{6 \times 5 \times \cancel{4!}}{\cancel{4!}\,(2)!} \times \frac{5 \times 4 \times \cancel{3!}}{2!(\cancel{3!})} = 15 \times 10 = 150$$

98. Outcomes ( )

Choice A
Classification: Combination Problem
Snapshot: This bonus problem exists to test permutation and combination theory at a grass roots level. A two-chili rating is assigned because it is meant to be completed within two minutes (the average time allocated for a GMAT math problem). A strong understanding of theory will allow the test taker to avoid doing any calculations.

Statement I:

    True. $_5P_3 > {}_5P_2$

    $_5P_3 = 60$ and $_5P_2 = 20$. Order matters in permutations and more items in a permutation equals more possibilities.

Statement II:

    False. $_5C_3 > {}_5C_2$

    $_5C_3 = 10$ and $_5C_2 = 10$. Strange as it may seem, the outcomes are equal! "Complements in combinations" result in the same probability. Complements occur when the two inside numbers equal the same outside number. Here 3 + 2 = 5. Note this phenomenon only occurs in combinations, not permutations.

Statement III:

    False. $_5C_2 > {}_5P_2$

    $_5C_2 = 10$ and $_5P_2 = 20$. Order matters in permutations and this creates more possibilities relative to combinations. Stated in the reverse, order doesn't matter in combinations and this results in fewer outcomes than permutations, all things being equal.

99. Reunion (🌶🌶🌶)

Choice D

Classification: Combination Problem

Snapshot: This problem, *Reunion,* is a rather complicated sounding problem, but its solution is actually quite simple. We're essentially asking: "How many groups of two can we create from eleven items where order doesn't matter?" or "How many ways can we choose two items from eleven items where order doesn't matter?"

$$_nC_r = \frac{n!}{r!(n-r)!}$$

$$_{11}C_2 = \frac{11!}{2!(11-2)!} = \frac{11 \times 10 \times \cancel{9!}}{2!(\cancel{9!})} = 55$$

100. Display (🎋🎋🎋)

Choice B
Classification: Combination Problem
Snapshot: This problem combines combinations and probability theory.

First, the total number of ways she can choose 3 computers from 8 is represented by the following combination.

$$_nC_r = \frac{n!}{r!(n-r)!}$$

$$_8C_3 = \frac{8!}{3!(8-3)!} = \frac{8 \times 7 \times 6 \times \cancel{5!}}{3!(\cancel{5!})} = 56$$

Second, the total number of ways in which the two most expensive computers will be among the three computers is 6. For example, one way to visualize the situation is to think of the eight computers as A, B, C, D, E, F, G, and H. If A and B are the most expensive computers, then there are six ways that these two computers could be among the three computers chosen, namely ABC, ABD, ABE, ABF, ABG, and ABH. Yet another way of arriving at this figure is to visualize the two most expensive computers as fixed within any group of three. Thus, we ask "How many ways can we choose a final computer from the group of eight, given that A and B are already in our group?" The answer to this part of the problem is derived by the following combination.

$$_6C_1 = \frac{6!}{1!(6-1)!} = \frac{6 \times 5!}{1!(5!)} = 6$$

The final answer: $\dfrac{6}{56} = \dfrac{3}{28}$

Here is perhaps the most succinct way to view this problem:

$$\frac{_nC_r}{_nC_r} = \frac{_6C_1}{_8C_3} = \frac{6}{56} = \frac{3}{28}$$

The following is an alternative solution:

$$\frac{1}{8} \times \frac{1}{7} \times 6 = \frac{6}{56} = \frac{3}{28}$$

The above scenario might be translated as: "The probability of choosing the most expensive computer, followed by the next most expensive computer, multiplied by the number of ways that a third computer could be chosen (given that there are six remaining computers to choose from)."

CHAPTER 3

DATA SUFFICIENCY

Mathematics possesses not only truth, but supreme beauty—a beauty cold and austere, like that of sculpture.
—Lord Russell Bertrand

OVERVIEW

Official Exam Instructions for Data Sufficiency

Directions

This data sufficiency problem consists of a question and two statements, labeled (1) and (2), in which certain data are given. You have to decide whether the data given in the statements are sufficient for answering the question. Using the data given in the statements, plus your knowledge of mathematics and everyday facts (such as the number of days in July or the meaning of the word counterclockwise), you must indicate whether—

Statement (1) ALONE is sufficient, but statement (2) alone is not sufficient to answer the question asked.

Statement (2) ALONE is sufficient, but statement (1) alone is not sufficient to answer the question asked.

BOTH statements (1) and (2) TOGETHER are sufficient to answer the question asked, but NEITHER statement ALONE is sufficient to answer the question asked.

EACH statement ALONE is sufficient to answer the question asked.

Statements (1) and (2) TOGETHER are NOT sufficient to answer the question asked, and additional data specific to the problem are needed.

Numbers:

All numbers used are real numbers.

Figures:

A figure accompanying a data sufficiency question will conform to the information given in the question but will not necessarily conform to the additional information given in statements (1) and (2).

Lines shown as straight can be assumed to be straight and lines that appear jagged can also be assumed to be straight.

You may assume that the positions of points, angles, regions, etc., exist in the order shown and that angle measures are greater than zero.

All figures lie in a plane unless otherwise indicated.

Note: In data sufficiency problems that ask for the value of a quantity, the data given in the statement are sufficient only when it is possible to determine exactly one numerical value for the quantity.

Strategies and Approaches

1. *Evaluate each statement independently (one at a time); if each statement is insufficient then evaluate both statements together as if they were a single statement.*

    It is critical to analyze each statement independently. Be careful not to let information from a previous statement be carried over to the next statement. Be sure to memorize the unique pattern of answer choices for Data Sufficiency.

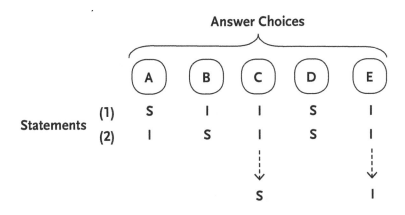

"S" stands for Sufficiency while "I" stands for Insufficiency.

If the first statement provides information sufficient to answer the question, but the second statement provides information that is insufficient to answer the question, then the answer is choice A. If the first statement provides information that is insufficient to answer the question, but the second statement provides information that is sufficient to answer the question, then the answer is choice B. If both statements individually are insufficient, but together they are sufficient, then the answer is choice C. If both statements alone are sufficient then the answer is choice D. If both statements individually are insufficient, and together they are still insufficient, then the answer is choice E.

2. *In a Yes/No Data Sufficiency question, each statement is sufficient if the answer is "always yes" or "always no," while a statement is insufficient if the answer is "sometimes yes" and "sometimes no." In a Value Data Sufficiency question, each statement is sufficient if the answer results in a single value, while a statement is insufficient if the answer results in a range of values.*

3. *When picking numbers, particularly for number properties, think first in terms of the "big seven" numbers, namely 2, –2, 1, –1, $\frac{1}{2}$, $-\frac{1}{2}$, and 0.*

Picking numbers is a popular and often necessary approach to use on Data Sufficiency problems. This is especially true with respect to number properties that lie at the heart of Data Sufficiency problems. But how does one best pick numbers for Data Sufficiency problems? The secret lies in learning how, and when, to use a manageable set of numbers to attack problems.

The beauty of the "big seven" numbers is that they offer a consistent, controlled base of numbers to pick from. See *Exhibit 3.1*. Think first in terms of the *big seven* numbers when picking numbers for *inequality problems* that appear within Data Sufficiency. "Open-ended" inequality problems might be defined as problems in which a very wide range of numbers can be chosen for substitution. These involve problems that include expressions such as $x > 0$, $x < 0$, $x > y$, $x < y$, $xy > 0$, $xy < 0$, $x^2 > 0$, $x^2 < 0$, $x^2 > x$, and $x^2 < x$.

4. *Employ elimination or guessing strategies, when possible.*

In terms of guessing, remember that "sufficiencies are our friends on Data Sufficiency." Once we discover that a statement is sufficient, the odds of us getting this problem right are 50–50. For instance, if the first statement is sufficient, the answer can only be choices A or D. If the second statement is sufficient, the answer can only be choices B or D. On the other hand, knowing that a statement is insufficient only eliminates two answers, still leaving three choices.

How are Answers Chosen in Data Sufficiency?

To understand *sufficiency* and *insufficiency*, let's familiarize ourselves first with *yes/no* data sufficiency questions. Here are five examples, each representing one of answer choices A through E:

Yes/No Data Sufficiency Question:

Is x an even number?

(1) x is a prime number less than 3.

(2) x is an integer greater than 1.

> Statement (1). Knowing that x is a prime number less than 3, tells us that x is 2. After all, 2 is the only prime number less than 3. We can answer this question with an unequivocal "yes"—x is an even number. This statement is sufficient.

> Statement (2). Knowing merely that x is an integer greater than 1 does not tell us whether x is even or odd. This statement, by itself, is insufficient.

Choice A is correct. To remember this combination, pronounce each letter: "S—I—A."

Is x an even number?

(1) x is an integer less than 3.

(2) x is the product of two even integers.

> Statement (1). Knowing merely that x is an integer less than 3 does not tell us whether x is even (e.g., 2, 0, −2, −4) or odd (e.g., 1, −1, −3). Because x could equally be even or odd, this statement is insufficient.

> Statement (2). Knowing that x is the product of two even integers guarantees that x is an even integer.

Choice B is correct. To remember this combination, pronounce each letter: "I—S—B."

Is x an even number?

(1) x is an integer greater than 1.

(2) x is an integer less than 3.

> Statement (1). Knowing merely that x is an integer greater than 1 does not tell us whether x is even or odd.

> Statement (2). Knowing merely that x is an integer less than 3 does not tell us whether x is even or odd.

Choice C is correct. Say *"Double I—C."* Because this is a double "I" situation (both statements are individually insufficient), we now combine both statements and evaluate them together. Knowing that x is an integer greater than 1 but less than 3 tells us that x must be 2. This is an even number. Therefore, this question is sufficient overall. The answer to this question is "yes"—x is even.

Is x an even number?

(1) x is the sum of two even integers.

(2) x is the product of an even and an odd integer.

> Statement (1). If x is the sum of two even integers, the sum must always be an even number.

> Statement (2). If x is the product of an even and an odd integers, the result must always be an even number. E.g., $2 \times 3 = 6$; $5 \times 4 = 20$.

Choice D is correct. Say *"Double S—D."*

Is x an even number?

(1) x is an integer greater than 1.

(2) x is an integer less than 4.

> Statement (1). Knowing that x is an integer greater than 1 does not tell us whether x is even or odd. This statement is insufficient.

> Statement (2). Knowing merely that x is an integer less than 4 does not tell us whether x is even or odd. This statement is insufficient.

Choice E is correct. Say *"Double I—E."* Because this is a double "I" situation (both statements are individually insufficient), we now combine both statements to evaluate them together. Knowing that x is an integer greater than 1 but less than 4 tells us that x must be 2 or 3. However depending on which of these two numbers we pick, the answer will either be even or odd. Thus, we cannot answer the question entirely yes or entirely no. The overall answer is insufficient.

Extra:

Is x an even number?

(1) x is the product of two odd integers.

(2) x is the sum of an even and an odd integer.

> Statement (1). The product of two odd integers results in an odd integer. The answer to this question is "no"—x is not an even integer; it's an odd integer. This statement is sufficient, not insufficient.

> Statement (2). The sum of an even and an odd integer always results in an odd integer. The answer to this question is "no"—x is not an even integer; it's an odd integer. This statement is also sufficient, not insufficient.

Choice D is correct. This "extra" question is included to highlight a interesting feature of *yes/no* data sufficiency questions. A definitively negative answer—"no"—does not indicate insufficiency; it indicates sufficiency. Insufficiency occurs when the answer can be either yes or no. If the answer is absolutely yes or absolutely no, this translates as sufficiency.

Another type of question is the *value* Data Sufficiency question.

Value Data Sufficiency Question:

What is the value of x?

(1) $x \geq 2$

(2) $x \leq 4$

> Statement (1). Knowing that $x \geq 2$, tells us that x could be numbers like 2, 3, 4, 5, etc., not to mention numbers like 2.5, 3.3, etc. We obviously can't tell the value of x. Therefore this statement is insufficient.

> Statement (2). Knowing that $x \leq 4$, tells us that x could be numbers like 4, 3, 2, 1, 0, −1, etc., not to mention non-integers (decimals). We can't tell if x is even. Therefore this statement is insufficient.

The answer to the above question is choice E. Since both statements are *insufficient,* we put them together. Knowing that $x \geq 2$ and that $x \leq 4$ tells us that x could be 2, 3, or 4, as well as those decimals in between. We cannot find a single value for x so the answer is *insufficient.*

How do the Big Seven Numbers Work?

EXHIBIT 3.1   BIG-SEVEN NUMBER CRACKER FOR NUMBER PROPERTY PROBLEMS™

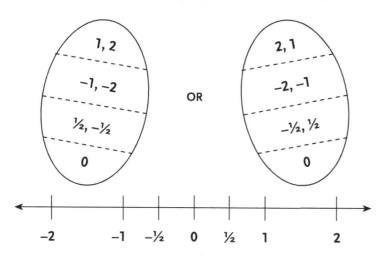

The "big seven" numbers—2, 1, $\frac{1}{2}$, 0, $-\frac{1}{2}$, −1, and −2—are excellent tools for use in solving inequality-type Data Sufficiency problems (see problems 14–20 in this chapter). Per *Exhibit 3.1*, why do the big seven numbers appear in the "ovals" in pairs and on different levels? Answer: To indicate hierarchy when picking numbers. Always try picking positive numbers first, then negatives, and then fractions. In other words, we should consider the positive numbers 1 and 2, before the negative numbers −1 and −2 and these before the fractions $\frac{1}{2}$ and $-\frac{1}{2}$. This is simply a matter of ease and simplicity. If a statement can be proven insufficient using only positive numbers, then there is no need to concern ourselves with negative numbers or fractions. Only if the statements contain squares or cubes should we also consider trying $-\frac{1}{2}$ and $\frac{1}{2}$. Note that the integer 0 is a reserve number; it's used infrequently.

Why do the "big seven" numbers work so well when picking numbers? Their secret lies in their ability to embody the behavior of all numbers on a number line (i.e., positive and negative whole numbers and fractions). For example, how do numbers behave when squared or cubed? Think of the big seven numbers as representatives. The way the number 2 behaves when squared or cubed is the same way any number greater than 1 behaves when squared or cubed. So the number 2 is our representative for numbers greater than 1 and it would make little sense to try other numbers such as 3 and 4. The way fractions such as $\frac{1}{2}$ behave when squared or cubed is identical to the way in which fractions between 0 and 1 behave when squared or cubed. In other words, it makes little sense to pick other fractions for substitution such as $\frac{1}{4}$ or $\frac{3}{4}$ because $\frac{1}{2}$ is our "big seven" representative for fractions between 0 and 1.

Here is a very useful summary of how each of the big seven numbers behave when squared or cubed:

The number 2:   <u>Squaring</u> a number greater than 1 (e.g., 2) results in a larger number.

Example $2^2 = 2 \times 2 = 4$
Result   4 is bigger than 2

<u>Cubing</u> a number greater than 1 (e.g., 2) results in a larger number.

Example $2^3 = 2 \times 2 \times 2 = 8$
Result   8 is bigger than 2

176

The number 1:   Squaring or cubing the number 1 results in the same number.

Examples $1^2 = 1 \times 1 = 1$; $1^3 = 1 \times 1 \times 1 = 1$
Result   1 is equal to 1

The fraction $\frac{1}{2}$:   Squaring a positive fraction between 0 and 1 (e.g., $\frac{1}{2}$) results in a smaller number.

Example $(\frac{1}{2})^2 = \frac{1}{2} \times \frac{1}{2} = \frac{1}{4}$

Result $\frac{1}{4}$ is smaller than $\frac{1}{2}$

Cubing a positive fraction between 0 and 1 (e.g., $\frac{1}{2}$) also results in a smaller number.

Example $(\frac{1}{2})^3 = \frac{1}{2} \times \frac{1}{2} \times \frac{1}{2} = \frac{1}{8}$

Result $\frac{1}{8}$ is smaller than $\frac{1}{2}$

The number 0:   Squaring or cubing the number 0 is still zero.

Examples $0^2 = 0 \times 0 = 0$; $0^3 = 0 \times 0 \times 0 = 0$

The fraction $-\frac{1}{2}$:   Squaring a negative fraction between 0 and −1 (e.g., $-\frac{1}{2}$) results in a larger number.

Example $(-\frac{1}{2})^2 = -\frac{1}{2} \times -\frac{1}{2} = \frac{1}{4}$

Result $\frac{1}{4}$ is bigger than $-\frac{1}{2}$

This is no surprise because all negative numbers when squared get bigger. Why? Because they become positive and "jump to the other side" of zero on the number line.

Cubing a negative fraction between 0 and −1 (e.g., $-\frac{1}{2}$) also results in a larger number.

Example $(-\frac{1}{2})^3 = -\frac{1}{2} \times -\frac{1}{2} \times -\frac{1}{2} = -\frac{1}{8}$

Result $-\frac{1}{8}$ is bigger than $-\frac{1}{2}$

Note that $-\frac{1}{8}$ is closer to zero than is $-\frac{1}{2}$. Thus, $-\frac{1}{8}$ is a larger number.

The number −1:   Squaring −1 results in a larger number.

Example $-1^2 = -1 \times -1 = 1$
Result   1 is bigger than −1

Cubing −1 results in the same number.

Example $-1^3 = -1 \times -1 \times -1 = -1$
Result   −1 is equal to −1

The number −2:   Squaring −2 results in a larger number.

Example $(-2)^2 = -2 \times -2 = 4$
Result   4 is bigger than −2

Cubing −2 results in a smaller number.

Example $(-2)^3 = -2 \times -2 \times -2 = -8$
Result   −8 is smaller than −2

MULTIPLE-CHOICE PROBLEMS

Odds and Evens

1. **Even Odds ( )**

    If x and y are positive integers, is $y(x-3)$ even?

    (1) x is an odd integer.
    (2) y is an even integer.

2. **Consecutive ( )**

    If p, q, r are a series of three consecutive positive integers, is the sum of all the integers odd?

    (1) Two of the three numbers p, q, r are odd numbers.

    (2) $\dfrac{p+q+r}{3}$ is an even integer.

Averaging

3. **Vote ( )**

    Each person in a club with 100 members voted for exactly one of 3 candidates for president: A, B, or C. Did candidate A receive the most votes?

    (1) No single candidate received more than 50% of the votes.
    (2) Candidate A received 32 votes.

Positives and Negatives

4. **ABC ( )**

    If a, b, and c are distinct nonzero numbers, is $\dfrac{(a-b)^3(b-c)}{(a+b)^2(b+c)^2} < 0$?

    (1) $a > b$
    (2) $b > c$

Integers and Non-Integers

5. Integers ($\int$)

    How many integers are greater than x, but less than y?

    (1) $y = x + 5$
    (2) $x = \sqrt{5}$

6. A & B ($\int\int$)

    How many integers n are there such that $a > n > b$?

    (1) $a - b = 4$
    (2) a and b are not integers.

Squares and Cubes

7. Units Digit ($\int\int$)

    What is the units digit of the non-negative integer y?

    (1) y is a multiple of 8.

    (2) The units' digit of y^2 is the same as the units' digit of y^3.

Factors and Multiples

8. Multiples ($\int$)

    If x and y are positive integers, is $2x$ a multiple of y?

    (1) x is a multiple of y.
    (2) y is a multiple of x.

9. Factors (🌶🌶)

How many distinct factors does positive integer k have?

(1) k has more distinct factors than the integer 9, but fewer distinct factors than the integer 81.

(2) k is the product of two distinct prime numbers.

Prime Numbers

10. Prime Time (🌶🌶)

If n is an integer, is $n + 1$ a prime number?

(1) n is a prime number.

(2) $n + 2$ is not a prime number.

11. Prime Time Encore (🌶🌶🌶)

If x and y are distinct integers, is $x + y$ a prime number?

(1) x and y are prime numbers.

(2) $x \times y$ is odd.

Factoring

12. F.O.I.L (🌶)

What is the value of a?

(1) $a^2 - a = 2$

(2) $a^2 + a = 6$

13. X-Factor ( )

Is $x = 1$?

(1) $x^2 - x = 0$

(2) $x^3 - x = 0$

Inequalities

14. Z-Ray ( )

Is $z < 0$?

(1) $-z < z$

(2) $z^3 < z^2$

15. Reciprocal ( )

If x and y cannot be equal to zero, is $\dfrac{x}{y} > \dfrac{y}{x}$?

(1) $x > y$

(2) $xy > 0$

16. Fraction ( )

If a and b cannot be equal to zero, is $0 < \dfrac{a}{b} < 1$?

(1) $ab > 0$

(2) $a - b < 0$

17. Kookoo (🌶🌶)

Is $k + k < k$?

(1) $k^2 > k^3$

(2) $k^3 > k^2$

18. Ps & Qs (🌶🌶)

Is $pr > 0$?

(1) $pq > 0$

(2) $qr < 0$

19. ABCD (🌶🌶)

Is $a + b > c + d$?

(1) $a > c + d$

(2) $b > c + d$

20. Upright (🌶🌶🌶)

If $\dfrac{a}{b} > \dfrac{c}{b}$, then is a greater than c?

(1) a is positive.

(2) c is negative.

Statistics

21. Dispersion ( )

What is the standard deviation of the terms in Set S?

(1) Set S is composed of 7 consecutive even integers.
(2) The average (arithmetic mean) of the terms in Set S is 49.

22. Central Measures ( )

Set A and Set B each contain three whole numbers ranging from 1 to 10. With regard to the data contained in each set, is the arithmetic mean of Set A greater than the arithmetic mean of Set B?

(1) The median of Set A is greater than the median of set Set B.
(2) The mode of Set A is greater than the mode of Set B.

ANSWERS AND EXPLANATIONS

The problems included here in *Chapter 3* focus on *number properties* and *statistics* in so far as these represent the majority of Data Sufficiency problems found on the math (quantitative) section of the GMAT. *Word problems* and *geometry*, for example, are tested in Data Sufficiency but with far less frequency.

1. Even Odds (🌶)

Choice D
Classification: Number Properties (Odds & Evens)
Snapshot: This problem highlights the basic concept that an even number times either an even or odd number is always even (e.g., $2 \times 2 = 4$; $2 \times 3 = 6$).

Statement (1) is sufficient. Knowing that x is odd tells us that the expression "$x - 3$" is even because x is odd and an odd number subtracted from an odd number must be even. Once we know that the expression "$x - 3$" is even, we also know that the whole expression "$y(x - 3)$" is even. It doesn't matter whether y is even or odd; an even number multiplied by an odd or even number is always even.

Statement (2) is also sufficient. Knowing that y is even tells us that the whole expression "$y(x - 3)$" is even regardless of whether "$x - 3$" is odd or even. An even number (i.e., y) multiplied by an even or odd number is always even. So in answering the question "Is $y(x - 3)$ even?" the answer is definitely yes because the whole expression is even.

It might be interesting to point out that this problem does not include the words "distinct positive integers." So it is possible that x and y could be the same number at the same time. Say, for example, y and x equal 2 such that $2(2 - 3) = -2$. This is still okay because -2, although negative, is still an even number. Also what if y and x were equal to 3 such that $3(3 - 3) = 0$. This is also okay because 0 is an even number! That's right—as strange as it may seem—the integer 0 is neither positive nor negative, but it is considered an even integer.

2. Consecutive (🌶 🌶)

Choice D
Classification: Number Properties (Odds & Evens)
Snapshot: When picking numbers for sets, try picking sets of three numbers. A set containing only one number is too small while a set of four or five numbers will likely prove cumbersome.

Both statements are again sufficient. Pick some numbers. If two of the three numbers are odd numbers, their sum will always be <u>even</u>: 1, 2, 3 (sum to 6) and 3, 4, 5 (sum to 12). Therefore, based on Statement (1), we can answer the question "Is the sum of all integers odd?" The answer is no because the answer will always result in an even number. Statement (1) is sufficient, not insufficient.

Statement (2) – Let's pick some groups of three consecutive numbers:

$$\frac{1 + 2 + 3}{3} = 2 \qquad \cancel{\frac{2 + 3 + 4}{3} = 3} \qquad \frac{3 + 4 + 5}{3} = 4 \qquad \cancel{\frac{4 + 5 + 6}{3} = 5}$$

Since $\frac{a+b+c}{3}$ must be an even integer, it must also be true that two of the three numbers must be odd and this is exactly where we started with Statement (2). Therefore, the sum of all integers will be even and the answer to the question will be no—the sum of all integers is not odd.

NOTE ❧ This problem also serves as a reminder that "a negative answer to a Yes/No Data Sufficiency question does not equal *insufficiency*—it equals *sufficiency*. The likely reason that this proves tricky for students who are first encountering GMAT Data Sufficiency is that it is intuitive to view positive and negative answers as extremes or polar opposites. In real life, the answer to the questions "Is the light on or off?" or "Is the project complete or not?" can only result in an unambiguous yes or no answer and, as these answers are in opposite camps, we let this influence us in Data Sufficiency. However, in Data Sufficiency, a definitely yes or no answer results in sufficiency.

3. Vote (🌶)

Choice B
Classification: Number Properties (Average Problem)
Snapshot: Sometimes we don't know much about what is true, only what can't be true.

Statement (1) does not tell you anything about the number of votes A received. Statement (2) tells us that Candidate A received 32 votes. Therefore, the other candidates received 100 – 32 = 68 votes. If we divide 68 by 2, we find that the other two candidates averaged 34 votes each: 2 more votes than A received. That means that there's no way that at least one of B or C did not get more votes than Candidate A. So Statement (2) allows us to answer no to the question in the statement, and is therefore sufficient.

4. ABC (🌶🌶)

Choice C
Classification: Number Properties (Positives and Negatives)
Snapshot: This problem highlights the value in picking from the following numbers: 2, –2, 1, –1, $\frac{1}{2}$, $-\frac{1}{2}$, and 0. In this problem, we need only try two pairs of numbers, namely 1, 2, and –1, –2.

The first statement is insufficient. Here is a solution for the first statement:

$$a > b \qquad \text{Is } \frac{(a-b)^3(b-c)}{(a+b)^2(b+c)^2} < 0?$$

$$\text{Is } \frac{(+)(\pm)}{(+)(+)} < 0?$$

First of all, we can tell that the denominator of this fraction will always be positive. Both expressions $(a+b)^2$ and $(b+c)^2$ are always positive because a positive number squared, or negative number squared, is always positive. Looking at the numerator, if $a > b$, we know that $(a-b)^3$ is positive. Pick some numbers to prove this including: $a = 2$ and $b = 1$; $a = -1$ and $b = -2$; and $a = 2$ while $b = -2$.

It all comes down to the expression, $b - c$, in the numerator. If $b > c$, then $b - c$ will be positive, and the whole fraction will be positive. If $b < c$, then the expression $b - c$ will be negative and the whole fraction will be negative. Therefore, we can't tell whether the whole expression is greater than zero or less than zero.

Statement (2) is insufficient. Here is a solution to the second statement:

$$b > c \qquad \text{Is } \frac{(a - b)^3(b - c)}{(a + b)^2(b + c)^2} < 0?$$

$$\text{Is } \frac{(\pm)(+)}{(+)(+)} < 0?$$

If $b > c$, this tells us that the expression $b - c$ is positive. Again, pick some numbers to prove this including: $a = 2$ when $b = 1$; $a = -1$ when $b = -2$; and $a = 2$ when $b = -2$. But we don't know anything about a or b. If $a > b$, then $a - b$ will be positive and the whole fraction will be positive. If $a < b$, then $a - b$ will be negative and the whole fraction will be negative. Therefore, we can't tell whether the whole expression is greater than zero or less than zero.

Now we combine the statements. Knowing that $a > b$ and $b > c$ tells us that both expressions in the numerator are positive. Therefore, the entire expression will always be positive. Strangely, the trickiest part of this problem may not be the math—but rather how to interpret the result. Based on the information in Statements (1) and (2) combined, the answer to the original question is no because the whole expression is not less than zero; it is greater than zero. We must choose sufficiency!

5.   Integers (🌶)

Choice C
Classification: Number Properties (Integers and Non-Integers)
Snapshot: Do not assume all numbers are integers; think also in terms of non-integers, which includes fractions and decimals.

The first statement is insufficient! This is tricky. Of course, we will want to pick some numbers. The key is to think not only in terms of integers but also in terms of non-integers (i.e., fractions and decimals).

	Pick Numbers	Integers between x and y
Statement (1)	$y = x + 5$	
Examples:	$6 = 1 + 5$	4 (i.e., 2, 3, 4, 5)
	$5 = 0 + 5$	4 (i.e., 1, 2, 3, 4)
	$4 = -1 + 5$	4 (i.e., 0, 1, 2, 3)
	$5.5 = 0.5 + 5$	5 (i.e., 1, 2, 3, 4, 5)

In short, there is either four or five integers between x and y. There are four integers between x and y if we assume x and y are integers. But there are five integers between x and y if we assume x and y are non-integers.

The second statement is also insufficient. Knowing that $x = \sqrt{5}$ tells us nothing about y, which could be any number—1 or 1,000,000. Let's put the statements together, approximating $\sqrt{5}$ as 2.2.

Using Statement (1) & (2):

$y = x + 5$
$y = 2.2 + 5$
$7.2 = 2.2 + 5$

Therefore, there are exactly 5 integers between x and y (i.e., between 2.2 and 7.2) and these include the integers 3, 4, 5, 6, and 7.

6. A & B (🌶️🌶️)

Choice C
Classification: Number Properties (Integers and Non-Integers)
Snapshot: This follow-up problem is included to reinforce the need to think in terms of non-integers as opposed to just integers.

Statement (2) is the easiest statement to start with. Knowing just that a and b are not integers, leads to such a wide range of numerical possibilities, which quickly leads to insufficiency. Try picking numbers such as $a = 2.5$ and $b = 0.5$ or $a = 1,000,000.5$ and $b = 0.5$.

Statement (1) proves more difficult to catch. It looks to be sufficient but ends up being insufficient.

	Pick Numbers	Integers between a and b
Statement (1)	$a - b = 4$	
Examples:	$5 - 1 = 4$	3 (i.e., 2, 3, 4)
	$4 - 0 = 4$	3 (i.e., 1, 2, 3)
	$3 - (-1) = 4$	3 (i.e., 0, 1, 2)
	$4.5 - 0.5 = 4$	4 (i.e., 1, 2, 3, 4)

When combining the information is both statements, we are seeking to determine how many integers are between a and b, given that a and b are both non-integers and $a - b = 4$. The answer will always be four integers.

7. Units Digit (🌶️🌶️)

Choice E
Classification: Number Properties (Multiples/Squares and Cubes)
Snapshot: The spotlight is on those numbers—0, 1, 5, and 6—which have the same units' digit whether squared or cubed. Don't forget the number "6"!

Statement (1) states that y is a multiple of 8. Potential numbers for y become 8, 16, 24, 32, 40, etc. The units' digit of a non-negative positive integer y could be 8, 6, 4, 2, 0, etc. So this statement is insufficient.

Statement (2) states that y^2 is the same as the units' digit of y^3. What non-negative integers satisfy this requirement? Such single digit integers include 0, 1, 5, and 6. This statement is also insufficient.

Integers	Squaring	Cubing
0	$0^2 = \underline{0}$	$0^3 = \underline{0}$
1	$1^2 = \underline{1}$	$1^3 = \underline{1}$
5	$5^2 = 2\underline{5}$	$5^3 = 12\underline{5}$
6	$6^2 = 3\underline{6}$	$6^3 = 21\underline{6}$

Because both statements have a variety of numbers that satisfy them, they are individually insufficient. Combining the information in both statements together, the overlap occurs on the numbers 0 and 6. This makes for choice E. The trap answer is choice C because many students will fail to see that numbers that end in 6 will have the same units' digit whether squared or cubed.

NOTE ❧ For simplicity's sake, our four integers have included single digit integers, namely 0, 1, 5, and 6. Many other larger integers, which also end in 0, 1, 5, or 6, will also satisfy the precondition stipulated by Statement (2). These numbers include 10, 11, 15, 16, etc.

8. Multiples (🌶)

Choice A
Classification: Number Properties (Factors and Multiples)
Snapshot: Pick "easy numbers" for problems involving multiples. Remember that multiples are always greater than or equal to a given number; factors are always less than or equal to a given number.

Pick numbers. For Statement (1), if x is a multiple of y, then the following are possibilities:

x	1	2	4	8
y	1	1	2	1

Statement (1) is sufficient. Obviously, if x is a multiple of y, then $2x$ will also be a multiple of y.

Statement (2) however is insufficient. Let's pick the exact same numbers. For example, if y is 2 and x is 1 then $2x$ could be a multiple of y. Likewise, if y is 2 and x is 2, then $2x$ is a multiple of y. But $2x$ might not be a multiple of y. For example, if y is 8 and x is 1, then $2x$ is not a multiple of y because 2 (i.e., 2×1) is not a multiple of 8.

y	1	2	4	8
x	1	1	2	1

9. Factors (🌶️🌶️)

Choice D
Classification: Number Properties (Factors and Multiples)
Snapshot: This problem showcases factors and prime number theory.

Statement (1) is sufficient because it tells us that k has 4 distinct factors; one more than 3, but one less than 5. That is, the integer 9 has three distinct factors: 1, 3, and 9. The integer 81 has five distinct factors: 1, 3, 9, 27, and 81. Therefore, by implication, k must have four distinct factors.

Statement (2) also tells us that k has four distinct factors. If k is the product of two distinct prime factors, its factors are as follows: 1, x, y, and xy. Test this out. Take $2 \times 3 = 6$. The integer 6 is the product of two distinct prime factors. How many factors does 6 have? It has four factors: 1, 2, 3, and 6. How about $3 \times 5 = 15$? How many factors does 15 have? It has four factors: 1, 3, 5, and 15.

10. Prime Time (🌶️🌶️)

Choice E
Classification: Number Properties (Prime Numbers)
Snapshot: Since the number 2 is the only even prime number, look for it to play a pivotal role in the solution to a prime number problem.

Statement (1) is insufficient. Knowing that n is a prime number does not tell us if $n + 1$ is a prime number. For example: $2 + 1 = 3$ (prime number) but $3 + 1 = 4$ (non-prime number). Statement (2) is insufficient. Knowing that $n + 2$ is not a prime number does not tell us if $n + 1$ is a prime number. For example, the numbers which satisfy Statement (2) include 2, 4, 6, 7, and 8. Now using these numbers to answer the original question (i.e., Is $n + 1$ a prime number?), we find the following: $2 + 1 = 3$ (prime); $4 + 1 = 5$ (prime); $6 + 1 = 7$ (prime); $7 + 1 = 8$ (non-prime); and $8 + 1 = 9$ (non-prime). Putting the statements together, we have (at least) two numbers which satisfy both statements. These include 2 and 7. So finally, "Is $n + 1$ a prime number?" It depends. Proof: $2 + 1 = 3$ (prime) but $7 + 1 = 8$ (non-prime).

11. Prime Time Encore (🌶️🌶️🌶️)

Choice C
Classification: Number Properties (Prime Numbers)
Snapshot: Just because the product of two numbers is odd, does not mean that both of the numbers are positive (odd) numbers.

For Statement (1), let's pick from the prime numbers 2, 3, 5, and 7. We can quickly see that $2 + 3 = 5$ is a prime but that $3 + 5 = 8$ is not a prime. So just knowing that x and y are prime doesn't give us a definite yes or no answer as to the question, "Is $x + y$ a prime number?"

Let's also pick numbers for Statement (2): $3 \times 1 = 3$ and $3 \times 5 = 15$. Also, $3 \times -1 = -3$ and $5 \times -1 = -5$. This is particularly tricky because we will likely not think in terms of negative numbers. In short, Statement (2) is insufficient because $3 + 1 = 4$ is not a prime number but $3 + (-1) = 2$ is a prime number!

Putting the statements together, we must pick numbers which satisfy both statements—that is, numbers which are primes and which, when multiplied together, are odd. And we know that two odd numbers added together result in an even number. Thus, the answer to the question "Is $x + y$ a prime number?" is most certainly no, leading to an overall answer for this question of "sufficient."

12. F.O.I.L ( )

Choice C
Classification: Number Properties (Factoring)
Snapshot: When both statements are insufficient in a Value Data Sufficiency question, a single value in common between the sets will lead to choice C (i.e., "overall sufficiency").

Since there are at least two answers for each statement, both statements are individually insufficient. But since there is a single value, and only one single value shared by both statements (i.e., the integer 2), both statements are together sufficient.

Factoring is a math process that seeks to find those numbers that would cause an equation to be equal to 0. For this reason, it is standard practice to set the equation equal to 0 to find these numbers.

Statement (1):

$$a^2 - a = 2$$
$$a^2 - a - 2 = 0$$
$$(a - 2)(a + 1) = 0 \qquad \text{Factors: } a \Rightarrow 2, -1$$

Statement (2):

$$a^2 + a = 6$$
$$a^2 + a - 6 = 0$$
$$(a - 2)(a + 3) = 0 \qquad \text{Factors: } a \Rightarrow 2, -3$$

13. X-Factor ( )

Choice E
Classification: Number Properties (Factoring)
Snapshot: When both statements are insufficient in a Value Data Sufficiency question, two or more values in common between the sets will lead to choice E.

Since there are at least two answers for each statement, both statements are individually insufficient. And since there are two (or more) values in common between the statements, namely 0 and 1, the statements together are insufficient.

Statement (1):

$$x^2 - x = 0$$
$$x(x - 1) = 0 \qquad \text{Factors: } x \Rightarrow 0,1$$

Statement (2):

$$x^3 - x = 0$$
$$x(x^2 - 1) = 0$$
$$x(x - 1)(x + 1) = 0 \qquad \text{Factors: } x \Rightarrow 0, 1, -1$$

NOTE ᴥ There are two situations to watch out for with respect to *two-variable, two-equation* scenarios on the Data Sufficiency section of the GMAT exam. The first occurs with respect to *non-distinct equations* and the second occurs with respect to *variables which cancel out completely*.

What is the value of x?
(1) $3x + y = 7$
(2) $2y = 14 - 6x$

In the above problem, answer choice C looks to be correct. After all, each statement will by itself be insufficient, but together they will prove sufficient. This would be true assuming that both equations are distinct equations (and we would simply substitute for one of the variables and solve for the other variable). However, they are not. In fact they are identical equations. Therefore the value of x cannot be determined, and answer choice E is correct.

What is the value of r?
(1) $4r + 3s = 5r + 2s$
(2) $3(r + s) = 9 + 3s$

In the above problem, answer choice C also looks to be correct, but, in fact, answer choice B is correct. In the second statement, the variable s cancels and r is equal to 3. Although both equations are distinct equations, if a variable cancels in one of the equations, the value of the other variable will be determinable.

14. Z-Ray ( )

Choice A

Classification: Number Properties (Inequalities)

Snapshot: For problems in which the statements contain squares and cubes, we should instinctively try fractions (i.e., $\frac{1}{2}$, $-\frac{1}{2}$), in addition to positive and negative integers. All of these numbers are, of course, members of the *big seven* numbers.

Statement (1) is sufficient. If $-z < z$, then this tells us that z must be positive. Therefore, in answering the question "Is $z < 0$?" the answer, according to Statement (1), is clearly no. There is no need to substitute numbers to prove this.

Statement (2) is insufficient. Which of the *big seven* numbers satisfy the condition $z^3 < z^2$? Answer: $-2, -1$, $-\frac{1}{2}$, and $\frac{1}{2}$. However, upon substituting these numbers in order to determine if $z < 0$?, we find that three of these numbers, namely, $-2, -1, -\frac{1}{2}$, allow us to answer yes, but the positive fraction $\frac{1}{2}$ leads to a no answer. Note that, with respect to Statement (2), the numbers 1, 2, and 0 do not satisfy this pre-condition $z^3 < z^2$ and, therefore, do not qualify.

15. Reciprocal (🌶️ 🌶️)

Choice E

Classification: Number Properties (Inequalities)

Snapshot: This problem highlights the efficacy of picking from a small set of manageable numbers: 1, 2, $-1, -2, \frac{1}{2}, -\frac{1}{2}$, and 0.

Statement (1) is insufficient.

Since $x > y$, we try the following three pairs of numbers: 2, 1 and $-1, -2$ and 2, -2.

    i)   When $x = 2$ and $y = 1$ then $\dfrac{2}{1} > \dfrac{1}{2} \Rightarrow$ yes!

    ii)   When $x = -1$ and $y = -2$ then $\dfrac{-1}{-2} > \dfrac{-2}{-1} \Rightarrow$ no!

    iii) When $x = 2$ and $y = -2$ then $\dfrac{2}{-2} > \dfrac{-2}{2} \Rightarrow$ no!

Statement (2) is insufficient.

Since $xy > 0$, we try 2, 1 and 1, 2 (simply reverse the order of the numbers).

    i)   When $x = 2$ and $y = 1$ then $\dfrac{2}{1} > \dfrac{1}{2} \Rightarrow$ yes!

    ii)   When $x = 1$ and $y = 2$ then $\dfrac{1}{2} > \dfrac{2}{1} \Rightarrow$ no!

Since we have already discovered insufficiency for the second statement, there is no need to try negative numbers. The mere juxtaposition of the positive numbers (i.e., 1, 2 and 2, 1) is enough to create insufficiency. However, when we have a "double I" situation (meaning both statements are individually insufficient), we put the statements together and ask: "Is there a pair of *big seven* numbers that satisfy both statements at the same time and yet lead to completely different answers (i.e., yes or no)?" The answer to this question is yes. The numbers are 2, 1 and $-1, -2$. These are exactly the numbers that we tested in Statement (1). Depending on whether we use a set of positive or negative numbers, we get two different answers to the question, "Is $\frac{x}{y} > \frac{y}{x}$?" One answer is yes and the second is no. The answer is choice E.

NOTE ✎ "Should we have tried fractions in the problem above?" Answer—no. There is no need. Fractions, namely $\frac{1}{2}, -\frac{1}{2}$, are to be used only when we have squares or cubes in the statements themselves.

16. Fraction (🌶🌶)

Choice E
Classification: Number Properties (Inequalities)
Snapshot: In terms of picking numbers, observe the importance of picking from both positive and negative integers.

Statement (1) is insufficient. Since $ab > 0$, we try 1, 2 and 2, 1 (in that order):

i) When $a = 1$ and $b = 2$ then $0 < \dfrac{1}{2} < 1$ ⇨ yes!

ii) When $a = 2$ and $b = 1$ then $0 < \dfrac{2}{1} < 1$ ⇨ no!

Statement (2) is insufficient. Since $a - b < 0$, we try 1, 2 and –2, –1 (in that order):

i) When $a = 1$ and $b = 2$ then $0 < \dfrac{1}{2} < 1$ ⇨ yes!

ii) When $a = -2$ and $b = -1$ then $0 < \dfrac{-2}{-1} < 1$ ⇨ no!

So in putting the statements together, we ask the question: "Is there a pair of numbers that satisfy both statements simultaneously, but which lead to different answers to the original question?" And the answer is yes; the numbers 1, 2 and –2, –1, in that order, lead to one yes answer and one no answer. Overall, this results in *insufficiency,* so answer choice E is correct.

17. Kookoo (🌶🌶)

Choice B
Classification: Number Properties (Inequalities)

Snapshot: This is a very intimidating looking problem. The fractions $\frac{1}{2}$ and $-\frac{1}{2}$ become keys to solving it.

Statement (1) is insufficient. If $k^2 > k^3$, then k could only be one of –2, –1, $-\frac{1}{2}$, and $\frac{1}{2}$. The negative numbers just listed lead to a yes answer, but the positive number $\frac{1}{2}$ leads to a no answer. In the second statement, If $k^3 > k^2$, then k must be a positive number greater than 1 and the answer to the question—"Is $k < 0$?"—is no.

NOTE ↝ The question "Is $k + k < k$?" is also equivalent to "Is $k < 0$?" Just add $-k$ to both sides in order to simplify this expression. Now we are asking whether k is less than 0. Of course, this is equivalent to the original statement because the only way for $k + k$ to be less than k is for k to be a negative number.

18. Ps & Qs ( )

Choice C

Classification: Number Properties (Inequalities)

Snapshot: Although we could also substitute numbers into this problem, it is not necessary because it can be solved conceptually. This is an example where there is no need to substitute numbers to achieve an outcome.

The first and second statements are clearly insufficient. The first statement contains no information about r while the second statement contains no information about p. Taken together, however, they are sufficient and we can answer the question with no; $p \times r$ is not greater than 0 because $p \times r$ is less than 0.

Conceptually, the statement $pq > 0$ tells us that both p and q are both either positive or negative (they have the same signs). The statement $qr < 0$ tells us that one of either q or r is negative while the other is positive (they have different signs). So combining this information: If p and q are positive, then r is negative and that means $p \times r$ is less than 0. If p and q are negative, then r is positive and that means $p \times r$ is negative.

19. ABCD ( )

Choice E

Classification: Number Properties (Inequalities)

Snapshot: Many candidates will pick choice C for this problem. Force yourself to try negative numbers even if things look sufficient.

First of all, the two statements are individually insufficient. Statement (1) makes no mention of the variable b. Statement (2) makes no mention of the variable a. Therefore, neither statement is sufficient to answer the question of whether $a + b$ is greater than $c + d$.

The trap answer is choice C. Many candidates will try positive numbers but will forget to try negative ones. Also, don't worry if every number is not strictly a *big seven* number. The solution below makes use of the number 3.

First try some positive numbers:

Statement (1):

$a > c + d$ $3 > 1 + 1$

Statement (2):

$b > c + d$ $3 > 1 + 1$

Conclusion:

$a + b > c + d$ $3 + 3 > 1 + 1$

Since 6 is greater than 2, the answer is yes.

Next try some negative numbers:

Statement (1):

$a > c + d$ $-1 > -1 + -1$

Statement (2):

$b > c + d$ $-1 > -1 + -1$

Conclusion:

$a + b > c + d$ $-1 + -1 > -1 + -1$

Since −2 is not greater than −2, the answer is no.

And for the record:

Statement (1):

$a > c + d$ $-3 > -2 + -2$

Statement (2):

$b > c + d$ $-3 > -2 + -2$

Conclusion:

$a + b > c + d$ $-3 + -3 > -2 + -2$

Since −6 is not greater than −4, the answer is also no.

20. Upright (🌶️🌶️🌶️)

Choice C

Classification: Number Properties (Inequalities)

Snapshot: This problem provides the ultimate workout in terms of picking numbers. If we can quickly conceptualize all six scenarios below, we'll be able to tackle this type of question on the GMAT. Attack this problem using only four of the "big seven" numbers: 2, −2, 1, and −1.

Conceptual setup: Since we don't know whether b is positive or negative, we can first assign b the value of +1 (per Scenarios 1, 2, and 3) and then assign b the value of −1 (per Scenarios 4, 5, and 6). Six possibilities unfold:

	Substitution	Result	Conclusion
Scenario 1:	$\dfrac{2}{+1} > \dfrac{1}{+1}$	$2 > 1$	$a > c$
	(where $a = 2$, $c = 1$, $b = +1$)		

Scenario 2: $\dfrac{-1}{+1} > \dfrac{-2}{+1}$ $\qquad -1 > -2$ $\qquad a > c$

(where $a = -1$, $c = -2$, $b = +1$)

Scenario 3: $\dfrac{2}{+1} > \dfrac{-2}{+1}$ $\qquad 2 > -2$ $\qquad a > c$

(where $a = 2$, $c = -2$, $b = +1$)

Findings: As long as b is positive, a will be <u>greater</u> than c.

	Substitution	*Result*	*Conclusion*

Scenario 4: $\dfrac{1}{-1} > \dfrac{2}{-1}$ $\qquad -1 > -2$ $\qquad a < c$

(where $a = 1$, $c = 2$, $b = -1$)

Scenario 5: $\dfrac{-2}{-1} > \dfrac{-1}{-1}$ $\qquad 2 > 1$ $\qquad a < c$

(where $a = -2$, $c = -1$, $b = -1$)

Scenario 6: $\dfrac{-2}{-1} > \dfrac{+2}{-1}$ $\qquad 2 > -2$ $\qquad a < c$

(where $a = -2$, $c = 2$, $b = -1$)

Findings: As long as b is negative, a will be <u>less</u> than c.

Statement (1) is insufficient. Given the precondition $\frac{a}{b} > \frac{c}{b}$, and the fact that a is positive, only Scenarios 1, 3, and 4 are possibilities. In Scenarios 1 and 3, a is greater than c, but in Scenario 4, a is less than c. We do not know whether $a > c$.

Statement (2) is insufficient. Given the precondition $\frac{a}{b} > \frac{c}{b}$, and the fact that c is negative, only Scenarios 2, 3, and 5 are possibilities. In Scenarios 2 and 3, a is greater than c, but in Scenario 5, a is less than c. We do not know whether $a > c$.

Summary: Given that both statements are insufficient, and the fact that a is positive and c is negative, the only scenario that is possible is Scenario 3, where $a > c$. We have a definitive answer to the question, "Is a greater than c?"—and the answer rests with choice C.

Don't fall into the trap of multiplying the original equation through by b to get $a > c$ and conclude, outright, that $a > c$. Because we do not know whether b is positive or negative, multiplying through by $-b$ would change the inequality sign and reverse the result. That is, when we multiply or divide both sides of an inequality by a negative number, the inequality sign must be reversed.

If b is positive:

$$\frac{a}{b} > \frac{c}{b}$$

$$\frac{\cancel{b}}{1} \times \frac{a}{\cancel{b}} > \frac{\cancel{b}}{1} \times \frac{c}{\cancel{b}}$$

$$a > c$$

If b is negative:

$$\frac{a}{b} > \frac{c}{b}$$

$$\frac{-\cancel{b}}{1} \times \frac{a}{-\cancel{b}} > \frac{-\cancel{b}}{1} \times \frac{c}{-\cancel{b}}$$

$$a < c$$

21. Dispersion (ᕱ)

Choice A
Classification: Statistics (Standard Deviation)
Snapshot: We do not need to know the formula for standard deviation (nor are we required to know it for the GMAT exam). All we need to know is that "standard deviation is a measure of dispersion." The more dispersed data is, the higher the standard deviation; the less dispersed data is, the lower the standard deviation.

Pick two sets of seven consecutive even integers. For example: 2, 4, 6, 8, 10, 12, 14, and 94, 96, 98, 100, 102, 104, and 106. We can tell by glancing at these numbers that the arithmetic mean of these sets are 8 and 100 respectively. The relative distances that any of these numbers are from their respective arithmetic means are identical. That is, 2 is just as far from 8 as 94 is from 100 and 14 is just a far from 8 as 106 is from 100. Whatever the standard deviation may be, it will be identical for both sets and, for that matter, for any seven consecutive even integers.

In Statement (2), let's pick two numbers that average to 49, but that are greatly different. For example, we could pick 1 and 97 or 48 and 50. However, even though their arithmetic means are identical, the standard deviation of these two sets would be drastically different.

NOTE ᕱ Another term we need to know for the GMAT is *range*. Range is the smallest item in a set subtracted from the largest item (or the positive difference between the largest and smallest numbers). The range for both of the above sets is 12; that is, 14 − 2 = 12 and 106 − 94 = 12.

22. Central Measures (ᕱᕱ)

Choice E
Classification: Statistics (Measures of Central Tendency)
Snapshot: This problem highlights the need to understand the three measures of central tendency—mean, median, and mode. The GMAT exam requires us to know how to calculate measures of central tendency. Calculating the mean is easy because that's the way we typically calculate average: We add up all the items and divide by the number of items in a given set. Median is the *middle most* number. Mode is the *most*

frequently recurring number. Note that the median for an even set of data is calculated by averaging the two middle terms. Lastly, a given set of data may have more than one mode, but we never average modes.

Statement (1): Let's pick some numbers in which the median for Set A is greater than the median for Set B.

	Median	Mode	Mean
Set A: i) 1, 5, 10	5	n/a	$\frac{16}{3} = 5\frac{1}{3}$
ii) 1, 5, 6	5	n/a	$\frac{12}{3} = 4$
Set B: i) 1, 4, 10	4	n/a	$\frac{15}{3} = 5$

We can conclude that although Set A has a greater median than Set B, it may or may not have a greater arithmetic mean.

Statement (2): Let's pick some numbers in which the mode for Set A proves greater than the mode for Set B.

	Median	Mode	Mean
Set A: i) 5, 5, 10	5	5	$\frac{20}{3} = 6\frac{2}{3}$
ii) 1, 5, 5	5	5	$\frac{11}{3} = 3\frac{2}{3}$
Set B: i) 4, 4, 10	4	4	$\frac{18}{3} = 6$

We can conclude that although Set A has a greater mode than Set B, it may or may not have a greater arithmetic mean.

Statement (1) and Statement (2) are together insufficient. The data presented for Statement (2) above shows that although Set A has both a greater median and mode than Set B, it may or may not have a greater arithmetic mean.

CHAPTER 4

SENTENCE CORRECTION

Grammar and logic free language from being at the mercy of the tone of voice.
　　　　　　　　—Resenstock-Huessy

OVERVIEW

Official Exam Instructions for Sentence Correction

Directions

This question presents a sentence, part of which or all of which is underlined. Beneath the sentence you will find five ways of phrasing the underlined part. The first of these repeats the original; the other four are different. If you think the original is best, choose the first answer; otherwise choose one of the others.

This question tests correctness and effectiveness of expression. In choosing your answer, follow the requirements of standard written English; that is, pay attention to grammar, choice of words, and sentence construction. Choose the answer that produces the most effective sentence. This answer should be clear and exact, without awkwardness, ambiguity, redundancy, or grammatical error.

Strategies and Approaches

1. *Glance first at answer choices looking for vertical patterns. Try to determine what the pivotal grammar issue is and if the pivotal issue falls under one of the "big six" grammar categories: subject-verb agreement, modification, pronoun usage, parallelism, comparisons, and verb tenses.*

    Sentence Correction questions selected for inclusion in this book focus primarily on the "big six" grammar categories, as mentioned above. Consistent with a majority of GMAT questions, grammar and diction are the driving forces while idioms and style are interwoven subcomponents.

    Vertical patterns refer to the first word or words of each answer choice, and less often, last word or words of each answer choice. It is the first few words of each answer choice that will often offer clues as to where a grammatical distinction lies, particularly those that fall into the "big six" grammar categories. For example, if the first couple of answer choices contain the word "has" and the last three answer choices contain the word "have" then we can deduce that a grammatical distinction centers on subject-verb agreement.

2. *Read the original sentence carefully.*

3. *Read each answer choice looking for horizontal patterns.*

    Horizontal patterns may also uncover problems in grammar but more likely they will be used to spot-check idioms and style. We may even use our ear to hone in on the correct answer.

4. *Choose the best answer—the answer which is grammatically correct, idiomatically correct, and effective in terms of style.*

REVIEW OF SENTENCE CORRECTION

Overview

In the broadest sense, Sentence Correction requires mastering basic grammar, diction (word choice), idioms, and style. Grammar and diction are based on rules of English. Idioms are based on adopted expressions which are deemed right or wrong simply because "that's the way it is said." Style is not considered right or wrong but rather it is viewed as more effective or less effective. Examples of each follow:

Grammar: The choice between "They have arrived" and "They has arrived" is based on a rule of grammar: the plural subject "they" requires the plural verb "have."

Diction: The choice between "fewer pencils" and "less pencils" is based on diction; "fewer" is used with countable items such as pencils.

Idioms: The choice between "I prefer fish to chicken" and "I prefer fish over chicken" is based on idiomatic expression; in this case "to" is the correct preposition.

Style: The choice between "employees of the company" and "company employees" is based on a convention of style—brevity; here the simplest version ("company employees") is deemed more effective.

Consistent with a majority of GMAT Sentence Correction problems, grammar is the driving force while diction, idioms, and style are interwoven subcomponents. Arguably the most efficient way to review grammar, diction, and idioms is by working through the following 100-question quiz. This quiz is built around the "big six" grammar categories: subject-verb agreement, modification, pronoun usage, parallelism, comparisons, and verb tenses. These six categories are also consistent with those used to group the multiple-choice questions included in this chapter.

The following 100-question quiz provides a highly distilled review of grammar, diction, and idioms. The first segment—grammar—is built on the "big six" grammar categories. Answers to questions Q1 to Q100 can be found on pages 236–245. A *Review of Grammatical Terms* begins on page 216. If a more technical grounding is desired, this section can be reviewed before attempting the quiz questions.

100-Question Quiz on Grammar, Diction, and Idioms

SUBJECT-VERB AGREEMENT:

The overarching principle regarding subject-verb agreement is that singular subjects require singular verbs while plural subjects take plural verbs. Our objective is to identify the subject in order to determine whether the verb is singular or plural.

☞ Rule 1:   "And" always creates a compound subject.

Q1   An office clerk and a machinist (was / were) present but unhurt by the on-site explosion.

The only connecting word that can make a series of singular nouns into a plural subject is "and." In fact, "and" always creates a plural subject with but one exception, as noted in the next rule.

☞ **Rule 2:**   If two items joined by "and" are deemed to be a single unit, then the subject is considered singular, and a singular verb is required.

Q2   Eggs and bacon (is / are) Tiffany's favorite breakfast.

☞ **Rule 3:**   When the subject of a sentence consists of two items joined by "or," the subject may either singular or plural. If the two items joined by "or" are both singular, then the subject and verb are singular. If the two items joined by "or" are both plural, then the subject and verb are plural. If one of the two items joined by "or" is singular and the other plural, the verb matches the subject that comes after "or."

Q3   In the game of chess, capturing one knight or three pawns (yields / yield) the same point value.

☞ **Rule 4:**   "Pseudo-compound subjects" do not make singular subjects plural.

Pseudo-compound subjects include the following: *as well as, along with, besides, in addition to,* and *together with.*

Q4   A seventeenth-century oil painting, along with several antique vases, (has / have) been placed on the auction block.

☞ **Rule 5:**   Prepositional phrases (i.e., phrases introduced by a preposition) can never contain the subject of a sentence.

Some of the most common prepositions include *of, in, to, by, for,* and *from.* A glossary of grammatical terms, as well as a definition of the word "preposition," follows in this chapter.

Q5   The purpose of the executive, administrative, and legislative branches of government (is / are) to provide a system of checks and balances.

☞ **Rule 6:**   "There is/there are" and "here is/here are" constructions represent special situations where the verb comes before the subject, not after the subject.

The normal order in English sentences is subject-verb-object (think S-V-O). "There is/there are" and "here is/here are" sentences are tricky because they create situations in which the verb comes before the subject. Thus, these sentence constructions require that we look past the verb—"is" or "are" in this case—in order to identify the subject.

Q6   Here (is / are) the introduction and chapters one through five.

Q7   (Is / are) there any squash courts available?

EXHIBIT 4.1   CHART OF INDEFINITE PRONOUNS

Singular or Plural	Examples
Certain indefinite pronouns are always singular	anybody, anyone, anything, each, either, every, everybody, everyone, everything, neither, nobody, no one, nothing, one, somebody, someone, something
Certain indefinite pronouns are always plural	both, few, many, several
Certain indefinite pronouns can be either singular or plural	all, any, most, none, some

☞ **Rule 7:** **When acting as subjects of a sentence, gerunds and infinitives are always singular and require singular verbs.**

Q8   Entertaining multiple goals (makes / make) a person's life stressful.

☞ **Rule 8:** **"-One," "-body," and "-thing" indefinite pronouns are always singular.**

Q9   One in every three new businesses (fails / fail) within the first five years of operation.

☞ **Rule 9:** **Certain indefinite pronouns—"both," "few," "many," and "several"—are always plural.**

Q10   Few of the students, if any, (is / are) ready for the test.

☞ **Rule 10:** **"Some" and "none" indefinite pronouns may be singular or plural.**

Q11   Some of the story (makes / make) sense.

Q12   Some of the comedians (was / were) hilarious.

Q13   None of the candidates (has / have) any previous political experience.

☞ **Rule 11:** **In "either … or" and "neither … nor" constructions, the verb matches the subject that comes directly after the "or" or "nor."**

Q14   Either Johann or Cecilia (is / are) qualified to act as manager.

Q15   Neither management nor workers (is / are) satisfied with the new contract.

☞ **Rule 12:** Collective nouns denote a group of individuals (e.g., family, government, assembly, crew). If the collective noun refers to a group as a whole or the idea of oneness predominates, use a singular verb. If not, use a plural verb.

Q16   Our group (is / are) meeting at 6 p.m.

Q17   A group of latecomers (was / were) escorted to their seats.

☞ **Rule 13:** "The number" is a singular noun and takes a singular verb. "A number" is plural and takes a plural verb.

Q18   The number of road accidents (has / have) decreased.

Q19   A number of train accidents (has / have) occurred.

☞ **Rule 14:** Percents or fractions, when followed by an "of phrase," can take a singular or plural verb. The key lies in determining whether the noun within the "of phrase" is singular or plural.

Q20   Fifty percent of video gaming (is / are) having great reflexes.

Q21   Two-thirds of their classmates (has / have) wakeboards.

☞ **Rule 15:** Measurements involving money (e.g., dollars, pounds), time (e.g., five years, the fifties), weight (e.g., pounds, kilograms), or volume (e.g., gallons, kilograms) are always singular and take singular verbs.

Q22   Ten dollars (is / are) an average daily wage for many people in the developing world.

PRONOUN USAGE:

Problems relating to pronoun usage typically center on personal pronouns. Three areas of confusion may include: choosing between the subjective or objective forms of personal pronouns, making sure pronouns agree in number with their antecedents, and ensuring that pronouns are not ambiguous in context.

☞ **Rule 16:** As a general guide, pronouns at or near the front of a sentence take their subjective forms; pronouns at or near the back of a sentence take their objective forms. The precise rule, however, is that pronouns take their subjective form when they are subjects of a verb; they take their objective form when they are objects of a verb.

Q23   The present is from Beth and (she / her).

Q24   Cousin Vinny and (he / him) are both valedictorians.

EXHIBIT 4.2   CHART OF PERSONAL PRONOUNS

	Subjective	Possessive	Objective
first-person singular	I	my, mine	me
second-person singular	you	your, yours	you
third-person singular	he, she, it	his, her, hers, its	him, her, it
first-person plural	we	our, ours	us
second-person plural	you	your, yours	you
third-person plural	they	their, theirs	them
who	who	whose	whom

☞ **Rule 17:**   Pronouns take their objective form when they are the direct objects of prepositions.

Q25   Between you and (I / me), this plan makes a lot of sense.

Q26   Do not ask for (who / whom) the bell tolls.

Q27   People like you and (I / me) should know better.

☞ **Rule 18:**   When forming comparisons using "than" or "as … as," supply any "missing words" (e.g., a verb in the examples below) in order to determine whether the subjective or objective form of the pronoun is correct.

Q28   My nephew is taller than (I / me).

Q29   We skate as fast as (they / them).

Q30   During our group presentation, our teacher asked you more questions than (I / me).

☞ **Rule 19:**   Who vs. Whom. "Who" is the subjective form of the pronoun, and "whom" is the objective form of the pronoun. If "he," "she," or "they" can be substituted for a pronoun in context, the correct form is "who." If "him," "her," or "them" can be substituted for a pronoun in context, the correct form is "whom."

Q31   The woman (who / whom) is responsible for pension planning is Mrs. Green.

Q32   This gift is intended for (who / whom)?

☞ Rule 20: Do not use a reflexive pronoun (a pronoun ending in "-self") if an ordinary personal pronoun will suffice.

Q33   The tour leader told Julie and (me / myself) to turn off our cell phones.

Q34   Young Robert hurt (him / himself) while climbing alone.

☞ Rule 21: Pronouns must agree in number with their antecedents.

Q35   A not-for-profit, like any other organization, has (its / their) own rules and regulations to follow.

Q36   Everybody should mind (his or her / their) own business.

                NOTE ❧ There is something known today as the "singular they." Although it is not considered proper in formal writing (and formal speech), in informal writing (and colloquial speech), it is ever common to see or hear the word "they" used to refer to a singular subject. For example: "Any parent knows that they have to be involved in a child's education." Although "parent" is singular, it is matched with the plural pronoun "they."

☞ Rule 22: Pronouns should not be ambiguous in context. If a pronoun does not refer clearly to a specific noun, it results in a situation of "ambiguous pronoun reference."

Ambiguous   Sam never argues with his father when <u>he</u> is drunk.

Q37   Sam never argues with his father when _____ is drunk.

☞ Rule 23: "Pronoun shifts," also known as "shifts in point of view," involve the inconsistent matching of pronouns, either in terms of person or number. Within a single sentence (and perhaps within an entire paragraph or writing piece), first person should be matched with first person, second person matched with second person, and third person matched with third person. A common violation involves matching the third-person "one" or "a person" with the second-person "you." Another violation involves matching the third-person singular "he," "she," "one," or "a person" with the third-person plural "they."

Incorrect   To know that <u>a person</u> can't vote is to know that <u>you don't</u> have a voice.

Q38   To know that a person can't vote is to know that _____ have a voice.

Incorrect   <u>One</u> cannot really understand another country until <u>they</u> have studied its history and culture.

Q39   One cannot really understand another country until _____ studied its history and culture.

MODIFICATION:

Modifiers, including modifying phrases, must be placed as close as possible to the nouns they modify. As a mostly uninflected language, English depends heavily on word order to establish modifying relationships. Therefore, the position of words is important. Confusion occurs because most modifiers attach themselves to the first thing they can "get their hands on" in the sentence, even if it isn't the right thing.

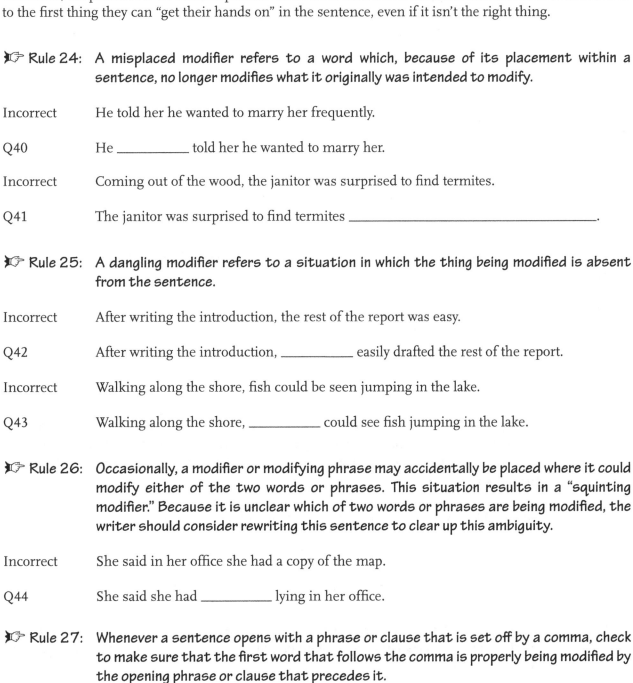

☞ Rule 24:   A misplaced modifier refers to a word which, because of its placement within a sentence, no longer modifies what it originally was intended to modify.

Incorrect   He told her he wanted to marry her frequently.

Q40   He _____ told her he wanted to marry her.

Incorrect   Coming out of the wood, the janitor was surprised to find termites.

Q41   The janitor was surprised to find termites _____.

☞ Rule 25:   A dangling modifier refers to a situation in which the thing being modified is absent from the sentence.

Incorrect   After writing the introduction, the rest of the report was easy.

Q42   After writing the introduction, _____ easily drafted the rest of the report.

Incorrect   Walking along the shore, fish could be seen jumping in the lake.

Q43   Walking along the shore, _____ could see fish jumping in the lake.

☞ Rule 26:   Occasionally, a modifier or modifying phrase may accidentally be placed where it could modify either of the two words or phrases. This situation results in a "squinting modifier." Because it is unclear which of two words or phrases are being modified, the writer should consider rewriting this sentence to clear up this ambiguity.

Incorrect   She said in her office she had a copy of the map.

Q44   She said she had _____ lying in her office.

☞ Rule 27:   Whenever a sentence opens with a phrase or clause that is set off by a comma, check to make sure that the first word that follows the comma is properly being modified by the opening phrase or clause that precedes it.

207

Incorrect	In addition to building organizational skills, the summer internship also helped me hone my team-building skills.
Q45	In addition to building organizational skills, _____.
Incorrect	An incredibly complex mechanism, there are some 10 billion nerve cells in the brain.
Q46	An incredibly complex mechanism, _____ has some 10 billion nerve cells.
Incorrect	Based on our observations, the project will succeed.
Q47	_____.

PARALLELISM:

Parallelism is both a style issue and a grammar issue. In other words, certain elements of parallelism are based on principle and are deemed to be more effective or less effective, better or worse, while other elements are based on rules and are considered correct or incorrect, right or wrong.

The overarching principle regarding parallelism is that similar elements in a sentence must be written in similar form.

☞ Rule 28: **Verbs should follow consistent form. Typically this means that all verbs should end in "-ed" or "-ing."**

Incorrect	In the summer before college, Max <u>was</u> a waiter at a restaurant, <u>pursued</u> magazine sales, and even had a stint at <u>delivering</u> pizzas.
Q48	In the summer before college, Max _____ tables, _____ magazines, and even _____ pizzas.

☞ Rule 29: **When prepositions are used before items in a series of three, there are two possibilities with regard to their use. Either a single preposition is used before the first item in a series (but not with the next two items) or prepositions are used before each item in the series.**

Incorrect	Our neighbors went <u>to</u> London, Athens, and <u>to</u> Rome.
Q49	Our neighbors went _____ London, Athens, and Rome.
Q50	Our neighbors went _____ London, _____ Athens, and _____ Rome.

☞ Rule 30: **Correlative conjunctions (e.g., "either … or," "neither … nor," "not only … but also," and "both … and") require that parallelism be maintained after each component part of the correlative.**

Incorrect	Jonathan not only likes rugby but also kayaking.

Q51   Jonathan _____ rugby but also kayaking.

Q52   Jonathan _____ rugby but also _____ kayaking.

☞ Rule 31: Gerunds and infinitives should be presented in parallel form. Where possible, gerunds are matched with gerunds and infinitives are matched with infinitives.

Less effective   <u>Examining</u> the works of William Shakespeare—his plays and poetry—is <u>to marvel</u> at one man's seemingly incomparable depth of literary expression.

Q53   _____ the works of William Shakespeare—his plays and poetry—is <u>to marvel</u> at one man's seemingly incomparable depth of literary expression.

☞ Rule 32: At times we can acceptably omit words in a sentence and still retain clear meaning. To check for faulty parallelism (in this context it is also known as improper use of ellipsis), complete each sentence component and make sure that each part of the sentence can stand on its own.

Incorrect   In the *Phantom of the Opera* play, the music is terrific and the stage props superb.

Q54   In the *Phantom of the Opera* play, the music <u>is</u> terrific and the stage props _____ superb.

Incorrect   The defendant's own testimony on the stand neither contributed nor detracted from his claim of innocence.

Q55   The defendant's own testimony on the stand neither contributed _____ nor detracted from his claim of innocence.

COMPARISONS:

The overarching principle in comparisons requires that we compare apples with apples and oranges with oranges.

☞ Rule 33: The superlative ("-est") is used when comparing three or more persons or things; the comparative ("-er") is used when comparing exactly two persons or things.

Q56   Between Tom and Brenda, Tom is (better / best) at math.

Q57   Among our group, Jeff is the (wealthier / wealthiest) person.

Q58   Of all the roses in our neighborhood, Chauncey Gardiner's grow the (more / most) vigorously.

Q59   Chauncey Gardiner's roses grow (more / most) vigorously than any other in the neighborhood.

☞ Rule 34: Remember to compare the characteristics of one thing to the characteristics of another thing, not the characteristics of one thing directly to another thing.

Incorrect   Tokyo's population is greater than Beijing.

Q60   Tokyo's population is greater than the _____ of Beijing.

Q61   Tokyo's population is greater than Beijing's _____.

Q62   Tokyo's population is greater than that of _____.

Q63   Tokyo's population is greater than _____.

Incorrect   Of all the countries contiguous to India, Pakistan's borders are most strongly defended.

Q64   Of all the countries contiguous to India, _____.

☞ Rule 35: Faulty or improper comparisons often leave out key words, particularly demonstrative pronouns such as "those" and "that," which are essential to meaning.

Incorrect   The attention span of a dolphin is greater than a chimpanzee.

Q65   The attention span of a dolphin is greater than _____ a chimpanzee.

Incorrect   The requirements of a medical degree are more stringent than a law degree.

Q66   The requirements of a medical degree are more stringent than _____ a law degree.

Incorrect   Like many politicians, the senator's promises sounded good but ultimately led to nothing.

Q67   Like _____ many politicians, the senator's promises sounded good but ultimately led to nothing.

☞ Rule 36: "Like" is used with phrases. "As" is used with clauses. A "phrase" is a group of related words that doesn't have both a subject and a verb. A "clause" is a group of related words that does have a subject and a verb. An easier way to remember the difference is to simply say, "A phrase is a group of words which doesn't have a verb; a clause is a group of words which does have a verb."

Q68   No one hits home runs (as / like) Barry Bonds.

Q69   No one pitches (as / like) Roy Halladay does.

☞ Rule 37: Consistent use of verb tenses generally requires that a single sentence be written solely in the present, past, or future tense.

Verb Tenses:

Exhibit 4.3   The Simple and Progressive Verb Forms

	Simple Form	Progressive Form
Present Tense	I travel	I am traveling
Past Tense	I traveled	I was traveling
Future Tense	I will travel	I will be traveling
Present Perfect Tense	I have traveled	I have been traveling
Past Perfect Tense	I had traveled…	I had been traveling…
Future Perfect Tense	I will have traveled…	I will have been traveling…

Q70   My dog barks when he (sees / saw) my neighbor's cat.

Q71   Yesterday afternoon, smoke (fills / filled) the sky and sirens sounded.

Q72   Tomorrow, we (will go / will have gone) to the football game.

☞ **Rule 38:   The present perfect tense employs the verbs "has" or "have." The past perfect tense employs the auxiliary "had." The future perfect tense employs the verb form "will have."**

Q73   We are raising money for the new scholarship fund. So far we (raised / have raised / had raised) $25,000.

Q74   By the time I began playing golf, I (played / had played) tennis for three hours.

Q75   Larry (studied / has studied / had studied) Russian for five years before he went to work in Moscow.

Q76   By the time evening arrives, we (finished / had finished / will have finished) the task at hand.

Rule 39:   The subjunctive mood uses the verb "were" instead of "was." The subjunctive mood is used to indicate a hypothetical situation—it may express a wish, doubt, or possibility. It is also used to indicate a contrary-to-fact situation.

EXHIBIT 4.4   VISUALIZING THE SIX VERB TENSES

Tense	Examples	Summary
Simple Present	I <u>study</u> physics.	Expresses events or situations that currently exist, including the near past and near present.
Simple Past	I <u>studied</u> physics.	Expresses events or situations that existed in the past.
Simple Future	I <u>will study</u> physics.	Expresses events or situations that will exist in the future.
Present Perfect	I <u>have studied</u> physics.	Expresses events or situations that existed in the past but that touch the present. Look for the verbs "has" or "have."
Past Perfect	By the time I graduated from high school, I <u>had decided</u> to study physics.	Expresses events or situations in the past, one of which occurred before the other. Look for the word "had" to signal the first of two past events.
Future Perfect	By the time I graduate from college, I <u>will have studied</u> physics for four years.	Expresses events or situations in the future, one of which will occur after the other. Look for the words "will have" to signal the first of two future events.

Q77   Sometimes she wishes she (was / were) on a tropical island having a drink at sunset.

Q78   If I (was / were) you, I would be feeling quite optimistic.

➤ Rule 40:   Conditional statements are most commonly expressed in an "If…then" format, in which case an "if" clause is followed by a "results" clause. Confusion often arises as to whether to use "will" or "would." The choice between these verb forms depends on whether a given conditional statement involves the subjunctive. For situations involving the subjunctive, the appropriate verb form is "would." For situations not involving the subjunctive, the verb form is "will." A helpful hint is that "would" is often used in conjunction with "were"—the appearance of both these words within the same sentence is the telltale sign of the subjunctive.

Q79   If economic conditions further deteriorate, public confidence (will / would) plummet.

Q80   If economic conditions were to further deteriorate, public confidence (will / would) plummet.

Q81   If my taxes are less than $10,000, I (will / would) pay that amount immediately.

Q82   If oil (was / were) still abundant, there (will / would) be no energy crisis.

Diction Review:

Diction may be thought of as "word choices." Choose the answer that conforms to the proper use of diction.

Q83   (A)   <u>Everyone</u> of the makeup exams is tough, but <u>anyone</u> who misses a scheduled test with good cause is entitled to write one.

        (B)   <u>Every one</u> of the makeup exams is tough, but <u>anyone</u> who misses a scheduled test with good cause is entitled to write one.

        (C)   <u>Every one</u> of the makeup exams is tough, but <u>any one</u> who misses a scheduled test with good cause is entitled to write one.

Q84   (A)   The green book, <u>that</u> is on the top shelf, is the one you need for math. The book <u>which</u> is red is the one you need for writing.

        (B)   The green book, <u>which</u> is on the top shelf, is the one you need for math. The book <u>that</u> is red is the one you need for writing.

        (C)   The green book, <u>which</u> is on the top shelf, is the one you need for math. The book <u>which</u> is red is the one you need for writing.

Q85   (A)   <u>Let's</u> cherish the poem "In Flanders Fields." Remembering those who fought for our freedom <u>lets</u> us live easier.

        (B)   <u>Lets</u> cherish the poem "In Flanders Fields." Remembering those who fought for our freedom <u>let's</u> us live easier.

        (C)   <u>Let's</u> cherish the poem "In Flanders Fields." Remembering those who fought for our freedom <u>let's</u> us live easier.

Q86   (A)   Once we turn these dreaded assignments <u>into</u> the professor's office, we'll feel a lot less obliged to pass any information <u>onto</u> our classmates.

        (B)   Once we turn these dreaded assignments <u>into</u> the professor's office, we'll feel a lot less obliged to pass any information <u>on to</u> our classmates.

(C)   Once we turn these dreaded assignments <u>in to</u> the professor's office, we'll feel a lot less obliged to pass any information <u>on to</u> our classmates.

Q87   (A)   The McCorkendales didn't <u>used to</u> enjoy warm weather, but that was before they moved to Morocco and got <u>used to</u> summer temperatures as high as 35 degrees Celsius.

        (B)   The McCorkendales didn't <u>use to</u> enjoy warm weather, but that was before they moved to Morocco and got <u>use to</u> summer temperatures as high as 35 degrees Celsius.

        (C)   The McCorkendales didn't <u>use to</u> enjoy warm weather, but that was before they moved to Morocco and got <u>used to</u> summer temperatures as high as 35 degrees Celsius.

IDIOMS REVIEW:

Idioms my be thought of as "word expressions." Idioms, like grammar and diction, are correct or incorrect, right or wrong. Here are fifteen common idioms.

Q88   (A)   A choice must be made <u>between</u> blue <u>and</u> green.

        (B)   A choice must be made <u>between</u> blue <u>or</u> green.

Q89   (A)   Many doctors <u>consider</u> stress a more destructive influence on one's longevity than smoking, drinking, or overeating.

        (B)   Many doctors <u>consider</u> stress <u>as</u> a more destructive influence on one's longevity than smoking, drinking, or overeating.

        (C)   Many doctors <u>consider</u> stress <u>to be</u> a more destructive influence on one's longevity than smoking, drinking, or overeating.

Q90   (A)   At first women were <u>considered</u> at low risk for HIV.

        (B)   At first women were <u>considered as</u> at low risk for HIV.

        (C)   At first women were <u>considered to be</u> at low risk for HIV.

Q91   (A)   Many <u>credit</u> Gutenberg <u>as having</u> invented the printing press.

        (B)   Many <u>credit</u> Gutenberg <u>with having</u> invented the printing press.

Q92   (A)   In the movie *Silence of the Lambs*, Dr. Hannibal Lecter is <u>depicted as</u> a brilliant psychiatrist and cannibalistic serial killer who is confined as much by the steel bars of his cell as by the prison of his own mind.

(B)   In the movie *Silence of the Lambs,* Dr. Hannibal Lecter is <u>depicted to be</u> a brilliant psychiatrist and cannibalistic serial killer who is confined as much by the steel bars of his cell as by the prison of his own mind.

Q93   (A)   Only experts can <u>distinguish</u> a masterpiece <u>and</u> a fake.

        (B)   Only experts can <u>distinguish</u> a masterpiece <u>from</u> a fake.

Q94   (A)   Although medical practitioners have the technology to perform brain transplants, there is no clear evidence that they can <u>do it</u>.

        (B)   Although medical practitioners have the technology to perform brain transplants, there is no clear evidence that they can <u>do so</u>.

Q95   (A)   <u>In comparison to</u> France, Luxembourg is an amazingly small country.

        (B)   <u>In comparison with</u> France, Luxembourg is an amazingly small country.

Q96   (A)   Roger Federer won Wimbledon with a classic tennis style, <u>in contrast to</u> Bjorn Borg, who captured his titles using an unorthodox playing style.

        (B)   Roger Federer won Wimbledon with a classic tennis style, <u>in contrast with</u> Bjorn Borg, who captured his titles using an unorthodox playing style.

Q97   (A)   There is <u>more</u> talk of a single North American currency today <u>compared to</u> ten years ago.

        (B)   There is <u>more</u> talk of a single North American currency today <u>compared with</u> ten years ago.

        (C)   There is <u>more</u> talk of a single North American currency today <u>than</u> ten years ago.

Q98   (A)   I <u>prefer</u> blackjack <u>over</u> poker.

        (B)   I <u>prefer</u> blackjack <u>to</u> poker.

Q99   (A)   Rembrandt is <u>regarded as</u> the greatest painter of the Renaissance period.

        (B)   Rembrandt is <u>regarded to be</u> the greatest painter of the Renaissance period.

Q100   (A)   The speaker does a good job of <u>tying</u> motivational theory <u>to</u> obtainable results.

        (B)   The speaker does a good job of <u>tying</u> motivational theory <u>with</u> obtainable results.

Review of Grammatical Terms

The Eight Parts of Speech

There are eight parts of speech in English: nouns, pronouns, verbs, adjectives, adverbs, prepositions, conjunctions, and interjections.

Noun	A noun is a word that names a person, place, thing, or idea.
	Example: <u>Sally</u> is a nice person and you can speak freely with her.
Pronoun	A pronoun is a word used in place of a noun or another pronoun.
	Example: Sally is a nice person and <u>you</u> can speak freely with <u>her</u>.
Verb	A verb is a word that expresses an action or a state of being.
	Example: Sally <u>is</u> a nice person and you <u>can speak</u> freely with her.
Adjective	An adjective is a word used to modify or describe a noun or pronoun.
	Example: Sally is a <u>nice</u> person and you can speak freely with her. The adjective "nice" modifies the noun "person."
Adverb	An adverb is a word that modifies an adjective, a verb, or another adverb.
	Example: Sally is a nice person and you can speak <u>freely</u> with her. The word "freely" modifies the verb "speak."
Preposition	A preposition is a word that shows a relationship between two or more words.
	Example: Sally is a nice person and you can speak freely <u>with</u> her.
	Prepositions are sometimes informally referred to as words that describe "the directions a squirrel can go." Squirrels, after all, seem to be able to run, climb, or crawl in nearly every possible direction.
	Examples of prepositions include: *after, against, at, before, between, by, concerning, despite, down, for, from, in, of, off, on, onto, out, over, through, to, under, until, up, with.*
Conjunction	A conjunction is a word that joins or connects words, phrases, clauses, or sentences. Three major types of conjunctions include coordinating conjunctions, subordinating conjunctions, and correlative conjunctions.
	Example: Sally is a nice person <u>and</u> you can speak freely with her.
Interjection	An interjection is a word or a term that denotes a strong or sudden feeling. Interjections are usually, but not always, followed by an exclamation mark.
	Example: Sally is a nice person and you can speak freely with her. <u>Wow!</u>

Parts of Speech vs. The Seven Characteristics

Each of the eight parts of speech has one or more of the following characteristics: (1) gender, (2) number, (3) person, (4) case, (5) voice, (6) mood, and (7) tense. The matching of a particular part of speech with its relevant characteristics is the primary "cause" of grammar.

NOTE ↫ Adjectives, adverbs, prepositions, conjunctions, and interjections do not have gender, number, person, case, voice, mood, or tense. Only nouns, pronouns, and verbs have one or more of these seven characteristics.

Gender	Gender may be feminine or masculine. Only nouns and pronouns have gender.
	Examples: Masculine—"boy" (noun), "him" (pronoun). Feminine—"girl" (noun), "her" (pronoun).
Number	Number may be singular or plural. Only nouns, pronouns, and verbs have number.
	Examples: Singular—"home" (noun), I (pronoun), "plays" (verb). Plural—"homes" (noun), "we" (pronoun), "play" (verb).
Person	Person may be first person, second person, or third person. A person doing the speaking is considered first person; the person spoken to is considered second person; a person spoken about is considered third person. Only pronouns and verbs have person.
	Examples: First person—"I write" (pronoun + verb). Second person—"you write" (pronoun + verb). Third person—"he writes" (pronoun + verb).
	NOTE ↫ When verbs are matched with personal pronouns, verbs differ only in number with respect to third-person singular pronouns. In the third-person singular, verbs are formed with the letter "s." For example: "He or she travels." But: "I travel," "you travel," and "they travel."
Case	Case may be subjective, objective, or possessive. Only nouns and pronouns have case.
	Examples: Subjective—"Felix has a cat." ("Felix" is a noun); 'He has a cat" ("he" is a pronoun). Objective—"The cat scratched Felix." ("Felix" is a noun); "The cat scratched him." ("him" is a pronoun). Possessive—"Felix's cat has amber eyes." (Felix's is a noun); "His cat has amber eyes." ("his" is a pronoun).
	NOTE ↫ Although nouns have case, noun forms remain virtually unchanged in the subjective, objective, and possessive cases.
Voice	Voice may be active or passive. Only verbs have voice.
	Examples: Active voice—"You mailed a letter." Passive voice—"The letter was mailed by you."

In the active voice, the doer of the action is placed at the front of the sentence; the receiver of the action is placed at the back of the sentence. In the passive voice, the receiver of the action is placed at the front of the sentence while the doer of the action is relegated to the back of the sentence.

Mood Mood can be described as being indicative, imperative, or subjunctive. Only verbs have mood.

Examples: Indicative mood (makes a statement or asks a question)—"It's a nice day." Imperative mood (makes a request or gives a command)—"Please sit down." Subjunctive mood (expresses a wish or a contrary-to-fact situation)—"I wish I were in Hawaii."

Tense Tense refers to time. There are six tenses in English—present tense, past tense, future tense, present perfect tense, past perfect tense, and future perfect tense. Each of these six tenses occurs within two forms: the simple form and the progressive form.

Examples: Present tense in the simple form—"I study." Present tense in the progressive form—"I am studying."

Other Grammatical Terms

Adjective clause An adjective clause is a subordinate clause that, like an adjective, modifies a noun or pronoun.

Example: "The house that sits on top of the hill is painted in gold." The adjective clause "that sits on top of the hill" describes the "house."

Antecedent An antecedent is the word to which a pronoun refers. It is the word that the pronoun is effectively taking the place of.

Example: "The clock is broken; it is now being repaired." The pronoun "it" is substituting for the antecedent "clock."

Appositive phrase An appositive phrase is used merely for description and is typically set off by commas.

Example: "The world's oldest book, which was discovered in a tomb, is 2,500 years old."

Article An article serves to identify certain nouns. English has three articles: *a, an, the. The* is known as a definite article; *a* and *an* are known as indefinite articles. Articles are often erroneously referred to as one of the eight parts of speech.

Clause A clause is a group of related words that does have a subject and a verb.

Example: "Many people believe in psychics even though they never hear of a psychic winning the lottery." The previous sentence contains two clauses. The first clause—"many people believe in psychics"—is an independent clause, containing the subject "people" and the verb "believe." The second clause—"even though they never hear of a psychic winning the lottery"—is a dependent clause, containing the subject "they" and the verb "winning."

Collective noun

Collective nouns are nouns which represent a group.

Examples: *audience, band, bunch, class, committee, couple, crowd, family, group, herd, jury, majority, people, percent, personnel, team.*

Complement

A complement is something that completes a subject and verb. Not all sentences have complements.

Examples: "I am."—This three-letter sentence (incidentally the shortest in the English language) does not contain a complement. "I am fit."—This sentence does contain a complement; the complement is the word "fit."

Coordinating conjunction

Coordinating conjunctions join clauses of equal weight.

Examples: There are seven coordinating conjunctions in English—*and, but, yet, or, nor, for,* and *so.*

Correlative conjunction

Correlative conjunctions join clauses or phrases of equal weight. They also impose a sense of logic.

Examples: *either…or, neither…nor, not only…but (also),* and *both…and.* The word "also," appears in brackets because it is deemed optional.

Demonstrative pronoun

Demonstrative pronouns serve to point out persons or things.

Example: There are four demonstrative pronouns in English: *this, that, these,* and *those.*

Dependent clause

A dependent clause is a clause that cannot stand on its own as a complete sentence. Dependent clauses are sometimes called subordinate clauses.

Example: "Keep an umbrella with you because it's forecast for rain." The dependent clause is "because it's forecast for rain."

Direct object

A direct object (of a verb) receives the action of that verb or shows the result of that action.

Example: "The outfielder caught the ball." The word "ball" is the direct object of the verb "caught."

See also Indirect Object.

Gerund

Gerunds are verb forms that end in "ing" and function as nouns. Informally they may be referred to as "words that look like verbs but function as nouns."

Examples: "Eating vegetables is good for you." "Learning languages is rewarding." "Seeing is believing." ("Eating," "learning," "seeing," and "believing" are all gerunds.)

Indefinite pronoun

Indefinite pronouns are pronouns that do not refer to a specific antecedent.

A more complete list of indefinite pronouns includes: *all, any, anybody, anyone, anything, both, each, either, every, everybody, everyone, everything, few, many, most, neither, nobody, none, no one, nothing, one, several, some, somebody, someone,* and *something.*

Independent clause

An independent clause is a clause that can stand on its own as a complete sentence. Independent clauses are sometimes called main clauses.

Example: "I'm going to backup my computer because it might crash." The independent clause is "I'm going to backup my computer" while the subordinate clause is "because it might crash."

Indirect object

An indirect object (of a verb) precedes the direct object and usually tells to whom or for whom the action of that verb is done.

Example: "The maître d' gave us a complimentary bottle of wine." The word "us" functions as the indirect object, even though it comes before the direct object. The words "bottle of wine" serve as the direct object.

See also Direct Object.

Infinitive

Infinitives are verb forms, in which the basic form of a verb is preceded by "to." Infinitives generally function as nouns but may also function as adjectives or adverbs. Informally they may be referred to as word pairings in which the preposition "to" is placed in front of a verb.

Examples: "To see is to believe." ("To see" and "to believe" are both infinitives.)

Interrogative pronoun

Interrogative pronouns are used in questions.

Examples: *who, which, what, whom,* and *whose.*

Intransitive verb

Intransitive verbs do not require an object to complete their meaning.

Example: "He waits." The verb "waits" does not require an object to complete its meaning.

See also Transitive Verb.

Nonrestrictive clause	A nonrestrictive clause is a clause that is not essential to the meaning of a sentence. Nonrestrictive clauses are generally enclosed by commas.

Example: "The green book, which is on the top shelf, is the one you need for math class." "Which is on the top shelf" is a nonrestrictive clause.

NOTE ✑ In choosing between "that" or "which," it is common practice to use "that" with restrictive (essential) phrases and clauses and "which" with nonrestrictive (nonessential) phrases and clauses. For this reason, "that" is used with clauses that are not set off by commas and to use "which" is used with clauses that are set off by commas.

See also Restrictive Clauses.

Object

An object (of a verb) is a word or words that receives the action of a verb. An object is a special kind of complement. Objects can be either direct objects or indirect objects.

See Direct Object and Indirect Object.

Parenthetical expression

Parenthetical expressions are expressions which are set off by commas and which seek to add some clarity to a sentence.

Example: "Yogurt, on the other hand, is a fine substitute for ice-cream." "On the other hand" is a parenthetical expression and could be removed from the sentence without destroying sentence meaning.

Words commonly used as parenthetical expressions include: *after all, by the way, for example, however, incidentally, indeed, in fact, in my opinion, naturally, nevertheless, of course, on the contrary, on the other hand, to tell you the truth.*

Participle

A participle is a verb form (ending in "ed" or "ing") that can function as an adjective. A participle is a type of verbal. Refer to the definition of "verbal."

Examples: "Cars parked near emergency exits will be towed." ("Parked" is a participle; it's an adjective describing "cars." The actual verb in the sentence is "will be towed.") "A sleeping dog never bit anyone." (The participle "sleeping" describes "dog." The actual verb in the sentence is "bit.")

Participle phrase

A participle phrase (also called a participial phrase) is a group of related words that contains a participle and, as a unit, typically functions as an adjective.

Examples: "Allowing plenty of time, Bill started studying twelve weeks before taking his College Board exams." ("Allowing plenty of time" functions as a participle phrase in describing "Bill.")

Personal pronoun

A personal pronoun is a pronoun designating the person speaking, the person spoken to, or the person or thing spoken about.

The following is a complete list of personal pronouns: *I, he, her, him, his, it, its, me, mine, my, our, ours, she, their, theirs, them, they, us, we, who, whom, whose, you, your, yours.*

Phrase

A phrase is a group of words which doesn't contain both a subject and a verb.

Examples: "Learning to be happy is difficult for a variety of reasons." The phrase "for a variety of reasons" does not contain a verb.

Predicate

A predicate is one of the two principal parts of a sentence. The predicate is "any word or words that talk about the subject"; the subject is "the word or words being talked about." Technically, the word "predicate" is a broader term than the word "verb," referring to both a verb and its possible complement. It is, however, much more common to refer to the *verb* and *complement* separately. In such cases, the *verb* can be referred to as the *simple predicate*; the *predicate* is referred to as the *complete predicate*.

Examples: "Water is the key to our survival." In this sentence, the subject is "water" and the predicate is "is the key to our survival." Breaking things down further, the predicate consists of the verb "is" and the complement "the key to our survival."

Reflexive pronoun

A reflexive pronoun refers back to a given noun or pronoun.

The following is a complete list of reflexive pronouns: *herself, himself, itself, myself, ourselves, themselves, yourself.*

Relative clause

A relative clause is a group of related words that begins with a relative pronoun, and as a unit, functions as an adjective. A relative clause is commonly referred to as an adjective clause (and sometimes as a subordinate adjective clause).

Examples: "Jim Thompson, who mysteriously disappeared while going for an afternoon walk on Easter Sunday, is credited with having revitalized the silk trade in Thailand." "Who mysteriously disappeared while going for an afternoon walk on Easter Sunday" is a relative clause which serves to modify "Jim Thompson."

See also Adjective Clause and Subordinate Clause.

Relative pronoun

A relative pronoun modifies a noun or pronoun (called its antecedent). A relative pronoun also begins a relative clause (also known as a subordinate adjective clause).

Examples: There are five relative pronouns in English: *that, which, who, whom,* and *whose.*

Restrictive clause

A restrictive clause is essential to the meaning of a sentence. Restrictive clauses are not enclosed by commas.

Example: "The book that is red is the one you need for English class." "That is red" is a restrictive clause.

222

Run-on sentence	A run-on sentence refers to two sentences that are inappropriately joined together, usually by a comma.
	Example: "The weather is great, I'm going to the beach." A comma cannot join two complete sentences.
Sentence	A sentence is a group of words that contains a subject and a verb, and can stand on its own as a complete thought.
	Example: "The world is a stage." The subject is "the world" while the verb is "is"; the complete thought involves comparing the world to a stage.
Sentence fragment	A sentence fragment is a group of words that cannot stand on their own to form a complete thought.
	Example: "A fine day." This statement is a fragment. It does not constitute a complete thought and cannot stand on its own. The fragment can be turned into a sentence by adding a subject ("today") and a verb ("is")—"Today is a fine day."
	Sentence fragments are not acceptable for use in formal writing. In contrast, sentence fragments are commonly used in informal writing situations (e.g., e-mail and text messaging), and frequently seen in creative communications such as advertising, fiction writing, and poetry.
	The following sentence fragments would be acceptable in informal written communication:
	Will Michael Phelps' feat of eight Olympic gold medals in a single Olympics ever be equaled? <u>Never.</u>
	We need to bring education to the world. <u>But how?</u>
	<u>Dream on!</u> No one beats Brazil at football when its star forwards show up to play.
Split infinitive	A split infinitive occurs when a word (usually an adverb) is placed between the two words that create an infinitive (i.e., between the word "to" and its accompanying verb). Splitting an infinitive is still considered a substandard practice in formal writing.
	Example: The sentence, "To boldly go where no one has gone before," contains a split infinitive. The sentence should be rewritten, "To go boldly where no one has gone before."
Subordinate clause	A subordinate clause is a clause that cannot stand on its own as a complete sentence. It must instead be combined with at least one independent clause to form a complete sentence. Subordinate clauses are sometimes called dependent clauses.
	Example: "We should support the winning candidate whomever that may be." The subordinate clause is "whomever that may be." The independent clause is, "We should support the winning candidate."

223

Subordinating conjunction	A subordinating conjunction is a conjunction that begins an adverb clause and serves to join that clause to the rest of the sentence.

Examples: *after, although, as, as if, as long as, as though, because, before, if, in order that, provided that, since, so that, than, though, unless, until, when, whenever, where, wherever, whether, while.*

Note that many of the words in the above list, when used in different contexts, may also function as other parts of speech.

Transitive verb	Transitive verbs require an object to complete its meaning.

Example: "She posted a parcel." The verb "posted" requires an object, in this case "parcel," to complete its meaning.

See also Intransitive Verb.

Verbal	A verbal is a verb form that functions as a noun, adjective, or adverb. There are three types of verbals: gerunds, infinitives, and participles. Gerunds, infinitives, and participles can form phrases, in which case they are referred to as gerund phrases, infinitive phrases, and participle phrases.

DICTION REVIEW:

Affect, Effect

Affect is a verb meaning "to influence." *Effect* is a noun meaning "result." *Effect* is also a verb meaning "to bring about."

The change in company policy will not <u>affect</u> our pay.

The long-term <u>effect</u> of space travel is not yet known.

A good mentor seeks to <u>effect</u> positive change.

All ready, Already

All ready means "entirely ready" or "prepared." *Already* means "before or previously," but may also mean "now or soon."

Contingency plans ensure we are <u>all ready</u> in case the unexpected happens. (entirely ready or prepared)

We've <u>already</u> tried the newest brand. (before or previously)

Is it lunchtime <u>already</u>? (now or so soon)

All together, Altogether

All together means "in one group." *Altogether* has two meanings. It can mean "completely," "wholly," or "entirely." It can also mean "in total."

Those going camping must be <u>all together</u> before they can board the bus.

The recommendation is <u>altogether</u> wrong.

There are six rooms <u>altogether</u>.

NOTE ✍ The phrase "putting it all together" (four words) is correct. It means "putting it all in one place." The phrase "putting it altogether" (three words) is incorrect because it would effectively mean "putting it completely" or "putting it in total."

Assure, Ensure, Insure

Assure is to inform positively. *Insure* is to arrange for financial payment in the case of loss. Both *ensure* and *insure* are now largely interchangeable in the sense of "to make certain." *Ensure,* however, implies a kind of virtual guarantee. *Insure* implies the taking of precautionary or preventative measures.

Don't worry. I <u>assure</u> you I'll be there by 8 a.m.

When shipping valuable antiques, a sender must <u>insure</u> any piece for its market value in the event it's damaged or lost.

Hard work is the best way to <u>ensure</u> success regardless of the endeavor.

Every large jewelry shop maintains an on-site safe to <u>insure</u> that inventory is secure during closing hours. (taking of precautionary measures)

Better, Best

Better is used when comparing two things. *Best* is used when comparing three or more things.

Comparing Dan with Joe, Joe is the <u>better</u> cyclist.

Tina is the <u>best</u> student in the class.

Between, Among

Use *between* to discuss two things. Use *among* to discuss three or more things.

The jackpot was divided <u>between</u> two winners.

Five plaintiffs were <u>among</u> the recipients of a cash settlement.

Complement, Compliment

Both complement or compliment can be used as nouns or verbs. As a verb, *complement* means "to fill in," "to complete," or "to add to and make better"; as a noun it means "something that completes" or "something that improves." *Compliment* is used in two related ways. It is either "an expression of praise" (noun) or is used "to express praise" (verb).

A visit to the Greek islands is a perfect <u>complement</u> to any tour of bustling Athens. Visitors to the Greek island of Mykonos, for instance, are always struck by how the blue ocean <u>complements</u> the white, coastal buildings.

Throughout the awards ceremony, winners and runner-ups received <u>compliments</u> on a job well done. At closing, it was the attendees that <u>complimented</u> the organizers on a terrific event.

Complementary, Complimentary

Both words are used as adjectives. Like complement, *complementary* means "to make complete," "to enhance," or "to improve" (e.g., complementary plans). *Complimentary* means "to praise" (e.g., complementary remarks) or "to receive or supply free of charge."

Only one thing is certain in the world of haute couture: fashion parties brimming with <u>complimentary</u> Champagne and endless banter on how colorful characters and <u>complementary</u> personalities rose to the occasion.

Differs from, Differ with

Use *differ from* in discussing characteristics. Use *differ with* to convey the idea of disagreement.

American English <u>differs from</u> British English.

The clerk <u>differs with</u> her manager on his decision to hire an additional salesperson.

Different from, Different than

These two word pairings are interchangeable. However, whereas *different from* is used to compare two nouns or phases, *different than* is commonly used when what follows is a clause.

Dolphins are <u>different from</u> porpoises.

My old neighborhood is <u>different than</u> it used to be.

Each other, One another

Use *each other* when referring to two people. Use *one another* when referring to more than two people.

Two weight lifters helped spot <u>each other</u>.

Olympic athletes compete against <u>one another</u>.

Farther, Further

Use *farther* when referring to distance. Use *further* in all other situations, particularly when referring to extent or degree.

The town is one mile <u>farther</u> along the road.

We must pursue this idea <u>further</u>.

Fewer, Less

Fewer refers to things that can be counted, e.g., people, marbles, accidents. *Less* refers to things that cannot be counted, e.g., money, water, sand.

There are <u>fewer</u> students in class than before the midterm exam.

There is <u>less</u> water in the bucket due to evaporation.

If, Whether

Use *if* to express one possibility, especially conditional statements. Use *whether* to express two (or more) possibilities.

The company claims that you will be successful <u>if</u> you listen to their tapes on motivation.

Success depends on <u>whether</u> one has desire and determination. (The implied "whether or not" creates two possibilities.)

NOTE ◈ In colloquial English, *if* and *whether* are now interchangeable. Either of the following sentences would be correct: "I'm not sure <u>whether</u> I'm going to the party."/"I'm not sure <u>if</u> I'm going to the party."

Infer, Imply

Infer means "to draw a conclusion"; readers or listeners infer. *Imply* means "to hint" or to suggest"; speakers or writers imply.

I <u>infer</u> from your letter that conditions have improved.

Do you mean to <u>imply</u> that conditions have improved?

Lie, Lay

In the present tense, *lie* means "to rest" and *lay* means "to put" or "to place." Lie is an intransitive verb (a verb that does not require a direct object to complete its meaning), while lay is a transitive verb (a verb that requires a direct object to complete its meaning).

Lie

Present	<u>Lie</u> on the sofa.
Past	He <u>lay</u> down for an hour.
Perfect Participle	He <u>has lain</u> there for an hour.
Present Participle	It was nearly noon and he was still <u>lying</u> on the sofa.

Lay

Present	<u>Lay</u> the magazine on the table.
Past	She <u>laid</u> the magazine there yesterday.
Perfect Participle	She <u>has laid</u> the magazine there many times.
Present Participle	<u>Laying</u> the magazine on the table, she stood up and left the room.

NOTE ✍ There is no such word as "layed." This word is the mistaken misspelling of "laid." Ex. "A magazine cover that is professionally laid out," not "a magazine cover that is professionally layed out."

Like, Such as

Such as is used for listing items in a series. *Like* should not be used for listing items in a series. However, *like* is okay to use when introducing a single item.

A beginning rugby player must master many different skills <u>such as</u> running and passing, blocking and tackling, drop kicking, and scrum control.

Dark fruits, <u>like</u> beets, have an especially good cleansing quality.

Might, May

Although *might* and *may* both express a degree of uncertainty, they have somewhat different meanings. *Might* expresses more uncertainty than does *may*. Also, only *might* is the correct choice when referring to past situations.

I <u>might</u> like to visit the Taj Mahal someday. (much uncertainty)

I <u>may</u> go sightseeing this weekend. (less uncertainty)

They <u>might</u> have left a message for us at the hotel. (past situation)

Number, Amount

Use *number* when speaking of things that can be counted. Use *amount* when speaking of things that cannot be counted.

The <u>number</u> of marbles in the bag is seven.

The <u>amount</u> of topsoil has eroded considerably.

Passed, Past

Passed functions as a verb. *Past* functions as a noun, adjective, or preposition.

Yesterday, Cindy found out that she <u>passed</u> her much-feared anatomy exam.

The proactive mind does not dwell on events of the <u>past</u>.

Principal, Principle

Although *principal* can refer to the head administrator of a school or even an original amount of money on loan, it is usually used as an adjective meaning "main," "primary," or "most important." *Principle* is used in one of two senses: to refer to a general scientific law or to describe a person's fundamental belief system.

Lack of clearly defined goals is the principal cause of failure.

To be a physicist one must clearly understand the principles of mathematics.

A person of principle lives by a moral code.

That, Which

The words *which* and *that* mean essentially the same thing. But in context they are used differently. It is common practice to use *which* with nonrestrictive (nonessential) phrases and clauses and to use *that* with restrictive (essential) phrases and clauses. Nonrestrictive phrases are typically enclosed with commas, whereas restrictive phrases are never enclosed with commas. This treatment means that *which* appears in phrases set off by commas whereas *that* does not appear in phrases set off by commas.

The insect that has the shortest lifespan is the Mayfly.

The Mayfly, which lives less than 24 hours, has the shortest lifespan of any insect.

That, Which, Who

In general, *who* is used to refer to people, *which* is used to refer to things, and *that* can refer to either people or things. When referring to people, the choice between *that* and *who* should be based on what feels more natural.

Choose a person that can take charge.

The person who is most likely to succeed is often not an obvious choice.

On occasion, *who* is used to refer to non-persons while *which* may refer to people.

I have a dog who is animated and has a great personality.

Which child won the award? (The pronoun which is used to refer to a person.)

Who, Whom

"Who" is the subjective form of the pronoun and "whom" is the objective form. The following is a good rule in deciding between *who* and *whom*: If "he, she, or they" can be substituted for a pronoun in context, the correct form is *who*. If "him, her, or them" can be substituted for a pronoun in context, the correct form is *whom*. Another very useful rule is that pronouns take their objective forms when they are the direct objects of prepositions.

Let's reward the person <u>who</u> can find the best solution.

Test: "He" or "she" can find the best solution, so the subjective form of the pronoun—"who"—is correct.

The report was compiled by <u>whom</u>?

Test: This report was drafted by "him" or "her," so the objective form of the pronoun—"whom"—is correct. Another way of confirming this is to note that "whom" functions as the direct object of the preposition "by," so the objective form of the pronoun is correct.

NOTE ✦ One particularly tricky situation occurs in the following: "She asked to speak to <u>whoever</u> was on duty." At first glance, it looks as though "whomever" should be correct in so far as "who" appears to be the object of the preposition "to." However, in fact, the whole clause "whoever was on duty" is functioning as the direct object of the preposition "to." The key is to analyze the function of "whoever" within the applicable clause itself; in this case, "whoever" is functioning as the subject of the verb "was," thereby taking the subjective form. We can test this by saying *"he or she was on duty."*

Let's analyze two more situations, each introduced by a sentence that contains correct usage.

(1) "I will interview <u>whomever</u> I can find for the job." The important thing is to analyze the role of "whomever" within the clause "whomever I can find" and test it as "I can find *him* or *her.*" This confirms that the objective form of the pronoun is correct. In this instance, the whole clause "whomever I can find" is modifying the verb form "will interview."

(2) "I will give the position to <u>whoever</u> I think is right for the job." Again, the critical thing is to analyze the role of "whoever" within the clause "whoever I think is right for the job." Since we can say "I think he or she is right for the job," this confirms that the subjective form of the pronoun is correct. In this instance, the whole clause "whoever I think is right for the job" is modifying the preposition "to." Therefore, this example mirrors the previous example, "She asked to speak to <u>whoever</u> was on duty."

200 Grammatical Idioms

Here is a list of the 200 most common grammatical idioms that a candidate is likely to encounter when preparing for the GMAT exam. Grammatical idioms are "grammatical phraseologies" that are deemed right or wrong simple because "that is the way they are written or spoken in English."

ABC

1. able to X
2. account for
3. according to
4. a craving for
5. a debate over
6. a descendant of
7. affiliated with
8. agree to (a plan or action)
9. agree with (person/idea)
10. allow(s) for
11. amount to
12. a native of
13. angry at/angry with
14. appeal to
15. apply to/apply for
16. approve(d) of/disapprove(d) of
17. a responsibility to
18. argue with/over
19. a sequence of
20. as a consequence of X
21. as...as
22. as...as do/as...as does
23. as a result of
24. as good as
25. as good as or better than
26. as great as
27. as many X as Y
28. as much as
29. as X is to Y
30. ask X to do Y
31. associate with
32. attempt to
33. attend to
34. attest to
35. attribute X to Y
36. assure that
37. averse to
38. based on

39. be afraid of
40. because of
41. believe X to be Y
42. better served by X than by Y
43. better than
44. between X and Y
45. both X and Y
46. capable of
47. centers on
48. choice of
49. choose from/choose to
50. claim to be
51. collaborate with
52. compare(d) to/compare(d) with
53. comply with
54. composed of
55. concerned about/concerned with (not "concerned at")
56. conform to
57. conclude that
58. connection between X and Y
59. consider(ed) (without "to be")
60. consider(ed) (with "to be")
61. consistent with
62. contend that
63. contrast X with Y
64. convert to
65. cost of/cost to
66. credit(ed) X with having

DEF

67. debate over
68. decide on/decide to
69. declare X to be Y
70. defend against
71. define(d) as
72. delighted by
73. demand that
74. demonstrate that

75.	depend(ent) on		111.	indifferent toward(s)
76.	depends on whether		112.	infected with
77.	depict(ed) as		113.	inherit X from Y
78.	descend(ed) from		114.	in order to
79.	desirous of		115.	in reference to/with reference to
80.	determined by		116.	in regard to/with regard to
81.	differ from/differ with		117.	in search of
82.	different from		118.	insists that
83.	difficult to		119.	intend(ed) to
84.	disagree with (person/idea)		120.	intersection of X and Y
85.	discourage from		121.	in the same way as...to
86.	differentiate between X and Y		122.	in the same way that
87.	differentiate X from Y		123.	introduce(d) to
88.	dispute whether		124.	in violation of
89.	distinguish X from Y		125.	isolate(d) from
90.	divergent from			
91.	do so/doing so (not "do it"/"doing it")		**JKL**	
92.	doubt that			
93.	draw on		126.	just as X, so (too) Y
94.	either X or Y		127.	less X than Y
95.	enable X to Y		128.	likely to/likely to be
96.	enamored of/with		129.	liken to
97.	enough X that Y			
98.	estimated to be		**MNO**	
99.	expect to			
100.	expose(d) to		130.	meet with
101.	fascinated by		131.	mistake (mistook) X for Y
102.	fluctuations in		132.	model(ed) after
103.	forbid X and Y		133.	more common among X than among Y
104.	frequency of		134.	more...than ever
105.	from X rather than from Y (not "from X instead of Y")		135.	more X than Y
			136.	native to
106.	from X to Y		137.	neither X nor Y
			138.	no less...than
GHI			139.	no less was X than was Y
			140.	not X but rather Y
107.	give credit for/give credit to		141.	not only X but (also) Y
108.	hypothesize that		142.	not so much X as Y
109.	in an effort to		143.	on account of
110.	in association with		144.	on the one hand/on the other hand

PQR

145. opposed to/opposition to
146. opposite of
147. inclined to
148. in comparison to
149. in conjunction with
150. in contrast to
151. in danger of
152. independent from
153. owing to
154. persuade X to Y
155. partake (partook) of
156. permit X to Y
157. potential to
158. prefer X to Y (not "prefer X over Y")
159. preferable to
160. prejudiced against
161. prevent from
162. prized by
163. prohibit X from Y
164. protect against
165. question whether
166. range(s) from X to Y
167. rates for (not "rates of")
168. recover from X
169. recover X from Y
170. regard(ed) as
171. replace(d) with
172. responsible for
173. resulting in

STU

174. sacrifice X for Y
175. seem to indicate
176. similar to
177. so as not to be hindered by
178. so X as to be Y
179. so X as to constitute Y
180. so X that Y

181. subscribe to
182. such X as Y and Z
183. sympathy for
184. sympathize with
185. tamper with
186. targeted at
187. the more X the greater Y
188. the same to X as to Y
189. to result in
190. to think of X as Y
191. tying X to Y
192. used to (not "use to")

VWXZY

193. view X as Y
194. whether X or Y
195. worry about (not "over")
196. X enough to Y
197. X instead of Y
198. X is attributed to Y
199. X out of Y (numbers)
200. X regarded as Y

Style Review

Style was not tested on the *100-Question Quiz*, although grammar, diction, and idioms were. Style is, however, tested within the multiple-choice problems that follow in this chapter.

Passive vs. Active Voice

As a general rule of style, favor the active voice, not the passive voice (all things being equal).

Less effective:	Sally <u>was</u> loved by Harry.
More effective:	Harry loved Sally.

Less effective:	In pre-modern times, medical surgery <u>was</u> often performed by inexperienced and ill-equipped practitioners.
More effective:	In pre-modern times, inexperienced and ill-equipped practitioners often performed medical surgery.

In a normal subject-verb-object sentence, the doer of the action appears at the front of the sentence while the receiver of the action appears at the back of the sentence. Passive sentences are less direct because they reverse the normal subject-verb-object sentence order; the receiver of the action becomes the subject of the sentence and the doer of the action becomes the object of the sentence. Passive sentences may also fail to mention the doer of the action.

Less effective:	Errors <u>were</u> found in the report.
More effective:	The report contained errors.
	The <u>reviewer</u> found errors in the report.

Less effective:	Red Cross volunteers should <u>be</u> generously praised for their efforts.
More effective:	<u>Citizens</u> should generously praise Red Cross volunteers for their efforts.
	<u>We</u> should generously praise Red Cross volunteers for their efforts.

How can we recognize a passive sentence? Here's a quick list of six words that signal a passive sentence: *be, by, was, were, been,* and *being.* For the record, "by" is a preposition, not a verb form, but it frequently appears in sentences that are passive.

Nominalizations

A guiding rule of style is that we should prefer verbs (and adjectives) to nouns. Verbs are considered more powerful than nouns. In other words, a general rule in grammar is that we shouldn't change verbs (or adjectives) into nouns. The technical name for this no-no is "nominalization"; we shouldn't nominalize.

Avoid changing verbs into nouns:

Less effective:	<u>reduction</u> of costs
More effective:	<u>reduce</u> costs

Less effective:	<u>development</u> of a five-year plan
More effective:	<u>develop</u> a five-year plan

Less effective:	<u>reliability</u> of the data
More effective:	<u>rely</u> on the data

In the previous three examples, the more effective versions represent verbs, not nouns. So "reduction of costs" is best written "reduce costs," "development of a five-year plan" is best written "develop a five-year plan," and "reliability of the data" is best written "rely on the data."

Avoid changing adjectives into nouns:

Less effective:	<u>precision</u> of instruments
More effective:	<u>precise</u> instruments

Less effective:	<u>creativity</u> of individuals
More effective:	<u>creative</u> individuals

Less effective:	<u>reasonableness</u> of the working hours
More effective:	<u>reasonable</u> working hours

In the latter three examples above, the more effective versions represent adjectives, not nouns. So "precision of instruments" is best written "precise instruments," "creativity of individuals" is best written "creative individuals," and "reasonableness of the working hours" is best written "reasonable working hours."

Brevity/Redundancy

As a general rule, less is more. Consider options that express the same ideas in fewer words without changing the meaning of a sentence. Sometimes opportunities exist to delete words that are merely redundant.

Less effective:	We want to hire the second candidate <u>owing to the fact that</u> he is humorous and has many good ideas.
More effective:	We want to hire the second candidate <u>because</u> he is humorous and has many good ideas.

Less effective:	A movie director's <u>skill</u>, <u>training</u>, and <u>technical ability</u> cannot make up for a poor script.
More effective:	A movie director's <u>skill</u> cannot make up for a poor script.

Weak Openers

Beginning a sentence with "it is" or "there is/there are" is grounds for a weak opener. Consider options which rephrase the sentence by deleting these opening words.

Less effective:	<u>It is</u> obvious that dogs make better pets than hamsters.
More effective:	Dogs make better pets than hamsters.

Less effective:	<u>There is</u> considerable evidence that a better diet will make you feel better.
More effective:	A better diet will make you feel better.

Answers to the 100-Question Quiz on Grammar, Diction, and Idioms

Q1   An office clerk and a machinist <u>were</u> present but unhurt by the on-site explosion.

Q2   Eggs and bacon <u>is</u> Tiffany's favorite breakfast.

The words "eggs" and "bacon" are intimately connected and deemed to be a signal unit.

Q3   In the game of chess, capturing one knight or three pawns <u>yield</u> the same point value

The subject "pawns" is plural and requires the plural verb "are."

Q4   A seventeenth-century oil painting, along with several antique vases, <u>has</u> been placed on the auction block.

Q5   The purpose of the executive, administrative, and legislative branches of government <u>is</u> to provide a system of checks and balances.

The subject of the sentence is "purpose." The prepositional phrase "of the executive, administrative, and legislative branches of government" does not affect the verb choice.

Q6   Here <u>are</u> the introduction and chapters one through five.

The compound subject "introduction *and* chapters one through five" necessitates using the plural verb "are."

Q7   <u>Are</u> there any squash courts available?

One helpful tip is to first express this as a declarative sentence: "There are squash courts available." Now it is easier to see that the subject is plural—squash courts—and a plural verb *are* is appropriate.

Q8   Entertaining multiple goals <u>makes</u> a person's life stressful.

"Entertaining multiple goals" is a gerund phrase that acts as the subject of the sentence (singular).

Q9   One in every three new businesses <u>fails</u> within the first five years of operation.

Q10   Few of the students, if any, <u>are</u> ready for the test.

The phrase "if any" is parenthetical, and in no way affects the plurality of the sentence.

Q11   Some of the story <u>makes</u> sense.

Q12   Some of the comedians <u>were</u> hilarious.

Q13   None of the candidates <u>have</u> any previous political experience.

Note that if "neither" was used in place of "none," the correct sentence would read: "Neither of the candidates <u>has</u> any political experience." "Neither" is an indefinite pronoun that is always singular. "None" is an indefinite pronoun that is singular or plural depending on context. The fact that "none" takes "have" and "neither" would take "has" is indeed a peculiarity.

Q14   Either Johann or Cecilia <u>is</u> qualified to act as manager.

Q15   Neither management nor workers <u>are</u> satisfied with the new contract.

Q16   Our group <u>is</u> meeting at 6 p.m.

Q17   A group of latecomers <u>were</u> escorted to their seats.

Q18   The number of road accidents <u>has</u> decreased.

Q19   A number of train accidents <u>have</u> occurred.

Q20   Fifty percent of video gaming <u>is</u> having great reflexes.

Q21   Two-thirds of their classmates <u>have</u> wakeboards.

Q22   Ten dollars <u>is</u> an average daily wage for many people in the developing word.

Q23   The present is from Beth and <u>her</u>.

Q24   Cousin Vinny and <u>he</u> are both valedictorians.

Q25   Between you and <u>me</u>, this plan makes a lot of sense.

The pronoun "me" (the objective form of the pronoun "I") is the direct object of the preposition "between."

Q26   Do not ask for <u>whom</u> the bell tolls.

The pronoun "whom" (the objective form of the pronoun "who") is the direct object of the preposition "for."

Q27   People like you and <u>me</u> should know better.

The objective form of the pronoun—"me"—must follow the preposition "like."

Q28   My nephew is taller than <u>I</u>.

In order to test this: My nephew is taller than <u>I am</u>.

Q29   We skate as fast as <u>they</u>.

Test this: We skate as fast as <u>they do</u>.

Q30   During our group presentation, our teacher asked you more questions than <u>me</u>.

Test this: During our group presentation, our teacher asked you more questions than <u>she or he asked me</u>.

Q31   The woman <u>who</u> is responsible for pension planning is Mrs. Green.

She is responsible for city planning; "he/she" is substitutable for "who."

Q32   This gift is intended for <u>whom</u>?

The gift is intended for *him* or *her*; "him/her" is substitutable for "whom."

Q33   The tour leader told Julie and <u>me</u> to turn off our cell phones.

Q34   Young Robert hurt <u>himself</u> while climbing alone.

Q35   A not-for-profit, like any other organization, has <u>its</u> own rules and regulations to follow.

Q36   Everybody should mind <u>his or her</u> own business.

Q37   Sam never argues with his father when <u>Sam</u> is drunk.

The sentence "Sam never argues with his father when he is drunk" is grammatically correct but contextually vague. It is contextually vague because we may feel that it is Sam who is drunk whereas, grammatically, it is Sam's father who is actually drunk (a pronoun modifies the nearest noun that came before it; here the pronoun "he" modifies the noun "father"). The sentence needs to be rephrased to clear up potential ambiguity. The most direct way to achieve this is to replace the pronoun "he" with the noun it is intended to refer to, namely Sam. Note that another way to clear up this ambiguity is to restructure this sentence as follows: "When <u>he</u> is drunk, Sam never argues with his father."

Q38   To know that a person can't vote is to know that <u>he or she doesn't</u> have a voice.

A "person" is a noun in the third person and the correct answer must be a pronoun that matches it in the third person.

Other correct options would include:

To know that a person can't vote is to know that <u>a person doesn't</u> have a voice.

To know that a person can't vote is to know that <u>one doesn't</u> have a voice.

Q39   One cannot really understand another country until <u>one has</u> studied its history and culture.

We have essentially five ways to validate this sentence—"one has," "a person has," "he has," "she has," or "he or she has." In the latter option, using "he or she has" keeps writing gender neutral (politically correct). The grammatical reason that the original does the work is because "one" is a third-person singular pronoun while "they" is a third-person plural pronoun. Thus, we have a pronoun shift or a shift in viewpoint. Any answer must also be in the third-person singular. Given the opportunity to rewrite the original sentence, two other correct options would also include:

You cannot really understand another country unless <u>you have</u> studied its history and culture.

Here, the second-person pronoun "you" is matched with the second-person pronoun "you."

We cannot really understand another country unless <u>we have</u> studied its history and culture. Here, the first-person plural pronoun "we" is matched with the first-person plural pronoun "we."

Q40   He <u>frequently</u> told her he wanted to marry her.

Q41   The janitor was surprised to find termites <u>coming out of the wood</u>.

Q42   After writing the introduction, <u>I</u> easily drafted the rest of the report.

Q43   Walking along the shore, <u>the couple</u> could see fish jumping in the lake.

Q44   She said she had <u>a copy of the map</u> lying in her office.

          She is presently not in her office but the map is.

          Also: While we were sitting in her office, she told me she had a copy of the map.

          She is in her office with or without the map.

Q45   In addition to building organizational skills, <u>I also honed my team-building skills during the summer internship</u>.

Q46   An incredibly complex mechanism, <u>the brain</u> has some 10 billion nerve cells.

Q47   <u>On the basis of our observations, we believe the project will succeed.</u>

          Firstly, "the project" is not based on our observations. Observations must be made by people, so "we" is an appropriate substitute. Secondly, the phrase "based on" is incorrect because we cannot be physically standing on our observations or attached to them. The correct phraseology is "on the basis of." In general, "based on" is not an appropriate modifier to use with people; but it's fine for inanimate objects, e.g., a movie based on a book.

Q48   In the summer before college, Max <u>waited</u> tables, <u>sold</u> magazines, and even <u>delivered</u> pizzas.

Q49   Our neighbors went <u>to</u> London, Athens, and Rome.

Q50   Our neighbors went <u>to</u> London, <u>to</u> Athens, and <u>to</u> Rome.

Q51   Jonathan likes <u>not only</u> rugby <u>but also</u> kayaking.

Here the verb "likes" is placed before the "not only…but also" correlative conjunction, creating parallelism between the words "rugby" and "kayaking."

Q52   Jonathan <u>not only likes</u> rugby <u>but also likes</u> kayaking.

Here, the verb "likes" is repeated after each component part of the "not only…but also" construction. Thus the words "likes rugby" and "likes kayaking" are parallel.

Q53   <u>To examine</u> the works of William Shakespeare—his plays and poetry—is <u>to marvel</u> at one man's seemingly incomparable depth of literary expression.

The infinitives "to examine" and "to marvel" are parallel.

Q54   In the *Phantom of the Opera* play, the music <u>is</u> terrific and the stage props <u>are</u> superb.

Since the verbs are different (i.e., "is" and "are"), we must write them out.

NOTE ✎ Rules of ellipsis govern the acceptable omission of words in writing and speech. There is no need to say, "Paris <u>is</u> a large and <u>is</u> an exciting city." We can say, "Paris <u>is</u> a large and an exciting city." The verb (i.e., "is") is the same throughout the sentence, so there's no need to write it out. Note, however, that the articles "a" and "an" are different and must be written out. Omitting the "an" in the second half of the sentence would result in an incorrect sentence: "Paris is a large and exciting city."

Q55   The defendant's own testimony on the stand neither contributed <u>to</u> nor detracted from his claim of innocence.

Since the prepositions are different, we cannot omit either of them

NOTE ✎ As a follow-up example, there is no need to say, "*The Elements of Style* <u>was written</u> by William Strunk, Jr., and <u>was written</u> by E. B. White." Since the verb form "was written" and the preposition "by" are the same when applied to both authors, we can simply say, "*The Elements of Style* was written by William Strunk, Jr., and E. B. White."

Q56   Between Tom and Brenda, Tom is <u>better</u> at math.

Q57   Among our group, Jeff is the <u>wealthiest</u> person.

Q58   Of all the roses grown in our neighborhood, Chauncey Gardiner's grow the <u>most</u> vigorously.

Q59   Chauncey Gardiner's roses grow <u>more</u> vigorously than any other in the neighborhood.

Q60   Tokyo's population is greater than the <u>population</u> of Beijing.

Q61   Tokyo's population is greater than Beijing's <u>population</u>.

Q62   Tokyo's population is greater than that of <u>Beijing</u>.

In the above example, the demonstrative pronoun "that" substitutes for the words "the population," and we are effectively saying: "Tokyo's population is greater than <u>the population of Beijing</u>."

NOTE ∽ It is incorrect to write: "Tokyo's population is greater than <u>that of Beijing's</u>." Such a sentence would read: "Tokyo's population is greater than the population of Beijing's (population)."

Q63   Tokyo's population is greater than <u>Beijing's</u>.

        Also: Tokyo's population is greater than <u>Beijing's population</u>.

        Also: Tokyo's population is greater than <u>that of Beijing</u>.

        Also: Tokyo's population is greater than <u>the population of Beijing</u>.

Q64   Of all the countries contiguous to India, <u>Pakistan has the most strongly defended borders</u>.

        The following would <u>not</u> be a correct solution: "Of all the countries contiguous to India, <u>the borders of Pakistan are most strongly defended</u>."

Q65   The attention span of a dolphin is greater than <u>that of</u> a chimpanzee.

Q66   The requirements of a medical degree are more stringent than <u>those of</u> a law degree.

Q67   Like <u>those of</u> many politicians, the senator's promises sounded good but ultimately led to nothing.

        Alternatively, we could use the words "like the promises of" in the following manner: "Like <u>the promises of</u> many politicians, the senator's promises sounded good but ultimately led to nothing." Ignoring the fill-in-the-blank, we could also write: "Like many politicians' promises, the senator's promises…"

Q68   No one hits home runs <u>like</u> Barry Bonds.

        "Like Barry Bonds" is a phrase. A phrase is a group of words that lacks a verb.

Q69   No one pitches <u>as</u> Roy Halladay does.

        "As Roy Halladay does" is a clause. A clause is a group of words that contains a verb.

Q70   My dog barks when he <u>sees</u> my neighbor's cat.

        The simple present tense "barks" is consistent with the simple present tense "sees."

Q71   Yesterday afternoon, smoke <u>filled</u> the sky and sirens sounded.

        The simple past tense verb "filled" is consistent with the simple past tense verb "sounded."

Q72   Tomorrow, we <u>will go</u> to the football game.

Q73   We are raising money for the new scholarship fund. So far we <u>have raised</u> $25,000.

Q74   By the time I began playing golf, I <u>had played</u> tennis for three hours.

        The playing of tennis precedes the playing of golf for these two past tense events.

Q75   Larry <u>had studied</u> Russian for five years before he went to work in Moscow.

        The past perfect tense is constructed using the auxiliary "had" and the past participle of the verb, in this case "studied." The past perfect tense clarifies the sequence of two past tense events. Here, it is clear that Larry first studied Russian and then went to Moscow.

        Question: What is the difference between the following two sentences?

        1) Larry <u>had studied</u> Russian for five years before he went to work in Moscow.

        2) Larry <u>studied</u> Russian for five years before he went to work in Moscow.

        Most grammar experts side with sentence 1 as the correct and preferable choice. However, some experts would argue that sentence 2 is equally correct. Sentence 2 uses two past tense verbs (i.e., "studied" and "went") as well as the temporal word "before." It can be argued that the combined use of the past perfect "had" and temporal words (e.g., *before, after, previously, prior, subsequently*), as seen in sentence 1, creates a redundancy, and that when the sequence of two past tense events is clear, particularly through the use of temporal word(s), the use of the past perfect tense is considered optional. Look for sentence 1 to be the correct choice for GMAT test-taking purposes.

Q76   By the time evening arrives, we <u>will have finished</u> the task at hand.

        The future act of finishing the task at hand will occur before evening arrives.

Q77   Sometimes she wishes she <u>were</u> on a tropical island having a drink at sunset.

        Expresses a wish; the subjunctive "were," not "was," is the correct choice.

Q78   If I <u>were</u> you, I would be feeling quite optimistic.

        Indicates a hypothetical, contrary-to-fact situation; "were," not "was," is the correct choice.

Q79   If economic conditions further deteriorate, public confidence <u>will</u> plummet.

        "Will" is correct in future events with implied certainty; we are making a statement about the future in absolute terms. The sentence is written in the form of "If *x* happens, then *y* will happen."

Q80   If economic conditions were to further deteriorate, public confidence <u>would</u> plummet.

Note that the inclusion of "were," when coupled with "would," signals the subjunctive mood.

Q81   If my taxes are less than $10,000, I <u>will</u> pay that amount immediately.

"Will" is correct when dealing with future events with implied certainty.

Q82   If oil <u>were</u> still abundant, there <u>would</u> be no energy crisis.

This situation is clearly contrary to fact. Oil is not abundant, and there is an energy crisis; "were" and "would" are used to signal the subjunctive.

Q83   Choice B
<u>Every one</u> of the makeup exams is tough, but <u>anyone</u> who misses a scheduled test with good cause is entitled to write one.

The words *anyone* and *any one* are not interchangeable. *Anyone* means "any person" whereas *any one* means "any single person or thing." Likewise, the words *everyone* and *every one* are not interchangeable. *Everyone* means "everybody in a group" whereas *every one* means "each person."

Q84   Choice B
The green book, <u>which</u> is on the top shelf, is the one you need for math. The book <u>that</u> is red is the one you need for grammar.

It is common practice to use *which* with nonrestrictive (nonessential) phrases or clauses and to use *that* with restrictive (essential) phrases or clauses. Nonrestrictive phrases are typically enclosed with commas, whereas restrictive phrases are never enclosed with commas. "Which is on the top shelf" is a nonrestrictive (nonessential) phrase. It is optional. We can omit it, and the sentence will still make sense. "That is red" is a restrictive (essential) phrase. It is not optional. Without it the sentence will not make sense.

Q85   Choice A
<u>Let's</u> cherish the poem "In Flanders Fields." Remembering those who fought for our freedom <u>lets</u> us live easier.

Let's is a contraction for "let us"; *lets* is a verb meaning "to allow" or "to permit." This sentence could have been rewritten: <u>Let us</u> cherish the poem "In Flanders Fields." Remembering those who fought for our freedom *allows* us to live easier.

Q86   Choice C
Once we turn these dreaded assignments <u>in to</u> the professor's office, we'll feel a lot less obliged to pass information <u>on to</u> our classmates.

The words *into* and *in to* are not interchangeable. Likewise, the words *onto* and *on to* are not interchangeable. Case in point: Turning assignments *into* the professor's office is a magician's trick! Passing information *onto* our classmates would mean physically putting the information on them.

Q87   Choice C

The McCorkendales didn't <u>use to</u> fancy warm weather, but that was before they moved to Morocco and got <u>used to</u> summer temperatures as high as 35 degrees Celsius.

Although *used to* and *use to* are largely interchangeable in spoken English, because the letter "d" is inaudible in many oral contexts, this is not the case in formal writing. The correct form for habitual action is *used to*, not *use to*. Example: "We <u>used to</u> go to the movies all the time." However, when *did* precedes "use(d) to" the correct form is "use to." This is commonly the case in questions and negative constructions. Example: Didn't you <u>use to</u> live on a farm? I didn't <u>use to</u> daydream.

Q88   Choice A
        Idiom: *Between X and Y*

A choice must be made <u>between</u> blue <u>and</u> green.

Q89   Choice A
        Idiom: *Consider(ed)* – not followed by *"to be"*

Many doctors <u>consider</u> stress a more destructive influence on one's longevity than smoking, drinking, or overeating.

Consider/considered is not followed by "to be" (or "as") when *consider(ed)* is followed by a direct object and used in the sense that some person or organization considers something to have some perceived quality. The word "stress" functions as a direct object of the verb *consider*, and the perceived quality is the "destructive influence" of stress.

Q90   Choice C
        Idiom: *Consider(ed)* – followed by *"to be"*

At first women were <u>considered to be</u> at low risk for HIV.

Consider/considered is followed by "to be" when *consider(ed)* has the meaning of "believed to be" or "thought to be."

Q91   Choice B
        Idioms: *Credit(ed) X with having*

Many <u>credit</u> Gutenberg <u>with having</u> invented the printing press.

Q92   Choice A
        Idiom: *Depicted as*

In the movie *Silence of the Lambs*, Dr. Hannibal Lecter is <u>depicted as</u> a brilliant psychiatrist and cannibalistic serial killer who is confined as much by the steel bars of his cell as by the prison of his own mind.

Q93   Choice B
Idiom: *Distinguish X from Y*

Only experts can <u>distinguish</u> a masterpiece <u>from</u> a fake.

Q94   Choice B
Idiom: *Do so*

Although doctors have the technology to perform brain transplants, there is no clear evidence that they can <u>do so</u>.

Q95   Choice A
Idiom: *In comparison to*

<u>In comparison to</u> France, Luxembourg is an amazingly small country.

Q96   Choice A
Idiom: *In contrast to*

Roger Federer won Wimbledon with a classic tennis style, <u>in contrast to</u> Bjorn Borg, who captured his titles using an unorthodox playing style.

Q97   Choice C
Idiom: *More…than/(Less…than)*

There is <u>more</u> talk of a single North American currency today <u>than</u> ten years ago.

Q98   Choice B
Idiom: *Prefer X to Y*

I <u>prefer</u> blackjack <u>to</u> poker.

Q99   Choice A
Idiom: *Regarded as*

Rembrandt is <u>regarded as</u> the greatest painter of the Renaissance period.

Q100   Choice A
Idiom: *Tying X to Y*

The speaker does a good job of <u>tying</u> motivational theory <u>to</u> obtainable results.

MULTIPLE-CHOICE PROBLEMS

Subject-Verb Agreement

1. Vacation (𝒮)

   Neither Martha or her sisters are going on vacation.

   A)   Neither Martha or her sisters are going on vacation.

   B)   Neither Martha or her sisters is going on vacation.

   C)   Neither any of her sisters nor Martha are going on vacation.

   D)   Neither Martha nor her sisters are going on vacation.

   E)   Neither Martha nor her sisters is going on vacation.

2. Leader (𝒮)

   The activities of our current leader have led to a significant increase in the number of issues relating to the role of the military in non-military, nation-building exercises.

   A)   have led to a significant increase in the number of issues relating to the role of the military in non-military, nation-building exercises.

   B)   have been significant in the increase in the amount of issues relating to the role of the military in non-military, nation-building exercises.

   C)   has led to a significant increase in the number of issues relating to the role of the military in non-military, nation-building exercises.

   D)   has been significant in the increase in the number of issues relating to the role of the military in non-military, nation-building exercises.

   E)   has significantly increased the amount of issues relating to the role of the military in non-military, nation-building exercises.

3. **Marsupial ( )**

According to scientists at the University of California, the pattern of changes that have occurred in placental DNA over the millennia <u>indicate the possibility that every marsupial alive today might be descended from a single female ancestor that</u> lived in Africa sometime between 125 and 150 million years ago.

A)   indicate the possibility that every marsupial alive today might be descended from a single female ancestor that

B)   indicate that every marsupial alive today might possibly be a descendant of a single female ancestor that had

C)   may indicate that every marsupial alive today has descended from a single female ancestor that had

D)   indicates that every marsupial alive today might be a descendant of a single female ancestor that

E)   indicates that every marsupial alive today may be a descendant from a single female ancestor that

4. **Critics' Choice ( )**

<u>In this critically acclaimed film, there are a well-developed plot and an excellent cast of characters.</u>

A)   In this critically acclaimed film, there are a well-developed plot and an excellent cast of characters.

B)   In this critically acclaimed film, there is a well-developed plot and an excellent cast of characters.

C)   In this film, which is critically acclaimed, there is a well-developed plot and an excellent cast of characters.

D)   In this film, which has been critically acclaimed, there are a well-developed plot and an excellent cast of characters.

E)   There is a well-developed plot and an excellent cast of characters in this critically acclaimed film.

5. **Recommendations** (𝄞 𝄞)

Implementing the consultants' recommendations is expected to result in both increased productivity and decreased costs.

A)   Implementing the consultants' recommendations is expected to result in

B)   Implementing the consultants' recommendations are expected to result in

C)   The expected result of enacting the consultants' recommendations are

D)   The expected results of enacting the consultants' recommendations is

E)   It is expected that enactment of the consultants' recommendations are to result in

Pronoun Usage

6. **Inland Taipan** (𝄞 𝄞)

The Inland Taipan or Fierce Snake of central Australia is widely <u>regarded to be the world's most venomous snake; the poison from its bite can kill human victims unless treated</u> within thirty minutes of an incident.

A)   regarded to be the world's most venomous snake; the poison from its bite can kill human victims unless treated

B)   regarded as the world's most venomous snake; the poison from its bite can kill human victims unless treated

C)   regarded to be the world's most venomous snake; the poison from its bite can kill human victims unless it is treated

D)   regarded as the world's most venomous snake; the poison from its bite can kill human victims unless they are treated

E)   regarded to be the world's most venomous snake; the poison from its bite can kill human victims unless they are treated

7. Medicare ( )

Although Medicare legislation is being considered by the House of Representatives, they do not expect it to pass without being significantly revised.

A) Although Medicare legislation is being considered by the House of Representatives, they do not expect it to pass without being significantly revised.

B) Although the House of Representatives is considering Medicare legislation, they do not expect it to pass without significant revision.

C) Although the House of Representatives is considering Medicare legislation, it is not expected to pass without being significantly revised.

D) If it is to be passed, the House of Representatives must significantly revise Medicare legislation.

E) Consideration and significant revision is expected if Medicare legislation is to be passed by the House of Representatives.

8. Valuation ( )

Financial formulas for valuing companies do not apply to Internet companies in the same way as they do to traditional businesses, because they are growing and seldom have ascertainable sales and cash flows.

A) Financial formulas for valuing companies do not apply to Internet companies in the same way as they do to traditional businesses, because they are growing and seldom have ascertainable sales and cash flows.

B) Internet companies are not subject to the same applicability of financial formulas for valuing these companies as compared with traditional businesses, because they are growing and seldom have ascertainable sales and cash flows.

C) Because they are growing and seldom have ascertainable sales and cash flows, financial formulas for valuing companies do not apply to Internet companies in the same way as they do to traditional businesses.

D) Because they are growing and seldom have ascertainable sales and cash flows, Internet companies are not subject to the same applicability of financial valuation formulas as are traditional businesses.

E) Because Internet companies are growing and seldom have ascertainable sales and cash flows, financial formulas for valuing these companies do not apply to them in the same way as to traditional businesses.

Modification

9. **Metal Detector** ( )

    Using a metal detector, old coins and other valuables can be located by hobbyists even though they are buried in the sand and dirt.

    A) Using a metal detector, old coins and other valuables can be located by hobbyists even though they are buried in the sand and dirt.

    B) Old coins and other valuables can be located by hobbyists using a metal detector even though they are buried in the sand and dirt.

    C) Using a metal detector, hobbyists can locate old coins and other valuables even though they are buried in the sand and dirt.

    D) Buried in the sand and dirt, old coins and other valuables can be located by hobbyists using a metal detector.

    E) A metal detector can be used to locate old coins and other valuables that are buried in the sand and dirt by a hobbyist.

10. **Management** ( )

    On the basis of their review of first quarter operating results, management's decision was to forgo expansion plans and pursue a more conservative marketing approach aimed at streamlining product offerings.

    A) On the basis of their review of first quarter operating results, management's decision was

    B) On the basis of its review of first quarter operating results, management decided

    C) Based on reviewing first quarter operating results, a decision was made by management

    D) Based on their review of first quarter operating results, management decided

    E) Based on first quarter operating results, management decided

11. Natural Beauty ( )

Plastic surgeons who perform surgery for non-medical reasons defend their practice on the basis of the free rights of their patients; many others in the health field, however, contend that plastic surgery degrades natural beauty, <u>which they liken to reconstructing a national park.</u>

A)   which they liken to reconstructing a national park.

B)   which they liken to a national park with reconstruction done to it.

C)   which they liken to reconstruction done on a national park.

D)   likening it to a national park with reconstruction done to it.

E)   likening it to reconstructing a national park.

Parallelism

12. Cannelloni ( )

<u>Cannelloni has and always will be my favorite Italian dish.</u>

A)   Cannelloni has and always will be my favorite Italian dish.

B)   Cannelloni was, has, and always will be my favorite Italian dish.

C)   Cannelloni was and always will be my favorite Italian dish.

D)   Cannelloni has been and always will be my favorite Italian dish.

E)   Cannelloni is, has, and always will be my favorite Italian dish.

13. Massage (🌶🌶)

Massage creates a relaxing, therapeutic, and rejuvenating experience <u>both for your body and your well-being.</u>

A)   both for your body and your well-being.

B)   for both your body and your well-being.

C)   both for your body and well-being.

D)   for both your body and well-being.

E)   both for your body as well as your well-being.

14. Europeans (🌶🌶🌶)

<u>Italy is famous for its composers and musicians, France, for its chefs and philosophers, and Poland, for its mathematicians and logicians.</u>

A)   Italy is famous for its composers and musicians, France, for its chefs and philosophers, and Poland, for its mathematicians and logicians.

B)   Italy is famous for its composers and musicians, France for its chefs and philosophers, Poland for its mathematicians and logicians.

C)   Italy is famous for its composers and musicians. France for its chefs and philosophers. Poland for its mathematicians and logicians.

D)   Italy is famous for their composers and musicians; France, for their chefs and philosophers; Poland for their mathematicians and logicians.

E)   Italy, France, and Poland are famous for their composers and musicians, chefs and philosophers, and mathematicians and logicians.

Comparisons

15. **Sweater ( )**

Although neither sweater is really the right size, <u>the smallest one fits best.</u>

A) the smallest one fits best.

B) the smallest one fits better.

C) the smallest one is better fitting.

D) the smaller of the two fits best.

E) the smaller one fits better.

16. **Sir Isaac Newton ( )**

Within the scientific community, the accomplishments of Sir Isaac Newton are referred to more often <u>than any</u> scientist, living or dead.

A) than any

B) than any other

C) than those of any

D) than are those of any

E) than those of any other

17. **Soya ( )**

In addition to having more protein than meat does, <u>the protein in soybeans is higher in quality than that in meat.</u>

A) the protein in soybeans is higher in quality than that in meat.

B) the protein in soybeans is higher in quality than it is in meat.

C) soybeans have protein of higher quality than that in meat.

D) soybean protein is higher in quality than it is in meat.

E) soybeans have protein higher in quality than meat.

18. Angel ( )

She sings like an angel sings.

A)   She sings like an angel sings.

B)   She sings like an angel does.

C)   She sings as an angel sings.

D)   She sings as if an angel.

E)   She sings as if like an angel.

19. Perceptions ( )

Because right-brained individuals do not employ convergent thinking processes, like left-brained individuals, they may not notice and remember the same level of detail as their counterparts.

A)   like left-brained individuals,

B)   unlike a left-brained individual,

C)   as left-brained individuals,

D)   as left-brained individuals do,

E)   as a left-brained individual can,

20. Assemblée Nationale ( )

As Parliament is the legislative government body of Great Britain, the Assemblée Nationale is the legislative government body of France.

A)   As Parliament is the legislative government body of Great Britain,

B)   As the legislative government body of Great Britain is Parliament,

C)   Just like the legislative government body of Great Britain, which is Parliament,

D)   Just as Parliament is the legislative government body of Great Britain, so

E)   Just as the government of Britain's legislative branch is Parliament,

21. **Geography ( )**

Despite the fact that the United States is a superpower, <u>American high school students perform more poorly on tests of world geography and international affairs than do</u> their Canadian counterparts.

A) American high school students perform more poorly on tests of world geography and international affairs than do

B) American high school students perform more poorly on tests of world geography and international affairs as compared with

C) American high school students perform more poorly on tests of world geography and international affairs as compared to

D) the American high school student performs more poorly on tests of world geography and international affairs than does

E) the American high school student performs more poorly on tests of world geography and international affairs as compared with

22. **Bear ( )**

<u>Like the Alaskan brown bear and most other members of the bear family, the diet of the grizzly bear consists</u> of both meat and vegetation.

A) Like the Alaskan brown bear and most other members of the bear family, the diet of the grizzly bear consists

B) Like those of the Alaskan brown bear and most other members of the bear family, the diets of a grizzly bear consist

C) Like the Alaskan brown bear and most other members of the bear family, the grizzly bear has a diet consisting

D) Just like the diet of the Alaskan brown bear and most other members of the bear family, the diets of the grizzly bear consist

E) Similar to the diets of the Alaskan brown bear and most other members of the bear family, grizzly bears have a diet which consists

23. Smarts ( )

Unlike the Miller Analogies Test, which follows a standardized format, <u>the formats for IQ tests vary considerably in both content and length.</u>

A)   the formats for IQ tests vary considerably in both content and length.

B)   the format for an IQ test varies considerably in both content and length.

C)   an IQ test follows a format that varies considerably in both content and length.

D)   an IQ test follows formats that vary considerably in both content and length.

E)   IQ tests follow formats that vary considerably in both content and length.

Verb Tenses

24. Golden Years ( )

A recent study has found that within the past few years, many executives <u>had elected early retirement rather than face</u> the threats of job cuts and diminishing retirement benefits.

A)   had elected early retirement rather than face

B)   had elected to retire early rather than face

C)   have elected early retirement instead of facing

D)   have elected early retirement rather than facing

E)   have elected to retire early rather than face

25. Politics ( )

Although he <u>disapproved of the political platform set forth by Senator Barack Obama during the 2008 U.S. presidential primaries, Senator John McCain had later conceded</u> that there must be a basis for a coalition government and urged members of both parties to seek compromise.

A)   disapproved of the political platform set forth by <u>Senator Barack Obama during the 2008 U.S. presidential primaries, Senator John McCain had</u> later conceded

B)   has disapproved of the political platform set forth by <u>Senator Barack Obama during the 2008 U.S. presidential primaries, Senator John McCain</u> had later conceded

C)   has disapproved of the political platform set forth by <u>Senator Barack Obama during the 2008 U.S. presidential primaries, Senator John McCain</u> later conceded

D)   had disapproved of the political platform set forth by <u>Senator Barack Obama during the 2008 U.S. presidential primaries, Senator John McCain</u> later conceded

E)   had disapproved of the political platform set forth by <u>Senator Barack Obama during the 2008 U.S. presidential primaries, Senator John McCain</u> had later conceded

26. Trend ( )

<u>The percentage of people remaining single in Holland increased abruptly between 1980 and 1990 and continued to rise more gradually over the next 10 years.</u>

A)   The percentage of people remaining single in Holland increased abruptly between 1980 and 1990 and continued to rise more gradually over the next ten years.

B)   The percentage of people remaining single in Holland increased abruptly between 1980 and 1990 and has continued to rise more gradually over the next ten years.

C)   The percentage of people remaining single in Holland increased abruptly between 1980 and 1990 and had continued to rise more gradually over the next ten years.

D)   There had been an abrupt increase in the percentage of people remaining single in Holland between 1980 and 1990 and it continued to rise more gradually over the next ten years.

E)   There was an abrupt increase in the percentage of people remaining single in Holland between 1980 and 1990 which continued to rise more gradually over the next ten years.

27. Fire (🌶🌶)

<u>Most houses that were destroyed and heavily damaged in residential fires last year were</u> built without adequate fire detection apparatus.

A)   Most houses that were destroyed and heavily damaged in residential fires last year were

B)   Most houses that were destroyed or heavily damaged in residential fires last year had been

C)   Most houses that were destroyed and heavily damaged in residential fires last year had been

D)   Most houses that were destroyed or heavily damaged in residential fires last year have been

E)   Most houses that were destroyed and heavily damaged in residential fires last year have been

28. B-School (🌶🌶)

<u>As graduate management programs become more competitive in the coming years in terms of their promotional and financial undertakings, schools have been becoming</u> more and more dependent on alumni networks, corporate sponsorships, and philanthropists.

A)   As graduate management programs become more competitive in the coming years in terms of their promotional and financial undertakings, schools have been becoming

B)   As graduate management programs are becoming more competitive in the coming years in terms of their promotional and financial undertakings, schools have been becoming

C)   As graduate management programs become more competitive in the coming years in terms of their promotional and financial undertakings, schools have become

D)   As graduate management programs are becoming more competitive in the coming years in terms of their promotional and financial undertakings, schools have become

E)   As graduate management programs become more competitive in the coming years in terms of their promotional and financial undertakings, schools will become

29. Summer in Europe (🌶 🌶)

<u>By the time we have reached France, we will have been backpacking for twelve weeks.</u>

A) By the time we have reached France, we will have been backpacking for twelve weeks.

B) By the time we have reached France, we will have backpacked for twelve weeks.

C) By the time we reach France, we will have been backpacking for twelve weeks.

D) By the time we will have reached France, we will have backpacked for twelve weeks.

E) By the time we reached France, we will have been backpacking for twelve weeks.

Answers and Explanations

1. Vacation ( )

Choice D
Classification: Subject-Verb Agreement
Snapshot: This problem is included to highlight the handling of correlative conjunctions, namely "either/or" and "neither/nor," which may involve the use of a singular or plural verb.

The consistent appearance in answer choices A through E, of "neither," indicates a "neither...nor" relationship. We can eliminate choices A and B outright. The correct verb should match the noun that comes after the word "nor." Since "her sisters" in D is plural, the plural verb "are" does the trick.

In summary, singular subjects following "or" or "nor" always take a singular verb; plural subjects following "or" or "nor" take a plural verb. Stated another way, when two items are connected by "or" or "nor," the verb agrees with the closer subject. That is, the verb needs only agree with the subject that comes after "or" or "nor."

There are two potentially correct answers; only the first alternative below is presented by answer choice D:

Correct: Neither Martha nor her sisters <u>are</u> going on vacation.
or
Correct: Neither her sisters nor Martha <u>is</u> going on vacation.

NOTE ⤳ In everyday writing and speaking, we may not think it necessary to know the intimate rules of grammar. As long as we reach our goal of communicating through our writing and speaking, why do we need to know precisely how everything works? After all, as long as we can drive a car, why do we need to know how the engine works? GMAT Sentence Correction requires that we become "grammar mechanics." It forces us to look under the "hood" and master how the writing and grammar engine works.

2. Leader ( )

Choice A
Classification: Subject-Verb Agreement
Snapshot: This problem is included to show subject-verb agreement and to highlight the role of prepositional phrases in disguising the subject and verb.

The subject of a sentence determines the verb (i.e., singular subjects take singular verbs; plural subjects take plural verbs) and the subject of this sentence is "activities" (plural). The intervening phrase "of our current leader" is a prepositional phrase, and prepositional phrases can never contain the subject of a sentence. Mentally cut out this phrase. Since the subject is "activities," the verb is "have," not "has." Another distinction that needs to be drawn relates to the difference between "number" and "amount." The word "number" is used for countable items and "amount" for non-countable items. Therefore, we have no problem choosing choice A as the correct answer after applying only two rules—the first is a subject-verb agreement rule followed by the "number" versus "amount" diction distinction. Also, per choices B and D, the clause "has/have been significant in the increase" is not only awkward but also passive.

3. Marsupial ( )

Choice D
Classification: Subject-Verb Agreement
Snapshot: This follow-up problem is also included to highlight the role of prepositional phrases within subject-verb agreement.

The subject of the sentence is "pattern," which is singular, and a singular subject takes the singular verb "indicates." An additional way to eliminate choices A and B is through the redundant use of the words "might" and "possibility" which express the same idea; either "possibility" or "might" is required. Also, the use of "might" in choice D is better than "may" (choice E) because "might" more clearly indicates "possibility" than does "may" and "might" is also the correct choice when referring to past events. In choosing between choices D and E, the idiom "descendant of" is superior to the unidiomatic "descendant from." Finally, note that in choices B and C, "had," the auxiliary of "lived," should be deleted because the simple past tense is correct. The past perfect, which employs "had," is not required; the past perfect tense is used to refer to an action that precedes some other action also occurring in the past.

NOTE ⤙ This problem complements the previous one. The former problem contained a plural subject ("activities") and a single item in the prepositional phrase ("current leader"). This problem contains a singular subject ("pattern") and a plural item in the prepositional phrase ("changes").

4. Critics' Choice ( )

Choice A
Classification: Subject-Verb Agreement
Snapshot: This problem is included to highlight "there is/there are" constructions in which the subject of the sentence comes after, not before, the verb.

The compound subject is plural—"well-developed plot <u>and</u> an excellent cast of characters"—and, therefore, requires the plural verb "are." Choices B, C, and E are out because of the incorrect verb "is." Choices C and D employ roundabout constructions that are inferior to "In this critically acclaimed film." Choice D also employs the passive construction "which has been critically acclaimed." Choice E rearranges the sentence, but still incorrectly employs the singular verb "is."

5. Recommendations ( )

Choice A
Classification: Subject-Verb Agreement
Snapshot: This problem is included to highlight gerund phrases which, when acting as the subject of a sentence, are always singular.

The gerund phrase "Implementing the consultants' recommendations" is the subject of the sentence. As gerund phrases are always singular, the correct verb here is "is." In choice C, "expected result" requires the verb "is," whereas in choice D, "expected results" requires the verb "are." In choice E, the "it is" construction creates an unnecessarily weak opener and an awkward sentence style.

6.   Inland Taipan ( )

Choice D
Classification: Pronoun Usage
Snapshot: This problem is included to highlight the occasional need to add personal pronouns in order to remove ambiguity.

This form of ambiguous reference is subtle. The original sentence is missing "they," and without the pronoun "they," the word "treated" might refer to "poison" or "victims"; "treated" is only supposed to refer to "victims." In choice C, the pronoun "it" logically but incorrectly refers to "bite." Technically it is not the bite that needs to be treated but the actual victims. Choices A, C, and E erroneously employ the idiom "regarded to be" when the correct idiom is "regarded as."

7.   Medicare ( )

Choice C
Classification: Modification
Snapshot: This problem is included to highlight the need to choose the correct pronoun—"it"—when referring to a collective singular noun or single inanimate object.

Choices A and B are incorrect because the pronoun "they" cannot refer to the House of Representatives. Not only is the House of Representatives a collective singular noun, but it is also an inanimate object; therefore, the proper pronoun choice is "it."

Choice D improperly employs the pronoun "it," which incorrectly refers to the House of Representatives rather than to Medicare legislation. Choice E may be the most passive of these sentences, in which the doer of the action, the House of Representatives, is now at the very back of the sentence.

In choice C, the pronoun "it" correctly refers to Medicare legislation. The subordinate clause "although the House of Representatives is considering Medicare legislation" is written in the active voice. The latter part of the sentence is written in the passive voice "without being significantly revised," and we just have to be willing to accept this wording given that it's the best of the remaining choices. For the record, two alternative wordings for the latter part of the sentence might include: "it is not expected to pass unless it is significantly revised" (active voice but employs two uses of the pronoun "it") and "it is not expected to pass without significant revision" (active voice but employs the nominalized "revision").

NOTE ✎ In general, the five most common signals of the passive voice include: "be," "was," "were," "been," and "being." In addition, the preposition "by" is also closely associated with the passive voice: e.g., "The ball was caught by the outfielder."

8. Valuation (🌶🌶🌶)

Choice E
Classification: Pronoun Usage
Snapshot: This problem is included to highlight ambiguity arising from the use of personal pronouns, and seeks to clear up such ambiguity, not by replacing pronouns, but by rearranging the sentence itself. Part of the reason it garners a three-chili rating is because the problem is long, and somewhat difficult to read and analyze in two minutes—the standard time allotted for completing any and all multiple-choice GMAT problems.

Choices A and B use the word "they" to refer to traditional businesses; this is illogical because traditional businesses are not growing, Internet companies are. Remember that a pronoun modifies the closest noun that precedes it. The structure in choice C makes it seem as if "financial formulas" are growing, and this, of course, is farcical.

Choices A and C use the awkward clause "do not apply to X in the same way as they do to Y." A more succinct rendition is found in choice E—"do not apply to X in the same way as to Y." In choices A, C, and E, the verb "apply" is more powerful and, therefore, superior to the noun form "applicability," which appears in choices B and D.

NOTE ❧ Beware of the high school wise tale that says you shouldn't begin a sentence with the word "because." If you learned this as a rule, forget it. According to the conventions of Standard Written English (SWE)—which, incidentally, this book abides by—the word "because" functions as a subordinating conjunction. Its use is effectively identical to that of "as" or "since," and we can think of these three words as substitutes. In short, there's actually no rule of grammar or style preventing us from beginning a sentence with the word "because."

9. Metal Detector (🌶)

Choice C
Classification: Modification
Snapshot: This problem is included to illustrate misplaced modifiers. In particular, an introductory modifying phrase (a phrase that begins the sentence) always modifies the first noun or pronoun that follows it (and which itself is in the subjective case). The general rule is that "modifying words or phrases should be kept close to the word(s) that they modify."

The only answer choice that is written in the active voice is choice C. The other four answer choices are written in the passive voice (the word "be" signals the passive voice). In choice A, coins and other valuables cannot *use* a metal detector; we must look for a person to act as the doer of the action. Choice E changes the meaning of the sentence, suggesting that the hobbyists bury the coins themselves. Whereas choices A and E are incorrect, choices B, C, and D are each grammatically correct. Choice C is the winner because, all things being equal, the active voice is deemed superior to the passive voice. This is a rule of style rather than grammar. Style is more or less effective, better or worse. Grammar is correct or incorrect, right or wrong.

NOTE ❧ Modification may involve the replacement of individual qualifying words, such as *almost, only, just, even, hardly, nearly, not,* and *merely.* Ideally, these words should be placed immediately before or after the words they modify lest they cause confusion.

In the memorable example below, consider how the placement of the word "only" changes the meaning of the sentence.

Original: Life exists on earth.

Let's add the word "only" and vary its placement:

Example 1:   <u>Only</u> life exists on earth.

                The meaning is that life is the sole occupier of earth. However, we know that there are things besides life that exist on earth, including inanimate objects like rocks.

Example 2:   Life <u>only</u> exists on earth.

                The meaning is that life merely exists on earth and doesn't do anything else.

Example 3:   Life exists <u>only</u> on earth.

                This is likely the intended meaning. The word "only" is appropriately placed in front of the word phrase it modifies—*on earth.*

Example 4:   Life exists on <u>only</u> earth.

                The meaning here is the same as above but slightly more dramatic. The implication is that life's sole domain is earth, and we're proud of it.

Example 5:   Life exists on earth <u>only.</u>

                The meaning is also the same as example 3, but with a flair for the dramatic. The implication may be that life is found only on earth, and isn't that a shame.

10. Management (🌶️ 🌶️)

Choice B
Classification: Modification
Snapshot: This problem is included to highlight a modification trap, particularly in the case of sentences beginning with the words "based on."

Choice A is incorrect because the opening clause, "On the basis of their review of first quarter operating results" cannot logically modify "management's decision"; it can only modify "management." In choice C is also incorrect for this reason. The clause "Based on reviewing first quarter operating results" cannot properly modify "a decision." Choice D is out because the pronoun "their" does not match its singular antecedent, "management"; the correct pronoun would be "its." In choice E, as well as choice D, "management" cannot, technically speaking, be "based on first quarter operating results" or "even a review of first quarter operating results."

NOTE ⊰ Watch out for sentences that are worded to suggest that people are "based on" something. For example, the sentence that begins, "Based on their research, scholars determined...," is erroneously stating that scholars are standing on their research or perhaps attached to it. On the other hand, it is completely acceptable to write sentences to suggest that one inanimate object is based on another (e.g., "A movie based on a book."). Here are two more examples:

"Based on simple line drawings, the new corporate logo looks quite catchy."

(The new corporate logo is based on our client's own drawings. Both "corporate logo" and "drawings" are inanimate objects).

"Brokers whose buy-recommendations were based on stock market fever."

(Both "buy-in recommendations" and "stock market fever" are inanimate objects.)

11. Natural Beauty ( )

Choice E
Classification: Modification
Snapshot: This problem is included to highlight another type of modification problem, known as "back sentence modification" because the phrase or clause set off by a comma occurs at the end of the sentence, not the beginning.

The final answer proves best—correct, logical, and succinct—in comparing *plastic surgery* to the act of *reconstructing a national park*. In short, the patient is being compared to a national park while the act of plastic surgery is being likened to the act of reconstructing a national park. The word "likening" functions as a participle; it introduces the participle phrase "likening it to reconstructing a national park." This phrase properly refers to "surgery," not "natural beauty."

In choices A, B, and C, the relative pronoun "which" refers, not to plastic surgery, but to the noun immediately preceding it, "(natural) beauty." As a result, "natural beauty" is compared to "reconstructing a national park" (choice A), to "a national park" (choice B), and to "reconstruction" (choice C). Choice D corrects this problem by eliminating the "which" construction and supplying the pronoun "it," thus referring clearly to "plastic surgery," but it illogically compares "plastic surgery" to "a national park." Moreover, the double use of "it" is awkward.

12. Cannelloni ( )

Choice D
Classification: Parallelism
Snapshot: This problem is included to highlight the use of parallelism as it relates to ellipsis (the acceptable omission of words).

To test choice D, simply complete each component idea, making sure each makes sense. "Cannelloni <u>has been</u> my favorite dish...Cannelloni always <u>will be</u> my favorite dish." Now check this against the original:

"Cannelloni <u>was</u> my favorite dish (doesn't work)...Cannelloni always <u>will be</u> my favorite dish." Choice E suffers the same fate as choices A and B, erroneously omitting *has been*. Choices B and C are muddled; the word "was" illogically suggests that Cannelloni was once a favorite dish, but no longer is.

13. Massage ( )

Choice B
Classification: Parallelism
Snapshot: This problem is included to highlight the use of parallelism when using correlative conjunctions.

There are four common correlative conjunctions in English. These include *either...or, neither...nor, not only...but also,* and *both...and.* The purpose of correlative conjunctions is to join ideas of equal weight. Therefore, things on both sides of each connector should be parallel in form and equal in weight.

The word pairing "both...as well as" is unidiomatic, so choice E can be eliminated. Here the correlative conjunction is "both...and," and the words that follow "both," and "and" must be parallel in structure. In choice B, the correct answer, the words "your body" follows the word "both," while the words "your well-being" follow the word "and"; this creates perfect parallelism. Choices C and D are not parallel. For the record, there are effectively two possibilities:

Correct: Massage creates a relaxing, therapeutic, and rejuvenating experience for <u>both</u> your body <u>and</u> your well-being.
or
Correct: Massage creates a relaxing, therapeutic, and rejuvenating experience <u>both</u> for your body <u>and</u> for your well-being.

Here's another example:

Incorrect: Sheila <u>both</u> likes to act <u>and</u> to sing.

Correct: Sheila likes <u>both</u> to act <u>and</u> to sing.
or
Correct: Sheila <u>both</u> likes to act <u>and</u> likes to sing.

14. Europeans ( )

Choice A
Classification: Parallelism
Snapshot: This problem is included to highlight the use of parallelism with regard to ellipsis, and to review semicolons, omission commas, sentence run-ons, and sentence fragments.

In choice A, the comma placed immediately after "France" and "Poland" is an *omission comma*—it takes the place of the missing words "is famous." Choice B provides an example of a run-on sentence. There must be an "and" preceding the word "Poland." As it stands, it is three sentences joined together by commas.

Choice C contains two sentence fragments: "France for its chefs and philosophers" and "Poland for its mathematicians and logicians." These phrases cannot stand on their own as complete sentences. Choice D improperly uses the pronoun "their," when what is called for is the pronoun "its." Moreover, we would need to have commas after both the words "France" and "Poland" in order to validate this choice; alternatively, we could omit commas after France and Poland. According to the rules of ellipsis, words can be omitted within a sentence if they're a readily understood in context.

Choice E changes the meaning of the original sentence (that's a no-no). There's little doubt that France and Poland have composers, musicians, chefs, philosophers, mathematicians, and logicians, but the focus is on what each country is specifically famous for.

In summary, there are four possible correct answers.

Correct: Italy is famous for its composers and musicians, France is famous for its chefs and philosophers, and Poland is famous for its mathematicians and logicians.

(The above version repeats three times the words "is famous.")

Correct: Italy is famous for its composers and musicians, France, for its chefs and philosophers, and Poland, for its mathematicians and logicians.

(The above is the correct rendition per choice A. The comma after "France" and "Poland" is effectively taking the place of the words "is famous.")

Correct: Italy is famous for its composers and musicians, France for its chefs and philosophers, and Poland for its mathematicians and logicians.

(The above version is likely the most subtle. The rules of ellipsis allow us to omit words that are readily understood within the context of any sentence. The words "is famous" are readily understood. This version is almost identical to choice B, except that it correctly inserts the word "and" before Poland.)

Correct: Italy is famous for its composers and musicians; France, for its chefs and philosophers; Poland, for its mathematicians and logicians.

(The above version uses semicolons along with commas. Note that the final "and" before Poland is optional. Unlike choice D, this choice correctly inserts a comma after "France" and "Poland" and replaces the pronoun "their" with "its.")

15. Sweater (🌶)

Choice E
Classification: Comparisons
Snapshot: This problem is included to highlight the handling of the comparative and superlative adjective forms.

The words "neither one" indicate that we are dealing with two sweaters. When comparing two things, we use the comparative form of the adjective, not the superlative. Thus, the correct choice is "better," not "best," and "smaller," not "smallest." "Better" and "smaller" (comparatives) are used when comparing exactly two things; "best" and "smallest" (superlatives) are used when comparing three or more things.

NOTE ∽ When two things are being compared, the *comparative* form of the adjective (or adverb) is used. The comparative is formed in one of two ways: (1) adding "er" to the adjective (for adjectives containing one syllable), or (2) placing "more" before the adjective (especially for adjectives with more than two syllables). Use one of the above methods, but never both: "Jeremy is wiser (or *more wise*) than we know," but never "Jeremy is more wiser than we know."

Some modifiers require internal changes in the words themselves. A few of these irregular comparisons are presented in the following chart:

Positive	Comparative	Superlative
good	better	best
well	better	best
bad	worse	worst
far	farther, further	farthest, furthest
late	later, latter	latest, last
little	less, lesser	least
many, much	more	most

16. Sir Isaac Newton (𝄐)

Choice E
Classification: Comparisons
Snapshot: This solution to this problem pivots on the use of the demonstrative pronoun "those."

The words "those" and "other" must show up in the correct answer. First, without the word "other," choices A, C, and D illogically compare Sir Isaac Newton to all scientists, living or dead, even though Sir Isaac Newton is one of those scientists. Second, without the word "those," choices A and B illogically compare "the accomplishments of Sir Isaac Newton" to "other scientists." Obviously, we must compare "the accomplishments of Sir Isaac Newton" to "the accomplishments of other scientists." In choices C, D, and E, the word "those" exists to substitute for the phrase "the accomplishments."

17. Soya (𝄐 𝄐)

Choice C
Classification: Comparisons
Snapshot: This problem highlights the use of the demonstrative pronoun "that."

Here, we must correctly compare "the protein in meat" to "the protein in soybeans." The demonstrative pronoun "that" is very important because it substitutes for the words "the protein." Choice C creates a sentence which effectively reads: "In addition to having more protein than meat does, the protein in soybeans is higher in quality than *the protein* in meat."

Choices A and B are out because the word "meat" must come after the opening phrase "in addition to having more protein than meat does." Choice D correctly employs "soybeans," but incorrectly uses "it" to make a comparison. The word "it" cannot stand for "the protein." Choice E incorrectly compares soybean protein to meat.

18. Angel ( )

Choice C
Classification: Comparisons
Snapshot: This problem is included to highlight proper comparisons involving "like" versus "as."

The basic difference between "like" and "as" is that "like" is used for *phrases* and "as" is used for *clauses*. A phrase is a group of words that does not contain a verb; a clause is a group of words that does contain a verb. Choices D and E ungrammatically employ "as" in phrases, in addition to being awkwardly constructed.

There are three potentially correct versions:

i)   She sings <u>like an angel</u>.

       "Like an angel" is a phrase (there is no verb), so "like" is the correct choice.

ii)   She sings <u>as an angel sings</u>.

       "As an angel sings" is a clause (contains the verb "sings"), so "as" is the correct choice.

iii)   She sings <u>as an angel does</u>.

       "As an angel does" is a clause (contains the verb "does"), so "as" is the correct choice.

NOTE ❧ Advertising is an arena where violations in English grammar may be turned to advantage. The American cigarette company Winston once adopted the infectious advertising slogan: "Winston tastes good like a cigarette should." The ungrammatical and somehow proactive use of "like" instead of "as" created a minor sensation, helping to propel the brand to the top of the domestic cigarette market. A more recent advertising campaign by DHL in Asia also contains a grammatical violation: "No one knows Asia like we do." The correct version should read: "No one knows Asia as we do."

19. Perceptions ( )

Choice D
Classification: Comparisons
Snapshot: This problem is included to highlight the comparative idiom "as … do"/"as … does."

The problem pivots on the "like/as" distinction. The intended comparison is between the convergent thinking processes of right-brain individuals and the convergent thinking processes of left-brain individuals. We cannot compare the convergent thinking processes of right-brain individuals directly to left-brain individuals (per answer choices A and B). The verb "do" is needed in order to substitute for the ability of left-brain individuals to employ convergent thinking processes.

Choices C, D, and E use the correct connector, "as," which is used with clauses, while choices C and E use "like" or "unlike," which is used with phrases. Choices B and E use the singular "individual" rather than the plural "individuals." Either of the following would be better:

Correct: Unlike left-brained individuals, right-brained individuals often do not employ their attention or perceptions systematically, and they may not notice and remember the same level of detail <u>as</u> their left-brained counterparts <u>do</u>.

Correct: Right-brained individuals often do not employ their attention or perceptions systematically, and, unlike left-brained individuals, right-brain individuals may not notice and remember the same level of detail <u>as</u> their left-brained counterparts <u>do</u>.

20. Assemblée Nationale (𝄞 𝄞)

Choice D
Classification: Comparisons
Snapshot: This problem is included to highlight the comparative idiom "Just as … so (too)." Note that the brackets indicate the optional use of the word "too."

In choices A and B, the use of "as" is incorrect. "As" functions as a subordinating conjunction, and this means that the reader expects a logical connection between the fact that Britain has a Parliament and France has the Assemblée Nationale. Try substituting the subordinating conjunction "because" in either choices A or B and the illogical relationship becomes more apparent. "Because Parliament is the legislative government body of Great Britain, the Assemblée Nationale is the legislative government body of France."

The "just as … so (too)" comparative idiom (choice D) can be used to express this type of meaning. "Just as something, so something else." Choice D provides a standard comparison: The Parliament of Great Britain is being compared to the Assemblée Nationale of France. In choice E, the comparison is awkward because we end up comparing the Government of Britain's Parliament with the Assemblée Nationale.

Choice C is clearly awkward and the omission of the verb "is" makes for an illogical comparison. Remember that for GMAT purposes, "just like" is considered an unnecessary redundancy of "like." In any event, "like" (or "just like") could only be used with phrases, not clauses, and what is needed here is a clause.

NOTE ↩ Savor this classic example:

Correct: <u>Just as</u> birds have wings, <u>so too</u> do fish have fins.

Incorrect: As birds have wings, fish have fins.

Incorrect: As birds have wings, fish, therefore, have fins.

Substituting "because" for "as" above, we can quickly see an illogical relationship. There is no logical connection between a bird's having wings and a fish's having fins. In other words, just because a bird has wings doesn't mean that a fish has to have fins.

21. Geography (🦶🦶)

Choice A
Classification: Comparisons
Snapshot: This problem is included to highlight the correct use of the "more...than" idiom, used in comparing two things.

Make an initial note that we should ideally be comparing American high school *students* with Canadian high school *students* (plural with plural) because the non-underlined part of the sentence contains the words "counterparts." Be suspicious of any of the answer choices which begin with "the American high school student." Verify also that in all cases verbs are correct. "Do" is a plural verb that matches the plural phrase "Canadian counterparts"; "does" is a singular verb that would be used to match the singular phrase "Canadian counterpart."

The last piece of the puzzle is to eliminate the non-standard comparative constructions, namely "more...compared to" as well as "more...compared with." The correct idiom is "more...than" or "less...than" (see *200 Common Grammatical Idioms*, page 232). Thus, choices B, C, and E cannot be correct.

22. Bear (🦶🦶🦶)

Choice C
Classification: Comparisons
Snapshot: When making comparisons, the most basic rule is to make sure to compare like things. That is, compare apples with apples and oranges with oranges. This is particularly true when comparing the characteristics of one thing to the characteristics of something else. In such cases, we must compare thing to thing, and characteristic to characteristic, and not compare the characteristics of one thing to another thing itself.

Here we want to compare "bears" with "bears" or "diets of bears" with "diets of bears." Choice A, the original, compares animals with diets by erroneously comparing the "Alaskan brown bear and most other members" of the bear family to the "diet" of the grizzly bear. Choice B is structurally sound ("those" is a demonstrative pronoun that takes the place of "the diets"), but unidiomatically refers to the "diets" of the grizzly bear. Idiomatic speech would require the use of "diet" to refer to a single bear species and "diets" to refer to more than one species of bear. Choice D uses the repetitious "just like" (when "like" alone is sufficient), as well as the unidiomatic "diets." Choice E commits the original error in reverse. Now "diets" of the Alaskan brown bear and most other members of the bear family are being compared directly to "grizzly bears," instead of to the diet of "grizzly bears."

All of the following provide potentially correct answers:

i)   Like the Alaskan brown bear and most other members of the bear family, the grizzly bear has a diet consisting of both meat and vegetation.

ii)   Like the Alaskan brown bear and most other members of the bear family, grizzly bears have a diet consisting of both meat and vegetation.

iii)   Like the <u>diets</u> of the Alaskan brown bear and most other members of the bear family, the <u>diet</u> of the grizzly bear consists of both meat and vegetation.

iv)   Like the <u>diets</u> of the Alaskan brown bear and most other members of the bear family, the <u>diet</u> of grizzly bears consists of both meat and vegetation.

23. Smarts (🐾🐾🐾)

Choice E
Classification: Comparisons
Snapshot: This problem is included as an "oddball" to demonstrate that we do not always compare a singular item with a singular item or a plural item with a plural item (e.g., Miller Analogies Test versus IQ tests). In context, a situation may necessitate comparing a singular item with a plural item or vice versa. Here the "apples to apples, oranges to oranges" comparison involves comparing one type of test to another type of test while comparing the format of one such test to the formats of another type of test.

Choices A and B erroneously compare "the Miller Analogies Test" with "the formats ..." We want to compare "one exam" to "another exam," or "the format of one exam" to the "format of another exam," or "the formats of some exams" to the "formats of other exams." Although choice C looks like the winning answer, upon closer examination, we realize that a single format cannot itself vary considerably in terms of content and length. Choice D correctly employs "formats," but now the problem reverses itself: A single IQ test does not have "formats." Choice E correctly combines "IQ tests" in the plural with "formats" in the plural.

Here's a follow-up example in mirror image to the problem at hand:

Incorrect: Unlike Canadian football, which is played on a standardized field, American baseball is played on a <u>field</u> that varies considerably in shape and size.

Correct: Unlike Canadian football, which is played on a standardized field, American baseball is played on <u>fields</u> that vary considerably in shape and size.

24. Golden Years (🐾)

Choice E
Classification: Verb Tenses
Snapshot: This problem is included to illustrate the difference between the present perfect tense and the past perfect tense. The correct answer employs the present perfect tense.

Only choice E uses the correct tense (present perfect), observes parallelism, and is idiomatic. Because the sentence describes a situation that continues into the present, choices A and B are incorrect in using the past perfect tense "had elected." The sentence begins in the present perfect tense ("has found"), and all things being equal, we want to maintain consistency with respect to tenses ("have elected"). In choice E, the noun forms "to retire" (infinitive) and "face" are more closely parallel than are the noun forms "retirement" and "facing." Note also that the dual expressions "x rather than y" and "x instead of y" are, according to Standard Written English, equivalent. However, the GMAT folks appear to side with the use of "rather than."

25. Politics ()

Choice D
Classification: Verb Tenses
Snapshot: This problem is included to highlight the past perfect tense and the precise use of the auxiliary "had" in forming this tense.

The original sentence contains two critical past tense verbs: "disapproved" and "conceded." It also contains the time word "later," as in "later conceded," which serves to further clarify the sequence of past events. This problem highlights an important characteristic of the past perfect tense, namely that the auxiliary "had" is used before the first of two past events. In this example, Senator John McCain "disapproved" before he "conceded." Thus, the auxiliary "had" must be placed before the first (not the second) of the two past events: "had disapproved...later conceded."

Choice A erroneously proposes a reversal in sequence ("disapproved...had later conceded"), while choice E doubles the use of "had" to create a verbal muddle ("had disapproved...had later conceded"). Both of these choices result in illogical alternatives. Choices B and C incorrectly employ the present perfect tense ("has") when the past perfect tense ("had") is what is called for.

NOTE ✑ Another correct answer would have included the following:

"Although he disapproved of the political platform set forth by Senator Barack Obama during the 2008 U.S. presidential primaries, Senator John McCain later conceded..."

This option is also correct, although it doesn't use the past perfect tense. It instead uses two past tense verbs, namely "disapproved" and "conceded," and the temporal word "later." Because the sequence of past tense events is clear, the use of the auxiliary "had" is considered optional. Refer to the explanation given for Q75 in *Answers to the 100-Question Quiz.*

26. Trend ()

Choice A
Classification: Verb Tenses
Snapshot: This problem is included to illustrate the difference between the past tense versus the past perfect tense and the present perfect tense. The correct answer sides with the past tense.

Here, the past tense is all that is needed to refer clearly to the time frame in the past (1980–1990). In choice B, the present perfect tense "has continued" is inconsistent with the timing of an event that took place in the distant past. In choice C, the past perfect tense "had continued" is not required because we are not making a distinction between the sequence of two past tense events.

In choices D and E, the focus switches from a rise in the "percentage of people" to a rise in the "abrupt increase." This shift in meaning is unwarranted and incorrect. The pronouns "it" (choice D) and "which" (choice E) are ambiguous and could refer to either the "percentage of people" or an "abrupt increase." Moreover, choices D and E employ the passive constructions "there had been" and "there was"; these are considered weak sentence constructions and are best avoided.

27. Fire ( )

Choice B
Classification: Verb Tenses
Snapshot: This problem is included to highlight the difference between the past perfect tense and the past tense and/or the present perfect tense. The correct answer employs the past perfect tense. This problem also addresses the passive verb construction "had been"/"have been."

The solution to this problem is conceptually similar to that of the preceding problem. The auxiliary "had" must be used in conjunction with the first of two past tense events. In short, only choice B uses the verb tenses correctly to indicate that houses were built or heavily damaged prior to their being destroyed by fire. Choices A, C, and E illogically state that some houses were both destroyed <u>and</u> heavily damaged; "or" is needed to indicate that each of the houses suffered either one fate or the other. In using only the simple past tense (i.e., the verb tense "were"), choice A fails to indicate that the houses were built before the fires occurred. Choices D and E erroneously employ the present perfect tense, saying in effect that the houses "have been constructed" after they were destroyed or heavily damaged last year.

28. B-School ( )

Choice E
Classification: Verb Tenses
Snapshot: This problem is included to illustrate the difference between the future tense and the present perfect tense (both simple and progressive verb forms). The correct answer uses the future tense.

Since all answer choices contain the words "in the coming years," we definitely know we are dealing with the future, and choice E complements our search for a future tense. In choices A and B, the tense "have been becoming" (present perfect progressive tense in the passive voice) doesn't work. In choices C and D, the present perfect tense is also out. The present perfect tense is useful only for events that began in the past and touch the present. Here we need a tense that takes us into the future.

29. Summer in Europe ( )

Choice C
Classification: Verb Tenses
Snapshot: This problem illustrates the correct use of the future perfect tense.

This problem demonstrates the correct use of the future perfect tense. Choices A and B, by employing the construction "have reached," offer incorrect versions based on the present perfect tense. Choices D and E create erroneous alternatives by commingling past tense constructions with those in the future tense. Choice D presents an incorrect version which doubles up the present perfect tense "have reached" with the future perfect tense "will have backpacked."

Choice E mixes the past tense "reached" with the future perfect tense (in the progressive form). For the record, an equally correct answer would have been: "By the time we reached France, we had been backpacking for 12 weeks." This would represent the correct use of the past perfect tense. Of course, the original sentence clearly indicates that the travelers are looking into the future—they have not yet arrived in France.

The future perfect tense and the past perfect tense are very much opposite in terms of time frame but structurally similar. Here are two more ways to draw a distinction between these two tenses:

Past perfect tense: By the time something happened (second event), something else had already happened (first event).

Future perfect tense: By the time something happens (second event), something else will have already happened (first event).

CHAPTER 5

CRITICAL REASONING

I can stand brute force, but brute reason is quite unbearable. There is something unfair about its use. It is hitting below the intellect.

—Oscar Wilde

OVERVIEW

Official Exam Instructions for Critical Reasoning

Directions

For this question, select the best of the answer choices given.

Strategies and Approaches

1. *Read the question.*

    There are four common Critical Reasoning question types: assumption questions, weakening questions, strengthening questions, and inference questions.

    Examples of each follow:

    Assumption question: "Which of the following is an assumption in the argument above?"

    Weakening question: "Which of the following would most weaken the above argument?"

    Strengthening question: "Which of the following would most strengthen the above argument?"

    Inference question: "Which of the following can be logically inferred from the passage above?"

2. *Read the passage.*

    Read the passage once carefully. By reading the question first and noting the type of question being asked, you are now reading with a purpose.

3. *Analyze the argument and try to anticipate what the likely answer is.*

    There are essentially two ways to analyze an argument. The first is according to classic argument structure. This entails breaking the argument down according to its three parts, namely conclusion, evidence, and assumption. The second and perhaps more direct method is to see if an argument's primary assumption falls under one of the six common categories of assumptions that commonly appear on the GMAT. These include: (1) comparisons assumptions, (2) representativeness assumptions, (3) cause-and-effect assumptions, (4) implementation assumptions, (5) number-based assumptions, and (6) logic-based assumptions.

    In terms of anticipating the likely correct answer, it is important to spend a few moments trying to summarize the argument in your own way by talking silently to yourself. Rushing this process, by failing to understand the argument and immediately proceeding to the answer choices, will hinder rather than help your quest to clarify things. You'll find yourself much more tempted by incorrect answer choices. Never fear taking a little time if it can aid understanding. Remember the test taker's adage: you paradoxically save time by spending time.

4. *Eliminate common wrong answer choices including out of scopes, irrelevancies, distortions, and opposites.*

In terms of common wrong answer choices, *out of scope* answer choices may be defined as answer choices that cannot be answered based on information presented in the passage. *Irrelevancies* are answer choices that are simply not pertinent to the question or issue at hand. *Distortions* are extreme answer choices. *Opposites* are answer choices that reverse meaning.

REVIEW OF CRITICAL REASONING

Defining Terms

What is an argument? An argument is not a heated exchange like the ones you might have had with a good friend, family member, or significant other. An argument, as referred to in logic, is "a claim or statement made which is supported by some evidence." A claim is part of a larger word called "argument."

"Oh, it sure is a nice day today." This statement is certainly a claim, but it is not an argument because it contains no support for what is said. To turn it into an argument we could say: "Oh, it sure is a nice day today. We have had nearly five hours of sunshine." Now the claim ("it sure is a nice day") is supported by some evidence ("nearly five hours of sunshine").

Let's get some definitions out of the way.

Conclusion	The conclusion is the claim or main point that the author, writer, or speaker is making.
Evidence	The evidence includes any facts, examples, statistics, surveys, and other information or data that the author (writer or speaker) uses in support of his or her conclusion.
Assumption	The assumption is the author's unstated belief (unstated evidence) about why his or her claim is right. An assumption is that part of the argument that the author, writer, or speaker assumes to be correct without stating so; it is "that which the author takes for granted." More poetically, the assumption may be said to be the "glue" that holds the evidence to the conclusion.

The ABCs of Argument Structure

The following expresses the relationship between the three elements of classic argument structure:

Conclusion = Evidence + Assumption
or
Conclusion – Evidence = Assumption

The ability to understand simple but formal argument structure is useful, if not essential, to advance critical thinking. After identifying the conclusion and evidence, we then proceed to examine the third element, called the assumption. So how do we go about identifying the first two elements, namely the conclusion and evidence?

Identifying the Conclusion and Evidence

Confusion may arise as to what part of an argument is evidence and what part is the conclusion. Certain "guide words" always signal the use of evidence or the start of the conclusion. *Exhibit 5.1* lists the most common guide words. If, for example, you hear someone say, "Because the economy is getting better, I'm going to buy a car," you may presume that the phrase "because the economy is getting better" is evidence. The reason for this is that the word "because" always signals the use of evidence. The remaining phrase "I'm going to buy a car" contains the conclusion. Note that these phrases may also be reversed without affecting what is the evidence and conclusion. For example, "I'm going to buy a car because the economy is getting better." If possible, use guide words to identify the conclusion and evidence in an argument.

EXHIBIT 5.1   GUIDE WORDS

Words that always signal "evidence"	Words that always signal "conclusion"
•As •As a result of •As indicated by •As shown by •Because •Given that •Since •The reason is that	•As a result •Clearly •Consequently •Hence •In conclusion •So •Therefore •Thus

It is important to note that guide words will not always be present to guide you, meaning that you cannot always rely on them to locate the conclusion and the evidence in a given argument.

Locating the Assumption

Whereas the conclusion and evidence in an argument are always explicit, the assumption is always implicit. The fact that assumptions are, by definition, implicit means that they will not be stated, that is, written down on paper by the author or spoken out loud by the speaker. They exist foremost in the mind of the author or speaker. Conclusions and evidence, on the other hand, are explicit. This means that they will be stated—physically written down on paper or spoken out loud.

EXHIBIT 5.2   THE PARTS OF AN ARGUMENT

Parts of an argument	Stated or implied	This means
Conclusion	Explicit	It is stated, i.e., written down or spoken out loud.
Evidence	Explicit	It is stated, i.e., written down or spoken out loud.
Assumption	Implicit	It is not stated (written down or spoken out loud), but remains in the mind of the person presenting the argument.

Evaluating Arguments

Evaluating arguments typically translates to attacking arguments. There are effectively two ways to attack an argument: attack the evidence or attack the assumption(s). Naturally, we must be able to identify the evidence and assumption in order to attack either.

Dorothy and Her College Entrance Exam

Exercise: In order to practice identifying an argument's assumption(s), fill in the missing pieces below.

Argument: Since Dorothy achieved a high score on her college entrance exam, she will surely succeed in college.

Conclusion: _____

Evidence: _____

Assumption: _____

Let's attack this argument.

Attack the evidence

Did Dorothy really score high on her college entrance exam? How high is high? In other words, we need to find out what score she actually got and then verify that it was indeed a "high" score.

Attack the assumption

This argument assumes that a high test score is not only enough to get accepted to college in the first place, but also that it's a good predictor of success in college. First, the college admissions process takes into account other factors, such as a candidate's written application essays, extracurricular activities, personal/academic references, and even an interview. Second, success in college depends on factors other than taking a test. Succeeding on a test requires no interaction with anyone except oneself. What about other factors, such as personal motivation, curiosity, independence, or emotional stability? Some courses may require group projects. In short, Dorothy may not have the personal qualities to succeed in college, even though she's mighty fine at taking an entrance exam!

Filling in the missing pieces, we may summarize the argument as follows:

Argument: Since Dorothy achieved a high score on her college entrance exam, she will surely succeed in college.

Conclusion: Dorothy will surely succeed in college.

Evidence: She achieved a high score on her college entrance exam.

Assumption: Success on a college entrance exam leads to success in college or, stated another way, success in college requires the same set of skills as is required to perform well on a college entrance exam.

The "Big Six" Assumption Categories

What again are the common types of assumptions that are encountered when tackling Critical Reasoning problems on the Verbal section of the GMAT exam? The six common categories of assumptions include: (1) comparison and analogy assumptions, (2) representativeness assumptions, (3) cause-and-effect assumptions, (4) implementation assumptions, (5) number-based assumptions, and (6) logic-based assumptions.

Comparison and Analogy Assumptions

Exhibit 5.3 provides a general strategy for attacking comparison and analogies assumptions.

EXHIBIT 5.3   ATTACKING COMPARISON AND ANALOGY ASSUMPTIONS

Topic	Formulaically	How to attack comparison and analogy assumptions
Are two things the same or nearly the same?	Does A = B?	Show that A is different from B and the comparison or analogy is weakened.
Are two things different?	Does A ≠ B?	Show that A is similar to B and the comparison or analogy is weakened.

In terms of evaluating or attacking comparisons, when two things are deemed similar, our goal will be to find dissimilarities in order to show that the two things are not alike. Consider the following example: "Martha did such a great job selling cutlery that we're going to promote her and put her in charge of condominium sales." What is being assumed is that sales ability is the key ingredient in making sales, and the type of product being sold is of secondary concern. How could we attack this argument? One way is to indicate that there could be a big difference between selling cutlery, a commodity product, and selling a condominium, a luxury good. A person effective at selling one type of product may be ineffective when selling another type. In the entrepreneurial context, a person successful in one industry may not be successful when switching to another industry.

In terms of evaluating or attacking comparisons, when two things are deemed dissimilar, our goal will be to find similarities in order to show that the two things are alike. For example, two male sports enthusiasts are having a beer, when one says to the other: "There is no comparison between athletes today and athletes of yesteryear. Mark Spitz won seven gold medals in swimming in the 1967 Mexico City Olympics, but his winning times are not good enough today to qualify for any of the men's Olympic swim events." To damage this argument, the second sports enthusiast might want to choose an example to show how athletes today are in some ways comparable to the athletes of yesteryear. For example, Jack Nicklaus' final round score of 271 in 1965 to win the Master's Golf Tournament in Augusta, Georgia, could be compared to Bubba Watson's final round score of 278 in 2012 to win the Master's Golf tournament on the exact same course.

In this respect, by comparing two athletes in this manner, things do not look so dissimilar after all. When comparing two things, particularly those across different time frames, we must be careful not to assume that information gathering techniques and, therefore, the quality of the data obtained are comparable. For example, any report comparing the findings of worker satisfaction levels in the 1940s to worker satisfaction levels today would be suspect, for no other reason than the difficulty of comparing the results of information gained under differing circumstances.

At the most fundamental level, we must ensure that the meaning and scope of words and terms used in an argument are consistently applied. Say, for example, we read that pollution is now ten times as bad in the suburban areas of our city as it was twenty years ago. Pollution may indeed by worse, but not by tenfold. What if the definition of pollution has changed to include air, water, noise, and garbage? This would certainly torpedo any attempt to establish a valid comparison.

Representativeness Assumptions

A sample is a group of people or things selected from a larger number of people or things that is presumably representative of the larger group or, as it is often said, "the population as a whole." We have all heard such statements as: "I've never met a person from country Z whom I liked" or "I highly recommend ABC Restaurant because the three times that I have dined there, the food has been delicious."

These two examples show representative sample assumptions in action. The first person obviously has not met all the people from country Z, and the second person obviously has not tried every dish in ABC Restaurant, and may even have tried the same dish on all three visits. For a sample to be representative, it must be both quantitatively and qualitatively representative. For a sample to be quantitatively sound, a large enough sample must be chosen. Obviously, the selection of one or two items is not enough. For a sample to be qualitatively sound, a random or diverse enough cross-sample of its members or items must be chosen.

What about a travel agency that claims: "Three out of every four tourists recommend Morocco as a tourist destination." For all we know, only eight tourists were surveyed, and six of these recommend Morocco as a tourist destination. In this hypothetical case, the sample of tourists chosen was too small. Now let's assume that the statistic "three out of every four tourists recommend Morocco" was based on a sufficiently large sample of several hundred tourists. But what if all the tourists were from Africa? Or suppose all the tourists were male or owned a travel agency specializing in trips to Africa? All of a sudden, we would have doubts as to whether these several hundred tourists were representative of tourists in general, and the statement that three of four tourists recommend Morocco would be suspect.

When evaluating situations involving representativeness, the objective is to show how a particular person, place, or thing is not representative of the larger "whole" and the argument is weakened or falls apart. On the other hand, show how a particular person, place, or thing is representative of the larger "whole" and the argument is strengthened.

Generally, the issue will not be whether a sample is large enough, but whether it is diverse enough. If the sample is not drawn from relevant representative subclasses, the sample size is of little consequence. A noteworthy real-life example is the Gallup poll, as originally devised by George Gallup, and used notably for predicting winning candidates in national political races. In order to generalize about the opinions of the people in an entire country with respect to a given candidate or political issue, data must be gathered from subclasses based on age, education, gender, geography, professional status, race, and perhaps even religion. Other subclasses, such as body weight and hair color, would be irrelevant. Even though there may well be millions of people in a given country, the Gallup poll requires a sample size of only about 1,800 people to be statistically accurate.

Note that a representativeness assumption is different from an analogy assumption. An analogy assumption might be thought of as a side-by-side comparison of two things whereas a representativeness assumption might be thought of as a vertical comparison stating that a "smaller something" is just like the larger whole. An analogy assumes big "A" is equal to big "B," but a representativeness assumption assumes little "a" is equal to big "A."

Cause-and-Effect Assumptions

Does one event really cause another? Cause and effect is concerned with the relationship (or non-relationship) between two events. The first event we call the *cause* and the second event we call the *effect*. Formulaically, we use A for the cause and B for the effect, which can be written A → B.

There are six categories under which potential cause-and-effect relationships arise. These include:

EXHIBIT 5.4   COINCIDENCE, CORRELATION, AND CAUSATION

No Cause and Effect	Cause and Effect
I. Mere coincidence	IV. Legitimate causation
II. Low correlation	V. Alternative explanation
III. High correlation	VI. Reverse causation

The first question we ask when a cause-and-effect assumption is on the horizon is whether any relationship exists between two items. There may not be any plausible relationship. For example: "The street light turned red just before the cat fell out of the tree; therefore, the red light caused the cat to fall out of the tree." These two events have no plausible causal relationship (mere coincidence). Next, assuming a relationship exists, we ask whether the two events are causally related or merely correlated. If a correlation exists, we seek to determine whether that correlation is low or high. If causally related, we seek to determine whether the two events are legitimately correlated or whether alternative or reverse causation is at work.

Here are further explanations of the categories outlined in *Exhibit 5.4*.

I.   Mere Coincidence

"Every time I sit in my favorite seat during a playoff game, our team wins." It is implausible that your "lucky" seat is causing your sports team to win. And it is equally implausible that a regular or "bad" seat will cause your team to lose.

II. Low Correlation

An example of low correlation might be the opening of new health clubs in your city and the general level of fitness among citizens in your city. Obviously, the opening of health clubs including weight-lifting classes, aerobic classes, and exercise machines will have some effect on the fitness level of people in general. But practically, it will not have a great deal of impact. The direct impact of a small number of health club members on the larger population of a city is limited. Even if there is a general trend toward more fitness in your city, it may be because people walk more, ride bikes more, and take hikes more often. Individuals may partake in these events and not be associated with health clubs.

III. High Correlation (but not causation)

There are certain items that have a strong correlation. We can safely say that there is a strong correlation between being tall and being an NBA player. Not every player in the NBA is tall but the vast majority of players are. A classic example in business is sales and advertising costs in a company. The more a company spends on advertising, the greater a company's sales. (Case in point: The correlation between advertising and sales is approximately 0.8) Other examples might include hot weather and ice cream sales, or rainy weather and umbrella sales. Strongly correlated events may be talked about as if they are causally related. It is important to be able to draw the line between high correlation and actual causation.

IV. Legitimate Causation

The law of gravity is a causal event. I throw an apple up into the air and it comes back down. Other events are so highly correlated that for all practical purposes they are assumed to be causally related. For example, the amount of coffee consumed and the amount of coffee beans used or the number of babies born and the number of baby diapers used. Note that it would not be accurate enough to say the number of coffee beans *grown* or the number of baby diapers *manufactured*.

V. Alternative Explanation

Alternative explanation can be technically called *alternative causal explanation*. Here we agree on a single conclusion (the effect), but differ as to which is the correct cause. We must always be on guard for the existence of another cause whenever it looks like two events are otherwise causally related. A business may have increased its advertising budget and seen an increase in sales. It is easy to view these two events as causally connected. But advertising may be having little effect on sales. The reason that sales have increased may be due to a major competitor of the company going out of business.

Another example occurs when John is speaking to Alice: "It's plain to see that the recent spike in high school shootings is the result of viewing violent TV programming." Who's to say that the high school shootings are not instead the result of lax gun laws, dwindling educational standards, or weakened religious following? In this case, it is not A that is causing B but rather C that is causing B. Or maybe there is a third factor causing both A and B. For example, perhaps both the increase in high school shootings and the increase in violent TV programming are the result of a third factor, e.g., breakdown of the family unit. In this latter case, it is not A that is causing B but rather C that is causing both A and B.

VI. Reverse Causation

Does your favorite commercial fiction author sell a lot of books because he or she is famous or is he or she famous as a result of selling lots of books? Reverse causation is tricky. You think X is causing Y but in reality it is Y that is causing X. The following example helps illustrate this point. Say you notice that a young woman at work named Sally is always working hard. And you say to yourself one day: "Sally is a hard worker. No wonder our boss gives her the toughest assignments." The argument becomes, "Because Sally is such a hard worker, our boss gives her the toughest assignments." But could the reverse be true? What if Sally is lazy and not naturally such a hard worker, but rather works hard only because she happens to be given the toughest projects. Now the argument becomes: "Because Sally is given such tough work projects, she is therefore forced to work hard!" Children may reveal funny examples to illuminate the concept of reverse causation. Young children may believe that firemen cause fires, for every time they see a picture or a video of a fire there are firemen at the scene. Eventually, the reverse is confirmed to be true: fires cause firemen.

As an historical example, when researchers first started testing the hypothesis that smoking causes cancer, one of the first things they considered was the reverse hypothesis—the idea that people who have cancer might go looking to start smoking (i.e., cancer causes smoking). Not surprisingly, this hypothesis proved groundless. However, in many other situations it is difficult to tell which is the cause and which is the effect. Consider the statement, "You're good at the things you like." The cause-and-effect argument becomes, "You like things (cause), and therefore you become good at them (effect)." But it could be that you find yourself good at some things and then learn to like them.

Implementation Assumptions

Implementation assumptions are a category of assumption that most closely mirror common sense. Although they sound so obvious when explained in simple academic terms, they are often spun into more complicated, convoluted scenarios when appearing on the GMAT (whether they appear as Critical Reasoning problems on the Verbal section or as Analysis of an Argument essays).

Some years ago, an article in a Western travel magazine stated: "Because air travel is becoming so convenient and because people have greater disposable incomes, soon everyone will have been to Africa to see the lions." Yet today, few people outside of Africa can claim to have been to Africa to see the lions. What accounts for the discrepancy between the travel magazine article and people actually going to visit Africa and the lions? Was the article wrong about plane travel becoming more convenient or people having higher levels of disposable income? The magazine was not likely wrong in these respects. However, the article was incorrect in its prediction that "everyone" (or, less literally, "many people") would go to Africa to see the lions. The discrepancy between an otherwise sound plan and action is based on the assumption that a sound plan must necessarily achieve its desired result. This is not necessarily so.

Why do plans not always work? There are essentially four major reasons that plans do not work: (1) an individual or organization's lack of desire, motivation, or perseverance; (2) an individual or organization's lack of prerequisite skill or technological capability to carry out the plan; (3) lack of required opportunity or wherewithal—e.g., economic resources—to commence or complete a given task; and (4) unanticipated bottlenecks or consequences (physical, financial, technological, or logistical) arising from the plan's implementation. "Implementation assumptions" are grounded on the idea that a plan will work because of an absence of the kinds of deficiencies cited here.

First, an individual or organization may lack desire, motivation, or perseverance to carry out a plan. There is a saying that "one who can read but doesn't is no better than one who cannot read." The ability to do something is not the same thing as actually using that skill. We all know of examples of extremely talented individuals who lack the focus or perseverance to achieve their true potential.

Second, the required skill or technological capability to carry out the plan may be lacking. Consider the statement a high school graduate made: "Either I'm going to medical school or I am going to join the military and become a member of the Special Forces." This assumes that the person has the talent and perseverance to get accepted to medical school en route to becoming a doctor. It equally assumes the physical and technical skill, mental toughness, and temperament to make it through training en route to being selected as a member of the Special Forces.

Third, we cannot assume that an individual or organization has the required opportunity or financial wherewithal, that is, economic resources, to complete a given task. In the example above, the high school graduate assumes that in the case of medical school, he or she has the ability to also obtain loans and other forms of financial aid required to complete medical studies.

Fourth, in terms of unanticipated bottlenecks or consequences, think what would happen if everyone pursued the proposed plan. For example, your office may be considering the installation of a new computer software system, which many believe will resolve your company's communication problems. But what if most workers find the system too complicated and difficult to use, they may avoid using it (physical and technological limitations).

Be suspicious of any claim that suggests that legislation can solve a problem. Legislation can certainly be used to discourage or limit undesirable actions, but it does not prevent them per se. Legislation to prevent discrimination, for instance, may not work if people themselves are unwilling to stop discrimination. Likewise, passing a law to increase fines for people parking their cars illegally in front of prestigious shopping venues will not necessarily stop shoppers from parking their cars, particularly wealthy consumers who may nonetheless decide to park illegally and accept higher fines.

Number-based Assumptions

Certain Critical Reasoning problems are based in math and an understanding of basic but tricky math may be essential in untangling these types of reasoning problems. The number-based assumptions presented here are broken down into five sub-categories. For the purposes of this overview, each sub-category below is supported with very simple examples.

I. Percentage vs. Actual Number Scenarios

We generally cannot compare percentages to numbers unless we know the exact numbers represented by the percentages. Percentages (like decimals, fractions, and ratios) are relative measures; actual numbers are absolute measures.

Suppose that there are only three females working at your company. Is this not gender discrimination? Not necessarily. What if there are only six persons working at your company? Then the three females represent 50 percent of total workers. Another example: In a given company, 10 percent of the employees in department A are salespersons whereas 20 percent of the employees in department B are salespersons. Does department B have more salespersons than department A? The answer is that we cannot tell. It could be that both departments have the same number of total employees, say 100, in which case department B would definitely have more salespersons than department A (see scenario 1). But there could be, say, 100 employees working in department A and 40 employees working in department B. In this case, the number of salespersons working in department A would be greater than the number of salespersons working in department B (see scenario 2).

Scenario 1:

	Dept A	Dept B
Number of total employees	100	100
% of employees who are salespersons	×10%	×20%
Number of salespersons	10	20

Scenario 2:

	Dept A	Dept B
Number of total employees	100	40
% of employees who are salespersons	×10%	×20%
Number of salespersons	10	8

Is train travel becoming more dangerous? Even if, in a given year, there are more train crashes and regrettably more deaths compared with a previous year, this does not necessarily mean that train travel is becoming more dangerous. We have to examine how many people are riding on trains (or, more precisely, "how many deaths per train miles logged"). If many more people are taking trains, it is likely that the percentage or ratio of train related deaths (to total passengers) is decreasing. In such a case, train travel would be deemed safer, not more dangerous. Ratios (or fractions, decimals, or percents) are necessary tools for drawing conclusions about qualitative measures such as "preferability," "danger," or "safety."

II. Overlap Scenarios

Overlap scenarios occur when items are members of either one group or another, but some items are members of both groups. Typically these are "either...or" situations which contain overlap. For example, a high school admissions office determined that of its 120 senior students, 78 were enrolled in math, and 63 were enrolled in physics. Here the total of both math and physics students adds up to 141. Some of these students must be taking both math and physics, and we cannot assume that all students must be either a math or physics student but not both.

Consider the following exchange:

Travel Agent: Of people who booked through our agency and traveled to Australia or New Zealand this past winter, 65 percent went to Australia and 55 percent went to New Zealand.

Customer: That doesn't sound right. You should check your numbers. How can more than 100 percent of your tourists travel to Australia or New Zealand?

The customer's response is likely invalid, because it is entirely possible that some tourists traveled to both Australia and New Zealand during their winter vacation.

III. Distribution or Allocation Scenarios

It cannot be assumed that data is divided into groups or sets of equal number. Distributions are not always proportional or linear. If a test has 100 problems and is divided into four sections, we can't assume that there are 25 problems per section. Likewise, we wouldn't assume that in a house that has three rooms covering an area of 750 square feet, that all rooms are exactly 250 square feet each.

IV. Total Costs vs. Per Unit Costs Scenarios

There are certain situations in which a distinction must be drawn between total costs and per unit costs. For example, a single piece of Dove chocolates and a single piece of Valentine chocolates are of equivalent size and of comparable quality. Since a box of Dove chocolates cost £5 (British pounds) and a box of Valentine chocolates costs £4 (British pounds), can we conclude Valentine chocolates are our best buy. Not necessarily—what if a box of Dove chocolates contains significantly more chocolates as compared with a box of Valentine chocolates? We cannot just assume that the number of units is the same.

V. Profit and Loss Scenarios

Profit and loss scenarios highlight the interplay of the three profit components: price, cost, and volume. Just because a computer store is selling more computers than last year does not mean that its profits are up. Why? Because an increase in the sales volume (i.e., number of unit sales) of a good or service item does not necessarily equal an increase in revenues or profits. Likewise, an increase in the price of a good or service does not necessarily equal an increase in profits. Moreover, an increase in the cost of a good or service does not necessarily equal a decrease in profits.

Variations of the profit formula appear below:

Revenue − Cost = Profit

$$(\text{Price}_{\text{per unit}} - \text{Cost}_{\text{per unit}}) \times \text{Volume} = \text{Profit}$$

$$(\text{Price}_{\text{per unit}} \times \text{Volume}) - (\text{Cost}_{\text{per unit}} \times \text{Volume}) = \text{Profit}$$

Logic-based Assumptions

For the purposes of studying for the GMAT, working with logic-based assumptions requires an understanding of the following two topics: "If...then" Statements and "No-Some-Most-All" Statements.

I. "If... Then" Statements

Consider the following statement:

Original: If you work hard, you'll be successful.

Now ponder these related statements.

Statement 1:   If you're successful, then you've worked hard.

Statement 2:   If you don't work hard, you won't be successful.

Statement 3:   If you're not successful, then you didn't work hard.

The question becomes: "Which of the above statements are logical deductions based on the original statement above?"

Upon closer examination, statement 1 isn't necessarily correct. The fact that you're successful (whatever this means!) doesn't mean that you have necessarily worked hard. There could be several other ways to become successful. For example, perhaps you're skillful, intelligent, or downright lucky.

Likewise, statement 2 is not necessarily correct. Just because you don't work hard doesn't mean that you won't be successful. As already mentioned, you might be skillful, intelligent, or lucky as opposed to hardworking. However, statement 3 is a perfectly logical deduction based on the original. If you're not successful, then you must not have worked hard. This doesn't mean, however, that there are not other explanations for why you might not have been successful. For example, perhaps you were neither skillful in your approach nor lucky in your application.

"If...then" statements are another way to represent causal relationships. Take the following generic statement: "If A, then B." This is sometimes written in a more formulaic manner: i.e., "If A → B." Consider the statement "If it is U.S. money (dollar bills), then it is green (colored)." This can also be written: If $US → Green. Another way to illustrate an "if...then" relationship is to draw circles. The "If" item always represents the innermost circle, while the "then" item always represents the outermost circle. See *Exhibit 5.5*.

EXHIBIT 5.5   DIAGRAMMING "IF...THEN" STATEMENTS

If it is U.S. money, then it is green (if US$, then Green)

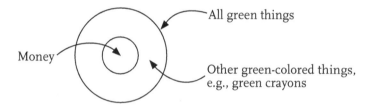

The above diagram illustrates in picture form the relationship between U.S. money and all green things. We can read from the inside circle to the outside circle, but we cannot read from the outside circle to the inside circle. "If U.S. money then green" does not equal "If green then U.S. money."

What can we logically infer from this type of statement? *Exhibit 5.6* contains four statements that may seem to the casual observer all to be inferable. However, only the fourth version is correctly inferable. In "if...then" statements, it is important that you read in one direction only, as the reverse is not necessarily true. Based on the original statement "If it is U.S. money, then it is green," the only thing we can infer logically from this statement is that it is true that "If it is <u>not</u> green, then it is <u>not</u> U.S. money."

EXHIBIT 5.6   AMERICAN MONEY

Statement	Are these statements logically inferable?
(1) If it is U.S. money, then it is green.	n/a – original statement
(2) If it is green, then it is U.S. money.	No. This statement now says that all green things are U.S. money, and this is obviously ridiculous. Many things in the universe are green, including green-colored crayons, Christmas trees, garbage pails, green paint, and Kermit the Frog. (Known as the fallacy of affirming the consequent.)
(3) If it is not U.S. money, then it is not green.	No. Why? Many things other than U.S. money are green in color. (Known as the fallacy of denying the antecedent.)
(4) If it is not green, then it is not U.S. money.	Yes. This statement is inferable. Why? Because being green is one of the requirements for something to be U.S. money.

To master "if...then" statements it is essential to memorize the information contained in *Exhibit 5.7*. According to formal logic, the contrapositive is always correct. That is to say, the only thing we can infer from an "If A, then B statement" is "If not B, then not A."

EXHIBIT 5.7   THE LOGIC OF "IF...THEN" STATEMENTS

Statement	Reference to formal logic	Are the statements logically inferable?
(1) If A, then B	n/a – (original statement)	n/a – (original statement)
(2) If B, then A	Known as the fallacy of affirming the consequent.	No, incorrect. This is not inferable.
(3) If not A, then not B	Known as the fallacy of denying the antecedent.	No, incorrect. This is not inferable.
(4) If not B, then not A	Known as the contrapositive.	Yes, correct. This is always logically inferable based on the original statement.

Another way of understanding "If...then" statements is through an understanding of necessary versus sufficient conditions. A necessary condition must be present for an event to occur, but will not, by itself, cause the given event to occur. A sufficient condition is enough, by itself, to ensure that the event will occur. In more technical parlance, a necessary condition is a condition which, if absent, will not allow the event to occur. A sufficient condition is a condition which, if present, will cause the event to occur.

When a person argues "If A, then B" and then argues "If B, then A," he or she erroneously reverses the conditional statement. The reason that a conditional statement cannot be reversed is that the original "If...then" statement functions as a necessary condition. When it is reversed, an "If...then" statement erroneously turns into a sufficient condition. In the example above, being "green" is a necessary but not a sufficient condition in order for something to be considered U.S. money. Obviously, other factors besides "green coloring" need be present, including special watermarked paper, unique insignia, and exact size. By reversing the "If...then" statement, we erroneously suggest that being green-colored is enough of a criterion for something to be considered U.S. money.

Try one more example: "I gave my pet hamster water every day and he still died." Giving your pet hamster water each day is a necessary condition for keeping him alive, but it is not a sufficient condition. Obviously, a hamster needs many other things besides water, one of which is food.

II. "No-Some-Most-All" Statements

Many errors are committed in drawing inferences because ordinary speech is inherently ambiguous. For example, take the four statements below:

Statement 1:   No As are Bs

Statement 2:   All As are Bs

Statement 3:   Some As are Bs

Statement 4:   Most As are Bs

To study the meaning of these four statements, refer to *Exhibit 5.8*. We can see that statement 1 corresponds to either diagram (1a) or (1b), but usually to diagram (1a). Statement 2 could represent either diagram (2a) or (2b), although usually diagram (2b). Statement 3 could typify any one of diagrams (3a), (3b), or (3c), although usually (3b). Statement 4 could refer to either diagram (4a) or (4b), but typically (4b). This is evidence that ordinary speech can hamper clear thinking, and that it is often necessary to use non-verbal symbols to reinforce clear thinking.

The diagrams in *Exhibit 5.8* summarize the concepts of mutual inclusivity, mutual exclusivity, and overlap. Either circles are completely separated, or circles overlap with one another circles, or circles are embedded inside one another. Basically, there are nine possibilities.

There are two major differences between "most" and "some" statements. First, it is assumed that "most" implies majority (greater than half), while "some" implies minority (less than half). Second, whereas "some statements" automatically imply reciprocality, "most statements" do not necessarily imply reciprocality. For example, the statement "some doctors are wealthy people" implies that some wealthy people are also doctors. But the statement "most doctors are wealthy people" does not necessarily mean that most wealthy people are doctors.

EXHIBIT 5.8   OVERLAP AND NON-OVERLAP SCENARIOS

Statement 1—*No As are Bs*—could refer to either diagram (1a) or (1b).

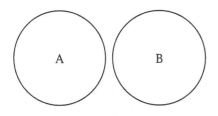

(1a)
A and B do not overlap
and are not touching.

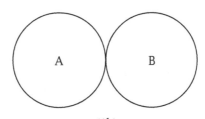

(1b)
A and B do not overlap
but are touching.

Statement 2—*All As are Bs*—could refer to either diagram (2a) or (2b).

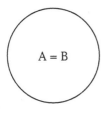

(2a)
A and B overlap perfectly.

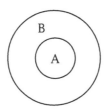

(2b)
A is completely inside B.

Statement 3—*Some As are Bs*—could refer to any of diagrams (3a), (3b), or (3c).

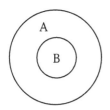

(3a)
B is completely inside A.

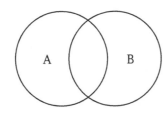

(3b)
A and B overlap.
A and B overlap partly.

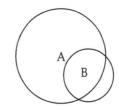

(3c)
A and B overlap. Most of B is inside
A, but most of A is not inside B.

Statement 4—*Most As are Bs*—could refer to either diagram (4a) or (4b).

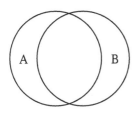

(4a)
A and B overlap. Most of A is
inside B and most of B is inside A.

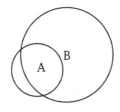

(4b)
A and B overlap. Most of A is inside
B, but most of B is not inside A.

MULTIPLE-CHOICE PROBLEMS

Comparison and Analogy Assumptions

1. **Crime ( )**

    According to an article in the *Life and Times* section of the Sunday newspaper, crime is on the downturn in our city. Police initiatives, neighborhood watches, stiff fines, and lengthened prison terms have all played a significant role in reducing the number of reported crimes by twenty percent.

    Which of the following would most weaken the belief that crime has decreased in our city?

    A)   In its Sunday newspaper, a neighboring city has also reported a decrease in crime.

    B)   Police officers were among those citizens who voted for a bill to support police initiatives to reduce crime in our city.

    C)   Most of the recent police arrests were repeat offenders.

    D)   The author of the article includes white-collar crime in his definition of crime, thus increasing the number of reported crimes.

    E)   It is possible for reported crime to have gone down while actual crime has remained the same or actually gone up.

2. **Hyperactivity ( )**

    Viewing children as more hyperactive today than they were ten years ago, many adults place the blame squarely on the popularity of video games and multimedia entertainment.

    Which of the following revelations would most undermine the argument above?

    A)   Even if children today are more hyperactive than they were ten years ago, they are widely viewed as more spontaneous and creative.

    B)   The claim that children are more aggressive today is a more serious charge than their being considered more hyperactive.

    C)   Children's books published in recent years contain on average more pictures than do children's books published in the past.

    D)   More types of behavior are deemed hyperactive today than there were ten years ago.

    E)   Incidences of ailments such as Attention Deficit Hyperactivity Disorder (ADHD) are reported to be on the increase in recent years.

3. **Banff National Park ( )**

A recent report determined that although only eight percent of drivers entering Banff National Park possessed yearly entry permits, as opposed to day passes, these drivers represented fifteen percent of all vehicles entering the Park. Clearly, drivers who possess yearly entry permits are more likely to enter Banff National Park on a regular basis than are drivers who do not.

The conclusion drawn above depends on which of the following assumptions?

A) The number of entries to Banff National Park by drivers with yearly entry permits does not exceed the number of yearly entry permits issued by the Park.

B) Drivers who possess yearly entry permits to Banff National Park are more likely to stay longer in the Park than drivers who do not.

C) All drivers with yearly entry permits to Banff National Park entered the Park at least once during the period of the report.

D) Drivers possessing yearly entry permits to Banff National Park are more likely to enter the Park regularly than are drivers who do not.

E) Drivers who entered Banff National Park with yearly permits during the period of the report were representative of the types of drivers who have entered other national parks with similar yearly permits.

Cause-and-Effect Assumptions

4. **SAT Scores ( )**

Parents are too easily impressed with the recent rise in average SAT scores at the top American undergraduate universities and colleges. Unfortunately, this encouraging statistic is misleading. Scores have risen not because students possess better math, English, and writing skills but because students are better at taking tests. For those students accepted at the top undergraduate universities and colleges, studies confirm that skills in the basics of reading, writing, and mathematics have been on the gradual decline over the past twenty years.

The author argues primarily by

A) denying the accuracy of his opponents' figures.

B) finding an alternative explanation for his opponent's evidence.

C) introducing irrelevant information to draw attention away from the main issue.

D) employing circular reasoning.

E) suggesting that his opponent's evidence may be flawed.

5. **Cyclists ( )**

Touring professional cyclists have been shown to have between four and eleven percent body fat. If we could all decrease our body fat to that level, we could all cycle at a world-class level.

Which statement(s) below accurately describe the flaw in the method of reasoning used in the above argument?

I. It assumes a causal relationship between two highly correlated events.

II. It suggests that low body fat is a sufficient condition rather than a necessary condition for becoming a world-class cyclist.

III. Its conclusion is based on evidence which, in turn, is based on its conclusion.

A) I only

B) II only

C) I & II only

D) II & III only

E) All of the above

6. **Valdez ( )**

Since Ana Valdez was installed as president of the Zipco Corporation, profits have averaged 15 percent each year. During her predecessor's tenure, the corporation's profits averaged only 8 percent per year. Obviously Ms. Valdez's aggressive international marketing efforts have caused the acceleration in the growth of Zipco's profits.

Which of the following, if true, would most weaken the conclusion drawn above?

A) During the tenure of Ms. Valdez's predecessor, the corporation began an advertising campaign aimed at capturing consumers in developing countries between the ages of nineteen and twenty-five.

B) The corporation's new manufacturing plant, constructed in the past year, has a 35 percent greater production capacity.

C) Since Ms. Valdez became president, the corporation has switched the primary focus of its advertising from print ads to radio and television commercials.

D) Ms. Valdez hired a well-known headhunting firm which found talented vice-presidents for two of the corporation's five divisions.

E) Just before Ms. Valdez took over as president, her predecessor, Mr. Jones, directed the acquisition of a rival corporation, which has nearly doubled the corporation's yearly revenues.

7. **Headline ( )**

The headline of the *Daily College Inquirer* reads: "Obesity Linked to Depression."

Which of the following, if true, would most weaken the implied conclusion drawn between becoming overweight and falling into depression?

A)   An obese person may not understand why he or she is depressed or how to escape from the throes of depression.

B)   Depression can result from things other than obesity.

C)   Low self-esteem is frequently cited as the cause of both obesity and depression.

D)   A person twice as overweight as another person is not likely to be twice as depressed.

E)   Depression has been further linked to desperation and suicide.

8. **TV Viewing ( )**

An investigator divided 128 adults into two distinct groups (high TV viewers and low TV viewers) based on the number of hours of violent TV programming they watched per day. A significantly larger percentage of the high-viewing group than of the low-viewing group demonstrated a high level of aggression. The investigator concluded that greater TV viewing, particularly of violent programming, caused higher aggression levels.

Which of the following, if true, most seriously weakens the conclusion above?

A)   Some subjects in the high-viewing group experienced lower levels of aggression than did other subjects in the high-viewing group.

B)   Some subjects in the low-viewing group did not experience any aggression.

C)   Fear of aggressive tendencies as a result of watching large amounts of TV was the reason some subjects restricted their viewing of TV.

D)   Some subjects watched live programming whereas other viewers watched pre-recorded TV programs.

E)   Some subjects' already high levels of aggression caused them to increase their viewing, particularly of violent TV programs.

9. Shark (𝄞𝄞)

In a marine reserve off the south coast of Australia, people are sometimes attacked by sharks. Here, it is believed that the sharks will only attack people who are mistaken for seals, which occurs when surfers wear entirely black body suits. So for the past few years, surfers have started wearing bright metallic body suits. While many area residents remain skeptical, no surfer wearing a metallic body suit has yet been attacked by a shark.

Which of the statements below, if true, would best support the argument of those who advocate the use of metallic body suits?

A) Surfers at other surf areas who wear metallic body suits have not been attacked recently by sharks.

B) A number of surfers in this marine area wearing black body suits have been attacked recently by sharks.

C) No sharks have been spotted in this marine reserve off the south coast of Australia in recent months.

D) Some of the surfers who wear metallic suits also wear wristbands that contain metal bells in order to frighten away any sharks.

E) Underwater divers have observed sharks attacking tuna and other ocean fish, some of them black in color.

Representativeness Assumptions

10. Movie Buffs (𝄞)

According to a recent survey, any sequel to the movie *Victim's Revenge* will not fare well. Respondents to a recent survey of moviegoers leaving the Sunday matinees around the country indicated that movies based on serial killers with psychopathic tendencies have fallen out of vogue with current movie buffs. Therefore, if movie studios want to produce films that are financially successful, they should avoid producing such films.

Which of the following would most weaken the idea that film studios should stop production of stories and dramas based on serial killers with psychopathic tendencies?

A) Movie stars have a significant following of individuals who see their every film.

B) People who attend of Sunday matinees are not representative of the views of the moviegoing population as a whole.

C) The film *Psycho,* originally directed by Alfred Hitchcock, was a big hit in 1960 and later remade in 1998.

D) Both student enrollment in college criminology courses and book sales based on the lives of real-life serial killers are up.

E) The cost of making such movies requires skillful actors who can portray emotional conflict and intellectualism, and these actors demand high salaries.

11. Putting ( )

Are you having trouble getting the golf score you deserve? Is putting your pariah? The new Sweet Spot Putter is designed to improve your golf game overnight without intensive lessons. Even rank amateurs can dramatically increase their putting accuracy by 25 percent. You too can achieve a low golf score with the new Sweet Spot Putter.

Someone who accepted the reasoning in the advertisement above would be making which one of the following assumptions?

A)   Without quality equipment, a golf player cannot improve his or her game.

B)   The new Sweet Spot Putter will improve an amateur's game more than it will improve a professional's game.

C)   The quality of a person's golf game is largely determined by the accuracy of his or her putting.

D)   The new Sweet Spot Putter is superior to any other putter currently on the market.

E)   Lessons are not as effective at improving the accuracy of a player's putting as is the use of quality equipment.

12. Critic's Choice ( )

In a newly released book, *Decline of the Novelist*, the author argues that novelists today lack technical skills that were common among novelists during the past century. In this regard, the book might be right, since its analysis of 200 novels—100 contemporary and 100 non-contemporary—demonstrates convincingly that few contemporary novelists exhibit the same skill level as that of non-contemporary novelists.

Which of the following points to the most serious logical flaw in the critic's argument?

A)   The title of the author's book could cause readers to accept the book's thesis even before they read the literary analysis of those novels that support it.

B)   There could be criteria other than the novelist's technical skills by which to evaluate a novel.

C)   The novels the critic chose to analyze could be those that most support the book's thesis.

D)   The particular methods novelists currently use may require even more literary skill than do methods used by writers of screenplays.

E)   A reader who was not familiar with the language of literary criticism might not be convinced by the book's analysis of its 200 novels.

13. Questionnaire (✦✦)

President: "I'm worried about the recent turnover in MegaCorp. If employees leave our company disgruntled, such negative feelings can hurt our reputation in the marketplace."

Human Resources Manager: "Your concerns are unfounded. As part of our post-employment follow-up process, we send questionnaires to each employee within thirty days of his or her leaving the company. These questionnaires seek honest answers and remind employees that all responses will be kept confidential. Of the last 100 employees who left our company, 25 have responded, and only five people have mentioned having had any negative employment experience."

The Human Resource Manager's argument is most vulnerable to criticism on the grounds that it fails to acknowledge the possibility that

A)   Opinions expressed in such questionnaires are not always indicative of how employees actually felt.

B)   Many of those who harbored truly negative feelings about their employment experience at MegaCorp did not respond to the questionnaire.

C)   The Public Relations firm, Quantum, recently hired by MegaCorp has successfully designed several programs specially aimed at boosting the company's public image.

D)   Questions asking about negative employment experiences have been placed at the end, not at the beginning, of the questionnaire.

E)   The response rate in general for questionnaires is 10 percent, meaning that only 1 in 10 questionnaires can be expected to be completed and returned.

14. Temperament ( )

Steve: Rick and Harriet, two of my red-haired friends, are irritable. It seems true that red-haired people have bad tempers.

John: That's ridiculous. Red-haired people are actually quite docile. Jeff, Muriel, and Betsy—three of my red-haired friends—all have placid demeanors.

Which of the statements below provides the most likely explanation for the two seemingly contradictory statements above?

A) The number of red-haired people whom Steve knows may be different from the number of red-haired people whom John knows.

B) The number of red-haired people whom both Steve and John know may not be greater in total than the number of non-red-haired people whom both Steve and John know.

C) It is likely that Steve or John has incorrectly assessed the temperament of one or more of his red-haired friends.

D) It is likely that both Steve and John have friends who are not red-haired and yet also have bad tempers.

E) The examples that Steve uses and the examples that John uses to support their conclusions are likely both valid.

Implementation Assumptions

15. Rainbow Corp ( )

"Tina obviously cares little about the environment. She continues to use Purple Rider Felt Pens even though the company that makes these pens, Rainbow Corp., has been the focus of several recent newspaper articles as a result of its indictment for several violations involving dumping toxic wastes in the harbor."

Which of the following would serve to most weaken the claim that Tina cares little about the environment?

A) Although the Rainbow Corp. has been the subject of several newspaper articles, it has been praised by consumers for its high-quality products.

B) Tina is not aware of the recent newspaper articles which feature Rainbow Corp. and its indictment for several violations involving dumping toxic wastes in the harbor.

C) The newspaper which ran the articles of Rainbow's indictments also owns a "gossip magazine" called the *Tipsy Tattler*.

D) The public relations department of Rainbow Corp. never issued a statement denying that the company had violated the law.

E) Tina held membership in an environmental protection organization during her freshman and sophomore years in college.

16. Public Transportation ( )

People should switch from driving their cars to work on the weekdays to taking public transportation, such as buses and subways. In major cities such as New York, London, or Tokyo, for example, cars are an expensive and inefficient means of transportation, and fossil fuel emissions are the major source of the city's pollution.

The argument above make all of the following are assumptions EXCEPT

A)   There may be easier ways to combat pollution in large cities than by having people switch to taking public transportation.

B)   There are enough people who actually own cars, which are currently being used to drive to work, to make this plan realistically feasible.

C)   Public transportation is both available and accessible should someone wish to switch.

D)   Current public transportation systems can accommodate all the people who decide to switch.

E)   The city can afford to pay public transport drivers and related personnel who may otherwise remain idle once the morning and evening rush hour periods are over.

17. Classics ( )

Any literate person who is not lazy can read the classics. Since few literate persons have read the classics, it is clear that most literate persons are lazy.

Which of the following is an assumption on which the argument above is based?

A)   Only literate persons can understand the classics.

B)   Any literate person should read the classics.

C)   Any literate person who is lazy has no chance of reading the classics.

D)   Any literate person who will not read the classics is lazy.

E)   Any literate person who can read the classics will choose to do so.

Number-based Assumptions

18. **Med School ( )**

A student activist group has released a report that suggests that female students have more difficulties in earning admittance to medical school. The facts in the report speak for themselves: seventy-five percent of all students in medical school are male, but fewer than half of all female applicants reach their goal of being admitted to medical school.

Which of the following data would be most helpful in evaluating the argument above?

A)   The portion of all admissions officers who are male versus female.

B)   The percentage of eligible female students admitted to medical school who accept a particular school's offer of admissions and the percentage of eligible male students admitted to medical school who also accept that particular school's offer of admission.

C)   The percentage of eligible female students admitted to medical school and the percentage of eligible male students admitted to medical school.

D)   Comparative records on acceptance rates of male and female applicants in other graduate programs such as business, law, and the sciences.

E)   The dropout rate for female and male students while in medical school.

19. **Military Expenditures ( )**

Proponents of greater military spending for the Reno Republic argue that the portion of their national budget devoted to military programs has been steadily declining for a number of years, largely because of rising domestic infrastructure development costs. Yet groups opposed to increasing military expenditure point out that the military budget of Reno Republic, even when measured in constant or inflation-adjusted dollars, has increased every year for the past two decades.

Which of the following, if true, best resolves the apparent contradiction presented above?

A)   Countries in the same region as the Reno Republic have increased the annual portion of their national budgets devoted to military spending.

B)   The advocates of greater military spending have overestimated the amount needed for adequate defense of the country.

C)   Domestic infrastructure development costs have indeed risen as sharply as the advocates of greater military spending claim they have.

D)   Military expenditures have risen at a rate higher than the rate of inflation.

E)   The total national budget has increased faster than military expenditure has increased.

20. Nova vs. Rebound ( )

Jill: "In our survey 53 percent of those questioned said they used Nova Running Shoes for jogging and 47 percent said they used Rebound Running Shoes for jogging."

Jack: "In that case everyone questioned used one product or the other."

Jill: "No, 24 percent said they didn't use either one."

Jill's statements imply that

A)   Not all of those questioned liked to go jogging.

B)   Some of those who said they used either Nova or Rebound Running Shoes for jogging were lying.

C)   Some of those who used Nova Running Shoes for jogging were among those who also used Rebound Running Shoes for jogging.

D)   Some of those who used neither product were nevertheless familiar with Nova and Rebound Running Shoes.

E)   Many Nova and Rebound Running Shoes are actually made in the same factory in various international locations.

21. Grapes ( )

It costs much less to grow an acre of grapes in California than it costs to grow an acre of watermelons in Oklahoma. This fact should be obvious to anyone who reads last year's annual farm report, which clearly shows that many millions of dollars more were spent last year growing watermelons in Oklahoma than were spent growing grapes in California.

Which of the following, if true, would most seriously call the reasoning above into question?

A)   Profits on the sale of Californian grapes are much higher than the profits derived from the sales of Oklahoma watermelons.

B)   There were far fewer total acres of grapes grown in California last year than total acres of watermelons in Oklahoma.

C)   An acre of grapes in Oklahoma costs much more to grow than an acre of watermelons in California.

D)   Part of Californian grown grapes were used to feed livestock whereas all of the watermelons grown in Oklahoma were used for human consumption.

E)   State subsidies accounted for a larger percentage of the amount spent growing watermelons in Oklahoma than of the amount spent growing grapes in California last year.

22. Act-Fast (🌶️🌶️)

One Act-Fast tablet contains twice the pain reliever found in a tablet of regular Aspirin. A consumer will have to take two Aspirin tablets in order to get the relief provided by one Act-Fast tablet. And since a bottle of Act-Fast costs the same as a bottle of regular Aspirin, consumers can be expected to switch to Act-Fast.

Which of the following, if true, would most weaken the argument that consumers will be discontinuing the use of regular Aspirin and switching to Act-Fast?

A)   A regular Aspirin tablet is twice as large as an Act-Fast tablet.

B)   Neither regular Aspirin nor Act-Fast is as effective in relief of serious pain as are drugs available only by prescriptions.

C)   Some headache sufferers experience a brief period of nausea shortly after taking Act-Fast but not after taking regular Aspirin.

D)   A regular bottle of Aspirin contains more than twice as many tablets as does a bottle of Act-Fast.

E)   The pain reliever in Act-Fast is essentially the same pain reliever found in regular Aspirin.

23. Fiction Books (🌶️🌶️🌶️)

A major publishing conglomerate released a survey concerning the relationship between a household's education level and the kind of books found in its library. Specifically, members of households with higher levels of education had more books in their libraries. The survey also indicated that compared with members of households with lower levels of education, members of households with higher levels of education had a greater percentage of fiction versus nonfiction books.

Which of the following can be properly inferred from the survey results cited above?

A)   People with the highest levels of education buy more fiction books than nonfiction books.

B)   Members of households with higher levels of education have more fiction books than nonfiction books.

C)   Members of households with lower levels of education have more nonfiction books than fiction books.

D)   Members of households with lower levels of education have more nonfiction books than do members of households with higher levels of education.

E)   Members of households with higher levels of education have more fiction books than do members of households with lower levels of education.

Logic-based Assumptions

24. **Intricate Plots (🌶)**

The ability to create intricate plots is one of the essential gifts of the scriptwriter. Strong plot development ensures that eventual moviegoers will be intellectually and emotionally satisfied by the story. If scriptwriting is to remain a significant art form, its practitioners must continue to craft intricate plots.

The author of the argument above would most probably agree with which one of the following statements?

A)   If a script has an intricate plot, it must necessarily be a significant art form.

B)   A script without an intricate plot will never become a blockbuster movie.

C)   If a script does not have an intricate plot, it will probably not be a significant art form.

D)   Scriptwriting is the most likely art form to become a significant art form.

E)   A scriptwriter must craft multiple plots within his or her scripts.

25. **Campus Pub (🌶🌶)**

During final exam week, our campus pub sells a lot of beer. But it isn't final exam week, so our campus pub must not be selling much beer."

Which of the following is logically most similar to the argument above?

A)   When people are happy, they smile, but no one is smiling, so it must be that no one is happy.

B)   When people are happy, they smile; our family members are happy, so they must be smiling.

C)   When people are happy, they smile, but one can smile and not be happy.

D)   When people are happy, they smile, but no one is happy, so no one is smiling.

E)   When people are not happy, they do not smile; our family members are smiling, so they must not be unhappy.

26. Balcony ( )

If your apartment is above the fifth floor, it has a balcony.

The statement above can be logically deduced from which of the following statements?

A)   No apartments on the fifth floor have balconies.

B)   An apartment does not have a balcony unless the apartment is above the fifth floor.

C)   All apartments above the fifth floor have balconies.

D)   All balconies are built for apartments above the fifth floor.

E)   Balconies are not built for apartments below the fifth floor.

27. Sales ( )

Debra: "To be a good salesperson, one must be friendly."

Tom: "That's not so. It takes much more than friendliness to make a good salesperson."

Tom has understood Debra's statement to mean that

A)   Being friendly is the most important characteristic of being a good salesperson.

B)   If a person is a good salesperson, he or she will be friendly.

C)   A salesperson only needs to be friendly in order to be a good salesperson.

D)   Most good salespersons are friendly people even though not all friendly people are good salespersons.

E)   If a person isn't friendly, he or she will not make a good salesperson.

28. Football ( )

Marie: "Every person on the Brazilian World Cup football team is a great player."

Beth: "What! The Italian World Cup football team has some of the best players in the world."

Beth's reply suggests that she has misunderstood Marie's remark to mean that

A)   Only Brazilian World Cup team players are great players.

B)   Marie believes that the Brazilian World Cup football team is the best overall football team.

C)   The Italian World Cup football team consists of less-than-great players.

D)   The Brazilian World Cup football team is likely to defeat the Italian World Cup football team should they meet in match play.

E)   Individual Brazilian World Cup team players will play as well as a unit as will the Italian World Cup team players.

29. Global Warming ( )

Jacques: "If we want to stop global warming, we must pass legislation to reduce fossil fuel emissions."

Pierre: "That's not true. It will take a lot more than passing legislation aimed at reducing fossil fuel emissions in order to stop global warming."

Pierre's response is inaccurate because he mistakenly believes that what Jacques has said is that

A)   Passing legislation to reduce fossil fuel emissions is necessary to reduce global warming.

B)   Only the passing of legislation to reduce fossil fuel emissions is capable of stopping global warming.

C)   If global warming is to be stopped, legislation to reduce fossil fuel emissions must be passed.

D)   Passing legislation to reduce fossil fuel emissions is enough to stop global warming.

E)   Global warming will not be stopped by passing legislation to reduce fossil fuel emissions.

Bolded-Statement Problems

30. Smoking (𝄞 𝄞)

The dangers of smoking, although well documented, are often ignored even today. According to numerous published accounts, a person who smokes habitually has a thirty percent greater chance of developing cancer or heart disease than someone who does not smoke. Many individuals residing outside the health and wellness fields either find research on the ill effects of smoking to be non-compelling or choose to ignore such evidence altogether. **They are likely to point to instances of individuals who smoke regularly despite living well into their nineties.** What these people fail to realize is that there is a difference between a highly correlated event and a causally related event. The absence of a causally related event does not negate the validity of a highly correlated event.

Which of the following best describes the purpose of the bolded statement?

A)   It is evidence used to support a conclusion that follows.

B)   It is a counter argument used as a persuasive device.

C)   It is evidence used to support a counterclaim.

D)   It is an assumption challenged through rebuttal.

E)   It is an unstated premise, linking the argument's evidence to its broader conclusion.

Answers and Explanations

1. Crime (🌶️)

Choice E
Classification: Comparison and Analogy Assumptions
Snapshot: Watch for "scope shifts" that occur when one term is inadvertently substituted for another as an argument unfolds.

The key to understanding this problem is to see the scope shift that occurs as a result of switching terms from "crime" to "reported crime." Obviously, reported crime is not the same thing as actual crime. As answer choice E states: "It is possible for reported crime to have gone down while actual crime has remained the same or actually gone up." In order to make valid comparisons, we need to stick to terms that are of equivalent meaning.

Choice A is incorrect. This answer choice slightly strengthens, not weakens, the original argument. In choice B, it does not matter whether police officers, as citizens themselves, voted for a bill on initiatives to reduce crime in the city. It also does not matter, as in choice C, whether most arrests were repeat offenders. Whether offenders were first-time offenders or repeat offenders, crime is crime.

The fact that crime has come to include white-collar crime (choice D) actually strengthens the argument. It suggests that there could be more incidences of crime (or cases of reported crime), which makes a decrease in crime (or cases of reported crime) potentially that much more significant.

2. Hyperactivity (🌶️🌶️)

Choice D
Classification: Comparison and Analogy Assumptions
Snapshot: Changes in definition destroy the ability to make comparisons. Make sure that the way terms are defined remains consistent.

The idea that more types of behavior are deemed hyperactive indeed weakens the claim that children today are more hyperactive than they were ten years ago. In short, there are more ways to "check off" and confirm hyperactive behavior. In order to compare the hyperactivity of children today versus ten years ago, we need an even playing field in terms of the comparability of terms: the definition of hyperactivity or the criteria for hyperactive behavior must remain consistent over time. Choices A and B are effectively out of the argument's scope. We are not talking about creativity and spontaneity, nor are we primarily concerned about other potentially more serious issues beyond hyperactivity. The impact of having more or fewer pictures in children's books remains unclear (choice C) as does an increase in ailments such as Attention Deficit Hyperactivity Disorder (ADHD) per choice E.

3. Banff National Park (🌶️🌶️🌶️)

Choice D
Classification: Comparison and Analogy Assumptions
Snapshot: This problem presents a very subtle "scope shift" that occurs with the addition of the words "on a regular basis." Without these words, the argument is otherwise on sound footing.

From a content standpoint, this problem is similar to an allocation or distribution scenario within number-based assumptions. Just because a driver with a yearly pass enters the Park more often than does a driver with a day pass, this does not technically mean that a driver enters the Park on a more regular or consistent basis. Case in point: a driver with a yearly pass might enter the Park ten times a month, but do so at the beginning and end of the month only, or even with multiple frequency on given days. Such "concentrated entries" would not constitute "regular" entries—"more" does not necessarily mean "more regularly."

The argument does not depend on choices A, B, C, or E. In fact, it is virtually certain that the number of entries made by drivers with yearly permits does exceed the number of yearly entry permits issued by the Park. After all, almost all drivers with yearly permits will likely enter the Park more than once during the year (that's why they have yearly permits). The argument does not depend on drivers with yearly permits staying longer in the Park (choice B); it is an "entry" that counts, not the duration of the stay. It is also not necessary for *all* drivers to have entered the Park at least once during the period of the report (choice C). Some of the drivers with yearly passes might not have entered the Park once. The only thing that is important is that the 8 percent of drivers possessing yearly permits do, in fact, constitute 15 percent of the vehicles entering the Park during the period of the report. In choice E, there is no need to compare drivers in this report to those who entered *other* national parks.

NOTE ∽ Here is another problem which is structurally similar in design and that makes the scope shift—"regular basis"—even easier to spot. Again the answer is choice D.

> A recent report by the Press Club determined that although only eight percent of its members were in fact correspondent members as opposed to non-correspondent members, these members represented fifteen percent of yearly food and beverage revenues earned by the club. Clearly, correspondent members are more likely to spend money for food and beverage in the Press Club on a regular basis than are non-correspondent members.
>
> The conclusion drawn above depends on which of the following assumptions?
>
> A)   The number of times individual correspondent members enter the Press Club does not exceed the number of entries by non-correspondent members.
>
> B)   Correspondent members are more likely to stay for longer periods of time per visit at the Press Club than non-correspondent members.
>
> C)   All members with correspondent memberships entered the Press Club at least once during the period of the report.
>
> D)   Correspondent members are more likely to spend money for food and beverage in the Press Club on a regular basis than are non-correspondent members, and are not prone to making large charges to their accounts for food and beverage during infrequent visits.
>
> E)   Correspondent members who entered the Press Club during the period of the report were representative of the types of members who frequent other affiliated press clubs.

4. SAT Scores ( )

Choice B
Classification: Cause-and-Effect Assumptions
Snapshot: This question was chosen as a classic example of an alternative explanation which serves to weaken cause-and-effect-type arguments. When tackling cause-and-effect scenarios, think first in terms of alternative explanations.

The argument basically says that SAT scores have gone up because students are better test takers, not because students possess better academic skills. Are students smarter or just better test takers?

Choices A and E may appear tricky. Actually the author doesn't deny his opponent's figures or suggest his evidence is flawed. In fact, the author agrees with his opponent's facts (test scores are getting higher). What the author is saying is that his opponent's evidence is incomplete, not flawed. Choice D is not correct. The argument is not flawed due to circular reasoning. In circular reasoning, a conclusion is based on evidence and that same piece of evidence is based on the conclusion. Choice D in this problem is incorrect for the same reason that choice E is incorrect in the previous problem, *Cyclist*. An argument that assumes what it seeks to establish is a circular argument.

Cause-and-effect fallacies exist when there is confusion as to the causal relationship between two events. See if the argument is set up in terms of some situation A causing some situation B. Ask, "Is A really causing event B?" Show that A does not necessarily lead to B and the argument is weakened or falls apart.

Here is a summary of how both arguments unfold:

Opponent's argument:

> Conclusion: Students are better skilled.

> Evidence: Test scores are getting higher.

> Assumption: There is a strong correlation between higher test scores and better skills. (That is, parents are impressed because higher scores are an indication that students are better skilled.)

Author's argument:

> Conclusion: Students are better test takers, not better skilled academically.

> Evidence: Studies confirm students are weaker in the basics (skills).

> Evidence: Test scores are getting higher.

> Assumption: There exists no strong correlation between higher test scores and better skills.

NOTE ⋘ SAT Scores is a problem that serves to highlight the importance of identifying the evidence and conclusion, as well as the underlying assumption which links the evidence with the conclusion. In advancing another example, consider the person who says: "No wonder Todd chose to attend a good university. He set himself up for the good job when he graduated." We cannot assume that Todd went to university for the purpose of getting a good job afterward. He may have gone to university to play on a varsity sports team with the hope of playing professional sports. He may have gone purely for the academic experience with no vocational thoughts at all, and then again, he may have gone just to get away from home, meet new friends, and enjoy himself socially.

Of the four arguments that follow, the first is the author's original argument. Argument #1, #2, and #3 provide counter arguments and act as alternative explanations as to why Todd went to university.

Author's original argument:

Conclusion:	The reason Todd chose to go to a good university was to get a good job upon graduation.
Evidence:	Todd went to a good university. He got a good job upon graduation.
Assumption:	Going to a good university caused Todd to get a good job upon graduation.

Argument #1: The sports person

Conclusion:	Todd went to a good university with a nationally recognized sports team because he wanted to play on that varsity sports team.
Evidence:	Todd went to a good university. He played on a nationally recognized varsity sports team.
Assumption:	A person would only go to a good university and play on a well-known varsity sports team unless that was his or her primary motivation for doing so.

Argument #2: The academic

Conclusion:	Todd went to university for the academic challenge.
Evidence:	Todd went to a good university. He excelled academically.
Assumption:	A person would not go to university and excel academically unless that was his or her primary objective for going to university.

Argument #3: The socialite

Conclusion:	Todd went to a good university to enjoy himself socially.
Evidence:	Todd went to a good university. He joined several well-known clubs on campus and met many new friends.
Assumption:	A person would not go to university and join several well-known clubs unless motivated to do so for social reasons.

5. Cyclists ( )

Choice C
Classification: Cause-and-Effect Assumptions
Snapshot: This problem is included to review *correlation* versus *causation* and *necessary* versus *sufficient* conditions.

Statement I ("It assumes a causal relationship between two highly correlated events") is true. Correlation does not equal causation. This argument assumes a causal relationship is responsible for a correlation. There is likely a high correlation between having low body fat and being a world-class cyclist. But there may well be a high correlation among other variables as well. For example, a high correlation also likely exists between having muscular strength and being a world-class cyclist, between having technical skills (maneuvering a bike) and being a world-class cyclist, and having mental toughness and being a world-class cyclist.

Statement II ("It suggests that low body fat is a sufficient condition rather than a necessary condition for becoming a world-class cyclist") is also true. Having low body fat is a necessary but not sufficient a condition for one being a world-class cyclist. In other words, having a low body fat does not make a person a world-class cyclist of and by itself. One needs other attributes too.

This problem can also be solved as an, "if...then"-type problem. The original reads, "If one is a world-class cyclist, then one has four to eleven percent body fat." When the "if...then" statement is erroneously reversed (as it is in the conclusion of this argument), the argument becomes, "If one has four to eleven percent body fat, then one can be a world-class cyclist."

Statement III is false. The argument is not flawed due to circular reasoning. In circular reasoning, a conclusion is based on evidence and that evidence is, in turn, based on the conclusion.

6. Valdez ( )

Choice E
Classification: Cause-and-Effect Assumptions
Snapshot: This follow-up problem reinforces the need to think first in terms of *alternative causal* explanations. If an argument suggests that A is causing B, check to see that another cause, namely C, is not instead causing B.

Choice E would most weaken the original argument. Citing a plausible alternative explanation serves to undermine the idea that Ms. Valdez's international marketing program was the reason for the jump in profits from eight percent to fifteen percent. The alternative explanation suggests that the increase in profits is due to a corporate acquisition prior to Ms. Valdez's appointment as president which doubled Zipco's annual revenues. We do have to assume in choice E that revenues and profits are linked proportionately; nonetheless, it is still the best choice.

None of the choices A through D bring us close enough to increased revenues or profits. They all mention potentially positive things, but we don't have a clear assurance that they brought in the bucks (dollars). Choice B, perhaps the best wrong answer choice, simply says that production capacity has increased. We do not know whether an increase in production *capacity* equals an actual increase in production, or if such an increase in production has resulted in more profits.

7. Headline (🌶️🌶️)

Choice C
Classification: Cause-and-Effect Assumptions
Snapshot: A more complex form of alternative explanation occurs when two effects result from a single cause. Thus, if the argument suggests that A is causing B, then consider the possibility that another cause, namely C, could be causing *both* A and B.

The idea that low self-esteem may be the cause of both obesity and depression most weakens this argument. Here, obesity and depression are deemed the joint *effects* of another single cause—low self-esteem.

Per choice A, it is not essential to the argument that one understands why he or she is depressed or how to escape from the throes of depression. It is only essential that obesity be the cause of depression. In choice B, it is not necessary for obesity to be the only cause of depression; there could be many ways to become depressed besides becoming obese. In choice D, it is not necessary that obesity and depression be linked proportionally, even if causally related. Depression could occur whenever one is declared "overweight," even though it would be logical to assume that one who is more overweight is also to some degree more depressed. Per choice E, the terms "desperation" and "suicide," even if linked to depression, are outside the scope of the claim—"obesity is linked to depression."

8. TV Viewing (🌶️🌶️)

Choice E
Classification: Cause-and-Effect Assumptions
Snapshot: This problem highlights the phenomenon of reverse causation. If A is thought to be causing B, the idea that B is causing A is called reverse causation and casts serious doubt on the notion that A is really causing B.

One way to destroy or seriously damage a causal relationship (e.g., A causes B) is to show that it is not A that causes B but B that causes A. This is what choice E does by suggesting reverse causation. It suggests that aggressive people go looking for violent TV programming, not that violent TV programming makes people aggressive.

Choice A may weaken things a bit, but not drastically. The fact that some viewers in the high-viewing group experienced lower aggression levels than did other subjects in the high-viewing group is not an improbable result. What matters is that more high-viewers experienced more aggression overall relative to low-viewers. Ditto for choice B. Choice C is incorrect because it is irrelevant whether fear did or did not cause some viewers to restrict their viewing. If it did, it will only mean that these viewers should have shown fewer signs of aggression because they weren't viewing as much. The reason that they are not viewing is effectively irrelevant. Choice D is also irrelevant; what matters is that people actually viewed the programs, not whether the programs were live or pre-recorded.

9. Shark (🌶️ 🌶️)

Choice B
Classification: Cause-and-Effect Assumptions
Snapshot: Test the "other side"—if you hear that a full moon causes the crime rate to rise, always ask what the crime rate is like when the moon is not full.

First, let's go to the incorrect answer choices. Answer A is the closest to the correct answer because it generally supports the idea that surfers in other areas are also not being attacked. Choice A slightly strengthens the original argument. Choice C weakens the argument, suggesting that there are no sharks left in the reserve. Choice D also weakens the argument by suggesting that an alternative explanation (i.e., wristbands with metal bells) may be key to understanding why sharks are not attacking surfers. Choice E is essentially irrelevant; we are talking about surfers, not divers or tuna. In choice B (correct answer), what we really want to know is whether sharks attack surfers wearing black suits while avoiding surfers wearing metallic suits.

What do you need in order to prove that metallic suits really work? The following framework is the basis for experimental design problems, as seen in real-life research.

	Shark attacks	No shark attacks	Total number of surfers
Black suits	(a)	(b)	xx
Metallic suits	(c)	(d)	xx
	xx	xx	xxx

This problem highlights the trap of *proof by selected instances*. People trying to prove the efficacy of wearing metallic suits cite examples from categories (a) and (d). That is, they cite instances of surfers wearing black suits and getting attacked by sharks (see a) and also cite instances of surfers in metallic wet suits who do not get attacked by sharks (see d). People trying to prove the efficacy of wearing traditional black suits cite examples from categories (b) and (c). That is, they cite instances of surfers wearing metallic suits and getting attacked by sharks (see c), while citing instances of surfers wearing black suits and not getting attacked by sharks (see b).

It is quite possible that in recent months there haven't been any shark attacks. In such an event, any comparison about the efficacy of wearing metallic suits would prove fruitless, as depicted in the following chart containing hypothetical numbers.

	Shark attacks	No shark attacks	Total number of surfers
Black suits	0	950	950
Metallic suits	0	50	50
	0	1,000	1,000

If we had actual numbers for all boxes, we could make a percentage comparison to determine if wearing a metallic suit really made a difference. The number of surfers wearing black suits who were attacked by sharks would be divided by the total number of surfers wearing black suits. The number of surfers wearing metallic suits who were attacked by sharks would be divided by the total number of surfers wearing metallic suits. A comparison of these two percentage figures would yield a conclusion.

NOTE ⁓ Which of the two statements below (1 or 2) add most support for the original statement?

Original: Firm ABC is spending money on advertising and seeing an increase in sales. Clearly advertising is causing the increase in sales.

Statement 1:   Other competing firms are also spending money on advertising and seeing an increase in their sales.

Statement 2:   Without spending money on advertising, Firm ABC would not have seen an increase in sales.

The answer is Statement 2. Although statement 1 lends some support to the proposition that advertising expenditure is leading to an increase in the sales of Firm ABC, what we really want to know is the opposite—what happens when we do not spend money on advertising. If we do not spend money on advertising, we would expect to see a resulting decrease in current sales levels. If not, then this would call into question whether advertising is really causing our sales to increase and suggest that another cause is responsible for the increase in sales.

10. Movie Buffs (🌶)

Choice B
Classification: Representativeness Assumptions
Snapshot: The word "survey" is a strong signal that a representativeness assumption is on the horizon.

This is a classic representativeness assumption question. The argument assumes that a sample based on people attending Sunday matinees (afternoon) is representative of the whole country of moviegoers. The question is, "How representative is the opinion of those attending Sunday matinees?" For example, Sunday matinee moviegoers might consist of a disproportionate number of family viewers (i.e., people with children) who prefer not to watch bizarre or violent movies during their Sunday afternoons. For this sample to be representative, we need to survey at least some Saturday night moviegoers, Saturday matinee moviegoers, and weekday moviegoers.

Choice A does weaken the argument somewhat by suggesting that people will see a movie regardless of its genre just so long as their star actor (or actress) appears. Choice C is incorrect because we are concerned about the *current* tastes of moviegoers (based on a recent survey) and not the movie hits of yesteryear.

Choice D is incorrect. We cannot assume that increased book sales and college enrollment in criminology courses is necessarily linked to trends among moviegoers. As far as we know, the moderate increase in course enrollments is the result of many other factors. Choice E is incorrect because it notionally strengthens the idea that movie producers should stop producing these types of movies because they are financially unsound. If actor salaries are high, then movie production costs will be higher, putting pressure on the bottom line.

11. Putting ( )

Choice C
Classification: Representativeness Assumptions
Snapshot: Representativeness assumptions are based on the idea that some smaller "thing" is representative of a larger whole.

The argument assumes that the ability to putt is the pivotal factor in determining whether a person can achieve a low golf score. A good golf game has many ingredients, including putting, driving, iron shots, chipping, sand-trap shots, judging weather, pacing, strategy, temperament, experience, physical fitness, and competitiveness. This passage assumes that it all happens on the putting green. Although it would be impossible to argue that putting is not an important component to achieving a low score in golf, it is certainly not the only factor.

Choice A is incorrect. We cannot assume that there is no way to improve a golf game other than with quality equipment. Practice itself might be enough to simply improve a golf game. The argument does suggest that if a person wants to make great improvements in his or her golf game, then he or she needs to make improvements in putting and, ideally, purchase a new Sweet Spot Putter.

Choice B is incorrect because it forms an unwarranted comparison that is not assumed in the argument. We do not know whether a new Sweet Spot Putter will improve an amateur's game more than it will improve a professional's game or vice-versa. Likewise, choice D is incorrect because we do not know whether the new Sweet Spot Putter is superior to any other putter currently on the market. For all we know, the Sweet Spot Putter is just one of three new miracle putters.

Per choice E, we also have no way of knowing whether lessons are, or are not, as effective at improving the accuracy of a player's putting as is the use of quality equipment.

12. Critic's Choice ( )

Choice C
Classification: Representativeness Assumptions
Snapshot: Check to see if evidence has been hand-picked to support a claim being made.

Since there are certainly far more than 100 contemporary novels and 100 non-contemporary novels to choose from, a question arises as to whether those novels chosen are representative of the entire population of contemporary and non-contemporary novels. It is possible that the author of *Decline of the Novelist* chose novels which best supported his/her thesis—that today's novelists are not as skillful as the novelists of yesteryear. Choice A might weaken the argument slightly but certainly wouldn't weaken it seriously. Choice B, while highly plausible, is irrelevant to the argument because the author focuses his/her argument on technical skill. Choice D is simply out of scope since we don't know anything about the literary skill required to do screenplays. Choice E is irrelevant; it doesn't matter whether the average reader is familiar with the terms of literary criticism; it only matters that the book's author is familiar with these terms.

13. Questionnaire ( )

Choice B
Classification: Representativeness Assumptions
Snapshot: Surveys or questionnaires completed and returned may not be representative of respondents' viewpoints in general if surveys or questionnaires not returned would have otherwise yielded conflicting information.

If those former employees of Mega Corp who harbor very negative feelings about the company remain silent (i.e., they don't respond to the questionnaire) then such views have been ostensibly omitted from inclusion. Choice A, may also be a concern, but it is impossible to tell whether it refers to employees who felt much better about their employment experience or much worse (we can't assume employees necessarily felt worse!). In choice C, we can't assume that the public relations efforts of Quantum have any affect on the employees who have left the company; besides, designing programs and implementing programs are two different things. The placement of questions within the questionnaire (choice D) is likely irrelevant or its impact, inconclusive. Choice E serves to strengthen the Human Resource Manager's claim because the response rate achieved by Mega Corp (i.e., 25/100 or 25 percent) is greater than the general response rate of 10 percent; of course, the higher the response rate the better.

14. Temperament ( )

Choice E
Classification: Representativeness Assumptions
Snapshot: "Evidence omitted" may hold the key to understanding the validity of an argument.

This is an example of *proof by selected instances*. Each person—Steve and John—will simply choose examples which support his intended claim. Steve picks red-haired people who have bad tempers to support his claim that red-haired people are bad tempered. John picks red-haired people who have good tempers to support his claim that red-haired people are not bad-tempered. The fact that the number of red-haired people (choice A) that one person knows is more or less than the number of red-haired people that the other person knows has no clear effect on reconciling the two statements. In fact, it is quite possible that the percentage of red-haired people that each knows is quite close, say five percent. After all, that's the magic of percentages as opposed to numbers—percentages express things in relative terms. In choice B, it is only plausible that the number of red-haired people both Steve and John know would be, in aggregate, less than the total of non-red-haired people both know. Confirmation of this likely reality will not reconcile the two seemingly contradictory statements.

It is also unclear whether choice C has any effect. Any mis-assessments may prove net positive or net negative or may have a counter-balancing effect. It is almost axiomatic that both Steve and John know of friends who are not red-haired and have bad tempers, but this will do nothing to reconcile the contradictory statements, so choice D is out. Note that the procedure for actually proving whether or not red hair is correlated with bad temper falls within the context of experimental design. Refer to the solution to problem 9, *Shark,* pages 316–317.

15. Rainbow Corp (🌶)

Choice B
Classification: Implementation Assumptions
Snapshot: An argument may depend on the assumption that a person or organization is aware of a pre-existing fact, situation, or condition.

If Tina is not aware of the recent newspaper articles featuring Rainbow Corp. as an environmental culprit, it does not make real sense to conclude that she does not care about the environment. Choices A and C are irrelevant. In choice D, even if the company's public relations department didn't issue a statement denying that the company violated the law, this doesn't mean that the company is guilty of any wrongdoing. Rainbow Corp's actual guilt or innocence has no impact on the issue at hand because Tina has no idea of the indictment. In choice E, the fact that Tina was a member of an environmental protection organization during her freshman and sophomore years in college weakens the claim a little, but not substantially.

NOTE ⤷ Let's review another example. Suppose that a certain global think tank is reviewing national anthems and their historical themes. It concludes that most national anthems have militaristic themes due in part to their creation during times of war or other conflict. Therefore, the think tank recommends that in the context of preserving global peace and stability, countries should consider changing their national anthems to rid them of any militaristic references. What would weaken this claim? Answer: Any explanation that suggests that citizens today are unaware of such militaristic themes present in their countries' national anthems.

16. Public Transportation (🌶🌶)

Choice A
Classification: Implementation Assumptions
Snapshot: One way to uncover implementation assumptions is to anticipate bottlenecks. This problem is also chosen to highlight the "all of the following would weaken/strengthen the argument EXCEPT" question format in which the correct answer is very often an *irrelevant* answer choice.

The fact that there may be better or easier ways to lower pollution levels in most large cities falls outside the scope of this argument. The argument only concerns itself with the idea that people should leave their cars at home and take public transportation to combat pollution.

This question was chosen to highlight implementation assumptions that can occur in Critical Reasoning problems. Choices B, C, D, and E are all valid implementation assumptions. Choice B questions whether there are enough people who actually own cars or who actually use cars to drive to work. In the most basic sense, if people do not own cars the argument is irrelevant. Choice C highlights a lack of required opportunity to make a plan work. Public transportation must be both available and accessible should someone decide to switch. Choices D and E highlight unanticipated bottlenecks, namely that the current public transportation system can accommodate all the people who decide to switch, as well as meet financial requirements.

NOTE ⌖ Here's a quick review problem written with a light-hearted tone:

People who often wear green shirts tend to score high on standardized exams because wearing green shirts makes you feel smarter and more optimistic.

All of the following would weaken the argument above EXCEPT

A) Many people who regularly wear green shirts have a tendency to read questions on standardized exams too quickly, thereby failing to grasp critical nuances within problems.

B) People who often wear green shirts are rarely among the best prepared students in terms of those sitting for a standardized exam.

C) Many people who frequently wear green shirts are especially unlucky on days when they sit for standardized exams.

D) The frequency with which green shirts are worn has been scientifically proven to have absolutely no effect on a person's performance on standardized exams.

E) People who often wear green shirts also like chocolate mint ice cream.

Choice E is correct in so far as it does not weaken the argument. This statement is simply irrelevant to the argument at hand.

17. Classics (🌶🌶🌶)

Choice E
Classification: Implementation Assumptions
Snapshot: The capability or ability to do something should not imply application of those abilities, whether due to choice or neglect.

In order for a plan to work, desire or motivation on the part of the individual or organization must be present. Here, the operative word is "can" and the ability to do something does not necessarily translate to the "will" to do something. "Can" does not equal "will."

Perhaps the easiest way to summarize the problem is to say that just because most literate people have not read the classics does not mean that they are necessarily lazy. Most literate people may simply choose not to spend their time doing so. Also, even if a person is lazy, he or she may still be able to read the classics. For example, the literate but lazy person may just read very slowly or in fits and starts but still arrive at the finish line. All we do know is that some people have likely read the classics. For all we know, some of these people might be motivated and some might be lazy. We cannot assume that all of the people who have read the classics belong to the motivated group.

Choice D is not correct because the original statement is not a true "if…then" statement and the contrapositive is not a valid inference, as it would otherwise be. The original statement only states that, based on a precondition, a person "can" read the classics.

NOTE ⋖ Here is an example which illustrates how choice D might have been a correct choice. Say the original statement was a true "if...then" statement as follows:

Hypothetical: If a person is literate and is not lazy, then he or she <u>will</u> read the classics.

Here, the contrapositive leads to a correct inference.

Statement: If a person has not read the classics, then he or she is a literate person who is lazy!

18. Medical School (𝄢 𝄢)

Choice C
Classification: Number-based Assumptions
Snapshot: Beware of comparing numbers directly with percents.

Percents and numbers do not always mix. Seventy-five percent cannot be compared with "half of all females applicants." This question only makes sense if we know the percentage of females accepted to medical school and compare this figure with the percentage of males accepted to medical school. A likely scenario is that 75 percent of all students in medical school are male because 75 percent of all applicants are male; 25 percent of all students accepted to medical school are female because 25 percent of the total applicants are female—little surprise.

Let's take a hypothetical example. Say that 10,000 applicants apply for a spot at a top medical school. What if 25 percent of the applicant pool is female while 75 percent is male? This means that 2,500 females will apply for admission and 7,500 males will apply for admission.

The opening class will consist of 500 students and only 1 in 20 applicants or 5 percent (500/10,000) of the applicants is accepted. Common sense tells us that with rules of fair selection in place, the opening class should be 75 percent male and 25 percent female, which directly reflects the applicant pool. Thus, the number of females in the opening class should be 125 (500 × 25%) while the number of males in the opening class should be 375 (500 × 75%).

Now, relate these facts to the scenario presented in the original passage: "The facts in the report speak for themselves: seventy-five percent of all students in medical school are male, but fewer than half of all the 2,500 female applicants reach their goal of being admitted to medical school." Of course less than half of all females are admitted; only 1 in 20 students overall is accepted!

Choices A, B, D, and E are all irrelevant to the issue at hand. In choice B there is no reason to suspect that the yield rates (percentage of offers given by medical schools that are accepted by students) would in any significant way be affected by gender. So although it might warrant some consideration, it is by no means a close contender with choice C.

19. Military Expenditures (👣👣)

Choice E
Classification: Number-based Assumptions
Snapshot: This problem presents a classic case where one or more items increase in dollar or absolute terms but decrease in percentage terms relative to a larger pie.

This problem highlights the concept of the *growing pie*. The apparent inconsistency is resolved if it is true that the portion or percentage of the national budget represented by military expenditures has increased by a greater amount than actual expenditures. If, for example, the national budget has increased ten-fold during the past two decades and the amount of actual expenditures (inflation adjusted) has increased by one percent per year, then the portion devoted to military expenditure has likely shrunk. Even if actual dollars spent on military expenditures is increasing each year, as long as overall (or total) expenditures is increasing more, the amount of military expenditures, in percentage terms, is falling.

The opposite of growing pies is *shrinking pies*. If this problem were a shrinking pie, actual dollars spent on military expenditures would be decreasing each year, but as long as overall expenditures were shrinking faster, the amount of military expenditures, in percentage terms, would be rising.

NOTE ✍ *Growing pies* or *shrinking pies* also present examples of the tangling of numbers and percents. Here are two examples from everyday living. Growing Pie—You may spend more money on personal phone calls this year compared with last year, but this does not mean that the percentage of your disposable income that you spend on phone calls has gone up. It is quite possible, for example, that you have enjoyed a significant increase in your disposable income. Therefore, although the actual money that you spend on personal phones calls has gone up, the percentage of your disposable income that you spend on phone calls has gone down. In short, a growing pie often results in an <u>increase</u> in *dollar* expenditures despite a corresponding <u>decrease</u> in the *percentage* of money being spent.

Shrinking Pie—You may spend less hours dining out than you used to, but this does not mean that you spend less of your free time dining out. What if you have a lot less free time these days? This would imply that an equal (or even fewer) number of hours dining out would mean that a greater portion (percentage) of your free time is spent dining out. In short, a shrinking pie often results in a <u>decrease</u> in *dollar* expenditures despite a corresponding <u>increase</u> in the *percentage* of money being spent.

20. Nova vs. Rebound (👣👣)

Choice C
Classification: Number-based Assumptions
Snapshot: Overlap occurs when the number of items in a group add up to more than 100 percent. Situations involving either A or B do not necessarily preclude the possibility of both A and B.

We cannot assume that a person liked either Nova or Rebound without taking into account the possibility that a person liked both name brand shoes at the same time. This situation results in overlap and accounts for the fact that the percentage appears to be greater than 100 percent. That is, 53% + 47% +24% = 124%.

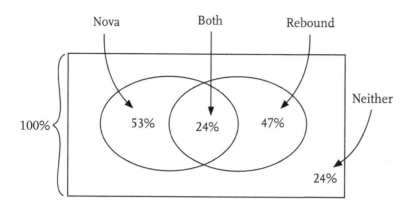

For the record, the following solution employs the two-groups formula:

Two-Groups Formula	Solve
+ Item #1	+ 53%
+ Item #2	+ 47%
− Both	− x%
+ Neither	+ 24%
Total	100%

The number who liked *both* is calculated as:

$$53\% + 47\% - x + 24\% = 100\%$$
$$124 - x = 100\%$$
$$x = 24\%$$

Therefore, 24 percent of the people liked both Nova and Rebound. This problem is both strange and tricky because 24 percent is the identical figure for the *both* and *neither* components in the calculation.

21. Grapes (🌶️🌶️)

Choice B
Classification: Number-based Assumptions
Snapshot: Total costs must be distinguished from per unit costs.

The assumption is that both crops were grown on the same number of acres. Of course, per acre costs in each U.S. state are determined as follows:

$$\frac{\text{Costs}}{\text{Acres}} = \text{Cost per acre}$$

In choice B, we cannot make an assessment on the cost per acre basis without knowing the total costs and the total acres. Despite the greater total costs to grow watermelons in Oklahoma (compared with

California), if many more acres of watermelons were grown in Oklahoma (as compared with grapes in California), then the cost per acre to grow watermelons in Oklahoma might very well be lower.

Answer choices A and C fall outside the scope of the argument. In choice A, we are talking about "costs to grow," not profits on the sale. Choice C switches terms around. In the original, we are only talking about watermelons in Oklahoma and grapes in California. We must stick with the information as presented. In choice D, how the crops are being *used* is irrelevant. In choice E, the source of money used to grow crops is also irrelevant. It does not matter who pays for the cost of growing the crops—farmers, the government (through state subsidies), or Aunt Jessie—costs are costs.

22. Act-Fast ( )

Choice D
Classification: Number-based Assumptions
Snapshot: Efficiency is calculated by dividing output by total hours (or units). Cost efficiency is calculated by dividing cost by total hours (or units).

This problem is built on the assumption that the number of tablets per bottle is equal. Therefore, if a bottle of Aspirin contains more than twice as many tablets as does a bottle of Act-Fast, then logic dictates that a bottle of Aspirin provides a greater amount of pain reliever. And since the cost per bottle is the same, it stands to reason that *cost efficiency* of Aspirin is greater than that of Act-Fast.

What we really want to determine is how much pain reliever we're getting and how much it is costing us. In choice A, there is no mention of the number of tablets per bottle so we cannot determine how much pain reliever in aggregate we're getting for our money. Furthermore, implied logic dictates that if one Act-Fast tablet contains twice the pain reliever found in a tablet of regular Aspirin then an Act-Fast tablet should be twice the size of a regular Aspirin tablet (or an Aspirin tablet should be one-half the size of an Act-Fast tablet). Whereas choice B is beyond the scope of the argument, choice C weakens the argument but not nearly to the extent choice D does. There is also no need for the pain reliever to be of a different type or strength as suggested by choice E.

23. Fiction Books ( )

Choice E
Classification: Number-based Assumptions
Snapshot: If student A spends a greater percentage of his or her disposable income on beer than coffee as compared with student B, then this does not mean that student A spends more money on beer than coffee.

This problem illustrates the ultimate tangling of numbers with percentages. Choice A is out of scope because we don't know about people with the highest levels of education; we only know about members of households with high levels of education (i.e., HEL—high education level households) and members of households with low levels of education (i.e., LEL—low education level households). Also, we do not know whether people really buy, are given, or inherit these books. Choices B, C, and D are out because we do not know for sure whether HEL households or LEL households have more or less fiction versus nonfiction books. We also do not know whether members of HEL households have more or fewer nonfiction books as compared with members of LEL households. The only thing we do know for sure is that if members of HEL households have more books in total than members of LEL households and a higher percentage of fiction versus nonfiction, then it must be true that HEL households contain a greater <u>number</u> of fiction books than LEL households.

All of the following are significant possibilities based on hypothetical numbers of books and percentages. Again, upon examination, the only thing that must be true is that for any given scenario the number of fiction books in HEL households must be greater than the number of fiction books in LEL households. Let's use 100 books and 50 books to test things out. The number of fiction books for HEL households, column (1), will always be greater than the number of fiction books for LEL households, column (3).

Scenario #1 – HEL households have 80 percent fiction books and 20 percent non-fiction books while LEL households have 50 percent fiction books and 50 percent non-fiction books.

Scenario #2 – HEL households have 70 percent fiction books and 30 percent non-fiction books while LEL households have 50 percent fiction books and 50 percent non-fiction books.

Scenario #3 – Get ready for this! HEL households could have 40 percent fiction books and 60 percent non-fiction books while LEL households have 20 percent fiction books and 80 percent non-fiction books. Note that this is possible because the percentage of fiction books for HEL households is still greater—40 percent—than the percentage of fiction books for LEL households—20 percent.

NOTE ◆ The following presents a problem which combines the concepts tested in the two previous problems: *Military Expenditures* and *Fiction Books*. Ponder the following statement:

"The percentage of white wine bottled to red wine bottled in Germany is greater than the percentage of white wine bottled in France."

Does this mean that there is more white wine bottled in Germany than white wine bottled in France? Answer—No. But why? Because the size of the wine industry in France is so much bigger than the wine industry in Germany. The French "pie," so to speak, is much bigger than the German "pie"; five times in fact.

Does the original statement mean that Germany bottles more white wine than it does red wine or that France bottles more white wine than it does red wine? The answer is no on both accounts.

Let's draw upon some plausible numbers in line with real statistics. France produces five times as much wine as Germany does. Of all the wine produced by Germany, 75 percent is white wine and 25 percent is red wine. Of all the wine produced by France, 25 percent is white wine and 75 percent is red wine. Even though the percentage of white wine bottled to red wine bottled in Germany is greater than the percentage of white wine bottled in France, France still produces more white wine than Germany does. Here are simple numbers to prove our point. Let's say that France produces 500 bottles of wine each year and Germany produces 100 bottles of wine each year. Therefore, France produces 125 bottles of white wine whereas Germany produces 75 bottles of white wine.

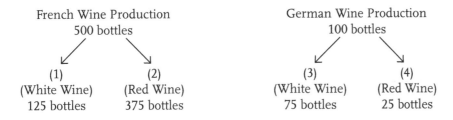

| French Wine Production | German Wine Production |
| 500 bottles | 100 bottles |

(1)	(2)	(3)	(4)
(White Wine)	(Red Wine)	(White Wine)	(Red Wine)
125 bottles	375 bottles	75 bottles	25 bottles

24. Intricate Plots (𝒮)

Choice C
Classification: Logic-based Assumptions
Snapshot: This problem highlights the valid use of the contrapositive. Formulaically, "If A, then B" is logically equivalent to "If not B, then not A."

The last line of the introductory blurb gives us an "if…then" statement which serves as the conclusion of the passage. "If scriptwriting is to remain a significant art form, its practitioners must continue to craft intricate plots." In determining what the author would most probably agree with, we need to look for logically deducible statements. Choice C, the correct answer, forms the contrapositive. "If a script does not have an intricate plot, it will probably not be a significant art form."

Choice A is an example of the fallacy of affirming the consequence. There are likely other factors that go into the making of a significant art form other than intricate plots. Choice B is the fallacy of denying the antecedent. Choice D is outside the scope of the argument; we do not know whether scriptwriting is the most likely art form to become a significant art form. Choice E is out; there is no reason to believe that more is better; perhaps one intricate plot per script is enough.

25. Campus Pub (🌶🌶)

Choice D
Classification: Logic-based Assumptions
Snapshot: This is known as the fallacy of denying the antecedent: "If A, then B" does not equal "If not A, then not B."

Looking back at the original, we find that just because it is not final exam week does not necessarily mean that the pub is not selling a lot of beer. For all we know the pub sells a lot of beer each and every week because it is a popular pub. It is certainly likely that the pub does sell a lot of beer during final exam week when students relieve stress. There could also be other lucrative weeks particularly when sports matches are being played such as football and basketball games.

In choice D, just because no one is happy doesn't necessarily mean some people won't smile. There could always be those people who smile regardless of whether they are happy or sad. Look at the original statement and concentrate on finding a similar structure.

Original Argument (albeit flawed!):

> If final exam week → sell lots beer
> ≠ final exam week → ≠ sell lots beer

Compare this with the similar structure found in correct choice D:

> If happy → smile
> ≠ happy → ≠ smile

26. Balcony (🌶🌶)

Choice C
Classification: Logic-based Assumptions
Snapshot: One way to think about an "if...then" statement in the form of "If A, then B" is that just because A leads to B does not mean that C, D, or E could not also lead to B.

We are told that all apartments above the fifth floor have balconies. We cannot, however, logically infer that apartments on or below the fifth floor do not have balconies. Answer choices B and E provide tempting traps. For all we know, every apartment from the first floor on up has a balcony.

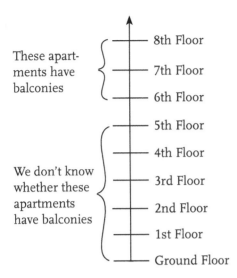

These apartments have balconies {
8th Floor
7th Floor
6th Floor

We don't know whether these apartments have balconies {
5th Floor
4th Floor
3rd Floor
2nd Floor
1st Floor
Ground Floor

NOTE ✍ The statement "If a person is rich, then he or she will vote in favor of a tax cut" does not mean that if a person is middle-class then he or she will not also vote in favor of a tax cut. Let's take another example from the world of advertising: The fact that increased expenditures on advertising has led to an increase in company sales does not mean that an increase in company sales could not have been achieved through other means—hiring more salespersons, lowering retail price, or hiring a famous, talented manager.

27. Sales (👣 👣)

Choice C

Classification: Logic-based Assumptions

Snapshot: The statement "If A then B" does not equal "Only As are Bs." For example, the statement "If one wants to make a good salad, one should use tomatoes" should not be interpreted to mean that tomatoes are the only thing necessary to make a good salad or that a good salad can be made merely by including tomatoes.

Choice C. Let's repeat what Debra said:

> To be a good salesperson, one must be friendly.

Debra's statement above is also equivalent to the following:

> If a person is a good salesperson, then he or she must be friendly.

Now let's summarize what Tom thought Debra said:

> If a person is friendly, then he or she will make a good salesperson.

Tom has effectively reversed the original "If…then" statement and erroneously committed the fallacy of affirming the consequent. Tom would have been correct had he instead responded, "Oh, what you mean is that only friendly people are capable of making good salespersons," or "I agree, a good salesperson must be friendly," or "That's right. If you're not friendly, then you're not going to make a good salesperson."

Choice B is a correct transcription of Debra's original statement. It cannot be correct because Tom disagrees with her. Choice E is a logical inference based on Debra's original statement (it is the contrapositive!). Choices A and D are not correct; regardless of whether the statements are true in themselves they do not lie at the crux of Tom's misunderstanding.

NOTE ❧ The following provides a snapshot of *logical equivalency statements*. All statements in the left-hand column are logically equivalent, meaning that they are equivalent ways of expressing the same relationship between A and B. Many reviewers find the last statement—Only Bs are As—the most difficult to grasp because it not only reverses the order of A and B, but also sounds peculiar.

Logical equivalency statements	Examples
If A, then B.	If it is a cat, then it is a mammal.
All As are Bs.	If it is not a mammal, then it is not a cat.
If not B, then not A.	All cats are mammals.
Every A is a B.	Every cat is a mammal.
Only Bs are As.	Only mammals are cats.

28. Football

Choice A
Classification: Logic-based Assumptions
Snapshot: The statement "Every A is a B" does not equal "Only As are Bs." For example, the statement "Every cat is a mammal" should not be interpreted to mean that "Only cats are mammals."

According to the rules of logical equivalency, the statement "<u>Every</u> person on the Brazilian World Cup football team is a great player" may be translated as "<u>If</u> a person is on the Brazilian World Cup football team, <u>then</u> he is a great player." And this may be further translated as "Only great players are Brazilian World Cup football players." Although the latter statement sounds awkward to the ear, it is logically correct. "If A, then B" statements must be translated as "Only Bs are As" in order to be correct.

Choice A is exactly what Beth has misunderstood Marie's remark to mean. Beth thinks Marie has said, "Brazil has all the great World Cup football players."

Choices B, C, D, and E are all unwarranted inferences.

29. Global Warming

Choice D
Classification: Logic-based Assumptions
Snapshot: Necessary conditions are not the same as sufficient conditions. The statement "A person needs water to remain healthy" does not mean that water alone is enough to keep a person healthy. Water is a necessary but not sufficient condition for someone to remain healthy.

If we want to stop global warming then we must pass legislation. As highlighted in tip #46, we must draw an important distinction between necessary and sufficient conditions. Passing legislation is necessary to stop global warming, but it is not a sufficient condition for doing so. It is not a sufficient condition because several other factors probably are necessary to stop global warming. For starters, in all cases we may need more than just legislation; we may need legal enforcement of approved laws. Furthermore, choice C is a near-identical restatement of the original statement. Answer choices A and B are all correct interpretations of Jacques' original "If...then" statement. However, since Pierre believes Jacques' statement is not true, we must look for an erroneous answer choice.

Choice E is an opposite answer choice. Pierre's mistake consists in believing that legislation is the sole causal agent in stopping global warming (as opposed to one of several factors); his misunderstanding does not lie in the belief that legislation is an ineffective step toward stopping global warming.

NOTE ⍋ Here's a related but simpler example:

Jacques: "If you want to keep your pet dog alive, you must give it water."

Pierre: "That's not true. It takes a lot more than water to keep your pet dog alive."

Pierre's response is inaccurate because he mistakenly believes that what Jacques has said is that

A)   Giving of water is necessary to keep your pet dog alive.

B)   Only the giving of water will keep your pet dog alive.

C)   If your pet dog is to be kept alive, it must be given water.

D)   Giving of water is enough to keep your pet dog alive.

E)   Your pet dog will not be kept alive merely by giving it water.

Choice D above is, of course, the correct answer. Jacques' statement correctly identifies water as a necessary condition for keeping your pet dog alive. Pierre has mistakenly assumed that Jacques has said that water is a sufficient condition for keeping your pet dog alive.

30. Smoking (🌶🌶)

Choice C
Classification: Bolded-Statement Problems
Snapshot: Bolded-statement questions now appear as regular "guests" on the GMAT exam.

The structure of the passage can be summarized as follows: An argument (consisting of two sentences) is put forth and a counter argument (consisting of two sentences) followed with a final rebuttal (consisting of one sentence).

Conclusion: The dangers of smoking, although well documented, are often ignored even today.

Evidence: According to numerous published accounts, a person who smokes habitually has a thirty-percent greater chance of developing cancer or heart disease than someone who does not smoke.

Conclusion: Many individuals residing outside the health and wellness fields either find research on the ill effects of smoking to be non-compelling or choose to ignore such evidence altogether.

Evidence: They are likely to point to instances of individuals who smoke regularly despite living well into their nineties. (Note: This sentence is recast from the problem verbatim.)

Rebuttal: What these people fail to realize is that there is a difference between a highly correlated event and a causally related event. The absence of a causally related event does not negate the validity of a highly correlated event.

Choices D and E are immediately out. It is impossible for any assumption to appear as a statement in the passage; assumptions are by definition implicit while conclusions and evidence are explicit. This bolded statement is also not a counter argument (choice B). An argument is a claim supported by evidence. What appears in this sentence just evidence—no claim. In choice A, what follows is not the conclusion but a rebuttal. The main conclusion appeared as the opening sentence.

CHAPTER 6

READING COMPREHENSION

*I took a speed reading course and read
War and Peace in twenty minutes. It
involves Russia.*

—Woody Allen

OVERVIEW

Official Exam Instructions for Reading Comprehension

Directions

The questions in this group are based on the content of a passage. After reading the passage, choose the best answer to each question. Answer all questions following the passage on the basis of what is stated or implied in the passage.

Strategies and Approaches

1. *Read for content, noting topic, scope, and purpose.*

   A GMAT test taker will encounter four Reading Comprehension passages per Verbal section and each passage will be accompanied by three or four questions each. Understanding the purpose of each passage is fundamental. As you read a passage, keep talking silently to yourself, "What's the purpose...where is the author going?" In other words, ask yourself, "Why did the author sit down to write the passage?"

2. *Read the first sentence first, then scroll down and read the last sentence next.*

   A good tip is to read the first sentence of the passage and then read the last sentence of the passage, then start back reading at the top. Why? Because the author of a passage might conclude on the last line, and if you read this as soon as possible, you will know where the author is going with his or her discussion, and then be better able to remember pertinent details.

3. *Read for structure, noting important "guide words" as well as the number of viewpoints and relationship among those viewpoints.*

   Keep close track of "guide words" such as "however," "but," "moreover," and "hence." These words are important and may influence dramatically the flow of the passage. Next, think in terms of the number of paragraphs and viewpoints presented. Usually one paragraph represents one viewpoint. Frequently, Reading Comprehension passages will contain two viewpoints and it may be helpful to try and simplify everything into simple black-and-white terms. For example, take a hypothetical passage written about personality development. Ask yourself what is the relationship between, say, the three paragraphs of the passage. Perhaps the first paragraph is the introduction, the second paragraph is how sociologists view personality development, the third paragraph is how biologists view personality development...now you've got it!

4. *Eliminate common wrong answer choices including out of scopes, distortions, and opposites.*

   There are three common wrong answer choices in Reading Comprehension. These include "out of scope," "opposite," and "distorted" answer choices. Note that "irrelevant" answer choices are not common wrong answer choices in Reading Comprehension, although they are not common wrong answer choices in Critical Reasoning.

REVIEW OF READING COMPREHENSION

There is an obvious difference between the kind of casual reading that takes place when reading a newspaper and the kind required when one sits for a standardized exam like the GMAT. There are essentially five areas to cover when discussing strategies for tackling Reading Comprehension passages and their accompanying multiple-choice questions. Mastering Reading Comprehension involves an understanding of passage type, passage content, and passage structure, as well as passage question types and common wrong answer choices.

I.   **Passage Type**

  - Social science
  - Science

II. **Passage Content**

  - Topic
  - Scope
  - Purpose (equals main idea)

III. **Passage Structure**

  - Transition or guide words
  - Number of paragraphs and their function
  - Number of viewpoints and their relationships

IV. **Passage Question Types**

  - Overview questions
  - Explicit-detail questions
  - Inference questions
  - Tone questions
  - Passage organization questions

V.   **Common Wrong Answer Choices**

  - Out of scope
  - Opposite
  - Distortion
  - Irrelevant
  - Too General
  - Too Detailed

Passage Type

There are three basic types of Reading Comprehension passages—social science, science, and business/economics. Since business and economics passages read more like social science than science passages, they fit easily under the umbrella of social science. The fundamental difference between social science and science is that science passages tend to be objective and generally exist to *describe*. Social science passages tend to be subjective and usually exist to *argue*. Social science (which deals with people, societies, and their institutions) is typically the domain of ideas, opinions, and conjecture while science (which deals with nature and the universe) is typically the domain of phenomena, theories, and details.

Viewpoints (ideas) and the flow or order of ideas are generally more important in social science readings than in science readings. In terms of understanding a social science passage, it is critical to understand the author's stance—"what side the author is on." A fitting analogy is to say that social science passages are "river-rafting rides" where the goal is to not fall off our raft amid the twists and turns—we must navigate a Reading Comprehension passage and stay with the author as he or she moves from one point to the next. Science passages are "archeological digs." Once we determine where to dig, we must keep track of the small pieces—we must be able to memorize and work with details.

Passage Content

Obviously, the better we understand what we have read, the better our chance of answering questions related to the subject at hand. In breaking down passage content, we can subdivide everything into three areas, namely topic, scope, and purpose.

Topic is defined as "the broad subject matter of the passage." *Scope* is defined as "the specific aspect of the topic that the author is interested in." *Purpose* is defined as "the author's main reason for writing the passage" or "why did the author sit down to write this passage." In short, *topic* and *scope* are "what" a passage is about while *purpose* is about "why" the passage was written.

One tip involves always performing a "topic-scope-purpose" drill (think T-S-P). That is, always ask yourself what is the topic, scope, and purpose. Let's test this.

> The whale is the largest mammal in the animal kingdom. When most people think of whales, they think of sluggish, obese animals, frolicking freely in the ocean by day and eating tons of food to sustain themselves. When people think of ants, on the other hand, they tend to think of hardworking underfed creatures transporting objects twice their body size to and from hidden hideaways. However, if we analyze food consumption based on body size, we find that ants eat their full body weight everyday while a whale eats the equivalent of only one-thousandth of its body weight each day. In fact, when we compare the proportionate food consumption of all living creatures, we find that the whale is one of the most food efficient creatures on earth.

What is the topic? The answer is clearly "whales." Don't be fooled into thinking that the topic is the "animal kingdom." This would be an example of an answer that is too general. What is the scope? The answer is "food consumption of whales." What is the purpose of the passage or why did the author sit down to write this? The author's purpose is to say that whales are food efficient creatures and to thereby counter the popular misconception that they are "biological" gas guzzlers.

Passage Structure

There are essentially two distinct ways to analyze passage structure: the micro and the macro. Micro analysis involves keeping track of transitions, which signal the flow of the passage. Guide words have been called the traffic lights of language. These words serve one of four primary purposes: to show continuation, illustration, contrast, or conclusion. See *Exhibit 6.1*.

Exhibit 6.1   Guide Words

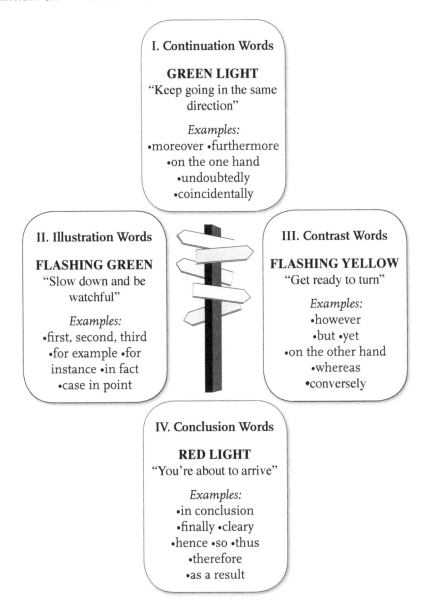

I. Continuation Words

GREEN LIGHT
"Keep going in the same direction"

Examples:
•moreover •furthermore
•on the one hand
•undoubtedly
•coincidentally

II. Illustration Words

FLASHING GREEN
"Slow down and be watchful"

Examples:
•first, second, third
•for example •for instance •in fact
•case in point

III. Contrast Words

FLASHING YELLOW
"Get ready to turn"

Examples:
•however
•but •yet
•on the other hand
•whereas
•conversely

IV. Conclusion Words

RED LIGHT
"You're about to arrive"

Examples:
•in conclusion
•finally •cleary
•hence •so •thus
•therefore
•as a result

Macro analysis involves noting the number of paragraphs and their function, as well as the number of viewpoints and their relationship. The relationships between or among viewpoints are finite and summarized in *Exhibit 6.2.*

In terms of paragraphs and their functions, the opening paragraph is usually the introduction and each succeeding paragraph takes on a single viewpoint or concept. Passages with one or two viewpoints are most common on reading passages, although three viewpoints within a single Reading Comprehension passage is a possibility. As already noted, viewpoints are more applicable to social science passages than to science passages because social science is typically subjective and argumentative.

EXHIBIT 6.2   PASSAGE STRUCTURE AND VIEWPOINT

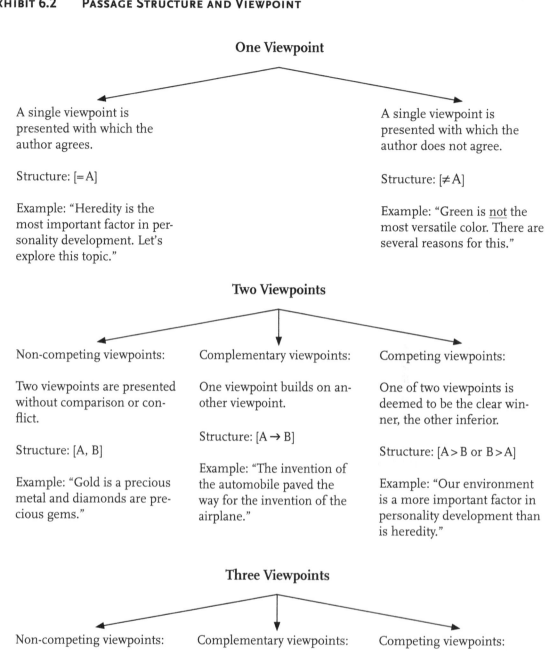

One Viewpoint

A single viewpoint is presented with which the author agrees.

Structure: [= A]

Example: "Heredity is the most important factor in personality development. Let's explore this topic."

A single viewpoint is presented with which the author does not agree.

Structure: [≠ A]

Example: "Green is not the most versatile color. There are several reasons for this."

Two Viewpoints

Non-competing viewpoints:

Two viewpoints are presented without comparison or conflict.

Structure: [A, B]

Example: "Gold is a precious metal and diamonds are precious gems."

Complementary viewpoints:

One viewpoint builds on another viewpoint.

Structure: [A → B]

Example: "The invention of the automobile paved the way for the invention of the airplane."

Competing viewpoints:

One of two viewpoints is deemed to be the clear winner, the other inferior.

Structure: [A > B or B > A]

Example: "Our environment is a more important factor in personality development than is heredity."

Three Viewpoints

Non-competing viewpoints:

Three viewpoints are presented without comparison or conflict.

Structure: [A, B, C]

Example: "Fruits, vegetables, and proteins are part of a healthy diet."

Complementary viewpoints:

A third superior viewpoint is considered to be the product of two original viewpoints.

Structure: [A + B → C]

Example: "The invention of the automobile and jet plane have led to the invention of the space craft.

Competing viewpoints:

One of the three viewpoints is deemed to be the clear winner, the others inferior.

Structure: [C > A or B]

Example: "Treatment C is a more effective cure than is treatment A or treatment B."

Passage Question Types

There are five basic kinds of Reading Comprehension questions. These include: (1) overview questions, (2) explicit-detail questions, (3) inference questions, (4) tone questions, and (5) passage organization questions. Examples of each question type are as follows:

Overview questions

"The primary purpose of this passage is to..." or "Which of the following is the author's main idea?" Not surprisingly, an overview question is sometimes called a primary purpose or main idea question.

Explicit-detail questions

"According to the passage, the author states that..." An explicit-detail question is a question which has a very literal answer. It is something that the reader has read and it can be confirmed based on words actually written in the passage.

Inference questions

"It can be inferred from the passage that..." or "The author implies that..." The artistry in answering an inference question lies in drawing that magic line between what can be logically inferred based on information in a passage and what is declared outside the scope of the passage.

Tone questions

"The attitude of the author toward mystics can best be described as..." A tone question asks the reader to comment on the "temperature" of some aspect of the passage.

Passage organization questions

"Which of the following best describes the way in which this passage is organized?" A passage organization question asks about the structure of the passage or the structure of a portion of the passage.

The four-quadrant grid that follows on the next page (see *Exhibit 6.3)* is a useful tool to ferret out common wrong answer choices on Reading Comprehension questions. The correct answer always appears in the middle where the bull's-eye is located. The four incorrect answers will almost always appear in one of the four corners.

Exhibit 6.3   The Four-Corner Question Cracker for Reading Comprehension™

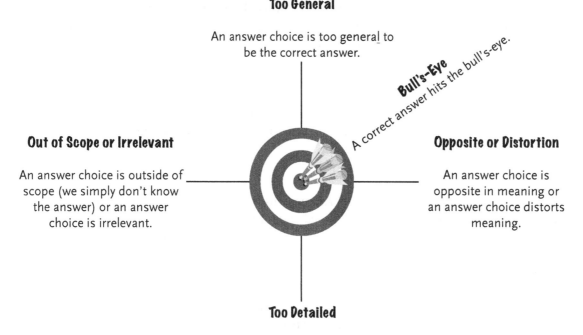

Too General

An answer choice is too general to
be the correct answer.

Bull's-Eye

A correct answer hits the bull's-eye.

Out of Scope or Irrelevant

An answer choice is outside of
scope (we simply don't know
the answer) or an answer
choice is irrelevant.

Opposite or Distortion

An answer choice is
opposite in meaning or
an answer choice distorts
meaning.

Too Detailed

An answer choice is too detailed to
be the correct answer.

Common Wrong Answer Choices

Out of Scope: An out of scope answer choice is an answer choice that cannot be answered based on information in the passage. An out of scope statement may, in fact, be right or wrong, but it is not something that can be determined based on information supplied by the passage.

Irrelevant: An irrelevant answer choice is an answer choice that in no way touches the topic; it is completely off target. We might contrast irrelevant answer choices with out of scope answer choices in that an out of scope answer choice is related tangentially to the passage, whereas the irrelevant answer choice is not. Think of an archer with bow and arrow. Out of scope means that the archer is missing the target, but at least he or she is shooting at the right target, and in the right direction. Irrelevant means that the archer isn't even shooting at the correct target.

Opposite: An opposite answer choice is an answer choice which is opposite in meaning to a statement or viewpoint expressed or implied by the passage. One common way answer choices are used to reverse meaning is through the inclusion or omission of prefixes such as "in," "un," and "dis," or the inclusion or omission of negative words such as "no" or "not." Thus, "ability" becomes "inability," "unfortunately" becomes "fortunately," "advantageous" becomes "disadvantageous," and "not applicable" becomes "applicable."

Distortion: A distorted answer choice is an answer choice that distorts the meaning of something stated or implied by the passage. Saying, for example, that something is "good" is not the same as saying that something is "best." Distortions are typically signaled by the use of extreme wording or by the use of categorical words such as "any," "all," "always," "cannot," "never," "only," and "solely."

Too General: This answer choice is relevant strictly to the overview question type. Examples: A discussion of "South American trade imbalances in the 1990s" is not the same thing as a discussion of "modern global economic practices." The latter is obviously broader in scope: "global" is broader than "South American"; "modern" is broader than "the 1990s"; "economics" encompasses more than just "trade imbalances."

Too Detailed: This answer choice is also relevant strictly to overview-type questions. Example: A discussion of "the propagation of the Venus Fly Trap" is a much more specific topic than is "plant reproductive systems." The correct answer to an overview-type question is, relative to the topic, neither overly general nor overly detailed.

Let's gain further insight into how test makers may create incorrect answer choices with respect to Reading Comprehension (as well as Critical Reasoning) questions. Take the following easy-to-understand statement:

Original: "Success is a strange phenomenon. You can achieve it through hard work, skill, or luck, or some combination of the three."

Here are several concocted statements derived from the original statement which showcase incorrect answer choices.

Out of scope: "The *most* important ingredient in success is hard work."

(Comment: No, we don't know whether hard work is the most important element in achieving success.)

"Hard work is a *more* important element in success than is skill."

(Comment: Unwarranted comparison—we don't know which element, in relative terms, is more important than the other.)

Irrelevant: "People who achieve success through hard work, skill, or luck sometimes find that their lives are meaningless."

(Comment: We are only concerned with how to achieve success, not what might happen beyond that juncture.)

Opposite: "People who are either hardworking, skillful, or lucky are *not* likely to achieve success."

(Comment: The word "not" reverses the meaning of the original statements.)

Distortion: "*Only* through hard work can one achieve success."

(Comment: No, we can also achieve success by being skillful or lucky. The word "only" creates a distortion.)

"A person who is hardworking does not run *any* risk of failure."

(Comment: The word "any" distorts the meaning of the original statements. How likely is the possibility of engaging in any human endeavor and having no chance of failure. Another way to view this statement is out of scope because the original statement makes no mention of the word "failure.")

"A person who is hardworking, skillful, or lucky can achieve *greatness*."

(Comment: The word "greatness" has an elevated meaning as compared with "success." Another way to view this statement is that it is out of scope because the original statement does not make mention of what it takes to achieve greatness.)

The Relationship Between Question Types and Common Wrong Answer Choices

How might the different Reading Comprehension question types be tackled based on an understanding of the common wrong answer choices?

(1) Overview questions

There are at least four ways to avoid wrong answer choices when tackling overview questions.

i)   Consider eliminating any answer choice which does not contain the words of the topic. Note that this advice works well for Q1, page 161.

ii)   Avoid any *overly detailed* answer choice, which may be a factually correct statement, but which is too detailed to be the correct answer choice to an overview question.

iii)   Avoid any *overly general* answer choice that is too broad to represent the topic at hand.

iv)   Use a verb scan, when possible. That is, look at the verb which begins each answer choice and eliminate those verbs which do not fit. Five common verbs found in Reading Comprehension passages include *describe, discuss, explain, argue*, and *criticize*. "Argue" is found frequently in social science passages; "describe" is found frequently in science passages. "Discuss" and "explain" are found in both social science and science passages. "Criticize" is usually not correct in an overview question involving a science passage because the author is typically endeavoring to describe something without being opinionated or judgmental.

(2) Explicit-detail questions and (3) Inference questions

On both explicit-detail questions and inference questions, common wrong answer choices include *opposites* and *out of scopes*.

Inference questions often contain wrong answer choices that are beyond the scope of the passage. In the context of a standardized test question, the test taker must be careful not to assume too much. Standardized test questions are notorious for narrowing the scope of what we can infer based on what we read. Contrast this with everyday life in which we generally use a loose framework and assume a lot.

(4) Tone questions

Tone is attitude and there are basically three "temperatures" for tone questions—positive, negative, or neutral. One trick is to avoid answer choices that contain "verbally confused word pairs." For example, the word pairs "supercilious disdain" or "self-mingled pity" are not terribly clear. Test makers like to include these types of answer choices believing that test takers will be attracted to confusing, complex sounding wrong answer choices.

(5) Passage organization questions

Two classic structures arise in Reading Comprehension passages. The first relates to social science passages, where a common structure is "A > B." Given that the hallmark of social science passages is their provocative, subjective, and often argumentative nature, such passages often contain competing viewpoints, where one view is favored over another. The other classic structure relates to science passages, which are often structured in the form of "A, B." An important distinction with regard to this latter structure (i.e., A, B) is that the two events are simply being described in detail, but not contrasted. Because science passages exist classically to describe (not to criticize), the author is unlikely to show favoritism to one side.

Regardless of the structure of the passage, a reader should always be careful to distinguish between the author's view and that of the information and evidence in the passage itself. For instance, the author may present information that clearly favors one side of an issue, especially if there is more support for that side or the stance is compelling. However, he or she may not necessarily endorse that viewpoint. Remember that "what the passage says" and "what the author thinks" may not always be one in the same. For example, an author of a passage may present evidence as to why the scientific community, in general, is skeptical about a belief in psychics, but that doesn't necessarily mean that the author is skeptical about a belief in psychics.

NOTE ✥ Two caveats that must be noted when using the *The Four-Corner Question Cracker for Reading Comprehension*™. The first is that it can only be used on three of the five question types, namely *overview* questions, *explicit-detail* questions, and *inference* questions. That said, this is hardly problematic because these three question types are by far the most common question types found in Reading Comprehension. In fact, they may even be referred to as the "big 3" question types for Reading Comprehension. Second, the vertical grid of the four-corner question cracker, which highlights <u>too general</u> answer choices and <u>too detailed</u> answer choices, can only be used when tackling overview questions. That is, the vertical grid cannot be used on *explicit-detail* or *inference* questions. In short, wrong answer choices on *explicit-detail* and *inference* questions are strictly referred to as being out of scope, opposite in meaning, or distorted in meaning.

MULTIPLE-CHOICE PROBLEMS

Sample Passage

The first passage below, and the accompanying questions (and answers and explanations), are presented to highlight analytical techniques for use in answering Reading Comprehension questions. Passage 1 exceeds 450 words in length and contains five questions. Reading Comprehension passages on the GMAT are usually not longer than 450 words in length and contain no more than four questions. Passages 2 and 3, on the other hand, typify the style, content, and length of difficult GMAT passages. Read each passage and answer the questions that follow.

Passage 1 (477 words)

1   For more than forty years, a controlling insight in my educational philosophy has been the recognition that no one has ever been—no one can ever be—educated in school or college. That would be the case if our schools and colleges were at their very best, which they certainly are not, and even if the students were among the
5   best and the brightest, as well as conscientious in the application of their powers. The reason is simply that youth itself—immaturity—is an insuperable obstacle to becoming educated. Schooling is for the young. Education comes later, usually much later. The very best thing for our schools to do is to prepare the young for continued learning in later life by giving them the skills of learning and the love
10   of it.

To speak of an educated young person or of a wise young person, rich in the understanding of basic ideas and issues, is as much a contradiction in terms as to speak of a round square. The young can be prepared for education in the years to come, but only mature men and women can become educated, beginning the
15   process in their forties and fifties and reaching some modicum of genuine insight, sound judgment and practical wisdom after they have turned sixty.

Those who take this prescription seriously would, of course, be better off if their schooling had given them the intellectual discipline and skill they need to carry it out, and if it also had introduced them to the world of learning with some
20   appreciation of its basic ideas and issues. But even the individual who is fortunate enough to leave school or college with a mind so disciplined, and with an abiding love of learning, would still have a long road to travel before he or she became an educated person. If our schools and colleges were doing their part and adults were doing theirs, all would be well. However, our schools and colleges are not
25   doing their part because they are trying to do everything else. And adults are not doing their part because most are under the illusion that they had completed their education when they finished their schooling.

Only the person who realizes that mature life is the time to get the education that no young person can ever acquire is at last on the high road to learning. The
30   road is steep and rocky, but it is the high road, open to anyone who has skill in learning and the ultimate goal of all learning in view—understanding the nature of things and mankind's place in the total scheme. An educated person is one who through the travail of his own life has assimilated the ideas that make him representative of his culture, that make him a bearer of its traditions and enable
35   him to contribute to its improvement.

The above excerpted passage was written by Mortimer J. Adler, author and former chairman of the board of directors of Encyclopedia Britannica and co-founder of The Center for the Study of The Great Ideas.

Q1. ( )

The author's primary purpose in writing this passage is to

A) Highlight major tenets in educational philosophy in the last 40 years.

B) Raise public awareness for the need of teachers with training in the liberal arts.

C) Contrast the words schooling and education.

D) Suggest that youth stands in the way of one becoming educated.

E) Cite the importance of reading with active discussion.

Q2. ( )

According to the passage, the best thing that our schools can do is to

A) Improve academic instruction at the grass roots level.

B) Advocate using the word "education" in place of the word "schooling" to better convey to adults the goal of teaching.

C) Convey to students that only through high scholastic achievement can one become truly educated.

D) Implement closely the opinions of adults who have already been through the educational process.

E) Help students acquire the skills for learning.

Q3. ( )

It can be inferred from the passage that the educated person must

A) Possess more maturity than passion.

B) Not be less than 40 years of age.

C) Be at least a university graduate.

D) Have read classic works of literature.

E) Have traveled widely in order to understand his or her own culture.

Q4. ( )

Which of the following pairs of words most closely describe the author's attitude toward adults as mentioned in the passage?

A)   Uninformed participants

B)   Unfortunate victims

C)   Conscientious citizens

D)   Invaluable partners

E)   Disdainful culprits

Q5. ( )

How is the previous passage organized?

A)   An objective analysis is put forth supported by factual examples.

B)   A single idea is presented with which the author does not agree.

C)   A thesis is presented and support given for it.

D)   Two ideas are contrasted and a conciliatory viewpoint emerges.

E)   A popular viewpoint is criticized from a number of perspectives.

Social Science Passage

Passage 2 (450 words)

1   How does ritual affect relationships between groups and entities external to them? According to traditional cultural anthropology, aggregates of individuals who regard their collective well-being as dependent upon a common body of ritual performances use such rituals to give their members confidence, to dispel their

5   anxieties, and to discipline their social organization. Conventional theories hold that rituals come into play when people feel they are unable to control events and processes in their environment that are of crucial importance to them. However, recent studies of the Tsembaga, a society of nomadic agriculturalists in New Guinea, suggest that rituals do more than just give symbolic expression to the

10   relationships between a cultural group and components of its environments; they influence those relationships in measurable ways.

Perhaps the most significant finding of the studies was that, among the Tsembaga, ritual operates as a regulating mechanism in a system of a set of interlocking systems that include such variables as the area of available land,

15   necessary length of fallow periods, size of the human and pig populations, nutritional requirements of pigs and people, energy expended in various activities, and frequency of misfortune. In one sense, the Tsembaga constitute an ecological population in an ecosystem that also includes the other living organisms and nonliving substances found within the Tsembaga territory. By collating

20   measurable data (such as average monthly rainfall, average garden yield, energy expenditure per cultivated acre, and nutritive values of common foods) with the collective decision to celebrate certain rituals, anthropologists have been able to show how Tsembaga rituals allocate energy and important materials. Studies have described how Tsembaga rituals regulate those relationships among people, their

25   pigs, and their gardens that are critical to survival; control meat consumption; conserve marsupial fauna; redistribute land among territorial groups; and limit the frequency of warfare. These studies have important methodological and theoretical implications, for they enable cultural anthropologists to see that rituals can in fact produce measurable results in an external world.

30   By focusing on Tsembaga rituals as part of the interaction within an ecosystem, newer quantitative studies permit anthropologists to analyze how ritual operates as a mechanism regulating survival. In the language of sociology, regulation is a "latent function" of Tsembaga ritual, since the Tsembaga themselves see their rituals as pertaining less to their material relations with the ecosystem than to

35   their spiritual relations with their ancestors. In the past, cultural anthropologists might have centered on the Tsembaga's own interpretations of their rituals in order to elucidate those rituals; but since tools now exist for examining the adaptive aspects of rituals, these anthropologists are in a far better position to appreciate fully the ecological sophistication of rituals, both among the Tsembaga

40   and in other societies.

Q6. ( )

The primary purpose of the passage is to

A)   Propose that the complex functions of ritual have been best analyzed when anthropologists and ecologists have collaborated in order to study human populations as measurable units.

B)   Criticize anthropologists' use of an ecological approach that ignores the symbolic, psychological, and socially cohesive effects of ritual.

C)   Evaluate theories of culture that view ritual as an expression of a society's understanding of its relationship to its environment.

D)   Point out the ecological sophistication of Tsembaga ritual and suggest the value of quantitative methods in assessing this sophistication.

E)   Argue that the studies showing that the effects of Tsembaga ritual on the environment can be measured prove that the effects of ritual on other environments can also be measured.

Q7. ( )

On the basis of the information in the passage, one might expect to find all of the following in the recent anthropological studies of the Tsembaga except

A)   An examination of the caloric and nutritive value of the Tsembaga diet.

B)   A study of the relationship between the number of Tsembaga rituals and the number of pigs owned by the Tsembaga.

C)   An analysis of the influence of Tsembaga forms of worship on the traditions of neighboring populations.

D)   A catalog of the ways in which Tsembaga rituals influence planting and harvest cycles.

E)   A matrix summarizing the seasonality of Tsembaga rituals and the type and function of weapons made.

Q8. ()

Which of the following best expresses the author's view of ritual?

A)   Rituals symbolize the relationships between cultural groups and their environments.

B)   As a cultural phenomenon, ritual is multifaceted and performs diverse functions.

C)   Rituals imbue the events of the material world with spiritual significance.

D)   A society's view of its rituals yields the most useful information concerning the rituals' functions.

E)   The spiritual significance of ritual is deemed greater than the material benefits of ritual.

Q9. ()

The author of the passage uses the term "latent function" (third paragraph) in order to suggest that

A)   The ability of ritual to regulate the environment is more a matter of study for sociologists than for anthropologists.

B)   Sociological terms describe ritual as precisely as anthropological terms.

C)   Anthropologists and sociologists should work together to understand the symbolic or psychological importance of rituals.

D)   Anthropologists are more interested in the regulatory function of rituals of the Tsembaga than they are the psychological function of rituals.

E)   The Tsembaga are primarily interested in the spiritual values that are embodied in their rituals.

Science Passage

Passage 3 (315 words)

1   Supernovas are among the most energetic events in the universe and result in the
complete disruption of stars at the end of their lives. Originally, the distinction
between Type I and Type II supernovas was based solely on the presence or absence
of hydrogen atoms (hydrogen lines). Supernovas without hydrogen lines were
5   called Type I, while those with hydrogen lines were Type II. Subsequent analysis
of many of these events revealed that this empirical classification schema instead
reflected two different mechanisms for the supernova explosion.

Type I supernovas happen in binary stars—two stars that orbit closely each
other—when one of the two binary stars is a small, dense, white dwarf star. If the
10   companion star ranges too close to the white dwarf that it is orbiting, the white
dwarf's gravitational pull will draw matter from the other star. When the white
dwarf acquires enough matter to become at least 1.4 times as big as the Sun, it
collapses and explodes in a supernova.

Type II supernovas occur when a star, much more massive than the Sun,
15   ends its life. When such a star begins burning out, the core of the star quickly
collapses releasing amazing energy in the form of neutrinos, a kind of particle
smaller than even an atom. Electromagnetic radiation—energy that is electric and
magnetic—causes the star to explode in a supernova. Whereas Type I supernovas
typically destroy their parent stars, Type II explosions usually leave behind the
20   stellar core.

The classification schema regarding the mechanism for supernova explosions
helps to more succinctly answer the question: Is the Sun in danger of becoming
a supernova? Neither does our Sun have a companion star orbiting it nor does
our Sun have the mass necessary to become a supernova. Furthermore, it will be
25   another billion years until the Sun runs out of fuel and swells into a red giant star
before going into a white dwarf form.

Q10.

How is this passage organized?

A)   A single phenomenon is introduced and two overlapping classification schemas are
contrasted.

B)   An original theory is mentioned before being overturned as a result of new findings.

C)   Two complementary mechanisms for describing a single phenomenon are discussed and
a conclusion is offered.

D)   A new classification schema is described and an example of how it works is provided.

E)   Two different classification systems are outlined and a question posed to help reconcile
both.

Q11. (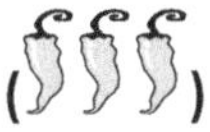)

Which of the following best summarizes the author's answer to the question: Is the Sun in danger of becoming a supernova?

A) The Sun is too large to have a white dwarf as a partner and lacks the physical size required to become a red giant.

B) Even if the Sun were paired with a white dwarf, the Sun does not have the mass necessary to create sufficient electromagnetic radiation.

C) The Sun is not a white dwarf with a companion star orbiting it, nor does it have the size to qualify as a Type II supernova.

D) Without a white dwarf orbiting the Sun, the Sun has no obvious way to increase its size to become a Type II supernova.

E) The Sun will inevitably become a supernova once it passes from a red giant to white dwarf but not for at least a billion years.

Q12. (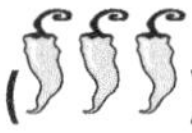)

It can be inferred from the passage that

A) Classifying a Type I or Type II event based on the presence or absence of hydrogen is not necessarily incompatible with a classification schema based on the mechanism by which these two events explode.

B) A dense white dwarf's gravitational pull on its companion star causes the companion star to collapse and explode as a supernova.

C) Before a star such as the Sun can become a red giant, it must first become a white dwarf.

D) In a Type II supernova, energy and electromagnetic radiation causes a star to collapse and explode.

E) Supernovas are rare events in our universe.

Q13. (🌶️🌶️)

According to the passage, which statement or statements below are true?

I. The energy created from a Type II explosion is greater than the energy created by a Type I explosion.

II. The sun is not a binary star.

III. Both Type I and Type II supernovas result in the complete destruction of the exploding star.

A) I only

B) II only

C) I and III only

D) II and III only

E) I, II, and III

Answers and Explanations

Q1. ( )

Choice D
Classification: Overview question
Snapshot: When attacking an overview question, look for the words of the topic and avoid both overly detailed or overly general answer choices.

Here's how the answers choices for Q1 are mapped using *The Four-Corner Question Cracker for Reading Comprehension™*.

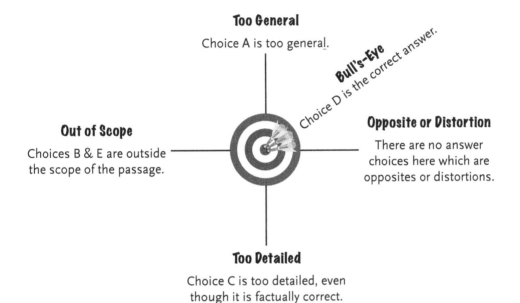

Too General
Choice A is too general.

Bull's-Eye
Choice D is the correct answer.

Out of Scope
Choices B & E are outside the scope of the passage.

Opposite or Distortion
There are no answer choices here which are opposites or distortions.

Too Detailed
Choice C is too detailed, even though it is factually correct.

Choice A is too general because a discussion of educational philosophy in the last forty years would likely incorporate the viewpoints of many individuals, not just the author's viewpoint. Choice B is outside the passage's scope. We do not necessarily know whether or not teachers should receive more liberal arts training. Choice C is a correct statement within the passage's context. However, it is too detailed to satisfy the primary purpose as demanded by this overview question.

For an overview question, there are effectively five reasons why wrong answers could be wrong. An answer choice will either be outside a passage's scope, opposite in meaning, distorted in meaning, too general, or too detailed. Whereas choice C was too detailed, choice A is an overly general answer choice. It is very useful to be on the lookout for answers that are out of the scope. This was the fate of answer choices B and E. Note that opposites or distortions are <u>not</u> common wrong answer choices with regard to overview questions.

A time-honored tip for answering overview questions involves performing a "topic-scope-purpose" drill. That is, we seek to identify the passage's topic, scope, and purpose. Topic is defined as the passage's broad subject matter. This is an "article on education." The topic is thus "education." Scope is defined as the specific aspect of the topic that the author is interested in. The scope here is "schooling versus education." Last, purpose is defined as the reason the author sat down to write the article. His purpose is to say:

"Colleges or universities can't educate; they exist to prepare students for later learning because youth itself makes real education impossible."

Understanding the topic, scope, and purpose should be enough to answer directly the overview question at hand. And knowing the author's purpose will likely set us up for another right answer on at least one of the remaining questions. Identifying the topic alone can help get us halfway to a right answer because the correct answer to an overview question almost always contains the words of the topic. In this case, the word "education" (or its derivative "educated") does not appear in answer choices B or E. We can feel fairly confident eliminating both of these choices.

Q2. (🌶🌶)

Choice E
Classification: Explicit-detail question
Snapshot: An explicit-detail question enables the reader to go back into the passage and "underline" the correct answer. Look for a literal answer.

Too General
Answer choices which are too general. (This option is not applicable to the explicit-detail question type.)

Bull's-Eye
Choice E is the correct answer.

Out of Scope
Choice A is outside the scope of the passage.

Opposite or Distortion
Choices B and D are opposites. Choice C is a distortion.

Too Detailed
Answer choices which are too detailed. (This option is not applicable to the explicit-detail question type.)

Where is the correct answer to be found? Consider the words "prepare the young for continued learning in later life by giving them the skills of learning," (lines 8–9) and "better off if their schooling had given them the intellectual discipline and skill" (lines 17–18). The word "skill" surfaces both times that the author talks about what schools should be doing.

Choice A is outside the passage's scope. The passage does not talk about improving academic instruction or anything to do with grass roots education levels. Nor does the passage talk about adults' opinions.

Choice B is essentially opposite in meaning. To be correct, this answer choice should read, "redefine 'education' as 'schooling' so to better convey to parents the goals of teaching." The author feels that adults have missed the point in thinking that finishing school is the same as finishing one's education; in fact, schools exist to school, and education comes later. Choice D may be classified as opposite in meaning, if we stick to the general spirit of the passage. The author believes that adults are very much uninformed and have missed the major point of education (lines 25–27); therefore, closely implementing their opinions is essentially opposite to the author's intended meaning.

Choice C is a distorted meaning. Distortions are most often created by the use of extreme wordings or by categorical or absolute-type wordings. Here, the word "only" signals a potential distortion. The author would likely agree that high scholastic achievement is a possible requirement for becoming educated, but not a sufficient condition in and of itself. In fact, the author really doesn't mention scholastic achievement, so we might classify it as being out of scope, if we did not happen to focus initially on the absolute-type wording.

Q3.

Choice B
Classification: Inference question
Snapshot: The challenge with inference questions is to find an answer that isn't explicitly mentioned in the passage, but one that can be logically inferred.

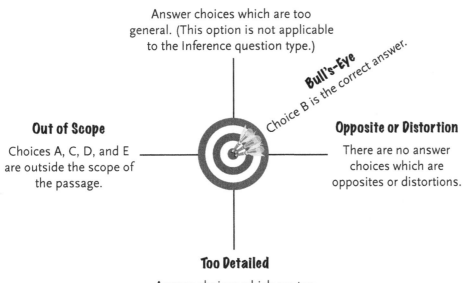

Too General
Answer choices which are too general. (This option is not applicable to the Inference question type.)

Bull's-Eye
Choice B is the correct answer.

Out of Scope
Choices A, C, D, and E are outside the scope of the passage.

Opposite or Distortion
There are no answer choices which are opposites or distortions.

Too Detailed
Answer choices which are too detailed. (This option is not applicable to the Inference question type.)

Although the author does not give an exact "education" formula, he effectively says that a number of factors are necessary to travel the high road to becoming educated. These include: passion, a knack for learning, discipline, and maturity. In terms of maturity, he clearly states: "The young can be prepared for education in the years to come, but only mature men and women can become educated, beginning the process in their forties and fifties and reaching some modicum of genuine insight, sound judgment and practical wisdom after they have turned sixty." Obviously, according to the author, if maturity begins in a person's forties and takes another ten to twenty years, then an individual cannot be less than forty years of age and still be considered educated.

Wrong answer choices in inference-type questions often fall outside the passage's scope. Choice A is outside the passage's scope and is specifically referred to as an unwarranted comparison. The author does not say whether he believes becoming educated takes more passion than maturity or more maturity than passion.

Choice C is perhaps the trickiest wrong answer choice. The author doesn't imply that one has to be a university graduate. In fact, he mentions "school and/or college" (lines 3, 21, 23, and 24), which suggests that he may well lump high school in with college and/or university. A high school graduate might have enough schooling to get onto the road of education. Moreover, the author doesn't claim one must be a four-year college or university graduate or even whether one has to attend college or university.

There is no mention of classic works of literature, so choice D is outside the passage's scope; we cannot answer this question based on information presented in the passage. Choice E is wrong because the author never mentions "travel." Don't mistake the word "travail" (meaning "struggle"; line 33) for "travel." Moreover, it is possible, without evidence to the contrary, that a person could never have left his or her own country and still understand those ideas that make him or her representative of his or her particular culture.

Q4. ( )

Choice A
Classification: Tone question
Snapshot: Tone questions ask about the author's feeling or attitude toward someone or something in the passage. Basically, the author will be either positive, negative, or neutral. In most cases, especially with respect to Social Sciences passages (as opposed to Science passages), the fact that the author would sit down to write something hints that he or she has some opinion about the topic at hand. Therefore, the neutral answer choice is not usually correct, even if available. For this question, we have, on the positive and supportive side, the following word pairs: "invaluable partners," "conscientious citizens," or "unfortunate victims." On the negative side, we have "uninformed participants" or "disdainful culprits."

The author's attitude toward adults is somewhat negative, but not excessively so. The feeling is more like frustration. The author believes that adults are not grasping the distinction between schooling and education (lines 25–27). Therefore, positive sounding choices C and D are out. Choice B, "unfortunate victims," is sympathetic, but the author thinks that adults are not victims, just misfocused. Choice E, "disdainful culprits," is too negative.

Q5. ( )

Choice C
Classification: Passage organization question.
Snapshot: Think in terms of the number of viewpoints and the relationship of these viewpoints.

The author introduces his thesis or summary in the very first sentence, "...a controlling insight in my educational philosophy...," then he goes on to support it with his personal observations, experiences, and opinions. Thus, choice A is not correct. No objective analysis is put forth; if there were, we would expect to see some surveys, statistics, or alternative viewpoints introduced. Choice B is wrong because there is a single idea presented, but the author agrees with it because it is his own idea. Choice D is incorrect as there are not two viewpoints presented, just one. Choice E suggests a popular viewpoint, but it is highly unlikely that many people have adopted this viewpoint because, according to the author, adults (and, by extension, laypersons) haven't really caught on. Last, a number of perspectives are not drawn upon. The author chooses to spend the entire article developing his single viewpoint "no one has ever been—no one could ever be—educated in school or college."

Q6. ( )

Choice D
Classification: Overview question
Snapshot: Make sure to read "the first sentence of the passage first then the last sentence of the passage next." Sometimes the author concludes at the bottom of the passage.

The major theme in this passage is that rituals are not only used by the Tsembaga society in a symbolic sense (that is, religiously, psychologically, or socially), but also in a practical or material way. Furthermore, these impacts or influences can be measured. Measurement is a key theme. Case in point: "they influence those relationships in measurable ways" (1st paragraph); "they enable cultural anthropologists to see that rituals can in fact produce measurable results in the external world" (2nd paragraph); and "newer quantitative studies permit anthropologists to analyze how ritual operates" (3rd paragraph). Choice D is a succinct rendition.

The passage does not suggest that anthropologists and ecologists collaborate for best results (choice A), even though the passage does suggest that anthropologists analyze ecological factors. Choice B is incorrect because the author does not criticize the symbolic role of rituals; he or she instead extends the discussion of rituals to include regulatory functions or mechanisms. The last sentence of the first paragraph makes this point: "However, recent studies of the Tsembaga, a society of nomadic agriculturalists in New Guinea, suggest that rituals do more than give symbolic expression to the relationships between a cultural group and components of its environment..."

The author does not evaluate theories of culture as indicated by choice C. His or her sole example is limited to the Tsembaga people. The author therefore does not prove that these studies show the measurable effects of rituals on other environments (per choice E).

NOTE ⇘ Performing the T-S-P drill for this passage proves beneficial. The topic of this passage is "rituals of the Tsembaga people." The scope is the "symbolic and material aspects of rituals for the Tsembaga people." The purpose is "to show that the benefits of rituals for the Tsembaga people are not only symbolic (spiritual) but also material (practical), and that these benefits can be measured."

Q7. (🌶🌶)

Choice C
Classification: Inference question
Snapshot: This inference question serves to introduce the "all of the following except" phraseology in Reading Comprehension.

The effects of rituals on neighboring populations is not described in the second paragraph so choice C would be the most unlikely candidate for inclusion in an anthropological study in support of the author's thesis. The influence of rituals on "the Tsembaga diet" (choice A), "the number of pigs owned" (choice B), "planting and harvest cycles" (choice D), or "type and function of weapons made" (choice E), all would be likely candidates for inclusion in such a report.

Q8. (🌶🌶🌶)

Choice B
Classification: Inference question
Snapshot: This question is similar to an overview question, but one which focuses on a specific subtopic within the passage.

The first sentence of the second paragraph lists many ways that rituals act as regulating mechanisms. It is obvious, therefore, that "ritual is multifaceted and performs diverse functions." Choice A is not incorrect per se, but rather it is incomplete. The author's view is that ritual does more than symbolize relationships. This is confirmed by the last sentence of the first paragraph: "However, recent studies of the Tsembaga, a society of nomadic agriculturalists in New Guinea, suggest that rituals do more than give symbolic expression to the relationships between a cultural group and components of its environment; they influence those relationships in measurable ways." Choice C is essentially opposite the author's view. The choice would have been better had it read: "Rituals imbue the events of the spiritual (symbolic) world with material significance." Choice D is also opposite in meaning. According to the last sentence of the passage (it's a long one), the author implies that anthropologists are in a better position to understand a society's culture than is the society itself. In choice E, we cannot confirm or negate this answer choice based on information presented in the passage. It is not clear whether the spiritual significance of ritual is deemed greater than the material benefits of ritual or whether the material benefits of ritual are deemed greater than the spiritual benefits of ritual.

Q9. (🌶🌶)

Choice E
Classification: Explicit-detail/Inference question
Snapshot: This is essentially a "vocabulary" question in which we are asked to interpret how a word or term in the passage is used.

The terms "latent function" and "hidden function" are worthy substitutes. Although the author states that "the Tsembaga themselves see their rituals as pertaining less to their material relations with the ecosystem than to their spiritual relations with their ancestors," this does not mean that such rituals do not, for them, perform other essential roles. The author brings up "latent function" to suggest there is "hidden benefit" in the use of ritual for the Tsembaga; these additional benefits are practical, not symbolic.

In choices A and B, the author is not pitting anthropologists and sociologists against one another, or for that matter, the study of anthropology and sociology. Nor is the author suggesting that the two sides work together as suggested by choice C. The author is also not concluding that anthropologists are more interested in the regulatory function of rituals than the psychological or symbolic importance of rituals (choice D), even though the former—regulatory functions of ritual—is the focus of this passage. Note that the use of the comparative word "more" (choices A and D) often creates answer choices that are out of scope.

Q10. (🌶🌶)

Choice D
Classification: Passage Organization question
Snapshot: Science passages typically exist to *describe* (as opposed to Social Science passages which typically exist to *argue*) and such passages frequently incorporate two theories, hypotheses, or explanations.

The new schema is based on the distinction between Type I and Type II supernovas; the original schema is one based on the absence of hydrogen (Type I) or the presence of hydrogen (Type II). The example of the Sun is provided as support for how the classification system works. Choice D best summarizes this structure.

In choice A, the schemas do not necessarily overlap. An event classified as a Type I supernova under one schema might not be classified as a Type I supernova under the other schema (and vice versa). Also, the two schemas are described, but not contrasted with each other. In choice B, it is inaccurate to describe the original theory as being overturned. The new theory is very much an "extension" of the old theory rather than a "replacement." In choice C, no conclusion is offered. For example, the author does not state that Type I is "better or worse" than Type II, or that Type I is easier to use in describing or explaining the occurrence of supernovas than Type II. No reconciliation between the two different classification systems is provided per choice E. The two different systems are very much distinct and do not lend themselves to reconciliation.

Q11. (🌶🌶🌶)

Choice C
Classification: Explicit-Detail/Inference question
Snapshot: This question requires linking information across multiple paragraphs in a passage, namely the last paragraph with paragraphs two and three.

Answer choice C describes accurately and completely the author's view in the final paragraph. The Sun is not a binary star because it doesn't have companion star orbiting it, so it can't qualify as a Type I supernova. Nor does the Sun have the size necessary to become a Type II supernova (it would have to be at least 1.4 times its own size).

In choice A, there is no relationship suggested between the size of the Sun and its ability to have a white dwarf partner (per Type I). Choices B and D create unwarranted linkages between Type I and Type II supernovas. It is the white dwarf, not the Sun, which would undergo collapse and explosion as a supernova. In choice E, even if the Sun does become a red giant before becoming a white dwarf, it does not mean that it will become a supernova. It would still need another star (i.e., binary star) that it could absorb en route to becoming a Type I supernova.

Q12. (🌶🌶🌶)

Choice A
Classification: Inference question
Snapshot: This question highlights the need to avoid choosing "reversed" cause-and-effect relationships and "fabricated" cause-and-effect relationships, which are the hallmarks of some incorrect inference answer choices that appear in difficult Reading Comprehension passages.

Choices B, C, and D represent examples of such reversed cause-and-effect relationships. In choice B, it is the dense white dwarf that explodes as a supernova, not the companion star! Choice C suggests that a star such as the Sun must first become a white dwarf before becoming a red giant. This stands in opposition to what is suggested in the last line of the passage: that a star such as the Sun "swells into a red giant star before going into white dwarf form." Choice D is more subtle. We know that Type II supernovas release energy from neutrinos and electromagnetic radiation. However the cause-and-effect relationship is reversed. It is the collapsing of the star that *causes* the release of energy as neutrinos and electromagnetic radiation, subsequent to the exploding of the star as a supernova. Choice D suggests that the energy and electromagnetic radiation is what *causes* the star to collapse and explode.

Choice A is readily inferable from the second and third sentences of the opening paragraph. Classifying Type 1 and Type 2 events based on the presence or absence of hydrogen or based on the different explosion mechanisms are not necessarily incompatible with one another. In other words, an event might be classified as a Type I supernova because it doesn't have hydrogen lines <u>or</u> because it explodes as a result of being a white dwarf that acquires matter from its orbiting binary star. An event might be classified as a Type II supernova because it does have hydrogen lines <u>or</u> because it explodes as a result of being a massive collapsing star.

There is no indication from the information given in the passage that supernovas are rare events in the universe at large (choice E). For all we know, they are common in some galaxies and rare in others. It is important not to draw upon outside knowledge when answering Reading Comprehension questions.

NOTE ❧ Per choice D, a simple example might serve to better clarify the nature of the potential overlap. Schema 1: Say, for example, we classify a good day versus a bad day by the absence or presence of rain. A good day will have the absence of rain while a bad day will have the presence of rain. Schema 2: We might also classify a good day versus a bad day based on the number of hours of sunshine received. A good day will have a substantial number of hours of sunshine while a bad day will have a minimum number of hours of sunshine. In short, between schemas 1 and 2, a good day might have the absence of rain and a substantial number of hours of sunshine. A bad day might have the presence of rain and a minimal number of hours of sunshine. As we can quickly see, a good day might be classified as a "good day" under either schema.

On the contrary, a day might have a little rain and also a substantial number of hours of sunshine. In this case, it is considered a bad day under schema 1 but a good day under schema 2. Likewise, a day might have no rain and a minimal number of hours of sunshine. In this case, it is considered a good day under schema 1 but a bad day under schema 2. Here, there is no overlap between the two schemas.

Q13. (🐾)

Choice B
Classification: Inference/Explicit-detail question
Snapshot: This question introduces the Roman numeral question-type in Reading Comprehension.

The statement represented by statement I cannot be proved or disproved from information gleamed from the passage. Although Type II stars appear bigger than Type I ("much more massive than the Sun" versus "at least 1.4 times as big as the Sun"), it is not certain which Type releases the greatest amount of overall energy.

Statement II is true. To be a binary star, the Sun must have an orbiting partner. Because the Sun does not, it does not qualify as a binary star (see first sentence of second paragraph as well as the last paragraph).

Statement III is false. The last line of the third paragraph clearly states: "Whereas Type I supernovas typically destroy their parent stars, Type II explosions usually leave behind the stellar core." Type II supernovas, therefore, do not result in "complete destruction of the exploding star."

NOTE ⤚ This passage did not contain an *overview* question. Nonetheless, it is always recommended to do a T-S-P drill, asking what is the topic, scope, and purpose of the passage. The topic is "supernovas." The scope is "Type I and Type II supernovas." The purpose is "to describe a new schema for classifying Type I and Type II supernovas."

CHAPTER 7

ANALYTICAL WRITING WORKSHOP

Put it before them briefly so they will read it, clearly so they will appreciate it, picturesquely so they will remember it and, above all, accurately so they will be guided by its light.

—Joseph Pulitzer

OVERVIEW

Official Exam Instructions for the Analytical Writing Assessment (AWA)

Directions

In this section, you will be asked to write a critique of the argument presented. You are NOT being asked to present your own views on the subject.

Writing your response: Take a few minutes to evaluate the argument and plan a response before you begin writing. Be sure to organize your ideas and develop them fully, but leave time to reread your response and make any revisions that you think are necessary.

Evaluation of your response: College and university faculty members from various subject matter areas, including management education, will evaluate the overall quality of your thinking and writing.

They will consider how well you—organize, develop, and express your ideas about the argument presented; provide relevant supporting reasons and examples; and control the elements of standard written English.

Strategies and Approaches

Analysis of an Argument Essay:

1. *Identify the conclusion and evidence contained in the argument.*

2. *Identify three (or more) assumptions contained in the argument.*

3. *Follow one of the outlines contained in the solutions template for an Analysis of an Argument essay.*

4. *Write (or type) a response and spend five minutes proofreading and tweaking your essay.*

REVIEW OF ANALYTICAL WRITING

Frequently Asked Questions

Here are answers to several frequently asked questions:

What is the basic goal in answering an Analysis of an Argument essay?

Writing the argument essay requires a test taker to analyze a statement or series of statements, called an argument, and discuss what is technically or logically wrong with it. How about an analogy? Responding to an Analysis of an Argument question requires us to respond to the argument at hand as if we are "overhauling a bicycle." We are required to break the argument down into its three parts, namely conclusion, evidence, and assumptions. This type of essay requires that we also show how to make the argument stronger, a requirement which is analogous to putting a bicycle back together once we have identified the problem areas.

An Analysis of an Argument essay is an "objective" essay because we are not required or encouraged to introduce personal examples, ideas, or opinions in order to make our case. Note that the GMAT official instructions to the Analysis of an Argument essay includes the sentence, "You are NOT being asked to present your own views on the subject."

How is the AWA used by business schools?

Although it is unclear how business schools use AWA (Analytical Writing Assessment) scores in the admissions process, there are three possibilities. Scores could be used in borderline admission decisions. They could be used to identify students who need a remedial writing course. Finally, they could be used to help verify that candidates wrote their admissions essays.

How is the AWA scored?

One human and one electronic e-grading machine called the "e-rater" score each AWA essay. Grades are assigned out of 6.0 based in intervals of 0.5 points. Your overall, final score is an average of both individual scores obtained. *Exhibit 1.4 (Chapter 1)* provides a snapshot of scaled scores and percentile rank for the Analytical Writing Assessment.

What do graders look for in terms of grading the AWA essay?

GMAT graders are looking for "good essays," defined in the most general sense as ones which have good grammar, structure, and content. Content is deemed most important.

For each 30-minute essay, what is the ideal way to allocate my time?

Spend five minutes thinking about and sketching your response; spend twenty minutes writing/typing your essay; and spend the last five minutes proofreading/tweaking your essay. The time allocation for each essay is therefore: 5–20–5.

How long should essays be?

Essays ("good essays") should be five to seven paragraphs, approximately 400 to 500 words in total word length. More is better on the AWA essays. All things being equal, longer essays correlate with higher grades.

Where do the AWA essays come from?

A complete list of the approximately 135 Analysis of an Argument essays may be downloaded from the GMAC website (www.mba.com). During the exam, a random generating device chooses one essay from the data bank. No one knows, therefore, which essay topic will be assigned to any given test taker.

The 4-Step Approach for Writing an Argument Essay

Step #1:   **Identify the conclusion and evidence in the argument.**

Logically, we identify the conclusion first, then the evidence, and finally the assumption(s). Again, the following formulas express the relationship between these three elements:

Conclusion = Evidence + Assumption
or
Conclusion − Evidence = Assumption

The conclusion is defined as the claim or main point that the author, writer, or speaker is making. The evidence includes any facts, examples, statistics, surveys, and other data or information that the author uses in support of his or her conclusion. The assumption is defined as "that which the author takes for granted."

Step #2:   **Identify three (or more) assumptions contained in your argument.**

The practical goal of answering an Analysis of an Argument essay is to identify three (or more) assumptions in the argument presented. Although there is no "right" way to go about finding assumptions, think of assumptions as falling into certain categories, including: comparison and analogy assumptions, representativeness assumptions, cause-and-effect assumptions, and implementation assumptions. The use of the *C-C-R-I-Q Assumption Cracker (Exhibit 7.3)* dovetails with the discussion of Critical Reasoning contained in *Chapter 3*.

Step #3:   **Follow one of the proposed solution templates for an argument essay.**

The recommended structure to use to answer an Analysis of an Argument essay is outlined in *Exhibit 7.1*. This method involves first identifying the assumptions and second showing how these assumptions can be strengthened. An alternative method involves mentioning how to strengthen each assumption directly after identifying a given assumption.

Begin by restating the argument and by answering the original question.

First and foremost, it is recommended that you begin your essay by answering the question at hand. That is, "How well-reasoned do you find this argument?" Note that the question of whether or not an argument is actually well reasoned is essentially unimportant because regardless of whether you think it is or is not well reasoned, you will still have to proceed to take the argument apart and examine the underlying assumptions. If you believe the argument is not well reasoned you may state: "I do not believe this argument is well reasoned as it is resting on several debatable assumptions." This approach makes sense since the game of answering an Analysis of an Argument essay is to attack an argument regardless of its actual reasonableness.

Should you believe the argument is well reasoned you may state: "I believe this argument is well reasoned; however, it is resting on several debatable assumptions." It is recommended that you simply replicate one of these two sentences when writing your Analysis of an Argument essay.

EXHIBIT 7.1   SOLUTION TEMPLATE FOR AN ANALYSIS OF AN ARGUMENT ESSAY

Standard Approach	Alternative Approach
The author concludes that (xxx) and uses as evidence (yyy). I do not find this argument to be well reasoned as it is resting on several debatable assumptions.	The author concludes that (xxx) and uses as evidence (yyy). I do not find this argument to be well reasoned as it is resting on several debatable assumptions.
First, identify assumption #1 and explain why it is potentially weak.	First, identify assumption #1 and explain why it is potentially weak. This assumption could be strengthened by showing that...
Second, identify assumption #2 and explain why it is potentially weak.	Second, identify assumption #2 and explain why it is potentially weak. This assumption could be strengthened by showing that...
Third, identify assumption #3 and explain why it is potentially weak.	Third, identify assumption #3 and explain why it is potentially weak. This assumption could be strengthened by showing that...
Next, show how assumption #1 could be strengthened...show how assumption #2 could be strengthened...show how assumption #3 could be strengthened.	
We could also strengthen the argument by softening its absolute-type wording...	We could also strengthen the argument by softening its absolute-type wording...
In conclusion, in order to better evaluate this argument, we need clarification as to what the word "xyz" means...	In conclusion, in order to better evaluate this argument, we need clarification as to what the word "xyz" means...

> Begin by summarizing the argument and answering the original question.

Use transition words to structure your argument essay.

As the traffic lights of language, *transition words* are extremely important words in the verbal and writing sections of the GMAT exam, and serve one of four primary purposes, namely to show contrast, illustration, continuation, or conclusion. See *Exhibit 6.1*, page 337.

Perhaps the most relevant transition words that you'll consider using when writing your Analysis of an Argument essay are the transition words for illustration: *first, second, third,* etc. What you are essentially going to do is to say that: "I don't find this argument to be well reasoned as it contains several debatable assumptions...first (assumption)..., second (assumption)..., and third (assumption)..."

Another way to view overall essay structure, particularly in terms of transition words, is to ponder the "simplest writing approach in the world." *Exhibit 7.2* depicts a sure-fire way to write on just about anything. It might not be the most exciting writing structure but it is clear and it works—take a stance, write your conclusion, say "there are several reasons for this," use transition words, and voila!

EXHIBIT 7.2   THE SIMPLEST WRITING APPROACH IN THE WORLD!

Example: Renaissance

I agree that the Renaissance Period was the most glorious time in human history to be an artist. There are several reasons for this. First,~~~~~~Second,~~~~~~Third,~~~~~~Fourth,~~~~~~Moreover,~~~~~~Finally,~~~~~~

Arguably the best way to visualize the structure for your essay is in terms of the classic *five-paragraph approach*—just as you learned in high school. The introduction is one paragraph, the body is three paragraphs, and the conclusion is one paragraph. Each point in the main discussion represents one paragraph in the body of the essay. In practice, however, you may use three paragraphs or even seven paragraphs depending on how you choose to combine the parts of your writing.

Question the use of one vague term used in the argument and ask for clarification.

Analysis of an Argument essay questions will invariably contain certain words which are inherently ambiguous. Examples of such words include: "success," "justice," "fairness," and "high-quality." What do each of these words mean exactly? Naturally, different people may interpret them differently. A good writing technique includes drawing attention to one vague word (or phrase) per each Analysis of an Argument essay and suggesting the need for a clearer, more precise interpretation. Perhaps the best place to draw attention to an inherently vague term is in the concluding paragraph of your essay. This is consistent with treatment seen in the sample essays for *Yuppie Café* and *Cars vs. Public Transportation* that follow in this chapter.

Suggest strengthening the argument by softening its absolute-type wording.

Analysis of an Argument essays appearing on the GMAT are typically written with absolute-type wordings. Absolute-type wordings have a stated or implied "all" meaning. For example, an argument will effectively say that "(all) corporations should do X or Y" or that "(all) people should take A or B course of action." You can make such arguments stronger by suggesting changing such extreme, categorical, or absolute-type wordings. For example, instead of "all corporations," you could suggest that the wording be changed to *"most* corporations should do X or Y." Instead of saying that people "should take such and such course of action," you could say that "people should *probably* take such and such course of action." Arguably the best place to address the *strengthening of absolute-type wording* would be at the end of the body of the essay (just before the conclusion), while the best place to address *clarification of a vague term* would be in the conclusion of the essay.

Step #4:   Write (or type) a response and spend five minutes proofreading your essay.

Plan to spend the final five minutes proofreading your work, looking for typos and tweaking your sentences. Naturally, variations in spelling and punctuation between British English and American English are both recognized and accepted by test graders in New Jersey, USA.

Using the Assumption Cracker

What is the best way to capture underlying assumptions in arguments? Most prospective test takers have no problem identifying the conclusion and evidence in an argument. But they do have trouble identifying assumptions. One question that is often in the minds of candidates is: "Is there a trick to being able to find a sufficient number of assumptions as well as a sufficient variety of assumptions?" The answer to this question is yes, and it comes in the form of the *C-C-R-I-Q Assumption Cracker for Analyzing Arguments™*, as showcased in *Exhibit 7.3*. The mnemonic C-C-R-I-Q is derived from the first letter of each of the five assumptions categories that make up the template: the "C" of comparison and analogy, the "C" of cause and effect, the "R" of representativeness, the "I" of implementation, and the "Q" of questionable evidence.

EXHIBIT 7.3   C-C-R-I-Q ASSUMPTION CRACKER FOR ANALYZING ARGUMENTS™

Comparison and Analogy Assumptions

Cause-and-Effect Assumptions

Representativeness Assumptions

Implementation Assumptions

Questionable Evidence

Mnemonic: C-C-R-I-Q

It is important to note that it may not always be possible to "check off" all five assumption categories for every given Analysis of an Argument essay. That said, the two arguments chosen in this chapter for our review, namely *Yuppie Café* and *Cars vs. Public Transportation*, each contain all five categories of assumptions.

One added bonus that comes from studying for the Analysis of an Argument essay (and using the *C-C-R-I-Q Assumption Cracker*) is the dual benefit of getting better prepared for the reasoning questions that appear on the Critical Reasoning (multiple choice) section of the GMAT (see *Chapter 3*). There are a few differences, however, between the arguments that appear on these two sections of the exam. First, whereas the arguments on the Critical Reasoning section center on a single, primary assumption, the arguments on the Analytical Writing Assessment contain multiple assumptions (and we are required to identify three or four of them to obtain a high score). Second, whereas we are only "allowed" to attack assumptions on the Critical Reasoning section of the exam, we are welcome to attack both assumption and evidence when evaluating an Analysis of an Argument essay. This approach is consistent with the discussion on evaluating assumptions as presented in *Chapter 3*. It is also the way we can attack arguments in real life: we attack the assumption(s) and attack the evidence.

The first four categories of the *C-C-R-I-Q Assumption Cracker* involve attacking assumptions. The final category involves attacking evidence. It appears that the GMAT AWA does not require the test-taker to make a technical distinction between evidence and assumption(s). Therefore, we can write "this argument assumes" when, in fact, we are attacking the argument's evidence.

Remember that all arguments have assumptions. It is never possible to say that an argument is weak because it is resting on assumptions. Note also that all arguments appearing on the GMAT are inductive as opposed to deductive. Inductive arguments are viewed as stronger or weaker rather than valid or invalid as is the case with deductive arguments. Therefore, it is also not possible to refer to arguments on the AWA section of the GMAT as valid or invalid or correct or incorrect.

1. Comparison Assumptions

Ask: Does the argument make logical comparisons? Are apples being compared to apples and oranges being compared to oranges (or are apples instead being compared to oranges or vice versa)? At the most fundamental level, we must ensure that the meaning (or definition) of words and terms used in an argument are being defined and applied consistently. Also, watch for "scope shifts" which occur when one term changes as an argument unfolds.

Rule: Show how two things are not logically comparable and the argument is weakened or falls apart.

2. Cause-and-Effect Assumptions

Ask: Does A really lead to B?

Rule: Show that A does not necessarily lead to B and the argument is weakened or falls apart. This may be achieved by finding another cause which explains the presumed cause-and-effect relationship or by showing that the two events in question are only strongly correlated, but not causally related.

3. Representativeness Assumptions

Ask: Does little "a" equal big "A"?

Rule: Show how a "part" does not equal the "whole" or that a sample is not representative of the larger population and the argument is weakened or falls apart.

4. Implementation Assumptions

Ask: Will a plan be implemented or used?

Rule: Show how no one will act on a plan or how the plan cannot be implemented due to financial, physical, logistical, or technological limitations and the argument is weakened or falls apart.

5. Questionable Evidence

Ask: Is the evidence used in the argument really good evidence? Are the numbers or statistics used really good? Are costs really as low as suggested, or are revenues or profits really as high as anticipated?

Rule: Show how the evidence (including any facts, examples, or statistics) is misleading or flawed and the argument is weakened or falls apart.

ESSAY EXERCISES

For the purposes of reinforcing techniques used to answer Analysis of an Argument essays, write or sketch a response to the following essay questions and compare them to the proposed solutions presented. *Yuppie Café* and *Cars vs. Public Transportation* are classic examples of argument-type essays.

Two Analysis of an Argument Essays

1. Yuppie Café ( )

> The following appeared as part of a campaign to get local businesses to advertise on the Internet and through social media.
>
> "The Yuppie Café began advertising on the Internet this year and was delighted to see its business increase by 15 percent over last year's total. Their success shows that you too can use the Internet to make your business more profitable."
>
> Discuss how well reasoned you find this argument. In your discussion, be sure to analyze the line of reasoning and the use of evidence in the argument. For example, you may need to consider what questionable assumptions underlie the thinking and what alternative explanations or counterexamples might weaken the conclusion. You can also discuss what sort of evidence would strengthen or refute the argument, what changes in the argument would make it more logically sound, and what, if anything, would help you better evaluate its conclusion.

Identify the conclusion and evidence and choose three (or more) assumptions:

Conclusion:

Evidence:

Assumptions:

-
-
-

2. Cars vs. Public Transportation ( )

"People living in cities should switch from driving their cars to work on the weekdays to taking public transportation such as buses and subways. In large cities such as New York, London, and Shanghai, cars are an expensive and inefficient means of transportation and fossil fuel emissions are the major source of the city's pollution."

Discuss how well reasoned you find this argument. In your discussion, be sure to analyze the line of reasoning and the use of evidence in the argument. For example, you made need to consider what questionable assumptions underlie the thinking and what alternative explanations or counterexamples might weaken the conclusion. You can also discuss what sort of evidence would strengthen or refute the argument, what changes in the argument would make it more logically sound, and what, if anything, would help you better evaluate its conclusion.

Identify the conclusion and evidence and choose three (or more) assumptions:

Conclusion:

Evidence:

Assumptions:

-
-
-

Outlines and Proposed Solutions

With respect to the two argument essays that follow, *Yuppie Café* and *Cars vs. Public Transportation*, the order in which assumptions and/or evidence appear may vary from outline to written solution. This is simply a matter of form, not substance.

1. Yuppie Café (🌶 🌶)

Solution in Outline Form

Opener:

The argument concludes that you can use the Internet to advertise and make your business more profitable. The author uses as evidence the fact that Yuppie Café advertised on the Internet and its business increased by 15% over last year's total. I do not find this argument to be well reasoned, as it rests on several debatable assumptions.

Identifying the assumptions:

- First, the argument assumes that a 15% increase in business is the same as a 15% increase in revenue or profit. The term "business increase" must be clarified in order to enable a proper comparison.

- Second, the argument assumes a cause-and-effect relationship between advertising on the Internet and the increase in business.

- Third, the argument assumes that Yuppie Café is representative of all other businesses—e.g., your own business.

- Fourth, the argument assumes that companies have access to the Internet in order to place company advertisements, and that they employ personnel capable of administering the system. The argument also assumes that a company has the money to spend on Internet advertising. These considerations create implementation assumptions. Finally, the argument likely assumes that the costs of Internet advertising do not outweigh the revenues to be received.

Questionable evidence:

- Fifth, the argument assumes that any business can achieve a 15% increase regardless of where it is in its natural growth cycle. This is easier for a younger, upstart business than for an older, more mature business.

Conclusion:

- In conclusion, to strengthen this argument, we need more information to substantiate all above-mentioned assumptions: cause-and-effect, representative sample, comparison and analogy assumptions, implementation, and questionable evidence.

- We could also strengthen the argument by "softening" the absolute-type wording as used in the original argument. The original sentence states, "Their success shows you how you too can use the Internet to make your business more profitable." The wording could instead read, "Their success shows how you too can probably use the Internet to make your business more profitable," or "Their success shows how a number of companies can use the Internet to make their businesses more profitable."

- Finally, we need clarification as to what exactly the word "success" means. How is it defined?

Solution in Essay Form (726 words)

The argument concludes that you can use the Internet to advertise and to make your business more profitable. The author uses as evidence the fact that Yuppie Café advertised on the Internet and its business increased by 15% over last year's total. I do not find this argument to be well reasoned, as it rests on several debatable assumptions.

First, the argument assumes that there is a cause-and-effect relationship between advertising on the Internet and an increase in business. It could be that Yuppie Café saw an increase in business for reasons not related to advertising on the Internet. For example, a major competitor of Yuppie Café may have gone out of business, the company may have started serving a higher-quality coffee product, business may have increased because word-of-mouth advertising lured customers, or perhaps there was a period of general economic prosperity.

Second, the argument assumes that Yuppie Café is representative of all other businesses, e.g., your own business. This creates a representative sample assumption. It may even be true that the Internet does help highly customer-oriented companies with their businesses, e.g., coffee shops, health spas, and book distribution companies. But what about an oil-and-gas or mining company? Obviously, it is difficult to generalize from a single example to all other companies.

Third, the argument assumes that other companies actually own computers, have access to the Internet in order to place company advertisements, and employ personnel capable of administering the system. Furthermore, the argument assumes that a company has the money or other financial wherewithal to spend on Internet advertising. Moreover, the argument assumes that the money a company spends on Internet advertising does not outweigh the revenues to be derived from increased sales. These considerations create implementation assumptions.

Fourth, the argument assumes that a 15% increase in business is the same as a 15% increase in profit. The word "business increase" likely refers to revenues, but, as we know, revenues and profit are not the same thing. Profit depends on the relationship between costs, revenues, and sales volume. Furthermore, the words "business increase" are vague. For example, a 15% increase in the number of customers served may not translate to a 15% increase in revenues or profits, particularly if the retail price of a cup of coffee has been significantly reduced or increased.

Fifth, the argument assumes that any business can achieve a 15% increase regardless of where it is in its natural growth cycle. Within any given industry, achieving a business increase is easier for a younger, upstart business than for an older, more mature business. The natural growth cycle for a typical business is characterized by an upward growth curve that flattens as the business matures. A younger business is more likely to have significant year-to-year growth. An increase in business will result in a higher percentage increase given that the increase is being compared to a relatively smaller base.

In conclusion, to strengthen this argument, we need more information to substantiate the cause-and-effect relationship between advertising and an increase in business. We need more examples in order to show that Yuppie Café is not merely an exceptional business example. We need some assurance that companies have the money and resources to pursue an Internet advertising program. We also need clarification as to whether an increase in business translates to an increase in revenues and/or whether an increase in revenues translates to an increase in profit. We need assurance that companies other than upstart companies can achieve a 15% increase in business and assurance that the 15% figure is accurate and can be relied upon.

One word—"success"—is particularly vague and needs clarification. Is a 15% increase in business a worthy criterion for "success"? To a venture capitalist, success might be defined by a return of 50% or more. Furthermore, should success be measured merely along a quantitative dimension? What about the qualitative dimensions of employee or consumer satisfaction? Finally, "softening" the wording in the original argument could strengthen the argument. The original sentence states, "Their success shows you how you too can use the Internet to make your business more profitable." The wording could read, "Their success shows how you too can probably use the Internet to make your business more profitable," or "Their success shows how a number of companies can use the Internet to make their businesses more profitable."

2. Cars vs. Public Transportation (🌶 🌶)

Solution in Outline Form

Opener:

The author concludes that people should switch from driving cars to work to taking public transportation such as buses and subways. The argument is based on the evidence that cars are an expensive and inefficient mode of transportation (in New York, London, and Shanghai) and fossil fuel emissions are the major source of the city's pollution. I do not find this argument to be well reasoned as it is resting on several debatable assumptions.

Identifying the assumptions:

- Cities? Do all people who live in cities necessarily live in *large* cities where pollution is a problem? This calls into question a scope issue—a city may not be a large city.

- Cars? The argument assumes that cars are the major source of the pollution in major cities. This may not be true. It could be that pollution comes from nearby factories or perhaps the toxicity of bus emissions is much greater than the toxicity of car emissions.

- Weekdays? It also assumes (and much more subtly) that pollution is caused by cars driven on the weekdays as opposed to the weekends. Could it be that many people only drive short distances to work on the weekdays and then go for joy rides on the weekends, making weekends the time when pollution really adds up?

- Three cities? The argument assumes that New York, London, and Shanghai are representative of other major cities. But is the public transportation in these cities typical of all major cities?—Probably not. What about Rome, Bangkok, or São Paulo? These cities likely do not have transportation systems as good as those of the cities mentioned in the argument.

- Own cars? The argument assumes foremost that people own cars. This may not be true.

- Available and convenient? It also assumes that public transportation is both available and convenient to use should a person decide to switch. What if there exists no convenient transportation in the far reaching suburbs of New York, London, or Shanghai? (Let's further assume that living in the suburbs still constitutes living in the city.)

- Bottlenecks? The argument also assumes that if people do switch, the current system of public transportation will be able to accommodate all the "switchers."

Questionable evidence:

- Expensive? The argument assumes that cars are an expensive means of transportation relative to public transportation. While this is quite compelling, it need not be necessarily true. First, there is car-pooling in which more than one person rides in a car. Second, a person might have to take more than a single form of public transportation. Third, let's view things from the city's standpoint, not the consumer's standpoint. If the city has to build or maintain a large public transportation system (e.g., building a subway system), it could prove very costly indeed. From the city's standpoint, the cheapest means of transportation may be privatized transportation (e.g., let consumers pay for and drive their own cars).

- Inefficient? The argument also assumes that cars are an inefficient means of transportation. However, if a person uses a car to get to work in a shorter period of time, gains in productivity may offset otherwise higher transportation costs. This is particularly relevant for high wage earners, e.g., chief executives, managing directors, doctors, etc.

Conclusion:

Strengthening the argument would require:

- More data to strengthen each of the above assumptions.
- Clarification as to the definition of the word "pollution."
- Softening the absolute-type wording from "people should switch" to "people should probably switch."

Solution in Essay Form (846 words)

The argument concludes that people living in cities should switch from driving their cars to work on the weekdays to taking public transportation such as buses and subways. It uses as evidence examples drawn from New York, London, and Shanghai, where cars are found to be an expensive and inefficient means of transportation and fossil fuel emissions are the major source of each city's pollution. I do not find the argument to be well reasoned as it is resting on several debatable assumptions.

First, the argument suggests that cars are an expensive and inefficient means of transportation. While this assumption is quite compelling, it need not be necessarily true. In terms of efficiency, a person using a car could get to work more quickly. This extra time could spell gains in productivity, particularly for high wage earners such as chief executives, managing directors, and doctors, whose time might be more than offset by the increased costs of private transportation. Also, there might be ways to directly offset the costs of using private vehicles. For example, car-pooling would mean that people share a single vehicle. Also, in the event that a person needs to take more than a single form of public transportation (e.g., a bus and the subway) to get to work, costs would increase. Finally, let us view things from the city's standpoint, as opposed to the consumers' standpoint. If the city has to build or maintain a large public transportation system (e.g., building a subway system), it could prove very costly indeed. From the city's standpoint then, the cheapest means of transportation may be privatized transportation, i.e., let consumers pay for and drive their own cars.

Second, the argument assumes that exhaust fumes from cars are the major source of each city's pollution. This may not be true. It could be that large factories are the major cause of fossil fuel emissions, not cars. Furthermore, could it be that buses and minibuses contribute disproportionately more to air pollution than do cars? This could be the case if buses, for example, run on a different type of fuel such as diesel and emit more harmful toxic fumes than do cars. This argument also assumes, and much more subtly, that pollution is caused by cars driven on the weekdays as opposed to the weekends. Could it be that many people only drive short distances to work on the weekdays and then go for joy rides on the weekends, making weekends the time when pollution really adds up?

Third, the argument made assumes that people actually own cars and that public transportation is an option both available and convenient should a person wish to switch. A person may not own a car and, even if he or she does, a choice to switch to different modes of transportation may not be possible. This latter point may be the case where a person lives in an out-of-the-way place where public transportation is virtually non-existent and cars provide the only transportation option. The argument also assumes that if people do switch, the current system of public transportation will be able to accommodate all the "switchers."

Fourth, there exists the assumption that people who live in cities, live in large cities. Even assuming this to be true, the situation in New York, London, and Shanghai regarding cars, public transportation, and pollution may not be representative of the situation in other cities. How comparable are these cities to other major cities? For example, it seems that these three cities have some of the most extensive public transportation systems in the world. Other major cities such as Rome, Bangkok, or São Paulo may not have an extensive, reliable, or convenient public transportation system. In the event that a person neither lives nor works in a major city, this argument quickly loses ground; cars may be the only efficient means of transportation.

Strengthening this argument would require evidence to support the supposed cause-and-effect relationship between driving cars and exhaust fumes which are contributing the majority of the city's pollution. We also need some data showing just how expensive and efficient cars are particularly considering how expensive it might be from the city's standpoint to build a brand-new transportation infrastructure. Furthermore, we encounter a representativeness assumption. Is Shanghai's transportation like that of other major cities? We need to be convinced that the public transportation in New York, London, and Shanghai is not just an aberration when compared to other major cities. Lastly, this argument could be strengthened by softening the absolute way the original sentence is worded. Instead of saying, "People should switch…," we could say, "People should probably switch…," or "A number of people should switch…" Also, instead of saying, "In major cities such as New York…," we could say, "In some major cities such as New York…"

Finally, the term pollution is inherently vague. Whereas cars might be the major source of the city's air pollution, they might not be the major source of the city's overall pollution if the term includes air, water, garbage, and noise.

CHAPTER 8

INTEGRATED REASONING WORKSHOP

The most important factor in the training of good mental habits consists in acquiring the attitude of suspended conclusion, and in mastering the various methods of searching for new materials to corroborate or to refute the first suggestions that occur.

—John Dewey

OVERVIEW

Official Exam Instructions for Integrated Reasoning

Graphical Interpretation

Interpret the graph or graphical image and select from each drop-down menu the option that creates the most accurate statement based on the information provided.

Table Analysis

Analyze the table, sorting on columns as needed, to determine whether each of the options presented meets the given criterion or not.

Two-Part Analysis

Read the information provided, review the options presented in the table, and indicate which option meets the criterion presented in the first column and which option meets the criterion presented in the second column. Make only two selections, one in each column.

Multi-Source Reasoning

Click on the tabs and examine all the relevant information from text, charts, and tables to answer the questions.

Strategies and Approaches

Graphical Interpretation

Ask yourself: "What is the purpose of this graph?" If there is more than one graph, ask yourself: "How do the graphs relate to one another?" For example, one graph might be a "blow up," showing one area of another graph in more detail. Always read closely the labels, legends, and any notes appearing in small type, which are placed at the bottom or at the sides of any graph.

Table Analysis

In sorting each column for the purpose of displaying information in ascending numerical order, ask yourself: "What numbers appear to be very large or very small?" Focus on the outliers as they will likely be the key to answering a question correctly. Note that the *type* of data across columns is likely to be mixed; some columns might be in dollars while others will show percents, decimals, or ratios.

Two-Part Analysis

Two-part analysis involves a written scenario or problem that contains two columns with choices, with each column connected to the other in some way. Ask yourself: "How do the 'variables,' as represented by each column, relate to one another?" For instance, do they move in tandem or do they trade off against one another.

Multi-Source Reasoning

Multi-Source Reasoning may present numbers, narrative, charts, or even diagrams. Immediately click on each of the tabs (usually three tabs but sometimes two) in order to examine what types of information are contained within each tab. Ask yourself: "What discrepancies can be found and what inferences can be drawn from the varying sources of information?"

REVIEW OF INTEGRATED REASONING WITH EXERCISES

This chapter, presented in workshop format, introduces candidates to the most fundamental skill areas tested on the Integrated Reasoning section of the GMAT exam. Notwithstanding the new formats within Integrated Reasoning, it could be argued that the only new skill that is being introduced is the ability to interpret graphs, charts, and information presented in tables. This chapter is specifically designed to reacquaint candidates with the most relevant, basic skills as they relate to working with graphs and interpreting data.

Frequently Asked Questions

How long is the new Integrated Reasoning section?

The Integrated Reasoning section is 30 minutes long and follows the 30-minute AWA writing section.

What types of questions are on the Integrated Reasoning section?

There are four types of questions on the Integrated Reasoning section:

Graphical Interpretation—Candidates need to analyze a graph or information in an image, and then complete a series of statements using drop-down menus.

Table Analysis—Candidates need to review a table of data, similar to a spreadsheet, and use this information to evaluate a series of "Yes/No," "True/False," "Consistent/Inconsistent," or "Can be determined/Cannot be determined" statements.

Two-Part Analysis—Candidates need to take two different sources of information or data and piece them together to answer the question asked.

Multi-Source Reasoning—Candidates need to click through several tabs containing data or information in various forms (including text, charts, and graphs) and answer a series of "Yes/No" questions based on the information.

How will Integrated Reasoning factor into my overall GMAT score?

The Integrated Reasoning section, like the AWA section, is scored separately. There are 12 questions in total, which yield a scaled scored of 0 to 8 in increments of 1 point. A percentile rank is assigned relative to the scaled score achieved.

How much time should be allotted to each question?

Test-takers have 12 questions to do in 30 minutes and can budget two and a half minutes per question.

How will MBA admissions officers use Integrated Reasoning scores?

Over the next five years, admissions officers will gain better insights into the supposed relationship between Integrated Reasoning scores and "success" in business school. Until this relationship is revealed, it is unlikely that schools will place significant weight on these scores. In the near term, one possible way to view Integrated Reasoning scores, as well as AWA scores for that matter, is that a decent score translates to "pass" while a substandard score translates to "fail."

How should I practice for the new Integrated Reasoning section?

The good news is that any practice and improvement made toward either the GMAT math or verbal section is likely to have spill over benefits in terms of the Integrated Reasoning section. One challenge is to get up to speed with graphs. This chapter directly addresses this challenge. Also, be on the look out for graphical and tabular information contained in newspapers and magazines such as *The Economist*. Test yourself by seeing how fast you can hone in on what the chart or graph is "really saying."

Why did GMAC (Graduate Management Admissions Council) opt to create the new Integrated Reasoning section?

In 2009, GMAC launched a major study to gather feedback from its member business schools about how it could improve the GMAT. It surveyed hundreds of business school faculty and administrators to find out what was working well, what could be better, and what ideas they had for improving the test. Some of the findings highlighted the need for business school students to be better able to 1) synthesize data and/or information, 2) see relationships among data and/or information, 3) work across multiple formats, namely words, numbers, and graphics, and 4) hone in on relevant data and/or information while side-stepping irrelevant data and/or information. What then is the Integrated Reasoning section really testing? The following might be a streamlined answer: "The Integrated Reasoning section tests a candidate's ability to deal with multiple formats and see relationships among data or information."

Are there any special concepts that are worth reviewing for use on the Integrated Reasoning section?

There are two sets of terms worth knowing when tackling the Integrated Reasoning section of the GMAT. The first set of terms is "mutually exclusive" and "not mutually exclusive." The second set of terms is "independent" and "not independent (dependent)." *Mutually exclusive* means that two events or outcomes do not overlap with one another or cannot occur at the same time. *Not mutually exclusive* means that two events or outcomes do overlap with one another or can occur at the same time. *Independent* means that two events or outcomes do not influence one another and occur randomly relative to each other. *Not independent (or dependent)* means that two events or outcomes influence one another and that the occurrence of one event has an affect on the occurrence of another event.

Here are some simple real-life examples to illuminate these terms. Say we are putting on a business conference and inviting attendees as well as guest speakers. The assignment of VIP seating and non-VIP seating is a mutually exclusive outcome. Either a person is in the VIP seats or he or she is not. The same holds true for determining who is an in-state versus out-of-state attendee. An attendee is either in-state or out-of-state with no overlap possible. However, in classifying attendees by profession, we might have overlap between who is a manager and who is an engineer and who is a salesperson and who is an entrepreneur. Obviously, some attendees might fall into more than one category. These categories would, therefore, not be mutually exclusive.

Two tasks might be independent and have no influence on one another. For example, in preparing for the conference, it wouldn't make any difference whether we made name tags first and then made copies of the conference handouts or made copies of the conference handouts and then made name tags. These events represent separate tasks that have no bearing on one another. On the other hand, two tasks may not be independent of one another; they may, in fact, be dependent on one another. This is true of events that must occur in a certain sequence. In preparing for the conference, we must plan the conference first before inviting speakers to speak at the conference. Likewise, attendees must be registered for the conference, before they can be admitted to the conference and before they ever fill out conference evaluation forms, which are handed out at the end of the conference. In other words, the filling out of a conference evaluation form is dependent upon a person actually attending the conference, which, in turn, is dependent upon a person having first registered for the conference.

Understanding Basic Graphs

Each of the twelve line graphs included in *Exhibit 8.1* has the following characteristics: It is either *flat* (horizontal) or *sloping* (upward or downward) and it is either composed of *straight lines* or *curves*.

All the graphs in *Exhibit 8.1* showcase two variables—money and time. *Money* appears on the vertical or y-axis, and *time* appears on the horizontal or x-axis. Graphs that are *flat* represent graphs with variables that do not vary with one another. On the other hand, graphs that are *sloping* represent variables that do vary with one another. If a graph *slopes upward* (whether a straight line or a curve), the two variables are said to be directly related to one another. This means that as one variable increases the other also increases or, conversely, as one variable decreases, the other deceases. Graphs that *slope downward* represent variables that are indirectly related to one another. This means that as one variable increases, the other decreases or, alternatively, as one variable decreases the other increases.

Finally, graphs that consist of *straight lines* have variables that are linearly related. "Linear" means that the variables increase or decrease proportionally. Graphs that consist of *curved lines* have variables that are non-linearly related. "Non-linear" means that the variables increase or decrease disproportionately.

Graphs composed of *straight lines sloping upward* depict variables that are both directly and linearly related to one another. For every unit of increase in one variable, there is a proportionate unit of increase in the other variable (and vice versa). A simple real-life example might involve the painting of a room. For every hour you spend painting, you get one more unit of work done.

Graphs composed of *straight lines sloping downward* depict variables that are indirectly, but linearly related to one another. For every unit of increase in one variable, there is a proportionate unit of decrease in the other variable (and vice versa). For every hour you spend painting your room, you get one less hour of leisure time.

Graphs composed of *curved lines sloping upward* depict variables that are directly, but non-linearly related to one another. For every unit of increase in one variable, there is a disproportionate unit of increase in the other variable (and vice versa). A simple real-life example might involve completing a difficult puzzle with many pieces. For each additional hour we spend working on it, we complete a disproportionate amount of the puzzle because the pieces start to fit.

Graphs composed of *curved lines sloping downward* depict variables that are both indirectly and non-linearly related to one another. For every unit of increase in one variable, there is a disproportionate unit of decrease in the other variable (and vice versa). Consider study time and retention over a sustained study period. For every hour spent studying, we gain a unit of benefit. But after two or three hours, we experience diminishing returns for our time and effort spent.

NOTE ⮞ Forward-slashing graphs indicate that two variables are directly related. Back-slashing graphs indicate that two variables are indirectly (inversely) related. Graphs formed with straight lines have variables which are linearly related. Graphs formed with curved lines have variables that are non-linearly related.

1. Quiz on Basic Graphs (🌶)

There are twelve graphs in *Exhibit 8.1*. Match each graph with one of the twelve statements that follow by placing the correct letter in the accompanying box. For your convenience, graphs are divided into three categories: rising graphs, flat graphs, and falling graphs. The topic is one that is dear to us all—salaries and wages. A one-chili rating is assigned to this problem as you only need to get six out of twelve questions correct in order to get the whole problem right!

EXHIBIT 8.1 BASIC GRAPHS

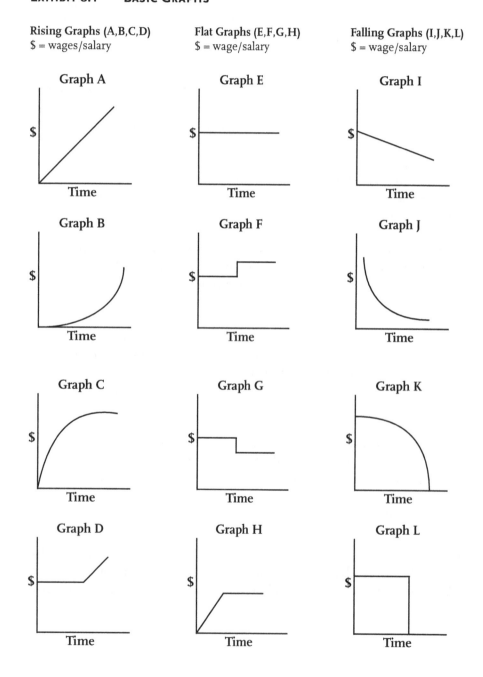

Rising Graphs (A,B,C,D)
$ = wages/salary

Flat Graphs (E,F,G,H)
$ = wage/salary

Falling Graphs (I,J,K,L)
$ = wage/salary

Rising Graphs (select from graphs A, B, C or D):

For every additional hour you work, you get paid incrementally more dollars for each hour worked. ❑

You get a fixed base salary but may also get additional pay based on hours worked which are not covered by your base salary. ❑

For every additional hour you work, you get paid incrementally fewer dollars for each hour worked. ❑

For every hour you work, you get paid y dollars per hour. ❑

Flat Graphs (select from graphs E, F, G or H):

You got a promotion at work that increased the fixed salary you now receive. ❑

Because of layoffs at work, you decided to take a reduction in your fixed monthly salary in order to keep your current job. ❑

You get paid a fixed (flat) wage regardless of the hours you work. ❑

You get paid by the hour, but cannot earn more than a certain dollar amount during the course of your working week. ❑

Falling Graphs (select from graphs I, J, K or L):

Your yearly pension decreases in terms of real dollars during each year of your retirement. ❑

Your wages decrease gradually with age until the time you stop working altogether. ❑

Your wages are fixed but stop the moment you retire. ❑

Your wages decrease dramatically with age, but you can still earn a little in your retirement. ❑

Line Graphs, Pie Charts, and Bar Charts

Three basic types of graphs and charts are commonly used to present data. Line graphs are best used to show how data changes over time. Pie charts are great for breaking data down by category. Bar charts are ideal for side-by-side comparisons of up to six pieces of data. Knowing the strength of each type of graph or chart and how they are best used to present information also helps us in interpreting the underlying data.

The following questions would precipitate the use of each of these graphs or charts in the commercial realm:

Line graphs

"How have corporate profits, sales, or earnings per share increased or decreased over time?" (Hint: A line graph is especially useful for showing trends.)

Pie charts

"How are corporate expenses broken down by major categories including the percentage of total corporate expenses that are administrative, salaries and wages, advertising, operating, and miscellaneous?" (Hint: Pie charts are especially useful for breaking things down.)

Bar charts

"How do the different corporate divisions stack up with one another in terms of head count (total number of employees)?" or "How does our company rank alongside its major competitors in terms of market share?" (Hint: Bar charts are most useful for showing side-by-side comparisons.)

Here's how these three types of visual tools might be used in a non-work setting:

Line graphs

"Am I watching too much television?" (Hint: After charting a week-by-week record of hours of TV viewing at home, you use the data to create a line graph showing the number of TV-free hours at home per week.)

Pie charts

"Where is all my money going?" (Hint: Use a pie chart to display what percentage of your disposable income is spent on different categories.)

Bar charts

"What are my greatest personal strengths and how do they rank?" (Hint: After identifying a half-dozen of your most salient personal or professional strengths, you assign values to them from 1 to 10—1 being lowest and 10 being the highest—and display them using a bar chart.)

Use the following two graphs to answer questions 2–4 regarding Grand Hotel & Casino's revenues for the month of January.

Grand Hotel

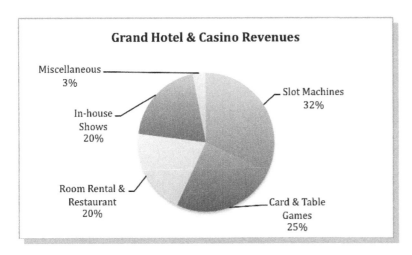

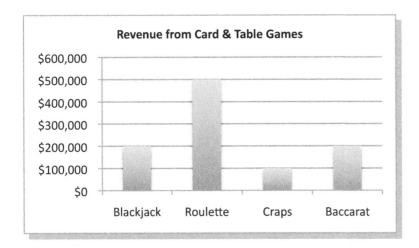

2. **Grand Hotel Q1** ( )

   What was the total dollar revenue earned by Grand Hotel & Casino for the month of January?

3. **Grand Hotel Q2** ( )

   For the month of January, revenue from *blackjack* provided what percent of the total revenue for Grand Hotel & Casino?

4. **Grand Hotel Q3** ( )

   Which of the following brought in more money during the month of January—*miscellaneous* revenues or revenues from *craps*?

Workforce

Use the following two graphs to answer questions 5–7 regarding the composition of Argentina's workforce between 1980 and 2010.

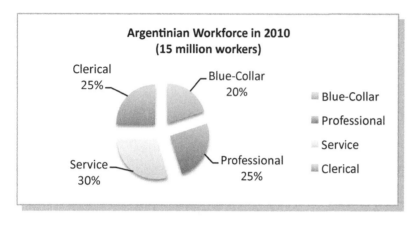

5. **Workforce Q1 (🌶)**

   The decrease in blue-collar workers from 45% in 1980 to 20% in 2010 represents a decrease of how many millions of people?

6. **Workforce Q2 (🌶🌶)**

   According to the data presented, the same number of people worked in the service sector in 2010 as worked in which sector in 1980?

7. **Workforce Q3 (🌶🌶🌶)**

   From 1980 to 2010, the number of Argentinians working in the service, professional, and clerical sectors increased. Calculate the percentage increases for each of these sectors in terms of the number of workers. Also, calculate the percentage decrease for the blue-collar sector in terms of the number of workers. Which sectors, if any, experienced a percentage increase that was greater than the percentage decrease attributed to the blue-collar sector?

Magna Fund

Use the following three graphs to answer questions 8–9 regarding Magna Fund's performance for the past four quarters.

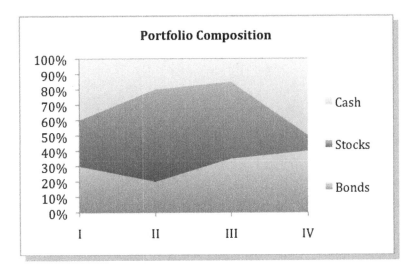

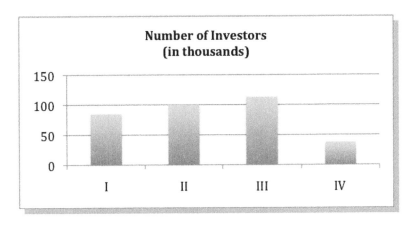

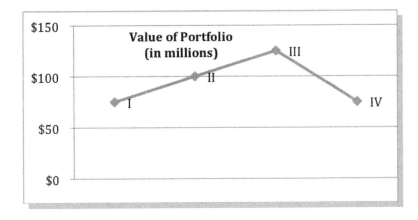

8. **Magna Fund Q1 ( )**

What was the percentage increase in the portfolio's value from the first quarter to the third quarter?

A) 40%

B) 50%

C) $66\frac{2}{3}\%$

D) 125%

E) $166\frac{2}{3}\%$

9. **Magna Fund Q2 ( )**

Which of the following statements can be inferred from the three graphs above?

I. The percent of the portfolio accounted for by cash declined from the third to the fourth quarter.

II. Bonds accounted for one-third or more of the portfolio in three of four quarters.

III. The average amount of dollar investment per individual investor was greatest during the fourth quarter.

IV. If the stock portfolio consisted of common and preferred shares only, and was maintained in a ratio of 70% common stock to 30% preferred stock, then the value of the preferred stock holdings was approximately $18 million during the second quarter.

    A) I & II
    B) II & III
    C) III & IV
    D) II, III & IV
    E) All of the above

CORRELATION ANALYSIS

Correlation is about the relationship between two (or more) variables. By relationship we are referring not only to how they are connected but also to the strength of their connection. Two variables can be connected in two basic ways: positively and negatively. Positively correlated variables are directly related (when one increases, the other increases; when one decreases, the other decreases). Negatively correlated variables are indirectly related (when one increases, the other decreases; when one decreases, the other increases).

The strength of the connection between two variables is measured by a value ranging from +1 to −1. A correlation of +1 is a positive-perfect correlation; a correlation of −1 is a negative-perfect correlation. In real life, positive-perfect or negative-perfect correlations are rare. Note that although the scatter points of perfect correlations appear as straight lines, positive-high correlations look like fat fountain pens, and positive-low correlations are shaped like squashes. *Exhibit 8.2* provides a flowchart to summarize the statistical relationships as they relate to correlation.

NOTE ✒ Positive correlations have graphs sloping upward; negative correlations have graphs sloping downward. The stronger the correlation between two variables, the nearer to a straight line will be their graph; the graph of a perfect correlation is a straight line.

EXHIBIT 8.2   CORRELATION FLOWCHART

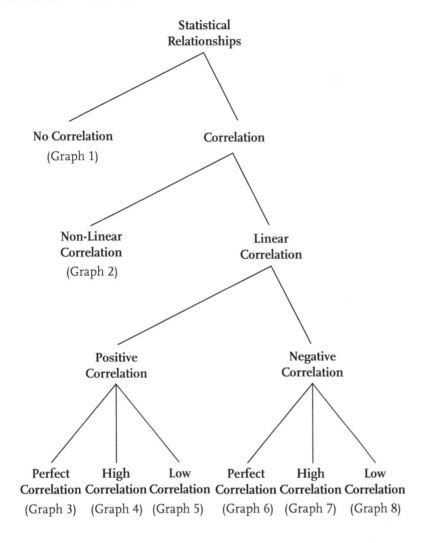

Exhibit 8.3 illustrates the different types of correlation using scatter plot graphs, which plot the intersection of data points.

Graph 1 indicates no correlation.

"What is the relationship between hair color and longevity?" We would expect the scatter points describing such data to be completely random.

Graph 2 depicts a non-linear correlation.

"How is performance affected by anxiety levels?" Whether it be an academic or athletic undertaking, a moderate level of anxiety is optimal, with low or high levels of anxiety suboptimal.

Graph 3 is a positive-perfect correlation.

The amount of coffee beans used and the number of cups of coffee consumed are directly related. Note that it would not be accurate to substitute the phrase "amount of coffee beans grown or produced" for "amount of coffee beans used" because coffee crop production might fluctuate independently of coffee beans actually consumed.

Graph 4 is a positive-high correlation.

"How are company sales affected by increasing dollars spent on advertising?" We expect to see a very strong correlation between these two variables. The more we advertise, the more sales increase (within certain limits). In the case of advertising and sales, we would typically expect to see a 0.8 positive correlation.

Graph 5 is a positive-low correlation.

"What is the relationship between height and weight?" The taller we are, the more we will likely weigh, but the correlation between height and weight is not particularly strong.

Graph 6 is a negative-perfect correlation.

"How does the life experience we gain with each year's passing vary with respect to the number of years we have left to live?" Well, for every year we live and gain experience, we have one fewer year to live. It's a trade-off: one year of experience traded for one year of our life.

Graph 7 is a negative-high correlation.

"How is our memory after drinking lots of beer?" It is a pretty good bet that for any individual, the more he or she drinks, the less remarkable will be his or her memory.

Graph 8 is a negative-low correlation.

"How is one's level of physical fitness linked to food consumption?" There might be some truth to the idea that the more we eat the less fit we are. But we also know of cases where highly fit individuals eat copious amounts of food, as is the case with many professional athletes, particularly those playing contact sports such as American football or rugby.

EXHIBIT 8.3   BASIC CORRELATION GRAPHS

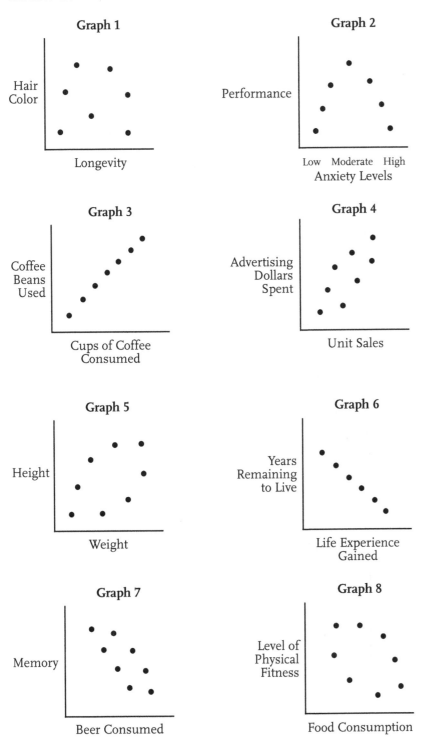

10. Quiz on Correlation Analysis ((🌶️🌶️))

Placing the appropriate letter in each box, match graphs A through H with the caption below that best describes the type of correlation depicted.

Positive-perfect correlation ☐   Negative-perfect correlation ☐

Positive-high correlation ☐   Negative-high correlation ☐

Positive-low correlation ☐   Negative-low correlation ☐

Non-linear correlation ☐   Zero correlation ☐

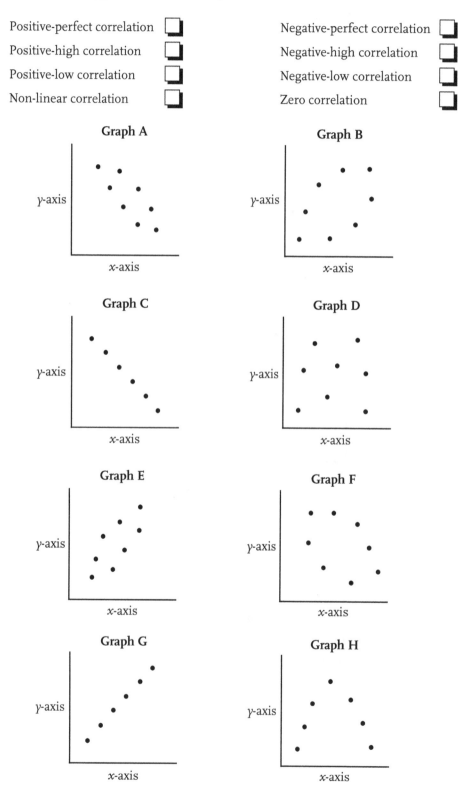

Graph A

y-axis

x-axis

Graph B

y-axis

x-axis

Graph C

y-axis

x-axis

Graph D

y-axis

x-axis

Graph E

y-axis

x-axis

Graph F

y-axis

x-axis

Graph G

y-axis

x-axis

Graph H

y-axis

x-axis

Answers and Explanations

1. Quiz on Basic Graphs ( )

Rising Graphs (select from graphs A, B, C or D):

For every additional hour you work, you are paid incrementally more dollars for each hour worked.   B

You get a fixed base salary, but may also get additional pay based on hours worked which are not covered by your base salary.   D

For every additional hour you work, you get paid incrementally fewer dollars for each hour worked.   C

For every hour you work, you get paid y dollars per hour.   A

Flat Graphs (select from graphs E, F, G or H):

You got a promotion at work that increased the fixed salary you now receive.   F

Because of layoffs at work, you decided to take a reduction in your fixed monthly salary in order to keep your current job.   G

You get paid a fixed (flat) wage regardless of the hours you work.   E

You get paid by the hour, but cannot earn more than a certain dollar amount during the course of your working week.   H

Falling Graphs (select from graphs I, J, K or L):

Your yearly pension decreases in terms of real dollars during each year of your retirement.   I

Your wages decrease gradually with age until the time you stop working altogether.   K

Your wages are fixed but stop the moment you retire.   L

Your wages decrease dramatically with age, but you can still earn a little in your retirement.   J

Grand Hotel

2. Grand Hotel Q1 ( )

Answer: $4,000,000. We know that card & table games revenue totals $1,000,000 and represents 25% of the pie. For example, total revenue from all card & table games—blackjack ($200,000), roulette ($500,000), craps ($100,000), and baccarat ($200,000)—amounted to $1,000,000 (see bar chart). Therefore, this relationship provides the key to solving for the total amount of money brought in by Grand Hotel & Casino.

$$\frac{25\%}{\$1,000,000} = \frac{100\%}{x}$$

$$25\%(x) = 100\%(\$1,000,000)$$

$$25\%(x) = \$1,000,000$$

$$x = \frac{\$1,000,000}{25\%}$$

$$x = \$4,000,000$$

3. Grand Hotel Q2 ( )

Answer: 5%. Blackjack is a type of card & table game. Blackjack accounted for $200,000 worth of total card & table game revenue. Again, total revenue from all card & table games, per bar chart, totaled $1,000,000 (blackjack, $200,000; roulette, $500,000; craps, $100,000; and baccarat, $200,000). Thus, blackjack accounted for 20% of card & table game revenue ($200,000/$1,000,000 = 20%). Since the percentage of total hotel and casino revenue attributable to card & table games was 25% (see pie chart), the final calculation is the product of these two numbers (percentages).

$$20\% \times 25\% = 5\%$$

NOTE ◅ With respect to bar charts and pie charts used in combination, concentrate on how one graph fits into the other. Because pie charts are best at breaking down information and bar charts are best at ranking information, the total dollar amount represented by the bar chart will most likely relate to a given percentage of the pie chart.

3. Grand Hotel Q3 ( )

Answer: miscellaneous revenues. The amount of money earned by craps was $100,000. This figure can be easily read from the bar chart. The amount of money earned from miscellaneous revenues was 3% of $4,000,000 or $120,000. Again, the $4,000,000 figure, as derived in Q1, represents the total dollar revenue earned by Grand Hotel & Casino.

Workforce

5. Workforce Q1 ( )

Answer: 1.5 million. First, the number of people working in the blue-collar sector in 1980 was 4.5 million (45% × 10,000,000 = 4.5 million). Second, the number of people working in the blue-collar sector in 2010 was 3 million (20% × 15,000,000 = 3 million). Therefore, the difference between 4.5 million and 3 million accounts for the 1.5 million decrease in the number of workers in this sector.

NOTE ⤚ When viewing two pie charts and comparing the percentage growth of items over two different time frames, beware of directly comparing the percentage figures of one pie chart with the other. To compare two figures, first translate these figures to actual dollars, based on the dollar size of each pie chart, and then make dollar or percentage comparisons.

6. Workforce Q2 ( )

Answer: The Blue-Collar Sector. The number of people working in the service sector in 2010 was 4.5 million (30% of 15,000,000). The number of people working in the blue-collar sector in 1980 was also 4.5 million (45% of 10,000,000). Although the absolute percentage of service sector workers in 2010 is smaller than the absolute percentage of blue-collar workers in 1980, the size of the workforce has grown by 5 million. The pie has gotten bigger. In this case, a smaller percentage of a bigger pie is equal to a larger percentage of a smaller pie.

7. Workforce Q3 ( )

Answer: Service, Professional, and Clerical Sectors. All three sectors experienced a higher percentage increase compared with the percentage decrease attributed to the blue-collar sector!

The tricky point here is that we cannot compare percentages directly. In other words, we cannot simply subtract the percentages for any particular sector to arrive at a percentage increase or decrease. For example, the absolute percentage decrease in the number of workers in the blue-collar sector (i.e., 45% − 20% = 25%) is obviously larger than any absolute percentage increase for any other sector. However, this type of calculation is not possible because we're asked for the percentage increase or decrease in terms of the number of workers in each sector. These are relative numbers and we must take into account the fact that the size of the pies we're comparing are not the same. The workforce was larger in 2010.

Service Sector (percentage increase):

$$\frac{\text{New} - \text{Old}}{\text{Old}} = \frac{4.5\,\text{M} - 1.5\,\text{M}}{1.5\,\text{M}}$$

$$\frac{3\,\text{M}}{1.5\,\text{M}} = 2 \times 100\% = 200\%$$

Professional Sector (percentage increase):

$$\frac{\text{New} - \text{Old}}{\text{Old}} = \frac{3.75\,\text{M} - 1.5\,\text{M}}{1.5\,\text{M}}$$

$$\frac{2.25\,\text{M}}{1.5\,\text{M}} = 1.5 \times 100\% = 150\%$$

Clerical Sector (percentage increase):

$$\frac{\text{New} - \text{Old}}{\text{Old}} = \frac{3.75\,\text{M} - 2.5\,\text{M}}{2.5\,\text{M}}$$

$$\frac{1.25\,\text{M}}{2.5\,\text{M}} = 0.5 \times 100\% = 50\%$$

Blue-Collar Sector (percentage decrease):

$$\frac{\text{Old} - \text{New}}{\text{Old}} = \frac{4.5\,\text{M} - 3\,\text{M}}{4.5\,\text{M}}$$

$$\frac{1.5\,\text{M}}{4.5\,\text{M}} = \frac{1}{3} \times 100\% = 33\frac{1}{3}\%$$

Magna Fund

8. Magna Fund Q1 (🌶)

Choice C. Refer to the chart titled *Value of Portfolio*. The y-axis is labeled in increments of $50 million. We can estimate the value of the portfolio during Q1 as being $75 million. The value of the portfolio during Q3 sits at $125 million. The difference between these two segments is $50 million. Therefore, $50 million divided by $75 million is equal to a $66\frac{2}{3}\%$ increase.

9. Magna Fund Q2 (🌶 🌶 🌶)

Choice C. Statement I is incorrect. The percentage of cash increases from the third to fourth quarter (Q3 to Q4). Although we see a black downward-sloping line, don't be deceived. This means that the percentage of cash is getting larger. In Q4, cash amounts to fully 50% of the value of the portfolio. When reading a cumulative line graph, concentrate on the space or area covered by each item in the cumulative line graph rather than on whether the lines enclosing these given areas are pointing upward or downward.

Statement II is also incorrect. Bonds accounted for one-third or more of the portfolio in exactly two of four quarters, namely the III and IV quarters. Note that one-third is $33\frac{1}{3}\%$, not 30%; bonds accounted for exactly 30 percent of the portfolio in Q1, not $33\frac{1}{3}$ percent.

Statement III is correct. The average amount of dollar investment per individual investor was greatest during the fourth quarter. Don't be deceived by the fact that Q3 has the greatest portfolio value and the greatest number of investors. Average means total dollars divided by total investors. So lots of money divided by fewer investors means rising investment per individual investor. Throughout the first, second, and third quarters, the investment per individual investor remains relatively stable. In the fourth quarter the value of the portfolio falls and so does the number of investors. However, the number of investors falls proportionately greater, meaning that more money is divided among fewer investors. Actual or approximate numbers are as follows:

Quarter 1:

$$\frac{\$75,000,000}{85,000} = \$882 \text{ per investor}$$

Quarter 2:

$$\frac{\$100,000,000}{100,000} = \$1,000 \text{ per investor}$$

Quarter 3:

$$\frac{\$125,000,000}{110,000} = \$1,136 \text{ per investor}$$

Quarter 4:

$$\frac{\$75,000,000}{40,000} = \$1,875 \text{ per investor}$$

Statement IV is also correct. In the second quarter, stocks account for 60% of the total portfolio (80% less 20%). This means that preferred shares are 30% of 60%, or preferred shares accounted for 18% of the total portfolio. Looking at the *Value of Portfolio* chart, we can see that total portfolio value during Q2 is $100,000,000.

The final calculation follows:

$$18\% \times \$100,000,000 = \$18,000,000$$

An alternative calculation is as follows:

$$(\$100,000,000 \times 60\%) \times 30\% = \$18,000,000$$

10. Quiz on Correlation Analysis ( )

Graph A – negative-high correlation
Graph B – positive-low correlation
Graph C – negative-perfect correlation
Graph D – zero correlation
Graph E – positive-high correlation
Graph F – negative-low correlation
Graph G – positive-perfect correlation
Graph H – non-linear correlation

APPENDIX I – GMAT & MBA INFORMATIONAL WEBSITES

Registering for the GMAT Exam

GMAC
- www.gmac.com

The GMAC (Graduate Management Admission Council) is responsible for administering the GMAT exam. The GMAT (Computer Adaptive Test) is offered on demand. For more information or to sign up on the Internet, go to gmac.com or mba.com. If you wish to call the U.S. and talk with a GMAT representative, contact customer service:

Tel: (800) 717-GMAT (4628)
Tel: (952) 681-3680

MBA Fairs & Forums

Annual MBA fairs and forums are organized by the following two companies. To determine the dates, cities, and venues applicable to you, check their websites:

World MBA Tour
- www.topmba.com

The World MBA Tour is sponsored by QS and headquartered in London, England.

The MBA Tour
- www.thembatour.com

The MBA Tour is headquartered in Lexington, Massachusetts, USA.

MBA Social Networks

The following two organizations are dedicated to providing information about the GMAT exam and the MBA admissions process and have a substantial number of visitors each month.

Beat the GMAT
- www.beatthegmat.com

MBA Club
- www.mbaclub.com

GMAT Courses

The following is a non-exhaustive listing (in alphabetical order by URL) of companies specializing in on-site and/or online GMAT courses.

- www.800score.com [800 Score]

- www.bestgmatprep.com [GMAT 20/20]

- www.dominatethegmat.com [Dominate the GMAT]

- www.edstarindia.com [Edstar]

- www.gmat-zone.com [GMAT Zone]

- www.gorillatestprep.com [Gorilla Test Prep]

- www.jamboreeindia.com [Jamboree]

- www.kaplan.com [Kaplan Educational Centers]

- www.knewton.com [Knewton]

- www.magoosh.com [Magoosh]

- www.manhattanreview.com [Manhattan Review]

- www.mba-center.net [MBA Center]

- www.mbahouse.com [MBA House]

- www.masterthegmat.com [Master the GMAT]

- www.mlic.net [MLIC]

- www.neworiental.org [New Oriental]

- www.oxfordseminars.ca [Oxford Seminars]

- www.perfectgmat.com [Shawn Berry GMAT Preparation]

- www.powerscore.com [Power Score]

- www.prep.com [Richardson Prep Center]

- www.primegmatprep.com [Prime GMAT Prep]

- www.princetonreview.com [The Princeton Review (TPR)]

- www.stratusprep.com [Stratus Prep]

- www.testmasters.net [Testmasters]

- www.veritasprep.com [Veritas Test Prep]

Other GMAT & MBA Websites

The following is a sampling of websites (in alphabetical order by website URL) that are dedicated to providing information about the GMAT exam and/or MBA admissions.

- www.accepted.com [Accepted]

- www.admissionsconsultants.com [Admissions Consultants]

- www.admitadvantage.com [Admit Advantage]

- www.amerasiaconsulting.com [Amerasia Consulting]

- www.businessweek.com [Businessweek]

- www.cgsm.org [The Consortium for Graduate Study in Management]

- www.clearadmit.com [Clear Admit]

- www.essayedge.com [Essay Edge]

- www.expartus.com [Expartus]

- www.foreignmba.com [Foreign MBA]

- www.gmac.com [Graduate Management Admission Council]

- www.gmat-mba-prep.com [GMAT MBA Prep]

- www.gmattutor.com [GMAT Tutor]

- www.gradloans.com [Grad Loans]

- www.gradschoolroadmap.com [Grad School Road Map]

- www.grockit.com [Grockit]

- www.ivyleagueadmission.com [Ivy League Admission]

- www.mbaadmit.com [MBA Admit]

- www.mbaexchange.com [The MBA Exchange]

- www.mbamission.com [MBA Mission]

- www.mbapodcaster.com [MBA Podcaster]

- www.mbastrategies.com [MBA Strategies]

- www.nbmbaa.com [National Black MBA Association]

- www.nshmba.org [National Society of Hispanic MBAs]

- www.stacyblackman.com [Stacy Blackman]

- www.thegmatcoach.com [The GMAT Coach]

Information on Business School Rankings

The following provides information about business school rankings. A number of major magazines and newspapers release annual or biannual rankings.

Title: The Best B-Schools (U.S. Schools)
Source: BusinessWeek
■ www.businessweek.com

The *BusinessWeek* ranking comes out every two years (even years) in the fall.

Title: America's Best Graduate Business Schools
Source: U.S. News & World Report
■ www.usnews.com

The *U.S. News & World Report* ranking comes out every year in the spring.

Title: The Top 100 Full-Time International MBA Programmes
Source: Financial Times
■ www.ft.com

The *Financial Times* ranking comes out every year in the month of January.

Title: Top Full-Time International MBA Programmes
Source: The Economist
■ http://www.economist.com/

The Economist ranking comes out in the fall of each year.

Title: Best US Business Schools
Source: Forbes
■ www.forbes.com

The *Forbes* ranking comes out every year in the month of August.

Latin America Business School Rankings
Source: America Economia
■ www.americaeconomia.com

The *America Economia* posts rankings on its website for Latin American business schools.

Australian Business School Rankings
Source: Australian Education Network
■ www.australianuniversities.com.au

The Australian Education Network posts rankings on its website for Australian business schools.

APPENDIX II – CONTACT INFORMATION FOR THE WORLD'S LEADING BUSINESS SCHOOLS

Business schools are listed in alphabetical order within each of the following regions—U.S., Canada, Europe, Australia, Asia Pacific, Latin America, South America, and South Africa. The schools listed in this appendix are compiled based on ranking information contained in various magazines and newspapers including, but not limited to, *BusinessWeek, US News & World Report,* and the *Financial Times.*

U.S. BUSINESS SCHOOLS:

Berkeley, University of California at – Haas School of Business
Berkeley, California
Tel: (510) 642-1405
- www.haas.berkeley.edu

Carnegie Mellon University – Tepper School of Business
Pittsburgh, Pennsylvania
Tel: (412) 268-2268
- www.tepper.cmu.edu

Chicago, University of – Booth School of Business
Chicago, Illinois
Tel: (773) 702-7743
- www.chicagobooth.edu

Columbia University – Columbia Business School
New York, NY
Tel: (212) 854-5553
- www.gsb.columbia.edu

Cornell University – Johnson Graduate School of Management
Ithaca, New York
Tel: (800) 847-2082 (U.S./Canada)
Tel: (607) 255-4526
- www.johnson.cornell.edu

Dartmouth College – Tuck School of Business
Hanover, New Hampshire
Tel: (603) 646-8825
- www.tuck.dartmouth.edu

Duke University – Fuqua School of Business
Durham, North Carolina
Tel: (919) 660-7705
- www.fuqua.duke.edu

Harvard Business School
Boston, Massachusetts
Tel: (617) 495-6128
- **www.hbs.edu**

Massachusetts Institute of Technology – MIT Sloan School of Management
Cambridge, Massachusetts
Tel: (617) 253-2659
- **http://mitsloan.mit.edu**

Michigan, University of – Ross School of Business
Ann Arbor, Michigan
Tel: (734) 763-5796
- **www.bus.umich.edu**

New York University – Stern School of Business
New York, New York
Tel: (212) 998-0100
- **www.stern.nyu.edu**

North Carolina at Chapel Hill, University of – Kenan-Flagler Business School
Chapel Hill, North Carolina
Tel: (919) 962-3236
- **www.kenan-flagler.unc.edu**

Northwestern University – Kellogg School of Management
Evanston, Illinois
Tel: (847) 491-3308
- **www.kellogg.northwestern.edu**

Pennsylvania, University of – Wharton School
Philadelphia, Pennsylvania
Tel: (215) 898-6183
- **www.wharton.upenn.edu**

Stanford University – Stanford Graduate School of Business
Stanford, California
Tel: (650) 723-2766
- **www.gsb.stanford.edu**

Texas at Austin, University of – McCombs School of Business
Austin, Texas
Tel: (512) 471-5893
- **www.mccombs.utexas.edu**

University of California at Los Angeles, Anderson School of Management
Los Angeles, California
Tel: (310) 825-6944
- **www.anderson.ucla.edu**

Virginia, University of – Darden Graduate School of Business Administration
Charlottesville, Virginia
Tel: (434) 924-3900
■ www.darden.virginia.edu

Yale University – Yale School of Management
New Haven, Connecticut
Tel: (203) 432-5932
■ www.mba.yale.edu

CANADIAN BUSINESS SCHOOLS:

McGill University – Desautels Faculty of Management
Montreal, Quebec
Tel: (514) 398-8811
■ www.mcgill.ca/desautels

Queen's University – Queen's School of Business
Kingston, Ontario
Tel: (613) 533-2302
■ www.queensmba.com

Toronto, University of – Rotman School of Management
Toronto, Ontario
Tel: (416) 978-3499
■ www.rotman.utoronto.ca

Western Ontario, University of – Richard Ivey School of Business
London, Ontario
Tel: (519) 661-3212
■ www.ivey.uwo.ca

York University – Schulich School of Business
Toronto, Ontario
Tel: (416) 736-5060
■ www.schulich.yorku.ca

EUROPEAN BUSINESS SCHOOLS:

Cambridge, University of – Judge Business School
Cambridge, United Kingdom
Tel: 44 (0) 1223 339700
■ www.jbs.cam.ac.uk

ESADE Business School
Barcelona, Spain
Tel: (34) 932 806 162
■ www.esade.edu

IE Business School
Madrid, Spain
Tel: 34 915 689 600
- **www.ie.edu**

IESE Business School – University of Navarra
Barcelona, Spain
Tel: (34) 93 253 4200
- **www.iese.edu**

IMD
Lausanne, Switzerland
Tel: 41 (0) 21 618 0111
- **www.imd.ch**

INSEAD
Fountainebleau, France
Tel: 33 (0) 1 60 72 40 05
- **www.insead.edu**

London Business School
London, United Kingdom
Tel: 44 (0) 20 7000 7000
- **www.london.edu**

Oxford, University of – Said Business School
Oxford, United Kingdom
Tel: 44 (0) 1865 278804
- **www.sbs.ox.ac.uk**

Rotterdam School of Management
Rotterdam, The Netherlands
Tel: 31 10 408 22 22
- **www.rsm.nl**

AUSTRALIAN BUSINESS SCHOOLS:

Australian Graduate School of Management (AGSM)
Sydney NSW, Australia
Tel: 61 2 9931 9490
- **www.agsm.edu.au**

Melbourne Business School
Carlton, Victoria, Australia
Tel: 61 3 9349 8400
- **www.mbs.edu**

ASIA-PACIFIC BUSINESS SCHOOLS:

Asian Institute of Management (AIM)
Makati City, Philippines
Tel: (632) 8924011 to5
- **www.aim.edu**

CEIBS
Pudong, Shanghai, PRC
Tel: 86 21 2890 5555
- **www.ceibs.edu**

(The) Chinese University of Hong Kong (CUMBA)
Shatin, New Territories, Hong Kong, PRC
Tel: (852) 2609-7783
- **www.cuhk.edu.hk**

Chulalongkorn University – Sasin Graduate Institute of Business Administration
Bangkok, Thailand
Tel: 66 2 (0) 2218-3856-7
- **www.sasin.edu**

(The) Hong Kong University of Science and Technology – HKUST Business School
Clear Water Bay, Kowloon, Hong Kong, PRC
Tel: (852) 2358-7539
- **www.mba.ust.hk**

Indian Institute of Management Ahmedabad (IIMA)
Ahmedabad, India
Tel: 91 79 2630 8357
- **www.iimahd.ernet.in**

Indian School of Business (ISB)
Hyderabad, India
Tel: 91 40 2318 7474
- **www.isb.edu**

International University of Japan – Graduate School of International Management (GSIM)
Niigata, Japan
Tel: 81 (0) 25-779-1106
- **gsim.iuj.ac.jp**

Nanyang Technological University – Nanyang Business School (NTU)
Singapore
Tel: (65) 67911744
- **www.ntu.edu.sg**

National University of Singapore – NUS Business School
Singapore
Tel: (65) 6516-2068
- www.bschool.nus.edu.sg

LATIN AMERICAN & SOUTH AMERICAN BUSINESS SCHOOLS:

EAPUC, School of Business
Santiago, Chile
Tel: 56-2 354-2238
- www.mbauc.ci

EGADE – TEC de Monterrey
Garcia, NL, Mexico
Tel: 52 81 8625 6030
- www.egade.itesm.mx

INCAE Business School
Alajuela, Costa Rica
Tel: 506 2433 9908
- www.incae.ac.cr

SOUTH AFRICAN BUSINESS SCHOOLS:

Cape Town, University of – UCT Graduate School of Business
Cape Town, South Africa
Tel: 27 (0) 21-406 1338/9
- www.gsb.uct.ac.za

Wits Business School
Johannesburg, South Africa
Tel: 27 11 717-3600
- www.wbs.ac.za

QUIZ – SOLUTIONS

Page numbers provide a point of reference.

1. False. The ratio of gold coins to total coins is $\frac{1}{6}$ or $16\frac{2}{3}\%$.

    Refer to *Chapter 2*, problem 52 (page 70).

2. False. The probability of tossing a normal six-sided die twice and getting at least one six is $\frac{11}{36}$, calculated as $\frac{1}{6} + \frac{1}{6} - (\frac{1}{6} \times \frac{1}{6}) = \frac{11}{36}$.

    Refer to *Chapter 2*, problem 87 (page 84).

3. False. The store item is now selling for a 44 percent discount or 56 percent of its original price. Example: $100 less 20 percent equals $80 and $80 less 30 percent equals $66. A $44 discount is 44 percent.

    Refer to *Chapter 2*, problem 40 (page 66).

4. False. The ratios of the length of the sides of a right triangle with corresponding angle measures of 30°–60°–90° is $1 - \sqrt{3} - 2$.

    Refer to *Chapter 2*, basic geometry formulas (page 41).

5. False. Multiplying a number by 1.2 is the same as dividing that number by the reciprocal of 1.2, which is 0.83, not 0.8.

    Refer to *Chapter 2*, problem 38 (page 65).

6. False. The following are grammatically correct sentences: "Jonathan *likes* not only tennis but also golf" or "Jonathan not only *likes* tennis but also *likes* golf."

    Refer to *Chapter 4*, problem 13 (page 252).

7. False. The statement "some doctors are rich people" does imply reciprocality because "some rich people must be doctors." That is, if some doctors are rich people, some rich people are doctors.

    Refer to *Chapter 5*, no-some-most-all statements (page 292).

8. False. The Analysis of an Argument essay neither requires personal examples or anecdotes nor is it made better by the use of personal examples and anecdotes.

    Refer to *Chapter 7*, frequently asked questions (page 365).

9. False. Whereas the conclusion and evidence of an argument are always explicit, the assumption is always implicit. The assumption is never explicit; it is invisible, existing in the mind of the speaker or the hand of the writer.

   Refer to *Chapter 5,* the ABCs of argument structure (page 279).

10. False. Arguably the best way to read a GMAT Reading Comprehension passage is to "read the first sentence first but the last sentence next." Then proceed to read the whole passage. The author might either conclude on the bottom line or hint at the passage's overall meaning, so reading the last sentence sooner rather than later is deemed advantageous.

   Refer to *Chapter 6,* overview (page 334).

ON A PERSONAL NOTE

Ruminations of a veteran GMAT test-prep instructor and MBA admissions coach.

Necessity is said to be the mother of invention. But so too is invention the mother of necessity. This book is a marriage of both processes. Although there was no initial mandate calling for this book's creation, once created there was little doubt it was needed. My early GMAT workshops in Hong Kong invited students to ask open-ended questions beyond the course script: "What are the different types of distance-rate-time problems found in math Problem Solving?...Are there any tricks to finding assumptions when writing an argument essay in Analytical Writing?...How do you pick numbers for Data Sufficiency problems?...Is there any special technique for solving math mixture problems?...What are the different kinds of cause-and-effect arguments that appear in Critical Reasoning? Can answer choices in Sentence Correction ever be grammatically correct and still not be the correct answer?...How are Reading Comprehension passages structured?"

The difficulty posed in answering such an array of questions is obvious. After all, fielding specific questions about the mechanics of a particular problem is not the same thing as being able to compare and contrast problems across a broad spectrum. The latter requires research and reflection. My research included a review of more than a thousand prior-released, official GMAT test questions as well as those materials used by numerous test-prep organizations. In short, my examination encompassed everything that was published and available.

My first discovery was "buckets of problems." I found that the best way to help students master the GMAT was to group problems by problem types (i.e., create buckets of similar problems). The next task was dividing these larger categories into sub-categories. It was then a matter of finding what specific problem-solving principles or techniques bind a given subcategory. "Buckets of problems" is, upon reflection, exactly how sports are practiced. Athletes, and inspired amateurs, never practice all tasks at the same time, unless they're trying to simulate competition. The game of golf provides a classic example. When practicing, a golfer practices one type of shot at a time: drives, long irons, chips, and putts. Only by breaking up the shots into "groups" can a golfer analyze what he or she is really doing en route to achieving a shot-making groove.

This book strikes a balance between representing problem categories and choosing thematic problems. A thematic or value-added problem is one that reveals much about how a particular type of problem works. Whereas representing each and every problem category and subcategory would have certainly resulted in a book of some 500 problems, ensuring that all problems are thematic enabled problem selection to be winnowed down to the 200 problems contained in this book. These "all-star" problems act as a template to represent the underlying math, verbal, writing principles that are likely to reappear on the actual GMAT.

In the same way that a blueprint is prerequisite for building a house, strong theory best precedes rigorous practice. In short, my four-tier recommendation for GMAT study is as follows:

I.   Achieve familiarity with the different types of problems on the test (do this book!).
II.   Do a sufficient number of additional practice problems.
III. Complete at least two full-length computer adaptive exams.
IV.   Take the real GMAT exam.

In terms of familiarizing yourself with the different types of problems, I recommend a two-pronged approach. First, if possible, sign up for a test-prep course. Second, study this book in conjunction with enrolling in a course. Most test-prep courses do a very good job of surveying the various problem types, but a generalizable criticism is that these courses are a little light in terms of content. The analytical approach embodied by *Game Plan for the GMAT* (and its spin-off editions, *Game Plan for GMAT Math* and *Game Plan for GMAT Verbal*) makes it an excellent complement and companion guide for anyone enrolled in a test-preparation course.

Whether you decide to take a test-prep course or study on your own, test preparation has three elements: content, structure, and strategy. Content is understanding what kinds of problems are on the exam. Structure is about following a specific plan of study in order to complete study, often within a limited time frame. Strategy refers to the need to find optimal ways to solve problems and understanding how, relative to the test, to maximize your strengths and minimize your weaknesses.

I'm a fan of test-prep courses and believe that every candidate should take one, notwithstanding availability, wherewithal, and the time required to complete a course. In my opinion, test-prep courses get results first and foremost because they provide structure. This should not be underestimated. We all know how difficult it is to motivate ourselves; any serious undertaking requires a schedule backed by commitment. The "best" test-prep courses typically provide live instruction and rely on "good" instructors. An experienced instructor is able to frame course material and add valuable examples and anecdotal information, which may not be part of the formal course offering. Many times the answer to the question "Which company has the best GMAT course?" may very well be the same as asking "Which company has the best GMAT instructor(s)?"

With respect to content, mastering any skill-based endeavor translates to having skills, knowledge, and confidence. As it relates to GMAT study, knowledge means being able to apply specific skills to new but analogous problems. Strategy is everything other than content—understanding the best approach to use to solve a given problem, choosing among different problem-solving techniques, learning how to eliminate answer choices and/or guess on questions (if necessary), adapting to a mix of questions on the test, dealing with time pressure, and maintaining concentration. One caveat: Although strategy is certainly a sexier word than content or structure, only common sense is needed to recognize that strategy alone is not enough to defeat the GMAT.

This book adheres to the philosophy that mastery of exam content is the only real way to conquer GMAT exam. *Game Plan for the GMAT* (and *Game Plan for GMAT Math* and *Game Plan for GMAT Verbal*) is unique in its analytical approach and its ability to reveal how problems work. This "recipe" book is steeped in best practices—those core strategies, techniques, and insights about how to score high on the GMAT, which were discovered, tested, and refined over a multi-year period. Sharing this knowledge with you brings me great satisfaction and it is an honor knowing that you invested your time in its review.

PRAISE FOR *GAME PLAN FOR THE GMAT*

These endorsements are applicable to a pre-released paperback edition of *Game Plan for the GMAT: Your Proven Guidebook for Mastering the GMAT Exam in 40 Short Days.*

"By not wasting a reader's time, Royal's *Game Plan for the GMAT* gives royal treatment to GMAT test takers. He clearly outlines useful strategies to solve real test problems, unlike any other book I have ever seen."

Steve Silbiger
Author of The Ten-Day MBA: The Step-by-Step Guide to Mastering the Skills Taught in America's Top Business Schools

"This book is the ultimate how-to GMAT skill-building book. As a French student whose first language is not English, I used this material to launch a successful second try on the exam. Practicing on former test questions is not enough. You have to get insights into why the test-makers choose the problems that they do."

Lionel Lopez
Graduate, Dartmouth Tuck School of Business

"Rigorous, analytical, thorough. A perfect companion for those wanting to take control of the GMAT."

Rosemaria Martinelli
Associate Dean, Student Recruitment & Admissions The University of Chicago Graduate School of Business; former Director of Admissions, The Wharton School

"This author's approach enabled me to increase my score from 650 to 730. I believe that his unique way of categorizing each type of question, giving insightful tips to master these problems, as well as the detailed analysis for each set of problems were key factors in my cracking the test. Moreover, I found in his materials, problems that I did not find anywhere else and which were critical on the D-day when answering a few extra questions right made the difference between a good score and an excellent one."

Cédric Gouliardon
Telecom Specialist
Graduate, INSEAD

"Brandon possesses a talent for clarity. The analytical writing section offers basic essay outlines that are both logical and easy to reproduce as well as wonderful sample essays that make a 6.0 seem simple. The 'classic problem' approach to learning provides a clear system for the test taker to follow, and the appendices are vital for last minute review. As my scores can testify, *Game Plan for the GMAT* delivers its claim."

Julia Travers
Graduate, Yale School of Management
GMAT: 740; AWA: 6.0

"I used *Game Plan for the GMAT* as my main source of study, supplementing it with practice from the *Official Guide for GMAT Review*. The *Official Guide* has lots of problems to practice on, but *Game Plan* is superb for helping understand conceptually how the problems work. Problems are organized by categories and the explanations also frame problems by introducing novel insights and techniques. I highly recommend this manual as your first line of defense. It helped me achieve a 700-plus GMAT score with only a month's practice, despite English not being my first language."

Sam Mottaghi, former consultant, Accenture (Sweden)
Graduate, Judge Business School (Cambridge)

For someone that didn't have a lot of time to prepare, this book provided a very effective way to study. I liked the approach of condensing the material into question types which made unfamiliar questions on exam day less daunting. Even as an engineering major (McGill University), I liked the idea of breaking the math in topic and subtopics and then summarizing important concepts. The author shows how difficult distance-rate-time problems can be solved by viewing distance as a constant, and how related D-R-T problems, although variants, conform to this model. There is a special barrel method for solving mixture problems and a template for solving overlap and matrix problems. Moreover, as a person who didn't consider herself strong in the verbal section, I appreciated how the grammar rules within sentence correction were broken down into the big six grammar categories. The preparation I did for the verbal section in the GMAT has also helped me to improve my overall writing skills which actually is more useful to me now than it was during the test. I love INSEAD and doing my MBA has been an incredible experience so far! It's easy to forget that this book helped make this possible.

Breanne Gellatly
Graduate, INSEAD

With the help of *Game Plan for the GMAT,* I achieved a plus 700 GMAT score. One section of the GMAT deals with mathematical concepts and acumen once learned in high school but long forgotten. For me, this book was highly effective in helping to 'recall' such lost math knowledge within a short period of time by selectively concentrating on relevant mathematical problems. Unlike conventional test preparation books which bombard you with irrelevant or overly-simplistic questions, mixed with gimmicks or tricks, *Game Plan for the GMAT* provides real principles which are ultimately useful over a wide range of problem type and difficulty level."

C. F. Pan
Graduate, Harvard Law School

"I can't thank you enough for the clarity and wisdom you impart in *Game Plan for the GMAT!* In terms of logical organization and exhaustive content, your GMAT guide has no equal."

Kemp Baker
Non-Profit Management Inc.
Washington, DC

ABOUT THE AUTHOR

Brandon Royal (CPA, MBA) is an award-winning educational author and a graduate of the University of Chicago's Booth School of Business. This book represents, in part, his distilled experience gained from having taught GMAT test-prep courses for Kaplan Educational Centers in Hong Kong and from having conducted hundreds of hours of individual tutoring sessions that helped scores of applicants beat the GMAT and achieve acceptance at the world's leading business schools.

To contact the author:

E-mail: contact@brandonroyal.com

Web site: www.mavenpublishing.com

Books by Brandon Royal

The Little Blue Reasoning Book:
   50 Powerful Principles for Clear and Effective Thinking

The Little Red Writing Book:
   20 Powerful Principles for Clear and Effective Writing

The Little Gold Grammar Book:
   Mastering the Rules That Unlock the Power of Writing

The Little Red Writing Book Deluxe Edition

The Little Green Math Book:
   30 Powerful Principles for Building Math and Numeracy Skills

The Little Purple Probability Book:
   Mastering the Thinking Skills That Unlock the Secrets of Basic Probability

Game Plan for Getting into Business School:
   100 Proven Admissions Strategies to Get You Accepted at the MBA Program of Your Choice

Game Plan for the GMAT:
   Your Proven Guidebook for Mastering the GMAT Exam in 40 Short Days

Game Plan for GMAT Math:
   Your Proven Guidebook for Mastering GMAT Math in 20 Short Days

Game Plan for GMAT Verbal:
   Your Proven Guidebook for Mastering GMAT Verbal in 20 Short Days

Lightning Source UK Ltd.
Milton Keynes UK
UKOW07f1951120715

255037UK00005B/84/P